In the last two decades international monetary relations have been characterized by latent instability, and more recently by severe tensions. Yet the issue of reforming the international monetary system does not appear on the agenda of the policymakers of the major countries involved. *The international monetary system* tries to analyse this apparent contradiction. It brings together contributions from some of the most authoritative academic economists and monetary officials, and examines each of the fundamental functions of the international monetary system.

There is broad support for improving present monetary arrangements with the aim of ensuring more stable conditions in monetary and financial markets and of promoting the orderly adjustment of payments disequilibria. For political reasons a fully fledged reform exercise is unlikely, but very few experts seem to like the status quo. This book provides the reader with a comprehensive account of the institutional and policy changes required to manage an increasingly integrated and interdependent global monetary and financial system.

The international monetary system

The international monetary system

EDITED BY
PETER B. KENEN
FRANCESCO PAPADIA
AND
FABRIZIO SACCOMANNI

*Proceedings of a conference organized
by the Banca d'Italia*

Published by the Press Syndicate of the University of Cambridge
The Pitt Building, Trumpington Street, Cambridge CB2 1RP
40 West 20th Street, New York, NY 10011-4211, USA
10 Stamford Road, Oakleigh, Melbourne 3166, Australia

First published 1994

Printed in Great Britain at the University Press, Cambridge

A catalogue record for this book is available from the British Library

Library of Congress cataloguing in publication data
The international monetary system: proceedings of a conference
organized by the Banca d'Italia / edited by Peter B. Kenen,
Francesco Papadia, and Fabrizio Saccomanni.
    p.   cm.
Papers from a conference honouring the memory of Rinaldo Ossola
(1913–1990), who served at the Banca d'Italia from 1938 to August
1976 in various positions, including Director General.
   ISBN 0 521 45468 9
   1. Foreign exchange–Congresses.   2. International finance–
Congresses.   I. Kenen, Peter B., 1932–   .   II. Papadia, Francesco, 1947–
III. Saccomanni, Fabrizio, 1942–   IV. Ossola, Rinaldo, 1913–1990.   V. Banca
d'Italia.
HG3851.I543   1994
332'.042–dc20   93-21076   CIP

ISBN 0 521 45468 9 hardback

Contents

IV   THE INTERNATIONAL FRAMEWORK FOR NATIONAL ECONOMIC POLICIES

Conference participants

Robert Z. Aliber, *The University of Chicago*
Giorgio Basevi, *Università degli Studi di Bologna*
C. Fred Bergsten, *Institute for International Economics*
Bruno Bianchi, *Banca d'Italia*
Lorenzo Bini Smaghi, *Banca d'Italia*
William H. Branson, *Princeton University*
Guido Carli
Pietro Catte, *Banca d'Italia*
Zhaohui Chen, *London School of Economics*
Carlo A. Ciampi, *Banca d'Italia*
Pierluigi Ciocca, *Banca d'Italia*
Richard N. Cooper, *Harvard University*
Franco Cotula, *Banca d'Italia*
Andrew D. Crockett, *Bank of England*
Marcello de Cecco, *Università degli Studi di Roma*
Lamberto Dini, *Banca d'Italia*
Rudiger Dornbusch, *Massachusetts Institute of Technology*
Mario Draghi, *Treasury Ministry, Rome*
Barry Eichengreen, *University of California at Berkeley*
Antonio Fazio, *Banca d'Italia*
Jeffrey A. Frankel, *University of California at Berkeley*
Giampaolo Galli, *Banca d'Italia*
Giancarlo Gandolfo, *Università degli Studi di Roma*
Alberto Giovannini, *Columbia University and Treasury Ministry, Rome*
Leonhard Gleske, *Deutsche Bundesbank*
Morris Goldstein, *International Monetary Fund*
Giorgio Gomel, *Banca d'Italia*
Paolo Guerrieri, *Università degli Studi di Napoli*
Aldo Guetta
Toyoo Gyohten, *Bank of Tokyo*
Robert D. Hormats, *Goldman Sachs International*

Peter B. Kenen, *Princeton University*
Jacques de Larosière, *Banque de France*
André de Lattre, *Banque Française de Service et de Crédit*
Stefano Lo Faso, *Banca d'Italia*
Giovanni Magnifico, *Istituto Universitario Navale di Napoli*
Rainer S. Masera, *Istituto Mobiliare Italiano*
Ronald I. McKinnon, *Stanford University*
Stefano Micossi, *Confindustria*
Giuliano Monterastelli
Robert A. Mundell, *Columbia University*
Gilberte Ossola
Pier Carlo Padoan, *Università degli Studi di Roma*
Tommaso Padoa-Schioppa, *Banca d'Italia*
Francesco Palamenghi Crispi, *Centrobanca, Rome*
Silvano Palumbo
Francesco Papadia, *Banca d'Italia*
Jacques J. Polak, *The Per Jacobsson Foundation*
Salvatore Rebecchini, *Banca d'Italia*
Wolfgang Rieke, *Deutsche Bundesbank*
Fabrizio Saccomanni, *Banca d'Italia*
Adelheid Sailer-Schuster, *Deutsche Bundesbank, Rome*
Carlo Santini, *Banca d'Italia*
Ciro Schioppa, *Banca d'Italia*
Sergio Siglienti, *Banca Commerciale Italiana*
Robert Solomon, *The Brookings Institution*
Luigi Spaventa, *Università degli Studi di Roma*
Alexandre Swoboda, *Centre International d'Études Monétaires et Bancaires*
André Szász, *De Nederlandsche Bank*
Niels Thygesen, *University of Copenhagen*
Carlo Tresoldi, *Banca d'Italia*
Edwin M. Truman, *Board of Governors of the Federal Reserve System*
Ignazio Visco, *Banca d'Italia*
John Williamson, *Institute for International Economics*

Foreword

CARLO A. CIAMPI

When the Banca d'Italia decided to organize a conference to honour the memory of Rinaldo Ossola, the choice of the theme presented no difficulty: a discussion of the problems of the international monetary system was the obvious way to pay tribute to a person who devoted most of his long and distinguished career to the goal of creating the procedures and instruments for the management of international monetary relations. At the same time, we were fully aware that the international monetary system is no longer at the centre of debate among either practitioners or academics.

Since the fateful August of 1971, the world has been living in what, in Ossola's days, was called a 'non-system': namely, an arrangement which is based on the single, and often disregarded, rule that each country should keep its own house in order and leave economic and monetary relations among nations to the 'magic of the market place'. International cooperation has therefore largely confined itself to *ad hoc* interventions in the context of 'crisis management' exercises. The traditional institutional fora for cooperation have been increasingly replaced by non-institutional arrangements such as the Group of Seven, where cooperation has not succeeded in going beyond the area of exchange rates to monetary, budgetary and structural policies. International monetary instability has not disappeared, however, and payments imbalances have widened. Thus, the question of what kind of international monetary arrangements would be required for the effective management of the problems facing the world economy is still waiting for an answer.

If the answer lies in a more structured international monetary system, certain preconditions will have to be fulfilled. Firstly, with the Maastricht Treaty ratified, European countries should devote more attention to international cooperation: the Community should develop an economic foreign policy reflecting the world's increasingly tripolar configuration. Secondly, the United States and Japan should take a more favourable attitude towards formal methods of international monetary cooperation, recognizing the advantages of ensuring the compatibility of their domestic

policies at the world level. Thirdly, the world trade system must be put back on the rails which have allowed the most prolonged period of growth in world history, since, if monetary stability fosters growth, the converse is also true.

If these conditions are met, there is a good chance that international monetary cooperation could develop very much along the lines foreseen by Rinaldo Ossola in an article published in the *Princeton Essays* in July 1971. In forecasting a world formed by three main economic areas, centred respectively on the United States, Japan and a European monetary union, Rinaldo Ossola envisaged that flexible exchange rates would be used between the various areas and that a well-organized international cooperative structure would ensure the orderly functioning of the system.

This book does not provide a unanimous answer to the problems confronting the international monetary and financial system of today. But from the valuable contributions of the outstanding economists and policy-makers assembled here, the request emerges clearly that the search for more stable international monetary arrangements be put again on the policy agenda of the leading industrial countries. If this call is heeded, it would be a most fitting tribute to the memory of Rinaldo Ossola.

Editors' note

The papers included in this book were first presented at a Conference organized by the Banca d'Italia in July 1992 to honour the memory of Rinaldo Ossola.

Rinaldo Ossola (1913–90) joined the Banca d'Italia in 1938, following studies at the Bocconi University in Milan and at the London School of Economics. In the Bank he served in various capacities at home and abroad, becoming Deputy Director General in 1969 and Director General in 1975. His involvement in international monetary issues was especially intense from 1967 to 1976, the period in which he served as Chairman of the Deputies of the Group of Ten. He left the Banca d'Italia in August 1976 to become Minister of Foreign Trade in the Italian Government. After leaving the government he was active in the Italian banking system as Chairman of the Board of major commercial banks.

The suggestion to hold a conference first came from Fabrizio Saccomanni, who was closely associated with Ossola in the years 1972–6. The programme of the Conference was designed with the encouragement and suggestions of Rainer Masera, Stefano Micossi, Robert Mundell, Jacques Polak, and Luigi Spaventa. The preparatory work for the Conference was conducted with the assistance of Salvatore Rebecchini and Ciro Schioppa, who also wrote a paper analysing the contributions of Rinaldo Ossola to the process of international monetary reform and prepared the relevant background documentation.

The organization of the Conference and the preparation of this volume would not have been possible without the invaluable work of Anna Buttarelli and Raffaella Giannini, validly assisted at a later stage by Stefania Secola.

In their contributions to this volume, all the authors paid unanimous tribute to Rinaldo Ossola for his endeavour to create a stable international monetary system, his diplomatic ability and his warm personality. We decided that their value would be enhanced by bringing them together here rather than leaving them scattered in the text.

PETER B. KENEN
FRANCESCO PAPADIA
FABRIZIO SACCOMANNI

Introduction

PETER B. KENEN, FRANCESCO PAPADIA, and FABRIZIO
SACCOMANNI

1 Premise

The reform of the international monetary system has not been on the
political agenda for many years. After the failed effort of the Committee of
Twenty (C-20) in 1972–4, and despite some brave attempts to revive the
issue, such as those by McKinnon (1984) and Miller and Williamson (1987),
it received scant attention in both academic and policy circles.

It was our great good fortune to be 'required' to organize a conference in
memory of Rinaldo Ossola as it provided an opportunity to reconsider the
state of the international monetary system and inquire about its prospects
in the light of its history. A common question runs through the contributions published in this book: does the lack of interest in reform of the system
derive from satisfaction with the way it is working or despair about the
likelihood of improving it? The authors give different answers but tend to
agree on one fundamental point: the present system is much less structured
than the grand design that came out of the Bretton Woods Conference, let
alone the yet grander design of John Maynard Keynes. The current system
is even less structured than the gold standard, which was not built on
institutional foundations, but derived its solidity from the belief that gold
was the necessary, ultimate monetary anchor.

The unstructured nature of the current international monetary system is
apparent in the way it deals with each of the three fundamental tasks of any
monetary system: (i) supplying international liquidity, (ii) determining
exchange rates, and (iii) providing an international framework for national
economic policies. Indeed, nothing in this book contradicts the assertion –
which is not necessarily a value judgment – that present arrangements must
be described as a non-system.[1] Andrew Crockett argues that international
liquidity is now created endogenously in the private markets to accommodate the demand of any creditworthy country. Peter Kenen suggests that
exchange rates are only loosely managed at the world level, with the limited
objective of preventing 'solipsistic' trips. Jacques Polak notes with concern
that the International Monetary Fund (IMF), the one global institution

1

concerned with monetary matters, has little influence on the policies and balance of payments adjustment of the large industrial countries – the only ones that matter for the world economy. These issues are handled by the Group of Seven (G-7) in an ineffective and sporadic manner that would have displeased not just John Maynard Keynes but also Harry Dexter White.

Some academics regarded the Bretton Woods system as too *dirigiste* and encouraged faint-hearted officials to try floating exchange rates, which they viewed as an extension of Adam Smith's invisible hand. Twenty years later, however, there is dissatisfaction among academics, shared by Robert Aliber, a Chicagoan, and Fred Bergsten, a former member of the Carter administration, both of whom stress that floating exchange rates have failed to display the promised self-equilibrating and welfare-improving characteristics.

Several contributions to this volume support indirectly the view that 'despair' rather than 'satisfaction' may explain the survival of the present non-system, suggesting that monetary arrangements may lead a life of their own, not amenable to restructuring by deliberate policy actions. First, as Ronald McKinnon argues, the asymmetric, dollar-based gold exchange standard which evolved after World War II was somewhat different than the regime designed at Bretton Woods. No one intended that the United States should be able to finance balance of payments deficits with its own liabilities in amounts exceeding the desire of other countries to acquire them. Robert Mundell shows how the gold parity of the dollar and the ensuing asset settlement obligation of the United States were supposed to have checked what President de Gaulle would characterize as the 'exorbitant privilege' of the United States. Second, floating exchange rates were not seen as a long-lasting alternative to the Bretton Woods regime.[2] The Smithsonian Agreement of December 1971, which tried to revive the exchange rate arrangements of Bretton Woods, reflected what Polak calls an 'unwillingness to administer euthanasia to a beloved system while there was still a glimmer of hope that it might survive'. Third, of the two attempts to reform the Bretton Woods system, one, the scheme to supplement international liquidity by creating Special Drawing Rights (SDR), was successful formally but took place just when the liquidity problem was about to vanish, and the other, the C-20, was an outright failure. Fourth, in the more limited European setting, the European Monetary System (EMS) transformed itself into an asymmetrical arrangement, based on German leadership, beyond the wishes or expectations of its founders. As Rainer Masera notes with prophetic concern, it likewise became over time a more rigid arrangement, only to suffer a very severe blow shortly after the conference on which this book is based. The analogy with the sequence of

events that characterized the evolution of the Bretton Woods system is extraordinary and deserves further analysis.

As Polak and Bergsten note incisively and wittily, economists and officials have contributed to these failures and surprises, by not seeing the need for shoring up the system – or to act on the need even when it was seen. But the failures and surprises, in and of themselves, suggest that monetary arrangements have their own internal dynamics, not readily amenable to modification by rational design. Markets, and in particular the 'green screen brigade' mentioned by Robert Hormats, with their Reuters and Telerate terminals, play a crucial role in this process. Political factors have also contributed importantly to the periodical oscillation of the monetary system between hegemony and cooperation, a *leit motiv* that runs through the recollections of Guido Carli, evoking a feeling of *dejà vu*.

This book does not pretend to give a final answer to the 'despair' or 'satisfaction' question. Rather, it hopes to help each reader form a personal opinion.

2 International liquidity

The authors of the chapters and comments in this section of the book agree, with only Mundell apparently dissenting, in declaring officially dead the problem of international liquidity: arrangements for providing reserves have ceased to play a major role in the working of the international monetary system. Quite exceptionally, moreover, they also agree in identifying the murderers: floating exchange rates and increased capital mobility. The point is made dramatically by Crockett, who contrasts the present system, in which liquidity is supplied endogenously on demand through recourse to private markets, with the one prevailing when the SDR was introduced, in which liquidity was supplied exogenously by gold mines, by the IMF, and by the US balance of payments. If capital is so mobile that, in Williamson's words, 'the external constraint on a country comes from its *creditworthiness* rather than from its *liquidity*', how can the supply of international liquidity influence the behaviour of the world economy?

William Branson never mentions international liquidity in his 'average' model, which treats the world, rightly, as a single closed economy; he simply and powerfully identifies changes in liquidity with shifts of an LM curve, resulting in turn from changes in money demand or in money supply. His substantive conclusion is that the present high level of real interest rates results primarily from actual and potential scarcity of saving and a tightening of monetary policy in Germany and only secondarily, if at all, from an autonomous shift of the demand for liquidity deriving from the accession of the Eastern European countries to international financial

markets. This is an interesting conclusion, not least because it applies to an actual economic situation the idea, previously relegated to theoretical analyses, that the expectation of a future fiscal expansion is contractionary. From the standpoint of this introduction, however, the most interesting feature of Branson's model is the important role it assigns to liquidity at the global level. The reader may agree or disagree with Branson's conclusions and with the qualifications offered by Alexandre Swoboda, that the international monetary regime may well affect the real interest rate, and by Marcello de Cecco, that low savings in the United States may be an important reason for high real rates. No reader, however, can conceivably claim that liquidity is irrelevant, unless he or she believes the unbelievable, i.e., that prices and wages are perfectly flexible.

We are thus left with an apparent conflict. Crockett and Williamson proclaim that 'international liquidity' is irrelevant; Mundell disagrees; and Branson's model of the global economy assigns a key role to liquidity. These disagreements, however, may be more semantic than substantive and may focus on the uses of the adjective 'international' rather than the noun 'liquidity'.

Crockett and Williamson explain that, at least for industrial countries, there is no longer any credit rationing: each country can obtain as much liquidity as it wishes at the going rate of interest. Branson shows how the equilibrium and dynamics of the world economy are influenced by aggregate liquidity. The two views are entirely consistent: together, they correspond with the statement made in a domestic setting that monetary policy influences macroeconomic conditions even when individual agents are not credit rationed. Indeed, both Crockett and Williamson state clearly that the global conditions under which individual countries can satisfy their demand for liquidity depend on the monetary policies of the countries issuing currencies of international importance, which is the basic premise of Branson's model.

Mundell, Masera, and Stefano Micossi contribute more elements to the analysis of liquidity by drawing additional analogies between domestic and global conditions. 'In the real world,' Mundell notes, 'uncertainty and transactions costs make money necessary, and this is as true at the international as it is at the intranational level.' Liquidity has utility for governments, as well as for individual agents. Masera and Micossi, elaborating on a point made by Crockett, draw attention to the distinction between 'owned' and 'borrowed' reserves, using words and arguments similar to those used in a closed economy setting to explain why access to credit facilities is not fully equivalent to the holding of liquid assets. There are links here to the logic of cash-in-advance models. The distinction between owned and borrowed reserves is particularly important for many

developing countries and for the countries of Eastern Europe, which are still credit constrained. The proposals by Polak and Williamson for a new allocation of SDRs are meant to address such needs rather than the old problem of international liquidity or, for that matter, the state of global liquidity.

To conclude succinctly, the issue of international liquidity is dead, but the issue of global liquidity is more important than ever. Moreover, attention must be paid to the liquidity needs of particular countries and groups of countries.

3 Exchange rates

It is in the exchange rate field that the present international monetary system differs most from the Bretton Woods system. Not only are there flexible exchange rates between the currencies of the three main regional blocs, as Ossola had foreseen as early as July 1971 (Ossola 1971), but, according to Kenen's calculations, about one-third of IMF member countries prefer some form of floating to pegging.

Two fundamental questions, but many answers, emerge from the contributions dealing with exchange rates: firstly, whether stable but adjustable exchange rates are a viable and lasting alternative to fully fixed rates, on the one hand, and fully flexible rates, on the other; secondly, whether the controversy over exchange rate arrangements can be best understood and resolved by coming at the problem from the standpoint of the monetary standard or the standpoint of economic interdependence and adjustment.

As regards the first question, Williamson, writing in 1977, had identified in the desire to restore the adjustable peg system, notwithstanding the development of capital mobility, the 'principal and crucial intellectual error of the C-20 . . .', dooming that reform effort to failure (Williamson 1977). As Polak notes in this book, however, most members of the European Community (EC) adopted that system only two years later. By 1991, moreover, the EMS, with an enlarged participation to the Exchange Rate Mechanism (ERM) and free capital movements for its members, was generally regarded as a striking success. Furthermore, Bergsten argues that the industrialized world should adopt arrangements intermediate between fixed and floating rates. Zhaohui Chen and Alberto Giovannini pose a blunt form of the same basic question by asking themselves 'are fixed but adjustable exchange rates a contradiction in terms?'

Academics are fond of posing questions in a stark way. Practitioners shy away from black and white statements, preferring qualified, greyer, formulations. Thus, the two non-academic authors of this introduction are inclined to conclude that the notion of 'fixed but adjustable exchange rates'

is not internally inconsistent and can be a workable option for a limited period of time, even with perfectly mobile capital, provided that economic fundamentals are not widely divergent and are expected to converge eventually. There are, of course, qualifications here. The phrases 'limited period of time' and 'not widely divergent' are nicely elastic. Lots of rubbish can be swept beneath them. To discourage that deplorable activity, it is important to articulate and quantify the basic trade-off between the feasible stringency of the exchange rate regime and the acceptable degree of divergence of fundamentals, with the latter reflecting, at least in part, the freedom that governments have to conduct autonomous economic policies. Chen and Giovannini shed some light on this basic trade-off. Using thirteen years of EMS data, they analyse the links between the stability of the exchange rate regime, exchange rate expectations, and economic fundamentals. Their preliminary findings lead them to conclude that there is indeed an internal inconsistency in the notion of stable but adjustable exchange rates. They find, in particular, that expectations of parity changes do not depend primarily on economic fundamentals, such as the level of economic activity, but are influenced most heavily by two 'non-fundamental' variables, i.e., the occurrence of a parity change in the previous month and the present position of a currency in its fluctuation band.

The results reported by Giovannini and Chen, while providing useful insights, do not bear conclusively on the view, which they ascribe to the Delors Report (Committee for the Study of Economic and Monetary Union 1989), that a pegged rate regime like the EMS risks being brought down by small divergences in monetary policies and can be held together only by the expectation of a transition to a full-fledged Economic and Monetary Union (EMU). Firstly, a failure to find significant links between past fundamentals and exchange rate expectations is not decisive; exchange rate expectations should not reflect past fundamentals but, rather, future fundamentals, which are by definition uncertain and difficult to quantify. Secondly, as noted by Luigi Spaventa, there are no monetary variables in the vector used by Chen and Giovannini to explain exchange rate expectations and thus they provide no evidence concerning the risk that discrepancies in monetary policies can destabilize the system through their effect on expectations. Nevertheless, since expectations seem to depend on what Spaventa euphemistically calls 'credibility variables', one could use Chen and Giovannini's results to support a view even more pessimistic than the one attributed to the Delors Report: convergence of fundamentals is not sufficient and may even be irrelevant for the stability of a system of stable but adjustable rates. Systemic stability depends on that most intangible element: credibility. A point made by Niels Thygesen is relevant here. The emphasis which the Maastricht Treaty has attached to a set of selected

convergence indicators should be welcomed, as it should concentrate the minds of market operators on fundamentals rather than on an elusive concept of credibility. In a way, if unintentionally, the Maastricht Treaty may have done what Giancarlo Gandolfo thinks central bankers and economists should do: increase the weight of 'fundamentalists' over that of 'chartists' in the foreign exchange market.

While acknowledging that it is impossible to test empirically the thesis of the Delors Report, one should consider as suggestive the events that started in the second half of 1992 and reached their climax in the Summer of 1993. With the 'no' vote in the Danish referendum on the Maastricht Treaty in June 1992, the whole EMU process was suddenly and dramatically surrounded by uncertainty. Interest rates rose in those European countries not belonging to the core of the Deutsche mark area; this was most striking in Italy and Spain but occurred also in France, Sweden, and other countries as well. The currencies of countries outside the Deutsche mark area came under severe pressure: sterling and the lira were eventually forced out of the exchange rate mechanism of the EMS; the peseta and the escudo were repeatedly devalued; the Nordic countries had to abandon their ECU pegs. The Irish punt, although supported by stronger fundamentals than those of some of the countries in the Deutsche mark area, eventually succumbed to devaluation pressures. The French franc was also attacked and, notwithstanding the soundness of the French economy, huge interventions and repeated increases in interest rates, the devaluation pressure forced, in August of 1993, the widening of the fluctuation bands of the ERM to an extraordinary 15 per cent. The Belgian and the Danish currencies followed, *de facto*, the French franc, leaving the Dutch guilder as the only remaining member of the Deutsche mark area. Conforming to a pattern noted by Masera, markets reacted tardily but violently to a worst case interpretation of the Danish vote, producing the most severe crisis in the history of the EMS and somehow vindicating the thesis of the Delors Report: the EMS is subject intrinsically to instability and can only be preserved if the market believes that it will be eventually superseded by EMU.

It is also hard to gather a body of evidence bearing on a weaker formulation of the hypothesis advanced above, i.e., that a system of stable but adjustable exchange rates is not sustainable in the very long run. Experience prior to World War II is not very relevant, because, under the gold standard, fixed exchange rates were not meant to be adjustable. And we have only three observations since World War II: the demise of the Bretton Woods par value system; the progressive transformation of the EMS into a fixed rather than adjustable exchange rate regime; and the EMS crisis of 1992–93. The direction was different in each instance. The first led to flexible rates; the second was leading to irrevocably fixed rates; and the

third has led again towards flexibility of exchange rates. They have in common, however, a movement away from the intermediate solution, a system of adjustable exchange rates, suggesting that the game which the authorities and markets play when fixity and adjustability coexist may not be sustainable for too long.

The bold step proposed by Richard Cooper, discussed below, takes the argument about the non-sustainability of fixed but adjustable rates to its logical, if extreme, conclusion. He discards, on normative grounds, the floating rate option in favour of a commitment by the major industrial countries to move eventually to a single currency. If one is willing to make an equally bold assumption, that societies and institutions, particularly those that are governed democratically, tend to optimize, if only in the very long run, one can convert Cooper's proposal into a prediction. There is only one stable resting point for exchange rate arrangements: irrevocably fixed rates or the economic equivalent of a single currency.

The other fundamental question raised above about exchange rate regimes is whether they should be evaluated from the standpoint of the monetary standard or for their contribution to the adjustment process. Kenen, supported warmly by McKinnon, recasts the exchange rate debate in light of concerns about the functioning of the monetary standard, rather than the more familiar concerns about balance of payments adjustment and macroeconomic interdependence. He examines recent arguments for fixing exchange rates to improve the quality of monetary policies but calls attention to several counterarguments. Foremost among the latter is the fact that a fixed exchange rate provides only a *relative* monetary standard, when, instead, an *absolute* standard is required. In some cases, such as the EMS, the need for a monetary standard can weigh heavily in favour of fixed exchange rates. But Gandolfo rightly notes that it is hard to generalize about these matters.

The statistics presented in Kenen's paper, which show that some form of exchange rate flexibility appealed to many countries in the 1980s, are consistent with the uncertain state of the debate about exchange rate arrangements. If there is a trend towards fixed exchange rates, and many contributors to this volume would deny that, it is weak and hard to quantify. Indeed, Kenen concludes that we are unlikely to see any substantial change in the exchange rate arrangements linking the three great economic areas. His conclusion rests on two features of the present situation. First, as Branson noted in a different setting, there was in 1992 an unprecedented differential in short-term interest rates between the United States and Europe, amounting to 6–7 per cent. It indicated that the economies and policies of those two regions were, and still are, far from being in phase. Second, the reforms required by the Maastricht Treaty, if

and when they are implemented, will institutionalize a significant difference between US and European attitudes. The European Central Bank (ECB) will be ruled by a statute establishing its independence and committing it to the maintenance of price stability in terms even stronger than those that apply to the Deutsche Bundesbank; since the ECB will be eager to establish its credibility and match action with words, it could evince attitudes quite different from those of the Federal Reserve System, making it very difficult to introduce or maintain a pegged exchange rate between the ECU and the dollar. Finally, a unified European economy will show about the same degree of openness as the American economy and a much lower degree than that of the economies of the individual EC countries; this may well diminish the interest of EC countries in stabilizing external exchange rates. An attitude of 'benign neglect' might well migrate from the western to the eastern shore of the Atlantic.

Summing up, one will find very few contributions to this part of the book that support flexible exchange rates *in principle*. But support for moving towards more exchange rate fixity is tempered by concerns about feasibility and the degree of political commitment.

The feasibility of exchange rate stabilization is the central focus of the chapter by Pietro Catte, Giampaolo Galli, and Salvatore Rebecchini. As any attempt to stabilize exchange rates is bound to rely significantly on interventions in foreign exchange markets, it is essential to ascertain their effectiveness. The debate on this topic began in the early 1970s, soon after the move to generalized floating. It took on ideological dimensions, with free marketeers, including most academic economists and some officials, arguing that intervention would interfere with the functioning of markets and would therefore be ineffective in the short run and counterproductive in the long run. Opponents of intervention characterized it pejoratively as 'dirty floating' and thus tried to stigmatize it. But advocates of intervention, not to be undone, invoked Bagehot's warning that 'money does not manage itself' and blamed freely floating rates for a litany of sins – the tendency to overshoot long-term equilibrium levels and to generate 'bubbles' and misalignments with adverse long-term consequences for inflation rates, competitive positions, and current account balances.

The debate on intervention went on without reaching a clear-cut conclusion. Even the study conducted in 1983 by the monetary authorities of the G-7 countries came to a split view, although tilting to the side of the skeptics, because of the sheer weight of the US position, then firmly aligned with the strict free-market ideology of the early Reagan administration. In 1985, however, the monetary authorities of the major industrial countries began to engage in large-scale intervention, individually and in groups involving three, five, seven, or more participants, in an effort to limit

excessive movements of the dollar exchange rate. There was, as a result, a revival of interest by academics in the effectiveness of interventions, although the profession, with few exceptions, continues to believe that the effects of sterilized intervention are at most quite small and do not last long; Jeffrey Frankel, whose work is included in this volume, represents one of the most notable exceptions. The academic view contrasts with the current view taken by practitioners, who regard official intervention as an important instrument to influence exchange rate expectations. Unfortunately, the monetary authorities themselves have made it harder for academic economists to study the effects of intervention. With few exceptions, they continue to treat daily intervention data as being confidential, historically as well as currently. It is equally hard to obtain time series data on the transactions or positions of private participants in the foreign exchange markets. Central banks have begun to conduct periodic surveys of turnover by currency and instrument, but these cover a single month in a three-year period. The shortage of relevant data, coupled with the well-known difficulties of modelling exchange rate behaviour, make it very difficult to conduct research on the effects of intervention.

Catte, Galli and Rebecchini try to shed some light on these obscure but vital issues by compiling data on concerted intervention intended to influence the US dollar. They study nineteen episodes during the 1985–91 period without using econometric methods but by carefully examining the behaviour of exchange rates, interest rates, and other variables. They conclude that intervention was successful, in that the trend of the dollar *vis-à-vis* the Deutsche mark and the yen was reversed in every case, although temporarily in some instances, and that eight of the nine major turning points in the dollar exchange rate coincided exactly with concerted intervention. Their work convinces them that 'no satisfactory history of the dollar in the 1985–91 period can be written without reference to the episodes of concerted intervention'. Not surprisingly, the discussants have focused on methodological issues. Both Frankel and Edwin Truman are uneasy about the absence of formal econometric testing, and they cite situations in which the criteria adopted to measure success or failure may be somewhat arbitrary or where, on close inspection, the results are inconclusive. Giorgio Basevi expresses similar reservations and suggests that the effectiveness of intervention can be measured decisively only in the context of a formal model of the exchange rate. Nevertheless, Frankel and Truman are impressed by the body of evidence assembled. In Frankel's words: 'Even a more skeptical view that judged some of the successes to be so short-lived as not to be successes at all, might still see the overall record as an impressive one.' And though Truman favours 'leaning against the wind' of optimism about intervention, he concedes that 'intervention was partially successful

in about five of the episodes and I think this is a good enough record to support the continued judicious use of intervention as a supplementary policy instrument'. This is a strong conclusion; even Catte, Galli, and Rebecchini were reluctant to state it in so many words, and it has far-reaching implications for the management of the international monetary system.

4 The international framework for national economic policies

The chapters and comments in the final part of this volume are not concerned with specific aspects of the system but with its general structure and its influence on the management of the world economy and the international adjustment process. The stage is set in the historical analysis by Tamim Bayoumi and Barry Eichengreen, who examine the performance of the international economy under the various regimes that have governed it over the years, beginning with the classical gold standard. They set an ambitious agenda for their chapter: ascertaining whether the successive episodes of exchange rate stability and instability resulted from the actions of policymakers, changes in the underlying economic environment, or the capacity of the national economies to adjust to disturbances reflecting changes in policies or underlying economic conditions.

Bayoumi and Eichengreen's methodology allows them to measure the effects of disturbances and of the subsequent adjustments to them. They distinguish between disturbances affecting output permanently (interpreted as supply shocks associated with the instability of the underlying environment) and disturbances affecting it only temporarily (interpreted as demand shocks associated with changes in macroeconomic policies). They conclude that no single factor can explain why exchange rates were stable in some periods but not in others. Decisive changes in exchange rate arrangements can be explained only by invoking combinations of factors. By comparing economic performance under the classical gold standard and under the Bretton Woods system, however, they conclude that, when it comes to fixing blame for the collapse of the Bretton Woods system, 'the culprit appears to be the steady loss of macroeconomic flexibility over time'. They believe, moreover, that this loss of flexibility persisted into the period of generalized floating and that we cannot begin to design better exchange rate arrangements before 'identifying the factors responsible for the decline over time in the speed of adjustment'.

This finding is quite consistent with the conclusions of Morris Goldstein, who examines the motives and achievements of policy coordination among the major industrial countries. Policy coordination among those countries originated in dissatisfaction with the workings of the balance of payments

adjustment process and its effects on the real economy. Goldstein credits policy coordination with averting a surge in protectionism and with pointing to the need for removing structural rigidities in the G-7 countries, but he believes that it has focused excessively on exchange rate management and has neglected the correction of fiscal imbalances. Not surprisingly, the proposals he presents for strengthening policy coordination go in the direction of broadening its scope, reflecting a blend of what can realistically be done and what would in principle be desirable. They include, for example, proposals aimed at establishing monitoring zones for key macroeconomic variables. Jacques de Larosière goes much in the same direction. He criticizes the G-7 process for failing to detect the implications of the surge of indebtedness in the United States and the United Kingdom and of asset inflation in Japan, both being responsible for the depth and duration of the current recession. Furthermore, the failure to address fiscal imbalances, particularly in the United States, and we would add Germany, has led to an overburdening of monetary policies, which Larosière blames for several other problems, including the 'overshooting' of interest rates and 'distortions' in capital flows. In light of the recent events that have shaken the EMS, these observations appear prophetic. But Larosière does not want to abandon policy coordination, despite its limitations. He would instead seek to strengthen the process by giving more attention to medium-term goals, by focusing on the evolution of the policy mix, and by working for better-balanced implementation.

Goldstein would probably agree with Larosière's recommendations, but he would make one more. The G-7 countries should loosen rather than tighten their exchange rate targets. He thus disagrees with Bergsten, who maintains that those countries have already established *de facto* target zones and should now endorse them formally. According to Goldstein, 'loud' target zones would be unhelpful. It would be better, he argues, for the anchor countries to give price stability the highest priority, using 'quiet' target zones to monitor and evaluate exchange rate developments; more forceful intervention and policy adjustments should be reserved for those unusual situations when there is evidence of large misalignments. His position is supported, not surprisingly, by Leonhard Gleske, Toyoo Gyohten and by Lamberto Dini, who remains skeptical about the willingness of leading industrial countries to 'subordinate their internal policy objectives to the pursuit of exchange rate stability'. Dini, like Goldstein, believes that there is a need to improve multilateral surveillance by the IMF and to intensify the coordination of fiscal policies.

Most of the contributors to this part of the book appear to believe that global policy coordination will be facilitated by the eventual achievement of EMU and the introduction of a single EC currency. Gleske, for example,

elaborating on the point made above, that EMU will reduce the sensitivity of the EC economy to exchange rate changes, predicts that this will lead quite naturally to the result desired by Goldstein: more emphasis in international cooperation on 'establishing macroeconomic and structural conditions that are necessary as foundation of domestic stability' and less emphasis on exchange rate stabilization.

The belief expressed by many authors that the international monetary system is heading towards consolidation and simplification is carried much further by Richard Cooper. In his view, 'the international monetary system should serve the broader aims of society and therefore should be instrumental in making life better for the ordinary people'. What they want, Cooper says, is PPP, namely 'peace, prosperity, participation'. These objectives would be best served in the long run by establishing 'a single currency, at least among the major manufacturing nations, e.g., the European Community, Japan, and the United States'. Cooper concedes that this proposal 'raises a host of management issues, since a single currency must have a single monetary policy' but concludes that this 'is challenging but not impossible to work out'.

5 Conclusions

No contributor to this volume defends the present international monetary system as the best of all possible regimes. The strongest defenses one can find are that it is functioning reasonably well and, more emphatically, that there is no obvious way to improve it. The criticisms are more passionate and blunt, ranging from accusations of inequity between developed and developing countries to those of inefficiency in the allocation of resources and of ineffectiveness in promoting adjustment, especially among the large industrial countries. Most contributors do not appear to be disturbed, however, by the untidy nature of the present system, which combines elements from archetypal models that should in principle be mutually exclusive. Indeed, *laissez faire* and interventionism appear to enjoy equal rights of citizenship; exchange rate flexibility coexists with arrangements designed to limit it, such as the EMS; the liberalization of capital movements progresses side by side with schemes, such as the Baker and Brady plans, for recycling capital into countries from which it fled.

Developments affecting the international monetary system since the conference on which this book is based are likely to alter the balance among these heterogeneous elements, but the ultimate outcome is hard to predict. Conflicting currents are at work. The EMS crisis initiated in September of 1992 has moved the EC towards more flexible exchange rate arrangements. But it could, over time, also have the opposite effect of accelerating the

progress towards EMU by some of the more convergent EC members, leaving open the opportunity for others to join at a later stage. Such a two-tier EMU, although posing political difficulties, may prove in the end to play a role resembling that of the two-band EMS, which fostered economic and monetary integration in the 1980s. The crisis has also revived interest in the relevance of international liquidity by suggesting, as does Masera in this book, that creditworthiness may not be the only variable that can affect the availability of balance of payments financing. Even creditworthy countries were obliged to rely on official assistance, either bilateral or multilateral, to supplement their own reserves. The problem of access to credit is no longer confined to developing countries, which must go to the market to finance their development programmes; it extends to countries with sound fundamentals, such as France, which may still have to supplement their reserves in order to defend a stable exchange rate, while sorting out their domestic problems through the normal democratic process. It is easy to blame the slow-moving democratic process for failing sometimes to keep up with the swift pace at with which financial markets can mobilize funds. But no one should want to abandon the democratic process, any more than one should want to 'throw sand' into the international financial mechanism, à la Tobin, in order to slow them down. The reintroduction of restrictions on capital movements would be a step backward, imposing a loss of efficiency on the international monetary system and on the world economy. One can nevertheless hope that politicians will learn something from the experience of 1992–93. Markets cannot be expected to refrain from placing bets on the outcome of a referendum or election, and the defenses against the consequences of such bets must be mobilized well in advance.

Finally, the events of 1992 and 1993 may have major implications for the aims and procedures of policy coordination. It would seem that markets reward policy coordination of the sort embodied in the Community's plan for EMU while penalizing lapses and inconsistencies. This is natural enough. The market is the place where people take their savings and bring their investment plans, and it is therefore extremely sensitive to risks affecting the security of savings and the profitability of investment. To price those risks correctly, the market must gather and assess information about economic and political developments. Policy coordination produces information of an especially useful sort, because it reduces the likelihood of divergent policies. If this lesson is properly learned by governments, it may herald a stronger process of policy coordination among the G-7 countries, not narrowly confined to exchange rate matters. We cannot expect every G-7 meeting to produce major policy changes. We can hope that they will cease to be mere media events, aimed at self-justification, and will get serious about the work needed to reduce external imbalances, correct the

policy mix within and between key countries, and improve the performance of the world economy.

The authors of this introduction are reluctant to bet on the ultimate outcome of recent events, and might even not make identical bets if they had to do so. Nevertheless, they agree on one fundamental point. There is greater dissatisfaction with the working of the international monetary system today, towards the end of 1993, than at the time of the conference on which this book is based, and one can only hope that this would help alleviating the 'despair' about the feasibility of international monetary reform.

Notes

1 The late Robert Triffin went much further, describing the present arrangements as an 'international monetary scandal' (Triffin 1987).
2 See Solomon (1982) and Rebecchini, S. and Schioppa, C. 'Rinaldo Ossola and the Reform of the International Monetary System', unpublished background paper prepared for the conference in memory of Rinaldo Ossola, Perugia 9–10 July 1992.

References

Committee for the Study of Economic and Monetary Union 1989. *Report on Economic and Monetary Union in the European Community* (Delors Report), Luxembourg, European Community.

McKinnon, R.I. 1984. 'An International Standard for Monetary Stabilization', *Policy Analysis in International Economics*, Washington DC, Institute for International Economics, 8.

Miller, M.H. and Williamson, J. 1987. 'Targets and Indicators: A Blueprint for the International Coordination of Economic Policy', *Policy Analysis in International Economics*, Washington DC, Institute for International Economics, 22.

Ossola, R. 1971. 'Toward New Monetary Relationships', *Essays in International Finance*, Princeton, International Finance Section, Princeton University, 87, July.

Solomon, R. 1982. *The International Monetary System, 1945–1981*, New York, Harper & Row.

Triffin, R. 1987. 'The IMS (International Monetary System . . . or Scandal?) and the EMS (European Monetary System)', *Banca Nazionale del Lavoro Quarterly Review*, September.

Williamson, J. 1977. *The Failure of World Monetary Reform, 1971–74*, Sunbury on Thames.

I

Overview of the issues: retrospects and prospects

1 The international monetary issues of the Bretton Woods era

JACQUES J. POLAK

1 Introduction

The key question addressed in this chapter can be formulated as follows: do we revisit the intellectual battlefields of the 1960s and 1970s, merely to reminisce about a *temps perdu*? Or do we find in this experience much that is of value to us in facing the problems of today's international monetary system?

There is no doubt, as Robert Solomon has pointed out recently, that there have been major shifts in the features of the international monetary system that preoccupy officials (Solomon 1991, pp. 67–77). We think differently about adjustment now than we did in the 1960s. We hardly think any more about international liquidity, which was our major preoccupation in the 1960s. Market fluctuations of 15 per cent in the exchange rates of the major currencies, though they make most of us feel somewhat uncomfortable, are pretty well tolerated by all concerned, in contrast to the four months of crisis it took in 1971 to reach agreement on more modest exchange rate changes. Of late, we have even developed an indifference to current account imbalances that would have given us apoplexy less than a decade ago.[1] Solomon attributes many of these changing perspectives on the international monetary system to the enormous increase in the international mobility of capital. In a broad sense, that characterization is surely correct. But I would want to register two important reservations.

First, even though today's problems may look radically different from yesterday's, that does not make yesterday's solutions irrelevant to today's policymakers. Let me refer to some examples that relate to exchange rate regimes. At the end of the 'reform exercise' of 1972–4 most observers would probably have agreed with what Williamson wrote in 1977 'that the principal and crucial intellectual error of the Committee of Twenty (C-20) lay in the decision to opt for restoration of the adjustable peg at a time when this system had ceased to be viable because of the development of capital mobility' (Williamson 1977, p. 181). Yet, two years later most members of the European Community (EC) readopted the adjustable peg. By 1991, an

enlarged European Monetary System (EMS), with freedom of capital movements for its members, is generally accepted as a striking success (I am not overlooking the special – and hence limiting – political factors that were necessary to this success). Not only the Bretton Woods experience, but also the gold standard experience, now seems quite relevant to the understanding and the design of the Economic and Monetary Union (EMU). To cite a quite different case, I find that what Nurkse wrote fifty years ago on the difficult exchange rate choices facing some sterling area countries is highly pertinent to the current problems of Australia and New Zealand (League of Nations 1944, pp. 134–6). The problems that populate the time-space universe in which economists roam belong to only a limited number of species. Old friends and enemies, or their close relatives, pop up all the time.

The other side of the relevancy question is that one should not assume that, at any time, officials are focusing their attention on issues that are relevant *even at that time*. As seen from a safe distance, the 1960s and 1970s – and I am sure many other decades as well – reveal a considerable amount of lost motion, pursuit of solutions to phantom problems, or of ill-considered solutions to real problems. I shall come to some interesting instances in the course of my chapter. Here, I shall just briefly recall a single major misdirected effort of the 1970s. In 1974–5, the Organization for Economic Cooperation and Development (OECD) and the Group of Ten (G-10) spent an intense six months in working out an SDR 20 billion 'Financial Support Fund' proposed by the US authorities and the Secretary General of the OECD. This facility, to be attached to the OECD, was designed 'to back up private capital markets and other financing mechanisms'.[2] The developed countries did not need this third line of defense; in fact, since 1977, they have not used the second line, the International Monetary Fund (IMF). When the US Congress refused to put up the US share of the money, the plan collapsed without a trace and with hardly a tear.[3]

On the question of relevancy I would put my intermediate conclusions as follows:

(1) Even though the system has changed, much of the experience of the 1960s and 1970s remains relevant. Many of the outlines of that experience have become blurred by the events of the past quarter century. They deserve to be brought back to light.

(2) The same period also saw some major preventable misdirections of international efforts. They too deserve our attention – first, as a general matter, to maintain a healthy skepticism with respect to the collective wisdom of officials, and second, more specifically, because in economics bad ideas seem to have almost as many lives as cats. (My favourite example of this proposition is the topic of 'commodity currency'.)

Guided by these two thoughts, I have selected five topics for discussion, all of them very much in the area in which Ossola played a leading role. Each contains some elements of theory that deserve to be brought out, some aspects of history that need straightening out and perhaps even some modest lessons to be learnt. The topics relate to the adjustment process, liquidity creation, the interest rate on the Special Drawing Rights (SDR), a substitution account, and objective indicators for exchange rate adjustment. I will not reveal in advance which of these belongs in category one (the past unjustly forgotten) and which in category two (if only we had been brighter). And, as will become clear, where I criticize 'officials', I do not exclude those in international organizations.

I realize that my selection of topics leaves out what some might regard as the most significant failure of financial officials in the period: the long and agonizing death of the par value system, lasting (at least) from the November 1968 Bonn Conference to the second devaluation of the dollar in February 1973. That topic deserves a full-scale study of its own. I shall leave it here with a question. Can one fault the official family (ministers, central bank governors, senior officials) for their unwillingness to administer euthanasia to a beloved system while there was still a glimmer of hope that it might survive?

2 Adjustment

There is a widespread impression that, in the period we are here considering, there was too much emphasis on financing payments disequilibria and too little on adjustment. Up to a point, this impression is correct: note, for example, the fact that the two industrial countries that used the Fund's oil facility, the United Kingdom and Italy, soon thereafter had to come to the Fund for standby credits. But it would be quite wrong to say that the need for adjustment was neglected.

The first G-10 Deputies Report (1964) on 'the monetary system and its probable future needs for liquidity' started out with a long chapter on the importance of adjustment and suggested that Working Party 3 (WP-3) of the OECD prepare a special study on this. It did not take too many meetings of the WP-3 to prepare this study, which was published in 1966 (OECD 1966). The members of the committee knew their Tinbergen and Meade, and they could readily agree that 'the adjustment process is therefore essentially a question for governments as to how to achieve a wide range of aims of an economic, political, and social nature with the limited number of policy instruments actually or potentially available to them' (para. 16). The report notes wide agreement on the policies appropriate in 'pure demand cases' (para. 45). It is recognized that it is more difficult to deal with cases of 'imperfectly adjusted competitive positions': surplus

countries don't want to inflate and deficit countries don't want to accept prolonged periods of stagnant demand. Exchange rate changes are mentioned (for deficit countries only!), but with considerable reservation. It should be remembered that in the mid 1960s, exchange rate changes were a near taboo subject among the G-10 countries, especially for the United States and the United Kingdom.[4]

Looking at this 1966 OECD report from today's perspective, there are at least two interesting and I would say endearing characteristics that have tended to get lost in the succeeding period. They are:

(1) Countries are, on the whole, responsible for their own payments imbalances. This presupposes, of course, that aggregate demand in the world is maintained on a broadly satisfactory level; but that condition was reasonably fulfilled in the 1950s and 1960s. Any country that had a large deficit or surplus could, in this setting, be expected to take remedial measures.

(2) The appropriate measures depended on the cause of the imbalance. This was accepted doctrine, following Meade.

Much of the harmony in WP-3 in the 1960s can be explained in terms of these two propositions. They led, in principle, to clear prescriptions as to which country should do what. In practice, they left room for discussion on the facts, on the urgency of action or on its political acceptability. But if deficits or surpluses persisted, a strong consensus that included the country under consideration was likely to evolve. Neither of these two propositions is still present as a strong element in the adjustment process as it currently works (or does not work) among the main industrial countries. The second proposition – that there are objective criteria for the choice of appropriate adjustment policies – succumbed first. This happened in the reform exercise of the C-20. Considering how many rules that exercise tried to impose on countries (asset settlement, reserve composition, indicators, etc.), and anxious to avoid the criticism that it treated every imbalance beyond a certain size as calling for an exchange rate change, the Committee thought it wise to leave countries the choice among possible adjustment policies. Its rule on that subject was brief and vague (IMF 1974, p. 8): 'Countries will take such prompt and adequate adjustment action, domestic or external, as may be needed to avoid protracted payments imbalances. In choosing among different forms of adjustment action, countries will take into account repercussions on other countries as well as internal considerations.'

It is not so easy to pinpoint when the first proposition was abandoned, among other reasons because it is sometimes difficult to give to it a concrete content. *Ex post* statistics show only surpluses and deficits. In the 1960s and early 1970s, these figures at least added up to about zero for the world as a

whole, but even that is no longer the case. To find causes, to find which countries are 'at fault', one has to dig below the surface. In some instances, the imbalances may be attributable in part to surplus, in part to deficit countries. This was certainly the case in the 1971 situation, which called for, and in the end produced, multilateral adjustment. But it is one thing to acknowledge the difficulties in assigning responsibilities for adjustment, and another to abandon the effort altogether and to replace it by a political mechanism that makes external adjustment among the major countries simply their 'shared responsibility', helped along by 'a regular dialogue at the political level' and 'peer pressure'. This is how a US Treasury Report to Congress describes the 'structured but judgmental framework' of the Group of Seven (G-7), which is taking the place of the 'automatic techniques [that] failed in the past' (US Treasury 1988). (It is not clear what failing automatic techniques or what past the authors of this report may have had in mind).

The point here is not to invoke nostalgic feelings about the coordination of adjustment measures as seen in the 1960s. There is no question that changes in the world financial system, among other factors, have made the design of adjustment rules much more difficult. But before we abandon the fundamentals of the approach of that period (and, at the same time, the rationale for the IMF's consultations with individual countries) we would do well to know what we put in its place.

3 Liquidity creation

In the 1960s the liquidity question took up much more time (elapsed time and meeting time) than the adjustment question. This was essentially because it raised intellectually far more difficult issues. Senior officials found themselves virtually without guideposts on the design of a system of reserve creation. In addition, coming from central banks and treasuries, they were naturally hesitant to engage in an activity that amounted to the creation of money *ex nihilo*. Steps in that direction were possible only if presented as 'contingency planning', to deal with a potential liquidity shortage. But beyond these very real intellectual and psychological difficulties, the process that finally culminated in the design of the SDR was held up by strongly negative feelings on the part of the US, the UK, and French authorities. In particular in the first year of the discussions (1963–4), the United States and the United Kingdom were concerned about the possible competition that a new international reserve asset would bring to the two main reserve currencies. Even after this reservation had been overcome, the United States continued a rearguard action to keep the interest rate on the SDR as low as possible. The French continued throughout the discussions

to ride their own hobby horses: to enhance the role of gold and to deprive the reserve centres – in particular the United States – of their 'exorbitant privileges'; when they did put forward a plan for reserve creation it was in fact a thinly veiled plan to raise the price of gold (Solomon 1982, p. 76). The patience of Ossola, as Chairman of the *Study Group on the Creation of Reserve Assets*, was sorely tested as large sections of his report had to be taken up by the discussion of two plans that never had a chance of broad support: the French Collective Reserve Unit (CRU) scheme and the British Mutual Currency Account (MCA) scheme (G-10 1965). A further retarding factor was the political ineptitude of the G-10, once they got around to designing a system for reserve creation, to limit the benefits of this system to themselves ('liquidity creation of the Ten, by the Ten, for the Ten', as Pierre-Paul Schweitzer characterized it), with at best a second window dispensing comparable amounts of credit to the rest of the Fund membership.

Against this background, the time and effort taken to design an agreed SDR system were not exorbitant; indeed, it is still somewhat of a miracle that officials and governments found the courage to agree to a novel mechanism, designed to protect the international monetary system against a threat that was only potential.

But, one may ask from today's vantage point, were these efforts necessary? Why all this commotion about a potential shortage of international liquidity? The last fifteen years have pretty convincingly shown that such a shortage is a non-problem. With free capital markets, creditworthy countries – like creditworthy corporations – can borrow the amount of liquidity they need. The supply of liquidity is a global one, to meet the total world demand of liquidity from private and official holders combined. That supply is set by the monetary policies of the major industrial countries whose currencies are used in reserves. These policies may, at any moment of time, be unduly tight or unduly lax by some sort of world standard, as judged for example by the weighted votes of the governors of the IMF. But the possibility that the sum of the monetary policies of a small number of key countries may not be optimal does not create the need for a collective power to create or destroy money, such as that provided by the SDR mechanism. If the main central banks agreed that more money was needed, they would supply it themselves; if not, they would have the votes to block SDR creation in the Fund.

It is easy to project this view of the liquidity question backwards and to pass the judgment that the question was not relevant in the 1960s either. I think this would be a wrong inference from the available evidence. At that time, capital markets were not yet free enough and deep enough to satisfy governments' legitimate needs for reserves. A few small countries (Norway, Australia) could satisfy their reserve needs in that market. Larger countries

could not. It took the petrodollar deposits of the mid 1970s to get the commercial banks into the sovereign lending business on a world scale.

By the late 1960s, this stage had not yet been reached and it would be hard to fault officials for not foreseeing it. What they did see was, instead, a certain tightening of international liquidity (gold and dollars) and emerging symptoms of a reserve shortage that their analysis had suggested as a possibility.[5] More detailed analysis of the 1969 decision to allocate SDRs would certainly be desirable. Were officials unduly influenced by the short-term tightening of credit in the United States and the resulting return flow of capital? Was there a certain itch to testdrive the new mechanism that had been put together with so much effort over the preceding six years? Perhaps there was a bit of both. But, mostly, this was a case where unpredictable events in the world economy turned a highly relevant problem into a marginal problem within a decade, creating a situation where it would be helpful to low-income countries, but hardly essential to the system, to continue SDR allocations (Polak 1988, pp. 175–90).

Could the problem come back – if not on the scale feared in the 1960s, but large enough to require the resumption of allocations? A good case can be made that it has come back. The countries making up the Commonwealth of Independent States (CIS) are making their entry in the international monetary system with negligible reserves. For one of them, Russia, the G-7 have announced a willingness to marshal a reserve fund of $6 billion, and commensurate action will no doubt prove necessary for the others. The G-7 and the G-10 have also acknowledged this as a system-threatening problem by announcing their willingness to activate the General Arrangements to Borrow (GAB) for this purpose.[6] But why invoke the GAB, which is designed for short-term lending, when what is needed is a permanent addition to the reserves of a major group of members and to the world reserve total?

To achieve that objective, the SDR mechanism is clearly the more appropriate one. This is not the place to enter into a discussion on how precisely that mechanism could best be used for this purpose, given the fundamental rule that SDR allocations are made to all members in proportion to quotas. Quite likely, the best technique would be a moderate-sized allocation, combined with an agreement that the main industrial countries would on-lend their allocations (perhaps through the Fund) to the CSI members and to the, equally needy, developing countries, as a second addition to all these countries' reserves.

4 The rate of interest on the SDR

One of the puzzling aspects of the long discussion (1963 to 1967) on the creation of the SDR was the almost total disregard of the interest rate on

this asset. Indeed, that discussion can only be understood on the implied assumption that the SDR would carry a zero interest rate and that hence, in the absence of mandatory reconstitution, SDR allocations were equivalent to 100 per cent grants. At one of the early G-10 meetings, the Canadian Deputy, Plumptre, shocked others by making this assumption almost explicit when he suggested that decisions to distribute reserve assets 'would presumably be taken just before Christmas'. But the response, then and later, was not to call for a proper interest mechanism to ensure that these were not gifts, but to argue that the benefits of receiving SDRs as gifts would be balanced by the potential 'burdens' to which participants in the scheme would be exposed.

In the 1960s, the Fund staff – I am sorry to say – was as much at fault as anyone else in treating SDR allocations as pure grants. This common misconception was responsible for much of the confusion in the semipublic debate that Ossola and I had in the fall of 1965 on the benefits of SDR allocations.[7] In the absence of a market interest rate on the SDR, the obligation to accept SDRs for a payments surplus would indeed be 'a burden', and a case could thus be constructed for limiting the distribution of SDRs to countries whose balances of payments could be expected to oscillate between deficits and surpluses. It then took only two (counterfactual) assumptions – that all G-10 countries qualified under this test and that the developing countries were not in the habit of building up reserves – to find a logical base for restricting the new reserve system to the G-10. That proposition was, in the end, abandoned by the G-10 but (as the Ossola correspondence shows) not because of a proper design of the SDR system with a market interest rate, but because it became untenable politically.

The Ossola Report dismissed the question of the SDR interest rate in a simple paragraph: 'The opinion has been expressed that payment of interest on all or some reserve claims would enhance their attractiveness as reserves, and some would make the rate variable in order to improve the flexibility of the scheme. Others, however, considered that, where a gold value guarantee is envisaged, the asset should be non-interest bearing' (G-10 1965, para. 146).

The initial interest rate on the SDR was set at 1.5 per cent *per annum*, which was copied from the interest rate set in 1962 under the GAB. In 1962, that had not been a negligible interest rate for a gold-guaranteed asset, but that was no longer so by the end of the decade.[8] By that time, many of the theoretical issues concerning the SDR had been clarified at a Fund-sponsored conference (IMF 1970) and the logic of moving the SDR interest rate to the market rate was recognized, at least by the technicians.

Once the SDR was severed from gold in 1974 and linked to a basket of currencies, the rate of interest was first raised to 5 per cent (about half the

market rate of the basket) and then gradually to the market rate by 1980. This helped to clarify the benefits of SDR allocations. Countries with ready access to the world's capital markets at the going rate now derive negligible benefits from SDR allocations – most of these countries have turned against further allocations, which has brought the SDR system to its current impasse. But countries with no access to capital markets, or that have to pay high premiums in such markets or for suppliers' credits, still benefit from allocations.

But on another contentious aspect of collective reserve creation, *viz*. the link to development financing, disregard of the interest rate question continued to produce needless controversy. A large part of the developing countries' case for the link rested on a zero SDR interest rate. As Ossola pointed out in 1972, 'if SDRs carry a market type rate of interest, a link would entail a long-term loan rather than an outright grant' (Ossola 1972). One of the very few points on which all participants in the debate on the link in the framework of the 1972–4 reform exercise could agree was that 'the overall benefit of link allocations to developing countries might not appear very large' at market interest rates, although these countries would at least get long-term credit at short-term rates without a risk premium (IMF 1974, p. 108). The developing countries – in particular those that were eligible for the zero interest credits of the International Development Assistance – could have taken the clue at this point and given up the struggle for the link. In fact, it took them until 1986 to do so.[9]

The muddle on the SDR interest rate is not an isolated example. On the contrary, it seems to fit into a pattern to use the rate on official assets and liabilities to pursue extraneous objectives. You will recall the proposal by Keynes (of all persons) to charge interest not only on debit but also on credit balances in the Credit Union in order to push creditors towards adjustment,[10] a proposal repeated to great acclaim by the French in the C-20 (Solomon 1982, p. 254).

Subordination of interest rates to other considerations is not entirely a thing of the past – it has recurred in the Fund (in a less extreme form) in recent years. It had taken the Fund about forty years to achieve (near) market interest rates: a credit rate equal to the SDR rate and a debit rate slightly below the SDR rate (the small element of concessionality made possible by the fact that the Fund had sold about one third of its gold in 1976–80, adding the book value of SDR 35 per ounce to its usable resources). But, as some countries fell into arrears in the 1980s, the Fund, anxious to keep up its income and to build up some additional reserves started adding basis points to the rate of charge and subtracting basis points from the credit interest rate, thus increasingly running the risk of pricing itself out of the market on two sides at the same time.

5 A substitution account?

Three times in the past twenty years the world's financial officials have laboured over the design of a substitution account – an account into which countries could deposit dollars (and perhaps other currencies) from their reserves against new SDRs or claims expressed in SDRs. The idea was studied as part of the 1972–4 effort to reform the international system, in 1978, as the counterpart of the decision to allocate SDRs, and again in 1979–80 in a period of widespread concern about a 'dollar overhang'. All these efforts remained unsuccessful. The reform effort at substitution disappeared from the scene together with the other hobby horses of that failed exercise: 'stable but adjustable par values', asset settlement, the link, and reserve indicators. In 1978, it turned out that agreement on an SDR allocation could after all be reached without reduction in the dollar component in reserves through substitution. And the last, the most determined, and nearly successful, attempt to create a substitution account failed in April 1980 when no agreement could be reached on the ultimate distribution of the risks of such an account and, perhaps more important, when the dollar began its ascent that lasted until early 1985.

Against this background of failure, it is important to put on record the single successful instance of substitution in the Fund. It occurred well before there were SDRs and it was Ossola's idea. Specifically, during the meeting of the G-10 Deputies in Rome in May 1966, Ossola, together with Governor Dewey Daane of the Federal Reserve System, approached me to explore whether a Fund transaction could be designed to solve the following problem. Italy considered that it had excess dollars and would like to deposit $250 million in the Fund. The United States was agreeable to the transaction. The operation was to be kept outside of the GAB, adopted in 1962, which would require agreement among the G-10. My reply was that this could indeed be handled in the Fund, provided that the transaction was executed by means of a series of steps allowed under the Fund's Articles. Italy would lend the Fund an amount of lire equivalent to $250 million. The United States would buy this amount of lire from the Fund, and then use the lire to purchase $250 million in US dollars from Italy. These three operations would give Italy a transferable gold-guaranteed claim on the Fund instead of its $250 million in dollars;[11] the United States would have a corresponding reduction in its reserve tranche (then still called 'gold tranche') in the Fund. While the Fund would describe the operation as a loan, it offered to find language that enabled Italy to describe it as 'depositing dollars with the Fund'. It took a few more months to tie down the details of the operation, which took place in August 1966.[12] In mid 1970, when Italy had a payments deficit, it used its claim on the Fund as a reserve asset by transferring it to Japan.

For the modest amount involved, thus, the attempt to use the mechanism of the Fund as a substitution account was entirely successful. It could have set an important precedent – although a more general use of a substitution facility would have had to overcome formidable difficulties. The United States had less than $500 million left for gold tranche drawings; would it have agreed to enter into a Fund standby arrangement in the credit tranches to accommodate other 'depositors'? What would have been the Fund's terms for such an unusual standby arrangement? Would it have been phased? None of these questions came up. The potential importance of the arrangement was barely noticed, and no other Fund member asked for the same treatment.[13]

But another feature of *this* substitution transaction is to be noted. Not only did Italy get a gold-guaranteed claim; the United States also accepted a gold-guaranteed liability. If the United States had agreed to the equivalent provision in later discussions on a substitution account (a liability expressed in SDRs), the negotiations in 1979–80 on such an account would have been materially simpler. As it was, the US insistence that its liability to a substitution account be expressed in dollars rather than SDRs made the problem of the financial balance of that account insoluble, thus posing the politically unmanageable problem as to how to distribute among the members any loss that such an account might incur.

It does not seem likely at present that the concept of a substitution account will again come to the fore as a conceivable answer to a real problem – or might it, when the European Central Bank (ECB) finds that the merged dollar holdings of the EC central banks far exceed its reserve needs? In any event, one lesson deserves to be carefully stored for possible future use, namely that expressing the claims on such an account in SDRs – the arrangement which the United States absolutely rejected at the time – would come very close to providing the magical 50/50 distribution of risk between creditors and the United States as debtor.[14]

6 'Objective indicators' for exchange rate adjustment

The trials of the Summer and Fall of 1971 had brought home to the United States the asymmetry of an adjustment system based on convertibility only: the deficit country is forced to take adjustment action, when reserves run out; the surplus country, on the other hand, while it may suffer an inflationary impact from the inflow of excessive reserves, is not put under the same necessity to adopt radical policy measures. Keynes had made the point in 1943; by 1972 the United States was ready to act upon it (Solomon 1982, p. 242).

In the first available forum for reform of the system – the preparation by the executive directors of the IMF, at the request of the governors, of a

report 'on the measures that are necessary or desirable for the improvement or reform of the international monetary system' – the US Director proposed a symmetrical system triggered by objective reserve indicators. Under this system, internationally agreed upper and lower limits for reserves would be established for each country to serve as 'objective indicators of par value changes'. If the reserves reached one or the other limit, 'this would be regarded as an indication, or as *prima facie* evidence, that a parity change was needed'.[15]

The reaction of the Executive Board to this proposal was overwhelmingly negative – not to the concept of symmetry, but to its implementation by reserve indicators. The Fund itself had an unsatisfactory experience with reserve statistics as a determinant of a far less important obligation of member countries, *viz.* the amount of past drawings they would have to repurchase. In the original Articles of Agreement this was linked to reserve levels and reserve increases, but members that wanted to delay repurchase had found it possible to manipulate reserve statistics. As part of the second amendment, the entire automatic provision was dropped and replaced by more judgmental rules.

More generally, the discussion made clear that most countries would not want to attach a decision to change their exchange rate, even presumptively, to reserve movements that might reflect short-term rather than fundamental developments, although they had to admit that experience with the alternative to indicators – 'balanced assessment' – had not been impressive.

When the reform discussion next moved to the Deputies of the C-20, the indicator proposal was again put on the table (C-20 1973, pp. 160–74). By now, some measure of flexibility had been introduced: the indicators would not give automatic, 'but strong presumptive', signals for adjustment, and some room was made for adjustment by measures other than changes in the exchange rate.

Even in its modified form, the American proposal could hardly be expected to find wide support. But an Italian counterproposal did much to avoid a head-on clash on indicators as such (Ossola and Palumbo 1972). In a paper circulated two days before the US paper, the Italian Deputies accepted the need for indicators. As they put it: 'The discretionary assessment of fundamental disequilibria has been tried, and it has been found wanting.' But they rejected reserve indicators as 'being too easily manipulated by the monetary authorities', giving rise to friction over their interpretation, and subject to random disturbances. Instead, they suggested the cyclically adjusted basic balance as 'the indicator least subject to official tinkering and most likely to provide correct information on the underlying trend of the balance of payments'. And they added that any information

provided by indicators would need to be supplemented by analysis of the current and prospective situation.

The Italian paper had the beauty of integrating the American proposal into a wider range of indicator plans with differing degrees of automaticity and judgment. A Fund staff paper comparing the two indicators from a variety of angles pushed further in this direction (IMF 1985b, pp. 57–67). Conceivably, if other elements of the reform exercise had fallen into place, this could have led to the adoption of some kind of judgmental indicator component as part of the reformed system. But the reserve indicator as a trigger of exchange rate changes could never have made it.[16] That, I am sure, was clear to Rinaldo Ossola in 1972. And a twenty-year jump to the present will provide confirmation, if any were needed. Article 104c of the Maastricht Treaty describes the consequences of an EC member state exceeding the fiscal objective indicators of that treaty. Although the EC members are pursuing an 'ever closer union', the punishment of fiscal transgression even in stage three is restricted to reports, the need to publish more information before issuing bonds, a possible cutoff from the European Investment Bank, possible fines and (our old standby since the days of Keynes) mandatory non-interest-bearing deposits! (Kenen 1992, pp. 73–4).

7 A moral?

Is there a moral to be drawn on the basis of these snapshots of the international monetary system, and of those who laboured at it, in the 1960s and 1970s? One lesson no doubt is that there was much lost motion, in part because of a true lack of understanding (the nature of the SDR, the role of interest rates), in part also because countries pursued political objectives rather than improvements of the system or even recognizable national economic or financial interests. The specific problems caused by these shortcomings are no longer relevant; at best, recognition of them may help future monetary negotiators to lose a little less time in dead-end streets. But the fundamental issues of adjustment and liquidity are still with us – and the constructive labour that Ossola and his colleagues performed in past decades will continue, not only to inspire us, but also, in a practical way, to guide us.

Notes

The author acknowledges valuable suggestions made by M. Goldstein and J. Williamson.

1 Compare Marris (1985) with Corden (1991, pp. 455–78).
2 OECD 1976, pp. 17–19. At the time this was known as the *Kissinger Plan*. The

total of quotas at SDR 20 billion about equalled the sum of the quotas of the OECD members in the IMF.

3 No reference to the plan can be found in Solomon (1982).

4 The first G-10 Deputies Report (chaired by Robert Roosa) had managed only barely, in a backhanded way, to recognize the exchange rate as an instrument of adjustment. The report did not include it in its listing of six instruments of economic policy, but then added: 'Such instruments must be employed with proper regard for obligations in the field of international trade and for the IMF obligation to maintain stable exchange parities which are subject to change only in cases of fundamental disequilibrium' (G-10 1964, para. 6).

5 'Proposal by the Managing Director on the Allocation of Special Drawing Rights for the First Basic Period' (1969), reprinted in IMF (1970, pp. 491–509).

6 Use of GAB resources for a non-participant requires a finding of 'an exceptional situation ... that could threaten the stability of the international monetary system' (GAB decision of 24 February 1983, para. 21 (b)).

7 Polak's letter to Ossola, 3 November 1965 and Ossola's letter to Polak, 24 November 1965 (documentation for the first joint Meeting of the IMF Executive Directors and the G-10 Deputies, Washington DC, 28–30 November 1965, unpublished).

8 This is evident from the consensus among economists who discussed the matter at the time. Sohmen described credit at the SDR rate as 'almost without charge' (Sohmen 1970, p. 18). Lindbeck speaks of 'gratis reserves' (Lindbeck 1970, p. 36). Fleming describes the SDR allocation mechanism as 'reserves [being] rationed out among countries virtually as a gift in predetermined proportions' (Fleming 1971, p. 36). Hirsch sees the full fruition of the SDR at risk from 'an artificially low interest rate' (Hirsch 1971, pp. 245–6).

9 When they agreed to para. 7 in the April 1986 Communiqué of the Interim Committee which stressed 'the monetary character of the SDR, which should not be a means of transferring resources' (IMF 1986, p. 116).

10 At the time, Dennis Robertson pointed out the ambivalence of this position in his wonderful ditty:
'Are we to love, honour, cherish, and thank or
to kick in the bottom the blokes who hold bancor?'
(Cited in Horsefield 1969, vol. I, p. 19).

11 The transfer was subject to Fund consent, as under the GAB, but Italy had every reason to expect the Fund to give its consent when asked.

12 The text of the exchange of letters setting out the condition of Italy's loan is found in de Vries 1976b, vol. II, pp. 211–13.

13 The Fund's history reports the operation in a brief paragraph that misses entirely its systemic significance: 'On only one occasion did the Fund engage in bilateral borrowing. In August 1966, when the United States sought to draw $250 million in Italian lire, the Fund's holdings of lire were down to $70 million. The Fund thereupon borrowed the $250 million in lire from Italy under a special arrangement similar to, but outside of, the GAB' (de Vries 1976a, I, p. 376).

14 With the weight of the dollar at 40 per cent of the SDR basket, the effect of expressing the claims of the account, like those of its liabilities, in SDRs would

have meant that the United States would have borne 60 per cent, and the creditors of the account 40 per cent, of the exchange risk.

15 Report by the IMF Executive Directors to the Board of Governors, 18 August 1972 (reprinted in IMF 1985a, vol. III, pp. 19–56). For the discussions leading up to the report, see de Vries 1976a, vol. I, pp. 130–7. Note that Solomon gives no inkling that at least this part of the 'Volcker plan' got an airing well before the famous Shultz speech at the 1972 Annual Meeting and the submission of the plan to the Deputies of the C-20 in November 1972.

16 As Williamson points out, that indicator also suffered from the handicap that it would, in a most unwelcome way, advertise impending par value changes (Williamson 1977, p. 182).

References

Committee of Twenty 1973. 'The US Proposals for Using Reserves as an Indicator of the Need for Balance of Payments Adjustment', Document of Deputies (27 November 1972), reprinted in Council of Economic Advisers, *Economic Report of the President*, January.

Corden, W.M. 1991. 'Does the Current Account Matter? The Old View and the New', in J.A. Frenkel and M. Goldstein (eds.), *International Financial Policy Essays in Honour of J.J. Polak*, Washington DC, IMF.

de Vries, M.G. 1976a. *The International Monetary Fund, 1966–71*, vol. I, Washington DC.

1976b. *The International Monetary Fund, 1966–71*, vol. II, Washington DC.

Fleming, J.M. 1971. 'The SDR: Some Problems and Possibilities', *IMF Staff Papers*, March.

Group of Ten 1964. *Ministerial Statement of the Group of Ten*, Annex prepared by Deputies, Paris, August.

1965. *Report of the Study Group on the Creation of Reserve Assets*, n.p., May.

Hirsch, F. 1971. 'SDRs and the Working of the Gold Standard', *IMF Staff Papers*, July.

Horsefield, J.K. 1969. *The International Monetary Fund, 1945–65*, vol. I, Washington DC.

International Monetary Fund 1970. *International Reserves – Needs and Availability*, Washington DC.

1974. *International Monetary Reform*, Documents of the Committee of Twenty, Washington DC.

1985a. 'Reform of the International Monetary System', Report by the Executive Directors to the Board of Governors (18 August 1972), reprinted in M.G. de Vries (eds.), *The International Monetary Fund, 1972–78, Cooperation on Trial*, vol. III.

1985b. 'Reserves and Basic Balances as Possible Indicators of the Need for Payments Adjustment', Document of Deputies, Committee of Twenty, (10 January 1973), reprinted in M.G. de Vries, *ibid*.

1986. 'Communiqué of the Interim Committee', *IMF Survey*, 21 April.

Kenen, P.B. 1992. *EMU after Maastricht*, Washington DC, Group of Thirty.

League of Nations 1944. *International Currency Experience*, Princeton.

Lindbeck, A. 1970. 'Comment on Sohmen', in International Monetary Fund, *International Reserves – Needs and Availability*, Washington DC.

Marris, S. 1985. *Deficits and the Dollar: the World Economy at Risk*, Washington DC, Institute for International Economics.

Organization for Economic Cooperation and Development 1966. *The Balance of Payments Adjustment Process*, Working Party No. 3 of the Economic Policy Committee, Paris, August.

1976. *Activities of OECD in 1975*, Report by the Secretary General, Paris.

Ossola, R. 1972. *Statement in the Second Meeting of the Deputies of Committee of Twenty*, 25 November.

Ossola, R. and Palumbo, S. 1972. *Adjustment Process and Exchange Rate Mechanism*, Document of Deputies, Committee of Twenty, 25 November.

Polak, J.J. 1988. 'The Impasse Concerning the Role of the SDR', in Wietze Eizenga *et al.* (eds.), *The Quest for National and Global Economic Stability*, Dordrecht.

Sohmen, E. 1970. 'General Reserve Supplementation: Some Central Issues', in International Monetary Fund, *International Reserves – Needs and Availability*, Washington DC.

Solomon, R. 1982. *The International Monetary System, 1945–81*, New York.

1991. 'Changing Perspectives on the International Monetary System', in J.A. Frenkel and M. Goldstein (eds.), *International Financial Policy: Essays in Honour of J.J. Polak*, Washington DC, IMF.

US Treasury 1988. *Report to the Congress on International Economic and Exchange Rate Policy*, 15 October.

Williamson, J. 1977. *The Failure of World Monetary Reform, 1971–74*, Sunbury on Thames.

2 Significant episodes in the evolution of the international monetary system

GUIDO CARLI

This chapter draws on my personal experience in international monetary issues over more than a quarter of a century in various international organizations, at the Italian Foreign Exchange Office, and at the Banca d'Italia. Together with Rinaldo Ossola, with whom I had a close association, I witnessed important events and will briefly mention some of them, selecting those that may be of interest today.

In 1950, I became chairman of the board of the European Payments Union (EPU), where we established what amounted to a system of multilateral surveillance, although we did not use such terminology at the time. The first exercise of surveillance was carried out on the occasion of the request by Germany for a line of credit to finance its balance of payments needs. We sent two economists to Germany, Per Jacobsson and Alec Cairncross. They came back and reassured us that Germany could be considered a reliable debtor. Since then Germany has been in permanent current account surplus, becoming, together with Japan, the most important net capital exporting country. This is a function that Germany has now given up, following the unification with the Eastern Länder: a change with potentially far-reaching repercussions for the world economy and the international financial system.

By the end of 1959 Robert Triffin sounded a warning about the implications of the US balance of payments deficit having become the only source of additional foreign exchange reserves and suggested considering alternative ways of supplementing international liquidity that would be less dependent upon the US payments deficit. I recall that the first suggestion that a new international reserve asset be established to replace gold and dollars was made in 1963 by Edward Bernstein. Bernstein recommended that the large industrial countries of the Group of Ten (G-10) establish a new Collective Reserve Unit, the CRU, that could be acquired by depositing in the IMF gold and reserve currencies (dollars, sterling, and French francs). Ideally a reserve unit might thus be regarded as a basket of reserve assets that could be used for settlement among countries. The participating

countries would be free to hold their reserves in any form, but holdings of gold would have to be matched by a minimum holding of reserve units, equal to at least one half of their gold reserves.

I see some analogies with some of the problems under discussion today: first, the idea of considering a basket of currencies as the equivalent of a reserve unit and, second, that of limiting the preponderant role of the currency of the dominant country. In 1964 the debate moved into the official arena at the International Monetary Fund (IMF). Following the indications of the report prepared by Ossola, the G-10 ministerial statement of 10 August 1964 admitted that the continuing growth in the volume of world trade and payments was likely to require additional international liquidity, perhaps in the form of a new reserve asset. Against this line of reasoning was the position of the President of France, General de Gaulle. He called for the abolition of the gold exchange standard and the settlement in gold of balance of payments deficits. In the opinion of the General the gold exchange standard lacked what he called reciprocity, because the dollar was considered as the equivalent of gold, unlike other currencies. That meant the United States was free to incur balance of payment deficits and finance them with dollars, a currency they could print, whereas other countries had to settle their deficits either in gold or in dollars, that is, in assets they had to earn. In this connection, it should not be forgotten that the gold exchange system was invented by Great Britain, in fact by John Maynard Keynes, to handle Britain's relations with India at the beginning of the century. It also worked only one way: when India was in deficit with Britain, it had to pay in gold, but when Britain was in deficit with India, it could pay in sterling.

General de Gaulle was also firmly against the idea of an 'abstract currency': he insisted that money concerns the public and has to be understood by everybody, while artificial currencies are not comprehensible to ordinary people. We have a similar situation today in Germany, where people know what a Deutsche mark is, but do not really understand what an ECU is, and therefore have a preference for the mark. It may be easy for central bank governors to understand what the ECU is, but explaining this to the public is not so easy. It takes time to convince people that money is something abstract, created by a group of wise persons, or pretending to be such.

The negotiations in the G-10 arrived at the conclusion that a deliberate, across-the-board creation of additional liquidity would be desirable. However, such a step raised the question not only of how to limit the creation of reserves but also of how to keep the amount of reserve assets within limits consistent with anti-inflationary policy. We are confronted with the same problems today regarding the ECU. What authority is

responsible for creating the ECUs? Can there be an obligation for creditor countries to accept settlement in ECUs in unlimited amounts?

In June 1971, Ossola and I went to Washington to discuss the situation of the international monetary system with the newly appointed Secretary of the Treasury, John Connally. Connally gave us an extremely forthright description of the policies of the United States of the time. More or less he said to us: 'America is no longer the land of unlimited opportunities, it is no longer possible to finance the Vietnam war, free health care, social security, and public works. Americans have become convinced that everyone is entitled to receive, in one form or the other, payments from the state. Something has to be done. The time of great decisions has come.' The great decisions were taken in 15 August 1971: the convertibility of the dollar into gold was abrogated. After an experiment with a fixed exchange rate system, but without the convertibility of the dollar into gold, the world moved to a floating exchange rate system. The first debate on how to manage the floating exchange rate system took place in September 1973 at the IMF Annual Meeting in Nairobi. The Managing Director of the Fund, Johannes Witteveen, spoke of the need for governments to allow a degree of exchange rate flexibility, subject to internationally agreed rules; I believe that this is still an issue of great importance today. The following year at the IMF Annual Meeting in Washington, the new American Secretary of the Treasury, William Simon, stated: 'Market forces must not be treated as enemies to be resisted at all costs but as necessary and helpful reflections of changing conditions in a highly interrelated world economy, with wide freedom for international trade and capital flows.' I have listened to similar statements in meetings in which I have participated recently and it seems to me that the debate has not come to a conclusion yet.

In this short recollection of events that Ossola and I witnessed, I have tried to select those that may be relevant today, particularly in the international debate on how to coordinate policies, keep exchange rates within limits consistent with the development of world trade, and avoid using high interest rates to protect the desired level of exchange rates. The problem of better policy coordination among countries in a floating exchange rate regime is still unresolved, and I believe that a contribution to its solution could come from the construction of the European Monetary Union. Establishing an area of true monetary stability could put Europe in a better position to deal with the United States and Japan in the domain of international monetary and trade relations.

Editors' note

This is an edited version of the remarks delivered by Dr Carli at the conference. Dr Carli died on 23 April 1993 without having had the time to review the final text.

Discussion

ROBERT Z. ALIBER

There are four reasons why I was eager to participate in this timely conference. The first is that for more than twenty years involvement with the Banca d'Italia has always been rewarding – I never seem to leave a meeting or conference without having learned something important. The second is the opportunity to comment on Polak's work, more than anyone else, Polak has been at the core of thinking in the international financial establishment. For more than thirty years his intellectual contribution to the 'The Monetary Theory of the Balance of Payments' was a singular achievement in a systemic view towards analysis of the causes of payments imbalances. And the third reason was that the title of Polak's chapter and I paraphrase, 'what can we learn from the Bretton Woods system that is now relevant for current international problems?' fits the mode of several papers I have been working on during the last three or four years. The fourth reason was that after so many conferences on whether forward exchange rates are biased or unbiased predictors of the future spot exchange rate, it seemed important to show appreciation for the initiative of Banca d'Italia in organizing a conference that takes a general equilibrium approach to analyse the system.

Polak's chapter provides an insider's view of the analysis and negotiations about five policy problem areas: adjustment, liquidity or reserve creation, the interest rate on the Special Drawing Rights (SDR), the substitution account, and objective indicators for changes in exchange rates that preoccupied Rinaldo Ossola and other members of the international financial establishment in the 1950s and 1960s; his chapter presents a fascinating intellectual history of this group's approach to these problems.

Polak is remarkably self-critical (more prone than many of my academic colleagues to admit of shortcomings of view). He presents a retrospective report card on how well those who met at the IMF worked their way through these adjustment and liquidity questions. Polak does not provide letter grades that our students demand; instead, there is a wistful tone in many of the comments: 'if only we had been smarter at that time'. My

interpretation is that the establishment deserves a relatively low grade on the interest rate on SDR and on the substitution account, and modestly higher grades on liquidity creation. He is too hard on himself on liquidity creation and too generous on the substitution account.

The key words in his paper are 'lost motion' – that, in some cases, the negotiations proved fruitless and that, in others, the achievements were modest. Indeed Polak concludes with the observation 'that there was much lost motion, in part because of a true lack of understanding (the nature of the SDR, the role of interest rates), in part also because countries pursued political objectives rather than improvements of the system or even recognizable national economic or financial interests'. The two key words in my comment are 'global consistency' – and I want to develop the analogy between the US payments deficits of the 1950s and the first half of the 1960s, and the massive US trade deficits of the 1980s.

Lost motion is inevitable in any intellectual exercise; many of us go through twenty or thirty drafts before an argument that seemed intuitive becomes clear and self-evident. National governments have a duty to pursue their national interests. A tension is almost inevitable because the interests of some members of the international financial establishment in seeking 'improvements in the system' may be inconsistent with the efforts of finance ministers of individual countries in seeking to advance national interests. One explanation for what Polak perceived as the 'lost motion' involved in the negotiations on liquidity creation, interest rate on SDR, and the substitution account concerns the way members of the establishment viewed (or more precisely, didn't view) competition among several national monies and gold, and SDR, which is a Gresham's Law problem.

The intellectual history that Polak describes might be summarized as the establishment's increasing familiarization with the impact of investor estimates of the total return and the risk of individual assets on their demand for each of these assets (and here I include monetary institutions as well as private parties). Thus Polak summarizes the problem of reserve shortage as a 'non-problem'. 'With free capital markets, creditworthy countries – like creditworthy corporations – can borrow the amount of liquidity they need.' Some countries, especially those with high domestic interest rates, may prefer a liability management approach to reserve management while others, primarily those with low interest rates, may prefer to accumulate reserve assets. As long as some countries prefer the asset management approach, the global consistency issue remains central.

The failure of the several initiatives toward developing a substitution account reflects the reluctance of the United States to accept a transfer of exchange risk without a compensating payment from the countries that would be relieved of this risk. A substitution account might be attractive to

the United States as long as there was a fixed US dollar price of gold; in the absence of the gold parity, the initiative seemed like an exercise without an economic rationale. The establishment's apparent lack of understanding about the relative price of various assets is highlighted by its inattention to the role of gold in private portfolios and official portfolios. Gold was 'inconvenient' partly because of the commitments about the retention of the parity; partly because it was competitive with the SDR and other securities in investor portfolios.

The reserve shortage of the 1960s reflected that gold had been under-priced since the early 1950s; the US Treasury sold gold from its buffer stock to maintain the $35 parity. The idea that the official price of gold might be increased – a recommendation that Milton Gilbert and Roy Harrod made in the 1960s – was slighted by extraneous arguments that involved the moral repugnance of apartheid in South Africa, and the reluctance to transfer wealth to the Soviet Union. Eventually market forces accomplished what the authorities were reluctant to initiate, the market price of gold surged far beyond anyone's expectations. The increase in the value of reserve assets that resulted from the increases in the market price of gold was ten to twenty times larger than the value of SDR extant. The logical implication of the arguments which had been used to justify the SDR arrangement in the 1960s was that the volume of SDR should have been reduced rather than increased in response to the surge in the oil price and the gold price.

A further explanation for Polak's 'lost motion' is the problem that the international financial establishment had, and still has, in dealing with the unique US role in international monetary arrangements. The United States is more than just another country, somewhat larger than any other, with a quota in the International Monetary Fund (IMF) sufficiently large to veto the initiatives of others. The tension here is between the establishment's implicit view that each country is one among equals and that arrangements among countries should be symmetric, and the attractiveness of US dollar securities in various portfolios. US dollar securities seemed to be favoured in the portfolios of foreign investors, and held in much larger amounts than would be predicted from the US share of world income. There is a tension between the symmetry in the types of arrangements favoured by the establishment, and the asset preferences of the various investors. The establishment was reluctant to recognize the US role in providing global consistency.

The distinction between the adjustment problem and the liquidity problem becomes blurred in the context of the persistent US payments deficits of the 1950s and the 1960s. A distinction is necessary between the US payments deficits of the 1950s and the early 1960s and then the later 1960s – or between a demand-determined US payments deficit and a

supply-determined US payments deficit. Did the US payments deficits of, say, 1964 reflect the excess foreign demand for dollar securities or did it reflect overvaluation of the US dollar, despite the then large US trade surplus? If we take Polak literally that 'countries are, on the whole, responsible for their own payments imbalances' and that 'any country that had a large deficit or surplus could, in this setting, be expected to take remedial measures' we are still left with the question 'should the United States or should the countries with the payments surpluses have taken the initiative in adjustment? Was the persistent payments imbalance a function of the excess demand for reserve assets by various industrial countries?'

To the extent that the monetary authorities in various countries believe that owned reserve assets are preferable to complete reliance on borrowed reserves, the United States may import a payments deficit. Similarly if investors in some countries conclude – as many did in the 1980s – that US dollar securities are preferable to securities denominated in their own currencies, the United States may import a trade deficit.

My answer to the question in Polak's chapter about the current relevance of the international monetary issues of the Bretton Woods system is, ironically more positive than his, perhaps because his reflections are focused on a set of negotiations while my concern is with the persistence of trade imbalances. The continued US trade deficit since the early 1980s seems analogous to the persistent US payments deficit of the 1950–65 period; both US deficits were imported: a result of the foreign demand for trade surpluses in the former case and trade deficits in the second case.

Many observers note that trade protectionism has increased in the last twenty years despite the growth in trade. That protectionism has increased while currencies have been floating may be only an association; if so, there are several examples of this association. Polak does not comment on one of the dominant problems of the 1970s and especially the 1980s, namely that movement of market exchange rates has been three or four times larger than the contemporary movement in the real or price level adjusted exchange rates. While there are some analogies between the operations of the pegged exchange rate system and the operation of the floating exchange rate system ('old problems in new guises' to use Polak's words), there seems to be no good or effective pegged exchange rate analogy to overshooting. Overshooting reflects the sluggishness of changes in market interest rates in response to changes in inflation rates.

Consider the current situation: within a decade the United States has moved from being the world's largest creditor country to being the world's largest debtor country. This change has no historical precedent, not even for those countries that have been on the losing side in a war. Moreover this remarkable change occurred even though the US Treasury did not borrow

in a foreign currency, and few US firms borrowed in a foreign currency to finance their activities or operations in the United States. How do the traditional textbook models explain a US trade deficit of 1–2 per cent of Gross National Product (GNP), at a time when the US dollar is undervalued by almost any test and the US economy is operating far below capacity levels of production? To my knowledge the answer to this question will not be found in Meade or Tinbergen, or in traditional text books in international finance. The US trade deficit has a counterpart in the trade surpluses of other countries; this statement is a definition and no causality is implied. At the causal level, the trade surplus of a Taiwan might reflect the desire of benevolent residents of that amazingly productive little country to finance the US trade deficit. An alternative interpretation is that the United States has accumulated a trade deficit because on the margin investors in Taiwan prefer the US dollar securities to securities denominated in the New Taiwan dollar or in some other currency.

Once the principle is accepted that some countries with trade surpluses are exporting imbalances, then the question becomes how far this argument can be extended. The change, following German unification, in the US trade and payments position with the European countries as a group suggests that, during most of the 1980s, the United States may have imported a trade deficit that was the counterpart of a level of German savings that was excessive with respect to German investment opportunities; to my knowledge the German authorities did not complain that foreign demand for German goods was 'crowding-out' domestic demand. Currently Japan has a trade surplus that is 3–4 per cent of its GNP. The counterpart of this increasing Japanese trade surplus is that some countries have trade deficits larger than they prefer – and the United States is one of these countries.

Let me conclude. There has been a remarkable change in international arrangements since Ossola and Polak and many others met in the 1960s to negotiate a reform of the system. Their objective was to develop a set of arrangements so that the policies of national governments could be globally consistent at the established parities for national currencies. Much of their effort became redundant with the move away from established parities. There is now increasing recognition that the system of floating exchange rates has delivered much less than we were promised; the imbalances among countries are much larger. And there is need for a new generation of Ossolas and Polaks to cope with the problems of global consistency.

Discussion

FRED C. BERGSTEN

I agree with most of Polak's chapter but I do have one very major difference with him that I will highlight immediately. The issue is what we can learn from the international monetary debates of the 1960s and 1970s. I find three main lessons, two of them general and one specific. The first is that both the officials and we economists can, and do frequently, make very major errors in diagnosing the problems of the monetary system and in proposing what ought to be done about them. Second, both groups can and do ignore reform options that would lead to a much better system, an issue that I think again is very much to be faced today. Third, on the specific issue of the substitution account which was addressed unsuccessfully in the late 1960s and again in the late 1970s, I would guess there may be a need for it in the late 1990s, because the creation of a truly European currency will result in the largest portfolio adjustment among currencies that we have seen in the postwar world, out of the dollar and into the European unit.

My first lesson is simply that the world constantly misdiagnoses the nature of international monetary problems. During the Bretton Woods system, as Polak reminded us in his paper, the focus was on a feared liquidity shortage. It was not an irrelevant problem, nor even a marginal problem, but it clearly was not the major problem as the very helpful background paper from the Banca d'Italia researchers points out (Rebecchini and Schioppa 1992). The main problem was clearly the lack of an effective adjustment mechanism, especially limits in the use of the exchange rate for that purpose. Therefore I believe that the focus of the international monetary negotiations in the 1960s was fundamentally misdirected. The Bretton Woods system did not collapse because of a liquidity shortage or the Triffin dilemma. It did not collapse because, I quote from Polak's paper, the United States ran out of reserves. To be sure, the decline in US gold holdings was a factor – Volcker in his book with Gyohten (1992) points out that it was a useful cover for the US action in August 1971 – but what happened was that the United States decided it wanted to adjust. It wanted to improve its internal economic situation by improving its trade balance. It

43

felt, rightly or wrongly, and Volcker's book again indicates how strongly this was felt in the United States at the time, that it could not adjust *via* the exchange rate under the rules of the Bretton Woods system as they applied at that time.

My conclusion is that the officials clearly focused on the wrong problem in spending a large amount of time on the negotiations of the Special Drawing Rights (SDR). Polak considers that the time spent on the SDR system was not exorbitant. I think that it was not only exorbitant but largely wasted. The main problem was essentially ignored, and if only Ossola and Polak and all those very creative minds had devoted as much effort to reforming the adjustment system in the 1960s as they did to creating the SDRs, we might have avoided the crises of the late 1960s and 1970s. May be, we could have avoided the breakdown of the Bretton Woods system. As the Banca d'Italia paper points out, Ossola's very enlightened views on exchange rate management and the use of the exchange rate for adjustment, expressed later in the exercise of the Committee of Twenty (C-20), suggest that, if given an option to do it, he would have pushed in a very constructive direction earlier on.

So much for the attitude of officials. But the officials were mainly following the intellectual consensus of the day, created by the economics profession. When I worked for Henry Kissinger, he gave me a very valuable lesson: 90 per cent of any public policy problem is creating the intellectual environment within which it's decided. The other 10 per cent is merely tactics. The shortage of liquidity exposed in the Triffin dilemma was underlying the views of all those who dealt with international monetary problems in the 1960s. I think *Gold and the Dollar Crisis* was probably the most influential single book ever published on international monetary affairs (Triffin 1960). The whole world, including the officials, had in their heads the Triffin dilemma, the liquidity problem, and the need to work on that. I have great respect for Triffin, but I think he derailed the world for a decade. His thesis set the international community off in the wrong direction, led them to ignore the main problem, brought on the crises of the late 1960s, and the breakdown of Bretton Woods. But the 1960s was only the first occasion for us to get it wrong. When the world moved to freely floating rates in the 1970s they did not solve all the problems, contrary, as Aliber courageously admitted, to what his colleagues at Chicago University maintained. Indeed floating rates may even have worsened them.

In the early 1980s, the conventional wisdom shifted to 'convergence': Beryl Sprinkel, the countries of the Group of Seven (G-7) in the Jurgensen Report (G-7 1983), and even the International Monetary Fund (IMF), told us that if national economies simply converged then international problems would be solved and there would be no need for international policy coordination. That, of course, was also wrong. The Ministers of the Group

of Five (G-5) stood up at the Plaza in 1985 and explicitly admitted it was wrong. The point is that in three successive periods – the 1960s, the 1970s, and at least the first half of the 1980s – the basic problem of the international monetary system was misdiagnosed by at least the mainstream of economists and acted upon in the wrong direction by the officials. The results were not very good.

Lesson number one also implies that these constant errors of enormous magnitude ought to instil a lot of humility in both the profession and the officials. It does mean we need to do much better in the future and must, in particular, keep our eyes on the ball, improving the adjustment process. In particular, we must find ways that will lead all countries to adjust, including the United States.

Closely related to lesson number one is lesson number two. In the breakdown phase of Bretton Woods, in particular, the officials, and those of us who supposedly were thinking about the problem, missed enormous opportunities to adopt the superior policy options that were available and that at least some of us were espousing at the time. In the late 1960s and even into the early 1970s, the world could have moved to limited forms of exchange rate flexibility in ways that would have preserved the Bretton Woods system and avoided much of the breakdown that occurred. At that time, there was no mention of reference ranges or target zones, but rather of wider bands and crawling pegs. However the basic idea was the same and some intellectual effort was being made in that direction. The Bürgenstock group, for example, was able to achieve a consensus in both academic and private-sector quarters (Bergsten *et al.* 1970). Those approaches were the subject of official consideration at the end of the Johnson administration, when the US government made a decision to start negotiating for at least some limited reforms in the exchange rate system. The Johnson administration did not get reelected, however, so they simply wrote up their idea in their final Annual Economic Report and monetary reform became another casualty of the Vietnam war.

At the start of the Nixon administration – this is also in the Volcker–Gyohten book – the United States did make some modest efforts to begin negotiating an adjustment mechanism in the direction of greater exchange rate flexibility. I was at the National Security Council at the time and recall that the Europeans stonewalled and reacted in a totally negative way to any such approach. The United States, I must admit, did not push very hard and therefore nothing much happened.

Contrary to what Polak said, I would not fault the unwillingness of the officials at that time to apply euthanasia to their beloved Bretton Woods system. What I would fault them on is the unwillingness to try to shore it up, amend it in the light of changing events. What is interesting is that the world, once again, began moving in the direction of more limited flexibility

of exchange rates in the 1970s. In Europe, the European Monetary System (EMS) was created. Managed floating began to become the norm internationally, particularly after the international cooperation to stop the fall of the dollar in the late 1970s. But that promising opportunity was snuffed out when the Reagan administration came in, rejected the idea of any kind of international monetary cooperation, and benignly neglected the dollar appreciation.

In this area, however, there was a promising move in the mid 1980s, building on the target zone idea of the early part of the decade and on the reference ranges that were embodied in the Louvre Agreement. There is still some echo of these today, though not in anything like the form that was agreed at the Louvre, flexible as it was. Nevertheless it seems to me that having tried both extreme versions – fixed rates in the 1960s, floating rates in the 1970s and early 1980s – we now should learn lesson number two: there are superior options and the time has come to choose an intermediate course – namely some limited and managed form of flexibility which could provide a much more stable and desirable system in the longer run.

McKinnon notes elsewhere in this volume that there are two different schools of thought about the use of the exchange rate: one is the international adjustment school, which I support, the other is the monetary standard view which he takes. McKinnon claims that his approach, the monetary standard approach, will create more trade and less protectionism and here I fundamentally disagree with him. It is certainly true that floating rates in the early 1980s led to massive dollar overvaluation, trade deficits, and protectionism. But so did the dollar overvaluation that emerged at the end of the Bretton Woods system of adjustable pegs in the late 1960s and early 1970s. Indeed that was the main trigger, in my view, of the first wave of US postwar protectionism. When John Connally and Richard Nixon broke the dollar–gold link in 1971, one of the objectives was to cope with the protectionist pressure of the time and they largely succeeded. Protectionist pressures derive from misalignments of currencies not their volatility. And misalignments can occur, and indeed have occurred in large degree, under both fixed rate systems and floating rate systems.

Thus, what is needed is an intermediate alternative. Kenen and others have argued that the exchange rate system has been behaving reasonably well over this recent period. But the chapter by Catte, Galli, and Rebecchini in Part III of this volume, as supported by Frankel, suggests that it is perhaps only because of active management by the authorities. In fact one could say we have a *de facto* target zone regime. If one looks at the tables in that chapter, you realize that the mark–dollar rate has been kept between 1.45 and 1.85 and the yen has been kept between 125 and 145. In other words, there is practically a target zone with a notional middle rate, plus or minus 10 per cent on either side (a little more for the mark, a little less for the

yen). One might conclude that if there has been some relative stability for the last five years it is because of the *de facto* establishment of a managed regime.

However, the stability is in nominal, not real exchange rates. Since the end of 1987, the real exchange rate of the yen has depreciated by about 25 per cent. As a result, Japan is headed this year towards a trade surplus of the order of $150 billion – the only big surplus in the world, adding once again to trade and protectionist pressure. What we need to do is modify the *de facto* target zone regime now in place by putting into it a mechanism to rebase the ranges more effectively and more consistently. That seems to me the next step in the systemic evolution. It clearly needs to be done right now in terms of the yen rate, not just *vis-à-vis* the dollar but *vis-à-vis* the Europeans too. I am not arguing that the dollar is overvalued but rather that the yen is undervalued. That is the big systemic problem at present. We need an Okura Hotel Agreement for the yen somewhat like the Plaza Hotel Agreement – or, in Frankel's terms, the February 1985 Agreement – for the dollar.

Lesson number three is that we may again in the future need a substitution account. I think Polak does us a great service in reminding us about the efforts on the substitution account in the past. I do not believe that the need for a substitution account will be triggered, however, as Polak suggested might be the case, when the Europeans pool their monetary reserves under Economic and Monetary Union (EMU). Even though that will create excess reserves in some sense, my guess is that it will not be a cause for reserve consolidation into a substitution account, though one would not want to rule it out. I do believe that, as Europe moves to an independent currency, as I think it will, despite the uncertainties created by the Danish referendum, currency markets will begin to experience the largest portfolio adjustment in the postwar period. The unified European economy will be the single biggest economy in the world, by far the world's biggest trader, and by far the biggest holder of monetary reserves. If it can create a single currency, that currency clearly will become a world currency. A natural portfolio adjustment will then take place out of all other currencies into that new world currency. The main shift will come out of the dollar, however, because the dollar remains the single most widely used currency in the world. This is the reverse of the portfolio adjustment that occurred when Japan liberalized its capital controls at the end of the 1970s: at that time the huge pent-up savings which had been held in yen, because of the exchange controls, began to spill out, adding to the enormous upward pressure on the dollar generated by Reaganomics. The resulting exchange rate disequilibrium added to the big trade imbalances and big trade protectionist problems of the early 1980s.

Now in reverse, as Europe will get an attractive world currency, money

will move into that currency out of the dollar. It will not be easy, of course, to handle such a shift through a substitution account because, in the first instance, the adjustment will come in private portfolios. One effect will obviously be to drive up the European exchange rate with adverse effects on European competitiveness, trade policy, domestic economies, and the like. I therefore suspect there could be a lot of intervention by the European System of Central Banks (ESCB), to buy dollars to limit the appreciation of their currencies. The United States may agree to that because it probably would like to prevent a sharp decline of the dollar. Therefore, a huge build-up of dollar holdings in the portfolio of the new European Central Bank (ECB) is likely to occur, which might then provide a suitable basis for some kind of substitution account.

As Gyohten points out in the Volcker–Gyohten book, the United States was very interested in a substitution account in the late 1970s. I happened to handle the last part of that negotiation when I was at the Treasury and the sticking point was that we did not feel that the US Congress would ever appropriate open-ended amounts of money to pay for a possible US liability incurred in the effort to reduce the role of its own currency. I suspect in the future some other technique, like the full use of IMF gold, may be needed to fund a substitution account, but I would certainly suggest that the item may come back on to the agenda in the late 1990s. I would venture to predict that all this may happen sooner rather than later. I know that the conventional view in Europe is that the progress towards EMU has been slowed down as a result of the Danish referendum, doubts in Germany about giving up the Deutsche mark, etc. But I recall that all of the major steps towards European economic and financial integration in the past have been political decisions, made by the top political leaders in Europe for political and somewhat personal reasons. In 1978 Giscard d'Estaing and Helmut Schmidt created the EMS over the objections of the Bundesbank and against the advice of most technicians. François Mitterrand and Helmut Kohl, maybe with some help from the other side of the Channel, are likely to make a similar decision within the next two or three years as the next major step towards European economic and monetary integration, with a very big political impact. So I would think that 1994 might turn out to be a year in which there is rapid movement towards EMU, the creation of a European currency, the next big portfolio adjustment in international finance, and possibly the need for a substitution account.

I have not made any effort to quantify the portfolio adjustment and I think that it should be a major research project. But if Europe does become a functional single economy with a single monetary policy, why should we not think that official and private monetary assets held in that European asset might not, over time, become half or more of the world total? That

would mean quite a substantial shift. My main point is that we should be thinking about it now. Governor Ciampi in the foreword to this volume makes the very welcome remark that the Europeans should be talking to the rest of the world about the international implications of EMU, but I think he qualifies the statement in saying they should do it only after EMU is in place. We, from the US perspective, often note that once European arrangements are in place and one tries to negotiate about them, the Europeans say: 'Those are firm, it is too late to talk about it.' That has been true with the Common Agricultural Policy and for other policies as well. The global implications of the massive structural change towards a single European market and monetary union for the international monetary system should be considered now in the appropriate fora. Then, maybe, it will be possible to find a consensus on how big the portfolio shift would be and whether something should be done about it.

Finally, I should make one correction to a misinterpretation of a point in Polak's chapter. This has to do with the Financial Support Fund of the Organization for Economic Cooperation and Development (OECD), the so-called Kissinger proposal, that was negotiated after the first oil shock. Polak said in his chapter that the proposal was rejected by the US Congress and died. That is not what happened. When the Carter administration came into office, we made a conscious decision to shift the project from the OECD to the IMF. What subsequently became the Witteveen Facility in the IMF was functionally the same idea as the Financial Support Fund in the OECD, the so-called third line of defence to deal with the recycling problem. In the Carter administration we were partly influenced by the Congressional attitude and we did think that the Congress would be more likely to support a facility in the IMF than in the OECD because of the IMF's track record as a financially sound lending agency. But the Carter administration also took the view that the IMF was the appropriate location for such an activity, partly because it would then be available for a wider universe of countries than those in the OECD. However, it was a conscious decision, right or wrong, by a new US administration: Congress did eventually support the Witteveen Facility, the objectives of the original Kissinger plan were implemented but *via* a different mechanism and one that I always felt was far superior.

References

Bergsten, C.F., Halm, G.N., Machlup, F., and Roosa, R.V. 1970. *Approaches to Greater Flexibility of Exchange Rates: the Bürgenstock Papers*, Princeton.
Rebecchini, S. and Schioppa, C. 1992. 'Rinaldo Ossola and the Reform of the

International Monetary System', unpublished background paper prepared for the conference in memory of Rinaldo Ossola.

Triffin, R. 1960. *Gold and the Dollar Crisis*, New Haven, Yale University Press.

Volcker, P. and Gyohten, T. 1992. *Changing Fortunes*, New York, Times Books.

Working Group on Exchange Market Intervention 1983. *Report of the Working Group on Exchange Market Intervention* (Jurgensen Report), March.

II

International liquidity

3 The rise and fall of the concept of international liquidity

JOHN WILLIAMSON

1 Introduction

Rinaldo Ossola was the leading exponent during the negotiations in the Committee of Twenty (C-20) of the mainstream European (or, at least, European economists') view of how the international monetary system should be reformed. It was to him that those of us who hoped for an outcome encompassing a Special Drawing Right (SDR) standard (not to mention limited exchange rate flexibility) always looked for an authoritative expression of our viewpoint.

A central element of an SDR standard would have been deliberate control of the volume of international liquidity. This concern to establish control over the volume of liquidity quickly evaporated once the C-20 had failed to reach any substantive agreement, and in consequence the world had drifted to what it has seemed natural to a number of us to describe as an international monetary non-system. This chapter seeks to illuminate the reasons for this striking change in intellectual attitudes. The chapter starts by tracing the emergence of the concept of international liquidity. It then explains the significance that was attached to the concept during the negotiations on international monetary reform that first created the SDR and then failed to follow through by agreeing on the other elements of a successor system to Bretton Woods in the C-20. The chapter next turns to an examination of the reasons for the demise of the concept. The final substantive section asks whether there is still a case for reviving SDR allocations.

2 Emergence of the concept

Discussion about the adequacy of international liquidity occurred already in the nineteenth century, in the form of the protracted debate about bimetallism. The impetus behind this proposal came from the declining price level in and after the 1870s, and the diagnosis that this stemmed from the inadequacy of a world monetary base that consisted solely of gold.

There was at the time a well-developed theory of how the international monetary system worked, which was centred on an explanation of the adjustment process along the lines of Hume's price-specie-flow mechanism. Well-managed countries had currencies that consisted essentially of gold, which was therefore mutually acceptable in settlement of deficits. The gold that central banks held in order to back the non-gold portion of their domestic money supplies in fact functioned very much as it did in subsequent periods, being exchanged to settle deficits and being defended through interest rate changes that were conspicuously successful in attracting gold in an era when the public had confidence that parities would remain unchanged. But since each country's money supply was limited by the amount of gold that it held, an 'inadequate' total stock of gold would force deflation on the world. In a period when demand was weak and prices were in consequence tending to decline, it was natural to look for some way to supplement the world monetary base. In due course the world found such a way, but it was through the use of reserve currencies by peripheral countries rather than through a switch of the centre countries to bimetallism.

Concern with a possible inadequacy of international liquidity emerged again after World War I, in parallel with the attempt to reestablish the prewar parities despite the large subsequent inflations in most of the belligerent economies. This attempt was unsuccessful in those economies where the war-time or postwar inflations had been too large, and those countries eventually repegged at exchange rates that roughly reestablished purchasing power parity (PPP) with the United States. Thus the net effect of the war was to reduce the real value of the gold stock roughly in proportion to US inflation.

Bernstein argues that this is quite typical of what had happened after all major wars prior to the World War II (see his account of his 1943 discussion of this topic with Keynes in Williamson 1983, p. 98). In any event, the fact that it meant that reserves were less abundant relative to the demand for them was recognized at the time, and the question of how to react to this situation was one of the major themes of both the Brussels conference in 1920 (Eichengreen 1992, pp. 154–7) and the subsequent Conference at Genoa in 1922. The latter conference had a very wide remit, since it was intended to clear up the political as well as economic issues left unsettled by the peace treaties. In the event, since agreement was reached on little else, the conference is famous chiefly for having encouraged non-centre countries to hold reserve currencies as international reserves so as to economize on the stock of gold. Although reserve currencies were in fact held fairly extensively prior to World War I (Lindert 1969, p. 76), the Genoa Conference marked the first official encouragement of the gold exchange standard.

As is well known, the interwar gold exchange standard was not a great success. A number of countries did build up their holdings of sterling and dollars during the 1920s. Nevertheless, a combination of high US interest rates intended to curb the stock market boom and the French refusal to act as a non-centre country (and instead demand gold when it moved into massive surplus following Poincaré's ultimate successful stabilization) sufficed to oblige Britain to maintain high interest rates to defend the pound, thus preventing British participation in the world boom of the 1920s. A run on the pound nonetheless occurred in 1931, forcing Britain to abandon convertibility into gold. The collapse of the gold exchange standard served to reduce international reserves and so to intensify the world recession.

A gold exchange standard reemerged after World War II, less by deliberate design than because it was not banned when the Bretton Woods system was agreed. That system had many attractive features. It largely succeeded in avoiding a waste of resources on unnecessary unemployment, in preventing the competitive use of exchange rate policy, and in desynchronizing the business cycle internationally, while building in an early warning signal of emerging inflationary pressures and providing an automatic stabilizer that would limit the damage caused by excess demand (in terms of a buildup of inflationary momentum) until needed deflationary measures could become effective (Williamson 1985a). While not all these features were fully appreciated at the time, there was sufficient awareness that the world was doing well, and that this was being helped rather than hindered by the international monetary system, to create a desire to preserve Bretton Woods.

Triffin (1960) was the principal exponent of the view that the system was in danger of collapsing. He claimed that the demand for reserves was growing faster than the supply could do unless the United States ran a deficit that would progressively undermine confidence in the dollar, so that the world was faced with a dilemma between a growing liquidity shortage that would threaten the expansion of the international economy and a collapse reminiscent of 1931. It was this thesis that, after several years' delay, inspired the negotiations that resulted in the creation of the SDR.[1] Triffin assumed that the growth in demand for reserves would match the growth in trade. This rested on two postulates. The first is that reserves are held for the purpose of permitting countries to mitigate internal fluctuations, by allowing them to finance trade deficits rather than being compelled to adjust immediately, a postulate first advanced by Thornton ([1802] 1962) but then abandoned in favour of the gold standard view that reserves are held to back the money supply. Thornton's view was revived after the collapse of the gold standard had led to the general abandonment of overt requirements to back the money supply, and, reflecting that view,

the Keynes Plan for an International Clearing Union proposed that bancor quotas – which would have been the main source of liquidity – be related to the value of trade. The second postulate is that the level of reserves needed to preserve a given degree of cover against reserve depletion could normally be expected to grow in line with trade. This argument was developed in an early paper by Triffin (1947). The postulate was criticized on the ground that reserves are needed to finance deficits, not trade, an argument first emphasized by Nurkse (1944). Triffin in fact incorporated this point into his analysis, since he recognized that countries with large export fluctuations would require higher reserves/imports ratios in order to reach a specified level of security, but he also argued that the size of payments imbalances could generally be expected to grow in line with trade so that reserves would still need to grow in proportion to trade. The contention was challenged by Olivera (1969), who derived a formula (analogous to the Baumol–Tobin theorem on the demand for money, though relying on a different rationale) which stated that the demand for reserves would grow only in proportion to the square root of trade. Similarly, Streissler (1969) used results from the theory of optimal stochastic processes to demonstrate the existence of economies in reserve holding. (Presumably these results apply only where trade growth consists of increases in volume rather than price.) Empirical estimates of demand for reserves functions found evidence that the variability of exports or trade balances was a significant determinant of demand, but they were inconclusive in determining whether there exist economies in reserve holding (the evidence is summarized in Williamson 1973, p. 697). It nonetheless remained customary to assume that the demand for reserves would be likely to grow roughly in parallel with trade if other things remained equal.

The recognition that reserves exist to finance deficits rather than trade led a number of economists to question whether 'international liquidity' should really be measured just by a country's reserves. Arndt (1948) was the first to argue that a country's 'liquidity position' should provide a measure of its ability to finance a deficit without resorting to adjustment measures. This suggests that a country's reserve holdings should be supplemented by its reserve-borrowing possibilities and, in the case of a reserve currency country, by the extent to which foreigners would build up holdings of its currency in the event of a deficit materializing, as well as the extent to which 'innocuous' interest rate fluctuations would attract a capital inflow.[2] Kane (1965) provided the most comprehensive treatment in this vein when he suggested that a country's international liquidity should be defined as a weighted average of its foreign assets, liabilities, commitments, and credit lines, where the weights would represent the authorities' estimates of the fractions of the various instruments or credits that they could expect to

activate or have drawn. This line of analysis was never further developed. Nevertheless, the crude interpretation of international liquidity as equal to reserves played a key role in the debate and negotiations on international monetary reform of the 1960s and early 1970s.

3 The significance of liquidity in the reform negotiations

The analysis as to why control over liquidity mattered was perhaps developed most explicitly at the conference on international reserves convened by the International Monetary Fund in 1970 (IMF 1970). The predominant standpoint at that conference was to follow Fleming (1961 and 1967) in viewing reserve creation as a policy instrument in the hands of the international authorities that should be set with a view to maximizing a world welfare function. The maximization is performed subject to a set of constraints imposed by the way in which the world economy operates, including the reaction patterns of the various national governments.

Virtually any positive theory of the behaviour of national governments will lead to the prediction that greater reserve ease will generate some combination of higher domestic demand, lower interest rates, currency revaluation, and the relaxation of restrictions on the import of goods or the export of capital. Conversely, a reserve shortage can be expected to generate some combination of tighter domestic demand, higher interest rates, currency devaluation, and tighter restrictions on imports of goods or exports of capital. The optimum rate of reserve growth is characterized by beneficial effects in the form of higher employment and fewer restrictions being equal at the margin to the costs of faster inflation. However, Polak (in IMF 1970, pp. 510–20) expressed a degree of scepticism about how far this framework could take one, primarily because for most countries the level of reserves was not a major determinant of economic policy, and certainly not of demand management policy.

A particular case of this approach rests on what I once termed the 'international quantity theory' (Williamson 1973). This assumes that reserve changes influence monetary policy on gold standard lines (in direct contradiction of the Polak view just described), that monetary expansion produces proportionate changes in nominal income as postulated by the quantity theory, and that changes in nominal income consist of price rather than quantity changes except in the very short run. Hence, reserve changes simply lead to changes in the world rate of inflation (in a world of fixed exchange rates).

Mundell (1971, ch. 14) argued that in the long run an increase in the rate of reserve creation was more likely to lead to a decrease than to an increase in the degree of reserve ease. The logic is that reserve creation induces

monetary authorities to try to dispose of the excess reserves they suddenly find themselves holding, which they do by inflating. This drives down the real return on reserve holding and therefore reduces the real level of reserves the authorities wish to hold. In the new equilibrium, when the system has adjusted to a faster rate of reserve creation, crises and their associated restrictions and forced devaluations will be more and not less frequent than before because reserve holdings are less adequate. Since it posits no benefits from a faster rate of reserve growth than that needed to preserve price stability, the international quantity theory implies that reserve creation should be targeted on stabilizing prices.

Of course, neither the Fleming view nor the international quantity theory imply that reserve creation can profitably be varied in the short run with the objective of stabilizing the world economy. In fact, faith in the efficacy of fine tuning was already diminishing as regards domestic stabilization policy when international monetary reform was under active discussion in the late 1960s and early 1970s. It was generally agreed (except possibly by the monetarists who developed the international quantity theory) that the links from reserve creation to an impact on nominal income were even more tenuous, and subject to longer lags, than those from monetary policy to nominal income. This is why it was early on resolved that SDR allocations would be determined for five years at a time ('basic periods') rather than year by year. In the words of the First Amendment to the IMF's Articles, SDR allocations were to be determined by the Fund seeking 'to meet the long-term global need ... to supplement existing reserve assets in such manner as will promote the attainment of its purposes and will avoid economic stagnation and deflation as well as excess demand and inflation in the world'.

Thus the mainstream view during the reform negotiations was that in a more or less fixed exchange rate world, such as it was desired to preserve, an appropriate rate of reserve creation was important in avoiding either a reserve shortage that might impose unnecessary deflation, a devaluation bias or excessive restrictions, on the one hand, or inflation and a revaluation bias, on the other. The ability to create reserves at an appropriate rate required three things: an ability to create reserves when the need to do so was judged to exist; an ability to judge how many reserves needed to be created; and an ability to prevent reserves being created from alternative sources. The first requirement was satisfied by the first stage of international monetary reform, the SDR agreement that was reached in outline at the Rio de Janeiro Annual Meetings in 1967 and finally ratified in 1969. The second requirement was addressed by the 1970 IMF Conference discussed at the beginning of this section, with the conclusions outlined above: that the rate of reserve creation should aim to keep a judicious

balance between higher employment and fewer restrictions, on the one hand, versus the risk of faster inflation, on the other, but that this could only involve crude long-term judgments rather than fine tuning. That left the third requirement, the need to establish control over other forms of international liquidity, which meant in practice over the accumulation of dollars in reserves. This provided one of the main points of controversy in the C-20 negotiations, along with the questions of when countries should adjust (notably the possible role of a reserve indicator system in signalling a need for adjustment), of how they should adjust (i.e., the exchange rate regime), and of a change in the formula governing SDR allocations so as to institute an aid link. Up to 1972 it had been assumed that gaining control over the stock of dollars would necessarily require an agreement to restrict dollar holdings to working balances of a specified size, with excess dollars funded into a substitution account that would issue SDRs in exchange. In the Summer of 1972, during the preparations of the IMF Executive Board for the forthcoming negotiations, the Italian chair argued that it would be possible to reconcile a much greater degree of freedom for countries to choose their reserve composition with what really mattered in regard to the stock of dollars, which was to stabilize the *aggregate* stock.[3]

The critical requirement was that the reserve centre, the United States (at that time there was only one reserve currency of any consequence), should always settle its imbalances by a transfer of reserve assets rather than by a change in its liabilities, an idea that was called *asset settlement*. This could be accomplished by creating a substitution account in the IMF from which countries that initially held excess dollar claims could draw SDRs. Suppose that subsequently a country that preferred accumulating dollars were to run a surplus with the United States: it could keep the dollars that it had earned, but (assuming the United States to be in balance with all other countries) the United States would be required to use SDRs to buy back an equivalent number of dollars from the substitution account. Hence, the aggregate credit extended to the United States could be insulated from the US balance of payments position, thus ensuring that the United States was subjected to the same pressures to adjust when in deficit as any other country.

Despite the efforts of Ossola, the proposals for asset settlement were not agreed in the C-20 negotiations. In fact, those negotiations ended with the publication of an *Outline of Reform* (IMF 1974) that must be among the most vacuous documents ever published by an international organization: it contained a list of aims and a taxonomy of alternative ways of achieving those aims on which no agreement had been reached. The world thereafter slid into an 'international monetary non-system', in the sense of acquiescing in a set of arrangements that allowed countries to do

essentially anything they wanted to. Interest in the subject of international liquidity quickly evaporated. The next section discusses why.

4 The fall of the concept of international liquidity

Two candidates suggest themselves as reasons to explain why people stopped worrying about the supply of international liquidity after the demise of the C-20. One is that the world moved away from fixed exchange rates; the other is that capital became even more mobile across international frontiers.

It had often been argued that one of the advantages of allowing exchange rates to float would be that it would dispense with the need for international reserves, although there was always a contrary view, voiced most strongly by Harrod (1966), which argued that countries would actually need more reserves under floating, essentially because they would forego what we would today describe as the benefits of credibility. In the event the evidence suggested some limited decline in the demand for reserves after the move to floating. Suss (1976) concluded that a majority of the industrial countries whose behaviour she examined had reduced their reserve use after the shift to floating, which would suggest that their demand for reserves could also be expected to have fallen. Likewise Heller and Khan (1978) found evidence of a once for all downward shift in the demand for reserves in late 1973. This evidence is consistent with the view that the strategic importance of maintaining a reserve target was diminished by the move to floating. It is certainly true that insofar as a country's primary objective is that of maintaining employment near some target value, then the abandonment of an exchange rate commitment will diminish its need to worry about the level of its reserves.

The advent of capital mobility is even more fundamental in undermining the whole idea that reserves can play a strategic role in permitting a degree of international management of the system. Consider the extreme case of perfect capital mobility, where a country can borrow an infinite sum at the exogenous world interest rate. If the SDR interest rate is equal to the borrowing rate of creditworthy countries, which will be necessary if countries are to be dissuaded from engaging in arbitrage operations designed to rid themselves of all their SDRs or to build up infinitely large SDR holdings (in the case where the SDR interest rate exceeded the borrowing rate), then it is a matter of total indifference to a creditworthy country as to whether or not it receives an SDR allocation. Any reserve shortage can be relieved by borrowing more on exactly the same terms as those on which it would have received allocations. And any excess reserves can be disposed of costlessly and without influencing the domestic economy by allowing a capital outflow. Under these circumstances countries will not

be placed under any pressure to alter their policies because of a shortage or surfeit of reserves.

The other casualty of increased capital mobility is the idea of asset settlement. Once again, it would make no difference to US behaviour if the United States had to settle all official settlement deficits by the transfer of reserve assets if it was also in a position to borrow or lend unlimited sums at the same interest rate. In fact, since 1974 the United States has become less and less unique in its ability to finance deficits through borrowing – not because the United States moved to asset settlement, but because other countries became equally able to increase their liability financing at their own discretion. There is still a difference in that the sort of liability financing that was supposed to be eliminated through asset settlement was own currency financing provided by foreign monetary authorities whereas that available to other countries is foreign currency financing provided by the private sector, but this is not a difference of strategic importance.

Of course, not all countries are part of the global financial market that allows unlimited sums to be borrowed at a given world interest rate. Indeed, probably none now satisfy that criterion perfectly nor are any likely to do so in the future, since the markets push up interest rates against countries that go too heavily into debt. Nonetheless, most industrial countries now have very substantial scope to borrow, and even more to lend, without much effect on the interest rate they pay or receive. In the 1970s many middle-income developing countries also found themselves in that situation, but the debt crisis reduced the number of developing countries considered creditworthy to a handful in East Asia. Even so, it is no longer possible to maintain that the concept of international liquidity has much relevance to the functioning of the international monetary system.

The fundamental reason is that under conditions of high capital mobility the external constraint on a country comes from its *creditworthiness* rather than from its *liquidity*. No formal theory of what this implies has been developed, but of course many of us recognize this change in our work. For example, my own attempts to estimate fundamental equilibrium exchange rates (Williamson 1985b) looked at countries' international debt positions and their likely sustainability, rather than at their liquidity, in order to formulate current account targets so as to give content to the concept of 'external balance'.

5 Is there a future for the SDR?

Does the conclusion that the concept of international liquidity has lost any strategic role in the operation of the international monetary system necessarily imply that the SDR scheme should be wound up? Or is there still a case for resuming SDR allocations?

So far as the industrial countries are concerned, the answer is clear. These countries are sufficiently creditworthy to be able to borrow what they need for reserve accumulation on essentially the same terms as they would receive SDRs, which means that allocations are pointless and the system should be wound up. But this is not true for most developing countries. Even those that have access to capital markets generally have to pay an interest premium substantially above the SDR rate, and many cannot borrow on any terms. These countries thus have to export real resources, or borrow on more costly terms than the interest they receive, in order to build up their reserves over time. In effect, the poor countries have to provide reverse aid to the rich in order to build up a prudent level of international liquidity. This is surely unjust, as was recognized by Ossola and his contemporaries when they agreed that developing countries should be included in the SDR scheme. A case for resuming SDR allocations can be made so as to remedy this injustice.

Is it possible to devise a formula that might conceivably entice the industrial countries to abandon their opposition to SDR allocations? Consider the following idea. The IMF would survey how many countries were unable to borrow internationally at an interest rate close to (say within 1 per cent of) the SDR interest rate. If a substantial block of countries (say those with IMF quotas totalling one quarter or one third of the total) were found to be in that situation, the Fund would aim to issue as many SDRs as those countries had revealed they wished to hold. Countries' revealed desires would be measured by the actual past increase in their reserve holdings during the preceding five-year ('basic') period. The IMF would then calculate the scale of SDR allocation that would be needed to supply those countries in aggregate with a similar reserve increase during the forthcoming basic period, and would issue SDRs on that scale. All participants would receive SDR allocations over the following five years on the scale needed to satisfy the revealed reserve needs of the less creditworthy countries. Since reserve needs tend to grow more rapidly in absolute terms over time, this would in general mean that the less creditworthy countries would not in fact be able to satisfy their entire reserve accumulation objectives through SDR allocations, but they should be able to satisfy the bulk of them that way. Receiving SDR allocations is a matter of complete indifference to an individual small creditworthy country; however, these countries would suffer collectively to the extent that the less creditworthy countries would no longer have to export real resources[4] to them in order to build up their reserves. The hope would be that allocation on the scale determined by this formula would enable the creditworthy countries to recognize that this loss would simply end existing payments of reverse aid (by the poor to the rich) rather than constitute additional aid.

The standard objection to the resumption of SDR allocations, that it would be inflationary, is inconsistent with the reasoning laid out above, which claims that SDR allocations have no impact on the policies pursued by major countries. A more persuasive explanation for the refusal to resume allocations is greed.

6 Concluding remarks

Unless capital mobility collapses, the set of ideas that underlay the debate on international liquidity and the reform negotiations in the C-20 has become irrelevant. The external constraint that the industrial countries (at least) face is imposed by creditworthiness rather than liquidity, and accordingly it would now be impossible to influence the state of the world economy by manipulating the rate of SDR creation. This evolution in events suggests that, even if the C-20 negotiations had succeeded in enthroning an SDR standard, the outcome would not have endured for long. This does not mean that it is impossible to conceive of a more structured international monetary system than the one that the world has endured for the last twenty years, but it does require that reform proposals be consistent with the fact of high international capital mobility among the leading countries. One such reform proposal that it would be equitable to introduce is a resumption of SDR allocations, on a scale adequate to fulfil the bulk of the reserve accumulation objectives of the less creditworthy countries. But this reform has nothing to do with managing the volume of international liquidity, it is just intended to remedy an injustice.

Notes

The author acknowledges with gratitude helpful comments on a previous draft by B. Eichengreen and J.J. Polak.

1 Eichengreen (1992, p. 20) points out that this thesis was anticipated in the 1929 analysis of one Feliks Mlynarski.
2 Some authors also suggested including a part of the foreign exchange holdings of its commercial banks and of inventories of tradable goods.
3 The argument was first revealed to the world in a report prepared by the IMF Executive Board as background to the C-20 negotiations (IMF 1972).
4 Or, for those with some creditworthiness, borrow; but, unlike the countries being described as creditworthy, paying a premium over the SDR interest rate.

References

Arndt, H.W. 1948. 'The Concept of Liquidity in International Monetary Theory', *Review of Economic Studies*, October.
Eichengreen, B. 1992. *Golden Fetters*, Oxford, Oxford University Press.

Fleming, J.M. 1961. 'International Liquidity: Ends and Means', *IMF Staff Papers*, December.

1967. 'Towards Assessing the Need for International Reserves', *Princeton Essays in International Finance*, 58.

Harrod, Sir Roy 1966. *Reforming the World's Money*, London, Macmillan.

Heller, H.R. and Khan, M.S. 1978. 'The Demand for International Reserves Under Fixed and Floating Exchange Rates', *IMF Staff Papers*, December.

International Monetary Fund 1970. *International Reserves: Needs and Availability*, Washington DC.

1972. *Reforming the International Monetary System*, Report by the Executive Directors to the Board of Governors, Washington DC.

1974. 'Outline of Reform', in *International Monetary Reform*, Documents of the Committee of Twenty, Washington DC.

Kane, E.J. 1965. 'International Liquidity: A Probabilistic Approach', Kyklos.

Lindert, P.H. 1969. 'Key Currencies and Gold 1900–1913', *Princeton Essays in International Finance*, 24.

Mundell, R.A. 1971. *Monetary Theory: Inflation, Interest and Growth in the World Economy*, Goodyear, Pacific Palisades.

Nurkse, R. 1944. *International Currency Experience*, League of Nations, Geneva.

Olivera, J.H.G. 1969. 'A Note on the Optimal Rate of Growth of International Reserves', *Journal of Political Economy*, March.

Polak, J.J. 1970. 'Money: National and International', in Interational Monetary Fund, *International Reserves: Needs and Availability*, Washington DC, IMF.

Streissler, E. 1969. 'A Stochastic Model of International Reserve Requirements During Growth of World Trade', *Zeitschrift fur Nationalökonomie*, December.

Suss, E.C. 1976. 'A Note on Reserve Use Under Alternative Exchange Rate Regimes', *IMF Staff Papers*, July.

Thornton H. 1962. *An Enquiry into the Nature and Effects of the Paper Credit of Great Britain*, third edition edited by F.A. von Hayek, Frank Cass, London (first published in 1802).

Triffin, R. 1947. 'National Central Banking and the International Economy', *Review of Economic Studies*, February.

1960. *Gold and the Dollar Crisis*, New Haven, Yale University Press.

Williamson, J. 1973. 'International Liquidity: A Survey', Economic Journal, September.

1983. 'Keynes and the International Economic Order', in D. Worswick and J. Trevithick (eds.), *Keynes and the Modern World*, Cambridge, Cambridge University Press.

1985a. 'On the System in Bretton Woods', *American Economic Review*, May.

1985b. *The Exchange Rate System*, Washington, Institute for International Economics (revised edition).

Discussion

RAINER S. MASERA

The aim of the chapter is to analyse the reasons for the rise and fall of the concept of international liquidity with particular reference to the last three decades. After reviewing the problem of international reserves at the end of last century and after World Wars I and II, Williamson examines the essential elements of the debate during the negotiations on international monetary reform at the end of the 1960s and at the beginning of the 1970s. He notes that the world 'slid into an international monetary non-system' and explains why interest in international liquidity 'quickly evaporated'. He also addresses the question whether there might be still a role for Special Drawing Rights (SDR) in the future and presents a proposal in this regard.

The concept of international liquidity cannot be viewed in isolation

I would state from the outset that the problem of (i) adequate international liquidity cannot be analysed and discussed separately from the concepts of (ii) the exchange rate regime, and (iii) adjustment rules. These three elements form a three-legged table. The table cannot stand if any one of the three legs is missing. Likewise, an international monetary system cannot hold if any one of those three components is lacking or poorly structured. Consequently, my main observation concerning Williamson's chapter is that it is fundamentally 'incomplete'. This may, of course, be due to the constraints imposed by the assigned topic.

Both in the gold and in the gold exchange standards all three elements had been considered: (i) exchange rates were fixed; (ii) the rules of the game were known;[1] and (iii) gold (and international currencies) constituted international reserves utilized to settle external imbalances.[2] It is a valid, if not exhaustive, argument to state that both standards ultimately failed because international reserves did not grow in a manner consistent with growth and stable prices in an international economic system characterized by an increasing downward rigidity in prices and wages.

In this respect an historical note may be necessary to underscore the *leitmotiv* of my comments. Between 1925 and 1928 the gold (exchange) standard was reestablished. The system was, however, flawed for three interacting reasons: (i) New gold parities implied very different competitive positions of the main currencies. Against Keynes's advice, the pound was reestablished at the prewar parity, leaving the currency exceptionally weak. Meanwhile, the French franc, which had been repegged at one fifth of its 1914 parity, was very strong. (ii) The rules of the game were no longer willingly respected. Non-cooperative games emerged, especially in relation to gold hoarding, but fundamentally as a consequence of the difficulty of downward adjustments of prices and wages (in spite of castor oil)[3] and the associated costs of monetary contraction. (iii) The total monetary base of the system, notwithstanding the suggestions of the Genoa Conference, was insufficient to foster non-inflationary growth. In 1931 the system collapsed. I would put the blame mainly on 'wrong' exchange rates, as indicated by the fact that it was the British pound which precipitated the crisis, but no doubt all three legs of the international monetary system were unstable and insecure (on this point see Clarke 1967). By 1935 attempts to reintroduce the system appeared to be successful: (i) new parities implied more realistic real exchange rates and (ii) the brake was released on the aggregate monetary base as a consequence of the dollar's devaluation *vis-à-vis* gold, which implied a two-thirds revaluation of the world's high-powered money in terms of current prices and incomes. However, political tensions were too high to allow countries to adhere to a consistent set of rules of the game in terms of policy adjustment. This was especially so because the *laissez faire*, automatic adjustment rules implicit in the orthodox theory of the gold standard were no longer applicable. The 1940 debate between Keynes and Lord Halifax on the 'new economic order' (see Funk 1940) as proposed by Walter Funk, President of the Reichsbank, articulated clearly the situation: Keynes refused to criticize Funk's ideas against the reestablishment of the gold standard, contrary to the orthodox official British views of the time.

The SDR

I agree with Williamson's view that SDRs did not work properly. However, this was not due to the intrinsic features of the instruments[4] but rather to the fact that they were introduced too late in the game.

The problem of international liquidity rose when it was clear that demand for international reserves could only by chance grow at the same rate as US international liabilities. Triffin was the first to pinpoint the paradox: growing demand for international liquidity could be satisfied only at the expense of growing deficits in the US balance of payments. But these

deficits would eventually undermine confidence in the dollar, risking the collapse of the entire system. The paradox made clear the need not only for additional own reserves at the international level, but also for symmetric rules to allow US payments imbalances to be reflected on the US money stock, without automatically affecting the stock of international reserves.

The discussion of alternative instruments of international reserves lasted too long. Results of this debate are well known: ideas to supplement gold with paper gold began to circulate in the 1960s (indeed, following Keynes's 1941 bancor approach), but the SDR supply scheme became operative far too late;[5] Ossola's 1972 proposal for asset settlement was not approved in the negotiations of the Committee of Twenty (C-20). By the beginning of the 1970s the international economic environment had greatly changed. Shortage of international liquidity no longer was a problem. On the contrary, liquidity at the international level had exploded and was out of control. In the new context, characterized by a dollar glut instead of a dollar shortage, the role of SDRs in providing additional own reserves had obviously declined.

Regarding the future role of SDRs, the question, in my view, is not properly addressed. Williamson's idea to resume SDR allocations for 'equitable' reasons is also questionable and perhaps even superseded at this point. The International Monetary Fund (IMF) currently is at an advanced stage of debating the redistribution of SDRs on the basis of conditionality, not equity.[6] Problems facing Third World countries with high real interest rates are, of course, of importance and should not be neglected. However, the use of SDRs to cope with such problems is mistargeted and changes improperly the original role for which SDRs were designed. In addition, with US interest rates as low as they are now, and with a relatively low exchange rate for the dollar, the proposal is not timely either.

The rationale behind SDRs was to create a liquid reserve with an international monetary function, capable of satisfying long-run demand for additional own reserves: if the supply of outside reserves does not grow, it is impossible for all countries to increase their official, high-powered reserves through balance of payments surpluses. This approach is not coherent with the use of SDRs as an instrument to finance growth of the Less Developed Countries (LDC). This is because the first requisite of any monetary asset – a stable store of value – may be jeopardized by the consideration of additional objectives governing its supply (on this point see G-10 1985). On the other hand, other instruments (for example grants, official transfers, credit facilities, and direct investments) are more properly suited to overcome the problem of real international interest rates being higher than real economic growth rates in LDCs. This is also true if one considers the more recent case of Eastern Europe, which has potentially

large financial needs. More explicit policies to reduce 'reverse aid' and transfer resources from rich to poor countries would be preferable.

Williamson's proposal to resume the use of the SDR to transfer real resources among countries has also other flaws. The idea of providing international reserves to less creditworthy countries in the form of SDRs on the basis of the needs revealed in the previous five years is hardly precise in today's world. A five-year lag in satisfying needs is too long a period, given high international capital mobility. Economic conditions and demands certainly will have changed during such a time period. Above all, the automatic mechanism according to which funds would be provided, independently of the country's past five-year economic policy and, even worse, of future commitments regarding its policies of adjustment, would introduce a dangerous element of moral hazard in the system. In this respect the relevance of creditworthiness in allocating funds should not be ignored in the allocation of SDRs. Creditworthiness imposes higher responsibility on the user of capital and any fall in creditworthiness penalizes less judicious countries. This represents a good criterion for efficient international financial resources allocation which also applies to industrialized countries, many of which are in fact not rated triple A.

Do flexible exchange rates and increased capital mobility explain the fall of the concept of international liquidity?

It is obvious that changes in the exchange rate and capital mobility regimes have deeply influenced not only the intellectual attitudes but also the practice of managing international liquidity and reserves.

Williamson presents the argument that the move to flexible exchange rates is one of the main causes for the fall in interest in international reserve management. I would not argue with the basic thrust of this proposition, although I feel that the case is somewhat overstated. To start with, the empirical evidence which he cites is unconvincing. The one-off downward shift in 1973 in the demand for reserves does not seem to be as conclusive as he suggests. The industrialized countries which moved to a flexible exchange rate system continued to maintain, and to make active use of, substantial reserve holdings.[7] Williamson himself pointed out in 1976 that central banks were continuing to intervene in the foreign exchange markets at least as, if not more, often under the current exchange rate regime than under the former exchange rate regime (Williamson 1976, p. 327). Indeed, with the current reappearance of very large differentials in interest rates between the dollar and other currencies, I wonder whether the very proposal of a substitution account may not resurface.

Regarding capital mobility, the international (private) capital markets

are no doubt playing an increasing role with respect to traditional, official channels in financing external imbalances. This permits, in principle, longer-term adjustment policies to be implemented. In practice, in many instances easy accessibility to financial markets may be responsible for the higher propensity of governments to finance imbalances without undertaking adjustment. Even at the expense of the higher interest rates that the markets require for weakened creditworthiness, those governments may have a short-run incentive to let their countries pay a higher service on their external debt in order to postpone the adoption of unpopular domestic policies. Having said that, I would not conclude, however, as Williamson does, that increased capital mobility has undermined the strategic role of reserves and of international liquidity because it is now possible to borrow any currency at market rates.

It continues to be necessary to distinguish the effects of high capital mobility on own reserves from the effects of high capital mobility on borrowed reserves. Regardless of the exchange rate regime, increased capital mobility insures a role for own reserves. The recourse to the latter tends to become very difficult precisely when they are needed. One may say that adequate own reserves are a necessary – even if not sufficient – factor in maintaining high creditworthiness. As to borrowed reserves, in any event, also in the present context of high capital mobility, it continues to be necessary to distinguish between reserves borrowed from the markets or from monetary authorities, such as those provided by agreements of the European Monetary System (EMS).

The EMS role in the present international monetary system

The EMS experience is omitted from Williamson's chapter, regrettably in my view, since it represents a significant innovation in the very field of international reserves.

With the already noted partial asymmetry of the dollar, the theory and practice of international reserves and foreign exchange intervention under fixed rates rests upon active use of the scarce currency, whereby there is a commitment of the weak currency to prevent depreciation below a certain threshold. To fulfil this commitment use must be made of the strong currency and/or of other international reserves. The liquidity problem – having enough reserves to cope with demands – cannot be isolated from that of adjustment, i.e., keeping broadly in line demand and supply. If there is inadequate growth of own reserves there is, of course, the risk of a deflationary bias for the system as a whole. On the other hand, it would not be possible to address the issue by reversing intervention roles. The liquidity problem would in fact, by definition, be resolved, since it would fall upon

the strong currency country to buy the weak currencies. This can always be done, because there is no difficulty in printing the domestic money. The system would, however, develop an obvious inflationary bias, since the latter agreement on intervention roles would *de facto* imply a commitment to making indefinite loans or to inflate at the pace dictated by the deficit country (Friedman and Roosa 1967).

The EMS provisions, especially after the Basel-Nyborg Agreement, represent a conceptually novel approach to the problem.[8] The so-called Very Short-Term Financing (VSTF) enables interventions to be made in currencies of the European Community (EC): to this end, EMS participating central banks open for each other very short-term credit facilities, unlimited in amount. In the short term, therefore, it is as if the fundamental exchange rate commitments previously referred to were reversed with the strong currency obliged to provide in unlimited amounts its currency to the weak one. The creation of official ECUs, or the extension of intra-EC credit facilities, deserves mention; the use of the VSTF, now also for intramarginal interventions, is a conceptual change which should not go unnoticed.

The infinite availability of reserves in the short run is by itself a significant deterrent against attacks on a currency. The vulnerability of the system implicit in the one-sided bets of private operators during the Bretton Woods system was thus greatly reduced in the EMS experience. Of course, the very functioning of the system was and is based upon mutual trust of the participating central banks, built upon time. Unlimited credit lines in the EMS are by no means a substitute for necessary adjustments in the medium and long term. Longer-term facilities are, in fact, progressively restricted, and eventually a country's reserve supply becomes rigid. This implies that the stability of the system relies heavily not only on a reciprocal expectation that rules will be respected but also on a strict coordination of monetary and fiscal policies among the member countries of the system. It is to be hoped that what to me appears to be an excessively long period of nominal exchange rate rigidity in the face of continuing divergences in inflation rates and in exogenous shocks will not strain the delicate balance of the system, before entering the phase of monetary unification proper (irrevocably fixed exchange rates).

Financial innovation

Changes in the international economic and financial environment have encouraged major innovation in the financial markets. In the 1980s and 1990s the engineers of the financial world adapted, produced, and combined a vast array of new and complex instruments (futures, options, interest rate and currency swaps, Forward Rate Agreements (FRAs)),

deeply changing the functioning of capital markets and treasury and investment management.[9] Swaps (technically back-to-back loans) between monetary authorities were – and are – an integral part of international reserve creation: I am clearly not referring here to this issue.

Contrary to Williamson, it is not capital mobility alone that has undermined the traditional approaches to international liquidity, but the joint availability of free capital movements and swaps and derivatives. It is only the interaction between these two phenomena that blurred the concepts of international reserves and international liquidity, thereby leading to 'endogeneization' of reserve supply. Without the hedging facilities of derivatives markets, capital mobility would not be as high as it is now. It is thanks to these markets that domestic interest and currency markets are welded together.

The growth of the markets of derivative products that we have witnessed in recent years is creating serious concerns about the need to strengthen the control and supervision of banks' off balance sheet activities.[10] Because of the sheer pace of innovation, both financial institutions and regulators are now under constant pressure to refine techniques to evaluate the potential risks implied in increasingly sophisticated products. In addition to market (or position) risks, i.e., risks deriving from movements in market rates, these risks also involve credit (or counterpart) risks, settlement risks, regulatory and legal risks. This is the grey side to the near perfect international capital mobility. Efficiency gains of financial innovation do not stem from the elimination of risk, but from its optimal allocation. This, however, does not guarantee that market participants are always able to evaluate the specific products correctly or, more importantly, that the possibility of 'systemic risk' is taken into proper consideration.

In conclusion, given the complementary roles of private markets and official channels in financing imbalances, discussions of international liquidity should consider the implications – advantages and risks – of recent financial innovation on the orderly evolution of the monetary and financial system.

Notes

I wish to thank L. Kay, S. Rebecchini, and G. Salsecci for helpful discussions on the issues of this comment.

1 As Triffin pointed out, the gold standard relied also on terms of trade adjustments between industrialized and developing countries (the colonies) (Triffin 1964).
2 There was, to a significant extent, gold economizing already in the gold standard (on this see Marini 1963).
3 'In Italy ... Signor Mussolini has threatened to raise the lira to its former value.

Fortunately for the Italian taxpayer and Italian business, the lira does not listen even to a dictator and cannot be given castor oil' (Keynes 1923, p. 119).

4 This does not mean that, in order to reinforce the role of the SDR, modifications in some of its features are not necessary (Masera and Sarcinelli 1985). In the main, it appears to me that the SDR should be made more useful by encouraging its use by both monetary authorities and market operators by establishing links between official and private SDRs; a proposal along this line was originally made by Kenen (Kenen 1983).

5 To recall, Ossola's Report is dated 1965, but the first allocation of SDRs took place in 1970.

6 The concept of conditionality suggests that 'the receipt of redistributed reserves – whether directly from the countries relinquishing them or indirectly through the Fund – should be *conditional* on implementing sound macroeconomic adjustment programmes, as well as on requirements relating to reserve holdings' (IMF 1992, p. 44).

7 The abandonment of the fixed exchange rate regime and the increased capital mobility seem to have had a bigger effect on the reasons why reserves are held than on the need for them (Frenkel 1983).

8 For a full description of the EMS see, for instance, Masera 1987.

9 According to BIS estimates, the outstanding notional principal of swaps in international markets was more than $4 trillion by the end of 1991. By the same period, the open interest of futures and options contracts was equal to $1,750 and $700 billion, respectively. To assess current market dimensions, it suffices to observe that the total of 'new' instruments traded both on organized exchanges and over-the-counter markets was, at the end of 1991, very close to the total of cross-border claims of BIS reporting banks (the traditional Eurocurrency markets) (Masera 1992).

10 A spate of recent articles published in the financial press testify to the increasing attention devoted to these issues in the marketplace and in regulatory fora.

References

Clarke, S. 1967. *Central Bank Cooperation: 1924–31*, New York, The Federal Reserve Bank of New York.

Frenkel, J. 1983. 'International Liquidity and Monetary Control', in G. von Furstenberg (ed.), *International Money and Credit: The Policy Roles*, Washington DC, IMF.

Friedman, M. and Roosa, R. 1967. 'The Balance of Payments: Free Versus Fixed Exchange Rates', American Enterprise Institute for Public Policy Research, *Rationale Debate Seminars*, Washington DC.

Funk, W. 1940. *The Economic Future of Europe*, Berlin, Terramare Office.

Group of Ten (Deputies) 1985. 'The Functioning of the International Monetary System' (Dini Report), in *Bollettino Economico*, Rome, Banca d'Italia.

Heller, R. and Khan, M. 1978. 'The Demand for International Reserves under Fixed and Floating Exchange Rates', *IMF Staff Papers*, December.

International Monetary Fund 1992. *International Liquidity and the SDR Mechanism*, SM/92/102, 27 May.

Kenen, P. 1983. 'Use of the SDR to Supplement or Substitute for other means of Finance', in G. von Furstenberg (ed.), *International Money and Credit: the Policy Roles*, Washington DC, IMF.

Keynes, J.M. 1923. *A Tract on Monetary Reform*, London, Macmillan.

Marini, L. 1963. *Evolution of Liquidity Concept under the Gold Standard*, Group of Ten (Liquidity Group), Washington DC.

Masera, R. 1987. *L'unificazione monetaria e lo SME*, Bologna, Il Mulino.

1992. 'Swaps and Financial Derivatives: Risks and Opportunities', paper presented at the IMI Group Seminar, *New Financial Products: Valuation, Risk Profiles and Management Techniques*, Rome, 11–12 June.

Masera, R. and Sarcinelli, M. 1985. 'Il ruolo del DSP nel sistema e un FMI completamente basato sul DSP', in Ministero del Tesoro, *Il Gruppo dei Dieci e il miglioramento del sistema monetario internazionale. Il contributo italiano*, Roma, Istituto Poligrafico dello Stato.

Ministero del Tesoro 1985. *Il Gruppo dei Dieci e il miglioramento del sistema monetario internazionale. Il contributo italiano*, Roma, Istituto Poligrafico dello Stato.

Triffin, R. 1960. *Gold and the Dollar Crisis*, New Haven, Yale University Press.

1964. 'The Myth and Reality of the So-Called Gold Standard', in *The Evolution of the International Monetary System*, Princeton, Princeton University Press.

Williamson, J. 1976. 'Exchange Rate Flexibility and Reserve Use', *Scandinavian Journal of Economics*, 78, 2.

1985. *The Exchange Rate System*, Washington DC, Institute for International Economics.

Discussion

ROBERT A. MUNDELL

Williamson's chapter on *The Rise and Fall of the Concept of International Liquidity* covers the ground Rinaldo Ossola walked on. It has a wide sweep, tracing the emergence of the concept of liquidity, stretching from the demise of bimetallism through the abortive attempt to restore the gold standard in the 1920s, and the breakdown of the gold-based dollar standard, to the uses of the concept of liquidity in the deliberations of the Committee of Twenty (C-20). Along the way, Williamson has an interesting discussion of alternative attempts to measure the adequacy of liquidity and its relation to the international version of the quantity theory of money. I suspect, however, that Ossola would have agreed more with Williamson's analysis than I do.

The core of Williamson's chapter offers the dramatic thesis that 'the concept of liquidity has lost its strategic role in the operation of the international monetary system . . .'. He considers two candidates in explanation for this demise: one is the move towards flexible exchange rates; the other, and what he considers the most important, is the increased mobility of capital. Williamson examines each in its turn.

Williamson notes that to some of its proponents, a system of flexible exchange rates would dispense with the need for reserves, but mentions the important exception of a few economists, and especially Sir Roy Harrod, who argued that more reserves would be needed under flexible exchange rates to offset the decline in credibility of monetary policy. The evidence Williamson cites from the 1970s suggests that there was some decline in reserve use; however, taking into account the following decade, it is clear that the global level of foreign exchange reserves, as a proportion of global imports, has not changed much. The use of foreign exchange reserves has grown more or less in proportion to trade, refuting the conjecture that reserves would be less necessary under flexible exchange rates. Because the dollar was by far the most important currency held in reserves, the importance of the dollar may even have increased under flexible exchange rates.

There is no doubt that the concept of global liquidity lost its strategic

74

importance as a policy tool under flexible exchange rates. Under flexible exchange rates, liquidity problems apply not to the world as a whole but to specific currency areas. When the currency area is a single nation, the country can acquire the liquidity it needs by buying it in the foreign exchange market. Because central banks can create high-powered national reserve money by buying foreign as well as domestic assets, they can acquire as many foreign assets as needed to keep 'international liquidity' rising with the demand for it, in the process of expanding the money supply more or less with nominal Gross National Product (GNP).

When countries form a fixed exchange rate area, they need to hold liquidity to maintain convertibility into the dominant currency of the area, as in the case of the Deutsche mark in the European Monetary System (EMS); the area as a whole needs to keep international reserves in dollars for purposes of pursuing any given exchange rate targets. Liquidity problems still exist under flexible exchange rates, but they are currency area specific, not global.

Williamson argues, however, that the 'advent of capital mobility is even more fundamental in undermining the whole idea that reserves can play a strategic role in permitting a degree of international management of the system'. He envisages 'the extreme case of perfect capital mobility where a country can borrow an infinite sum at the exogenous world interest rate . . . Any reserve shortage can be relieved by borrowing more . . . Under these circumstances countries will not be placed under any pressure to alter their policies because of a shortage or surfeit of reserves.' He notes that another 'casualty of increased capital mobility is the idea of asset settlement . . . it would make no difference to US behaviour if the United States had to settle all official settlements deficits by the transfer of reserve assets if it was also in a position to borrow or lend unlimited sums at the same interest rate'.

Williamson's analysis is interesting and provocative but it seems to me that it suffers from three limitations. One stems from his failure to incorporate the intertemporal budget constraint into his concept of perfect capital mobility; a second from his failure to make an adequate distinction between liquidity and wealth; and a third, from his failure to distinguish adequately between different forms of liquidity.

Even with a perfect capital market, countries cannot borrow beyond their wealth constraint, which determines their capacity to repay. If the rest of the world allowed a country to borrow an infinite amount at a positive interest rate, this country would find itself bankrupt as interest payments on the debt moved towards infinity or, at any rate, beyond the GNP and capital stock of the borrower. Capital mobility does not imply the sacrifice of the rationality implied by the absence of an intertemporal budget constraint which determines capacity to repay.

Capacity to repay can be roughly measured by potential export surpluses. Long before a country has borrowed a significant fraction of its national wealth, it would face rising risk premia in borrowing rates that cannot be assumed away by 'perfect capital mobility'. Williamson seems to recognize this, but almost as an afterthought, when he says that 'under conditions of high capital mobility the external constraint on a country comes from its *creditworthiness* rather than from its *liquidity*'. This is correct, but it is true of every capital market; creditworthiness limits borrowing even in a perfect capital market.

The fact that wealth or creditworthiness limits borrowing does not, however, mean that there is no liquidity constraint distinct from the wealth constraint. Assets can be ranked along a spectrum from the least to the most liquid asset. The wealth (or creditworthiness) and the liquidity constraints would be identical only if all assets were homogeneous with respect to liquidity. If that were true there would be no need for an international monetary system!

In the real world, uncertainty and transactions costs make money necessary; this is as true at the international as it is at the intranational level. The essence of the international monetary problem, as distinct from the international wealth or development problem, is that assets have different degrees of liquidity and that these liquid assets are often distributed unequally among countries in disproportion to differences in wealth. Very wealthy countries might be very illiquid and, conversely, very poor countries might be very liquid.

At the end of World War II, for example, Britain was by no means a poor country, yet it was extremely illiquid, and had to suffer the transactions costs (and indignity) of protracted negotiations for its American loan. Today, Russia is a country rich in natural resources and technological capacity but it is extremely illiquid; it could acquire liquidity by itself through forced sales of parts of its wealth at distress prices, but only at a tremendous sacrifice of wealth. Conversely, some non-belligerent countries emerged from World War II with abundant liquidity despite considerable poverty. Even today, some development success stories like Taiwan and Singapore are extremely liquid despite the fact that they remain only in the middle range of income levels. There is a vast difference between the wealth of a country and its liquidity.

Liquidity, thought of as a magnitude to be measured, includes only the most liquid forms of wealth. But the relevant concept for practical discussions of the international monetary system comprises only that share of liquid assets that can be commandeered by the government or international monetary authorities. In most free enterprise economies, liquidity held by the private sector is not available for purposes of supporting the

foreign exchange market. As measured by the International Monetary Fund (IMF), for example, reserve assets would include conditional liquidity from the IMF, gold, drawing rights, Special Drawing Rights (SDR), and foreign exchange; I have ranked these in order of their liquiditiness. These assets comprise only a tiny fraction of total wealth.

Of course in emergencies, such as war, even dedicated free enterprise governments feel little compunction about commandeering private sources of wealth. Under ordinary circumstances, the mobilization of private-sector liquidity for use in the foreign exchange market usually involves high transaction costs and uncertainty in the form of a substantial political effort with an uncertain result. Even the use of drawing rights from the Fund requires substantial transaction costs and uncertainty in the form of negotiating the standby arrangements and making commitments to new policies that are *ex ante* uncertain. One of the arguments for the creation of the SDR in the 1960s, as opposed to expansion of the use of ordinary drawings from the Fund, was that it would add to the total of 'unconditional liquidity'.

Within the group of government-controlled liquid foreign assets that constitute international liquidity, some assets are more liquid than others; therein lies the germ of what constitutes the Gresham's Law problem, or the 'confidence problem' as it was conceived by the Bellagio Group.[1] Gresham's Law comes into play whenever international assets exchange for the same price, but in some respects are unequal. The asset with the lowest opportunity cost drives out the other. Every country whose currency is fixed to some other currency or asset faces a potential confidence problem in that it must be prepared to supply reserve assets on demand to support its currency; but, from a global standpoint, it has a special significance in its application to the 'key' or 'centre' country in the system. Williamson deals with this under the heading of 'asset settlement', which, in the context of discussions in the C-20, was a code word for gold sales by the United States.

Whatever it is called, the Gresham's Law or asset settlement problem at the global level refers to convertibility of one asset into another at a fixed price. The country at the centre of the system takes upon itself the responsibility of maintaining the relative price of two assets.

Under bimetallism the centre country was France (with a background role played by an emerging United States). Following the gold discoveries in the middle of the last century France was inundated with gold which its bimetallic stance compelled it to buy in exchange for silver; its 'asset settlement problem' was that of supplying scarce silver in exchange for abundant gold; by so doing France exchanged most of her silver money, which was hoarded or exported, for gold. Two decades later, however, France opted for monometallic gold. When production conditions had

made silver abundant and gold scarce, France, which had suspended specie payments during war conditions in 1870, decided against bimetallism, which would have required her to exchange her entire gold currency back to silver.[2]

Britain, as a reserve currency and key currency country in the 1920s and early 1930s was confronted with an asset settlement problem in 1931; rather than submit to deflationary discipline it suspended its commitments to convertibility. The United States had an asset settlement problem of exchanging gold for dollars in 1933; instead of settling in gold, it went off the gold standard, rejecting European proposals for a return to gold at the World Economic Conference the following summer. The problem of asset settlement for the United States was reversed after devaluation of the dollar and a gold scare in 1937 temporarily created doubt that the United States would accept dollars in exchange for gold at the new price.[3]

The traditional (scarce metal, abundant currency) asset settlement problem reemerged for the United States in the 1950s and 1960s due to the unique obligations accepted by the United States under Article IV-4(b) of the Articles of Agreement of the IMF, by which the United States was absolved from the need to intervene in the foreign exchange market because of its commitment to buy and sell gold freely for international monetary purposes. The counterpart of what President de Gaulle called the 'exorbitant privilege' of the United States (to run up its dollar obligations) was the US commitment to convert dollars into gold. In maintaining its commitment to asset settlement, the bulk of the US gold stock was transferred to Europe. Asset settlement became a losing game for the United States and in practice it ended in the 1960s when the dollar became *de facto* inconvertible into gold.

The attempt to revive asset settlement in the 1970s in the guise of the gold substitution account was no doubt inspired by European exasperation at the inflationary pivot role played by the United States and envy of its seigniorage potential; it was greeted in the United States as a European attempt to clip the wings of the dollar, a lost cause both before and after the 1972 US elections. There was no *quid pro quo* for the United States in the proposal for the gold substitution account.

Williamson argues that the idea of asset settlement became a casualty of increased capital mobility. But when the phrase 'asset settlement' was coined, the United States, with its large net creditor position, had never lost its creditworthiness; there was no sudden increase in capital mobility that rendered the concept obsolete. The asset settlement problem ceased to be considered simply because the United States – and no other country – in the 1970s was not willing to return to a one-sided commitment to gold (or any other kind of) convertibility. The asset settlement problem exists only when

a country has made an asset settlement commitment; this was never the case after the introduction of flexible exchange rates. Nor was the disappearance of the concept due to the increased 'liability financing' of other countries. It is true that the rise of the Deutsche mark, and, to a lesser extent the yen, as reserve centres has reduced the asymmetric role of the dollar, but this evolution occurred long after the demise of the clamour for asset settlement.

The reason the concept of asset settlement ceased to be talked about at the global level was simply that neither the United States nor any other country undertook to make its currency convertible into the asset of settlement (whatever it was). In a world of completely flexible exchange rates, the concept of convertibility or asset settlement becomes an empty box.

This does not mean that the concept of asset settlement or convertibility has no longer any place in economic thinking about the international monetary system. In fact, the concept merely went underground when flexible exchange rates were adopted in 1973 and the 'dollar overhang' disappeared. The concept of asset settlement would be revived in any *anchored* fixed exchange rate area, where currencies were convertible into the area's anchor whether it be a commodity like gold or oil, or a currency like the dollar, yen, or ECU.

The foregoing should make it clear that I do not agree with Williamson's conclusion pertaining to the 'demise' of the concept of liquidity. If it is a valid concept, it has universal application. Because, as Williamson says, virtually any positive theory of the behaviour of national governments will lead to the prediction that greater reserve ease will generate some combination of expansionary policies, the adequacy of liquidity must be measured by its consequences: global inflation is a symptom of excess liquidity; global deflation of deficient liquidity.

After the Napoleonic wars, there was a period of global deflation and deficient liquidity; after the gold discoveries in mid century, there was excess liquidity; after the breakup of bimetallism in 1870, there was excess liquidity in the silver bloc and deficient liquidity in the gold bloc; after the mid 1890s, with the vast increase in gold from South Africa, there was inflation and excess liquidity in the gold bloc.

There was a gold shortage in the 1920s, but judged by inflation, no liquidity shortage; liquidity requirements had been made up by the use of foreign exchange, an unstable component. A liquidity shortage appeared, however, when the foreign exchange component of reserves was dismantled, with deflationary consequences. Deflation ended after the devaluation of the dollar and there was no longer a liquidity shortage in the late 1930s.

Sudden changes in demand for liquidity or large shifts in the composition

of reserves can have inflationary or deflationary consequences. The shift of countries from silver to gold in the 1870s and also in the early 1890s had deflationary consequences in the gold bloc and inflationary consequences in the silver bloc. The abandonment of the gold standard by belligerent European countries during World War I created an excess supply of gold liquidity, which created inflation in countries that, like the United States, remained on the gold standard.[4] A similar effect occurred in the late 1930s and early 1940s as the currencies of the belligerents became inconvertible and the United States reacquired the bulk of the world's stock of monetary gold. The increase in demand for gold by European countries in the late 1950s and early 1960s created a gold shortage at a time when, from a global standpoint, there was no liquidity shortage; the international monetary 'war' of the 1960s centred on the undervaluation of gold and a struggle for power, not a shortage of liquidity.

A reduction in demand for dollars in the course of a consolidation of dollar reserves as the European Monetary Union (EMU) proceeds would create excess liquidity and have inflationary consequences for the dollar area unless it were offset by an appropriately contractionary monetary policy on the part of the Federal Reserve System; similarly, a decline in European demand for gold in the course of EMU would lead to a fall in its price unless other countries reentered the gold market.

Williamson ends his essay with a proposal for allocations of SDRs to the least creditworthy countries. As Williamson says, this has nothing to do with the liquidity problem; it is an unabashed attempt to 'remedy an injustice'. I sympathize with his target, but not with his instrument. It has a double defect. First, it shares with the 'link' proposal the defect of mixing up a poverty problem with the liquidity problem; and second, it sends exactly the wrong signals to encourage sound economic policies among the developing countries. The IMF in any case is not the right international agency responsible for redressing poverty; and Williamson's proposal would destroy the potential of the SDR as a respectable component of the future international monetary system. It would be far better to channel resources for the alleviation of poverty explicitly through such institutions as the International Development Association.

'Is there a future for the SDR?' Williamson's question is worth asking. In my view, the SDR has a future as a universal unit of account at the heart of the international monetary system. To achieve this goal, it should be redefined from a basket of five inflating currencies to a unit that is stable in terms of its purchasing power.

Let me conclude by saying that, while I have disagreed with key points in

Williamson's analysis, I believe that he has made a thoughtful, challenging much-needed attempt to make more rigorous the concept of liquidity, and that he has raised questions that are useful subjects for research in the years to come.

Notes

1 An informal group of international economists and monetary officials from various countries which met regularly in the 1960s to discuss international monetary issues.
2 And, one might add, follow this up with submission to the inflation of the silver area.
3 The political history of the international monetary system can be characterized in part by the systematic attempt of the dominant financial power to resist the attempts of former great or future great powers to reduce the advantages to the centre country of being number one. I have traced this observation in Mundell 1991.
4 I have elsewhere referred to this as the 'Thornton effect' (Mundell 1989a and b). Thornton was the first to modify Hume's mechanism to take account of the fact that, when a country expanded credit and consequently lost gold, the world price level (and thus the home price level) would rise, presumably more or less in proportion to the fraction the gold exports were of the monetary gold stock of the rest of the world.

References

Mundell, R.A. 1989a. 'Trade Balance Patterns as Global Equilibrium: The Seventeenth Approach to the Balance of Payments', in *Rivista di Politica Economica*, 79 (6) (June): 9–60; reprinted in M. Baldassarri, L. Paganetto and E. Phelps (eds.) 1992. *International Interdependence and Economic Policy Coordination*, Rome: St Martin's Press/SIPA, 9–60.

Mundell, R.A. 1989b. 'The Global Adjustment System', in *Rivista di Politica Economica*, 79 (12) (December): 351–464; reprinted in M. Baldassarri, J. McCallum and R. Mundell (eds.) 1992. *Global Disequilibrium in the World Economy*, Rome: St Martin's Press/SIPA, 351–464.

Mundell R. A. 1991. 'World Financial Institutions and the Exchange Rate System', Proceedings of the Inaugural Conference on Inflation, Public Debts and Monetary Policy, University of Molise, Campobasso, Italy, in *Rivista di Politica Economica*; updated version was presented as 'EMU and the International Monetary System: A Transatlantic View', Austria National Bank Lecture Series, Vienna, June 1993.

4 The role of market and official channels in the supply of international liquidity

ANDREW CROCKETT

1 Introduction

International liquidity, as a topic of academic research and official concern, has suffered something of an eclipse over the past twenty years. The shifting perception of the importance of the subject is clearly associated with the growing role of markets in the provision of liquidity, replacing or supplementing official sources. But the issue is more complex than that. The purpose of this chapter will be to explore why views of international reserve supply arrangements have changed, and to what extent this reflects underlying changes in the world economy, as against developments in economic thinking, or even mere changes in fashion.

A quarter of a century or so ago, Rinaldo Ossola chaired the Group of Ten (G-10) deputies' meetings which produced the report that bears his name (G-10 1965). This report paved the way for the creation of the Special Drawing Rights (SDR) facility in the Fund. SDRs were seen as completing the unfinished work of Bretton Woods, by filling a gap in reserve supply arrangements. They would thus create a firm basis for the working of the adjustment process under fixed but adjustable exchange rates. Few international economists doubted that this was one of the key issues in ensuring stable growth of the world economy. The International Monetary Fund published a major conference volume on the theme of international liquidity in 1970 (IMF 1970) and Williamson surveyed over 200 contributions to the subject in his review article in the *Economic Journal* published in 1973 (Williamson 1973).

Twenty-five years on from the Ossola Report, it would be hard to find many economists who believed the management of international liquidity to be a major element in the performance of the world economy. In IMF Annual Reports, discussion of the subject of liquidity has shrunk from being a major focus, to a couple of pages or so. References to the need to create official liquidity have become increasingly sparse in international communiqués.

Changing views of the role and importance of reserve supply arrange-

ments reflect both changes in the world economy – in particular, the shift to more flexible exchange rate arrangements and the growth of international capital markets – and developments in thinking, as the economic signifi-cance of models of portfolio balance have come to be better appreciated. In the 1960s, it was still possible to use a paradigm in which a stable demand for international reserves confronted an exogenously determined supply. In such a context, the key policy questions revolved around the identification of the arguments of the demand function, and the maintenance of a supply/demand equilibrium. Now, the relevant paradigm is, to simplify somewhat, one in which reserves are endogenously created, with no direct external constraint on supply.

Later on in this chapter, we will consider these two paradigms in more detail, including the extent to which they were a reasonable representation of reality, and the factors that caused one to be replaced by the other. First, however, it will be useful to have some discussion of terms, in particular the relationship of the concept of reserves to that of liquidity, and the relevance of the distinction between market and official sources of liquidity. Against the background of these definitions, and in the light of changing views of reserve supply arrangements, we will review the growth of reserves in the postwar period, divided into five subperiods which, though somewhat arbitrary, represent distinct phases in the evolution of the system. Finally, the chapter turns to some problems and issues in present arrangements which continue to deserve attention, despite the overall 'message' that liquidity can be considered largely endogenous.

2 Definitions

Reserves and liquidity

Most writers recognize the distinction between reserves and liquidity, but nevertheless proceed as though the two were synonymous (see, for example, Williamson 1973, p. 687). *International reserves* can be defined as those assets held by monetary authorities that represent liquid international purchasing power. Traditionally, reserves include gold, foreign exchange, SDRs, and reserve positions in the IMF. *International liquidity* is a broader concept and encompasses access to borrowing, as well as the capacity of national authorities to convert non-reserve assets into international pur-chasing power through the use of markets. Liquidity is the more relevant concept in a behavioural sense, although reserves is the more easy to define. It is also useful to distinguish between *owned* and *borrowed* reserves. Owned reserves are those for which there is no counterpart external liability, whereas borrowed reserves are matched by foreign currency liabilities of the monetary authorities.

Even before the growth of international capital markets, it was recognized that countries had access to liquidity that was not captured by measures of reserves. In particular, 'conditional liquidity' was available in the form of borrowing rights at the IMF. To some extent, access to borrowing facilities reduces the need for 'owned liquidity'. But the extent to which it does so clearly depends on both the *size* of the borrowing facilities, and the degree of *conditionality* attached to their use. With the growth of international capital markets, countries can also satisfy their needs for liquidity through market borrowing. To the extent that countries borrow in markets, and add the proceeds to their reserves, the liquidity provided by the international capital markets will be reflected in reserve totals. However, to the extent that countries use *potential* access to international markets as a substitute for *actual* holding of reserves, it is very difficult to measure the liquidity that the existence of such markets affords. More generally, of course, the fact that private agents can use international financial markets to satisfy their needs has an effect on the reserves that monetary authorities need to hold in their own name. (The direction of the effect is, however, ambiguous; movements in private holdings of external assets may substitute for official reserve movements; or create a need for larger official reserves to offset shifts in private sector portfolios.)

Liquidity can also be created by bilateral or multilateral swap facilities. For the most part swap facilities amongst central banks are subject to little or no conditionality, and in that respect could be considered an addition to reserves, much like reserve positions in the Fund. However, swap positions have other restrictions on their use, such as the time for which they may remain outstanding, so that their utility is considerably more limited than that of owned reserves. A similar observation is applicable to the Very Short-Term Financing facility (VSTF) of the European Monetary System (EMS). Participants in the Exchange Rate Mechanism (ERM) of the EMS have automatic access to unlimited borrowing rights under the VSTF. But recourse to the VSTF is limited in time, and must be repaid by transfers of owned reserves after a short period.

The difficulty of providing quantitative content to the concept of liquidity in the broad sense just defined explains the approach used by most analysts, which is to use official reserves as a proxy for liquidity. But it should be borne in mind that it is an imperfect proxy. Not only do reserves fail to capture important elements that add to liquidity, they can also include assets that are, for practical purposes, no longer liquid. Since 1973, for example, holdings of gold have been virtually immobilized, in part because of the uncertain price at which such holdings could be realized, but perhaps also because of the potential criticism that national authorities

could face as a result of transactions in gold.[1] Gold holdings can, however, be more readily used by central banks as collateral for borrowing in markets.

Sources of reserve creation

A second definitional issue concerns the distinction between 'official' and 'market' sources of liquidity. It is sometimes implied that foreign exchange reserves are mostly created by market processes, while all other reserves can be viewed as 'exogenous' or officially created. This is something of a simplification. In fact, four sources of reserve creation can be identified, with differing degrees of exogeneity:

(i) Gold. So long as the price of gold is fixed, the availability of monetary gold can be considered exogenous to the system, being determined by the interaction of mining technology and private demand.

(ii) SDRs and Reserve Positions in the Fund. SDRs are owned reserves created by deliberate international decision, and the stock of them is exogenously determined. Reserve Positions in the Fund depend on the overall size of Fund quotas (exogenously determined), and the (endogenous) extent to which drawings on the Fund by some members create reserve positions for others.

(iii) Balance of payments deficits by reserve currency countries. These can be viewed as exogenous, if they arise from economic developments and policy decisions in the reserve currency countries, and not as a result of demands to hold foreign currency claims by creditor countries. However, deficits by reserve currency countries only give rise to an increase in international liquidity when other countries are prepared to hold the resulting claims. To this extent, there is an important element of endogeneity in this source of reserve creation.

(iv) Maturity transformation or currency exchange in financial markets. This is the most truly endogenous of reserve creation mechanisms, since reserve creation can occur entirely at the initiative of the reserve holding country and without requiring a deficit by the country whose currency is held in reserves. Reserve creation through the market can occur by straightforward maturity transformation, as for example when a country borrows at long term in foreign exchange and invests the proceeds in liquid assets in the same currency, or by the purchase of foreign currency against domestic currency through intervention in the foreign exchange market.

The distinction between endogenous and exogenous sources of reserve creation is based on whether the underlying transaction has, as its main

motive, the satisfaction of reserve demand by the holding country. As will be readily apparent, however, it is not easy to give empirical content to this distinction.

3 Two paradigms

Bretton Woods: exogenous reserve supply

At the time the Ossola Report was published in 1965, there was a straightforward, and pleasingly elegant, basic theory of how the adjustment process worked. The overall environment was one of fixed exchange rates, which were seen as necessary to avoid the risk of beggar-thy-neighbour exchange rate policies. Within this context, countries sought to combine internal and external balance. Internal balance was defined as reasonably full employment of factors of production, while external balance required a sustainable balance of payments. When a country's current account position weakened, the response was to adopt domestic deflationary measures so as to restrain domestic absorption and restore payments equilibrium. Similarly, when a balance of payments surplus emerged, a country would have more scope for relatively expansionary policies, that would allow an increase in absorption. Exchange rate adjustments were provided for only in cases of 'fundamental disequilibrium'.

In this model, international reserve holdings were viewed as a cushion against short-term fluctuations in payments positions, and as being subject to a relatively well-defined demand function. This made reserves a key element of the adjustment process. If the level (or, *pace* Machlup 1966, pp. 119–37, the rate of change) of reserves was inadequate, the result would be a preponderance of deflationary over expansionary policies, and possibly also the emergence of balance of payments restrictions. On the other hand, with an excess supply of reserves, inflation would be the result. So the task of international monetary management was to create and distribute the unique quantity of reserves that would appropriately balance expansionary and deflationary forces in the world economy, thus producing the optimum combination of price stability and global economic growth.

This broad model of the international economy directed the attention of policymakers to the demand and supply functions for international reserves. On the demand side, considerable research effort was expended in analysing the factors governing national holdings of reserves (see, for example, Britto and Heller 1973; Frenkel 1974). In the end, most researchers concluded that it was not possible to specify a demand function that would explain short-term movements in reserve holdings; and that in the longer term it was hard to improve on a rule of thumb whereby global

reserve needs would grow broadly in line with international trade. On the supply side, it was assumed that international liquidity was largely exogenous, and that increments to reserves would be closely dependent on deliberate reserve creation decisions. Additions to gold stocks were, of course, still a potential source of reserve growth. However, by the late 1960s, this form of international liquidity was adding relatively little to world reserves, and was obviously inadequate in itself. Holdings of reserve currencies, by contrast, had grown rapidly during the late 1950s and 1960s. A major cause of this development was the continuation of the US balance of payments deficit (on an official settlements basis), which initially permitted a welcome increase in the reserves of other countries. However, Triffin pointed out the potential instability of arrangements in which US official liabilities were continually growing relative to the US gold stock (Triffin 1960). Overall, it was generally assumed that the rate of growth of reserves held in foreign exchange would have to be cut back. In equilibrium, the total volume of world reserves could not grow faster than the stock of primary liquidity (i.e., gold and, prospectively, internationally created reserve assets).

In sum, therefore, the prevailing view in the mid 1960s was that there was a sufficiently stable demand function for reserves to influence the policy decisions of individual countries. The available supply of reserves could be managed by the international community through the deliberate creation of international liquidity. Thus the issue of international liquidity was central to the effective functioning of the adjustment process.

Post-Bretton Woods: endogenous reserves

It is less easy to identify the model of international economic adjustment that prevails in 1992. Simplifying somewhat, and realizing that not all will agree with the choice of emphasis, the main elements may be summarized as follows: all countries accept that there is no long-run trade-off between inflation and full employment and, moreover, accept that price stability is the best environment for stable and sustainable economic growth. Convergence towards internationally consistent price stability goals is a necessary, though not a sufficient, condition for exchange rate stability.

Concerning external adjustment, the combination of international capital mobility and flexible exchange rates should be allowed to reconcile divergences in relative economic performance among countries. It is recognized, however, that exchange rate movements can both reflect and cause problems of economic adjustment. Changes in relative policy mix, for example, can generate changes in savings/investment balances among countries that require shifts in exchange rates. But exchange markets can at

times overshoot equilibrium rates with adverse consequences for the working of the adjustment process. Even in a global system of flexible exchange rates, therefore, there may be a role for exchange rate policies, and a demand to hold international reserves. However, this demand is less likely to be stably related to the volume of international trade than it was under Bretton Woods arrangements.

On the supply side, the 1992 paradigm is one in which creditworthy countries can essentially acquire the volume of reserves they need through asset transformation in deep and liquid international capital markets. The extent to which they exploit this possibility will depend on shifting perceptions of the need to hold reserves for exchange rate management purposes, as well as on the terms and conditions under which such asset transformation can be effected. The creation of official liquidity (e.g., through SDR allocations) will have practically no influence on the aggregate holding of international reserves since it will merely substitute for, rather than add to, liquidity created through the market.

What happened between 1965 and 1992 to bring about this fundamental change of view concerning the role of reserves in the adjustment process? Important shifts took place both in the factors underlying the demand for reserves and, on the supply side, in the availability of liquidity. So long as the Bretton Woods system of fixed but adjustable exchange rates was regarded as the operational context, and reserves were held mainly to smooth out fluctuations in current account positions over time, it was possible to envisage a stable demand for reserves. The 'benefit' provided by reserve holding could be measured in terms of a reduction in the variability of domestic absorption. With the advent of flexible exchange rates, however, an alternative adjustment mechanism became available (at least potentially) which did not require the holding of reserves. At the same time, the growth of international capital markets meant that shifts in the current account no longer had such a direct impact on official reserves. Relatively minor changes in interest differentials could induce short-term capital flows that would protect the reserves against the consequences of movements in the current account position. A number of academic studies have attempted to measure the impact of floating exchange rates on the demand for reserves (Heller and Khan 1978, pp. 699–724). In general, and perhaps counterintuitively, the broad conclusion is that it is hard to detect any significant reduction in the demand to hold reserves, nor much of a shift in the stability of the demand for reserves function. Thus, the reduction in the importance ascribed to reserves as a tool of international economic management cannot easily be laid at the door of increased volatility in reserve demand.

The more important change is that in reserve supply arrangements. As described earlier, the growth of international capital markets has meant that reserve holding countries (in the aggregate, as well as individually) face

Table 4.1. *The Euro currency market 1964–91 (US$ billions)*

	Gross deposits	% growth of gross deposits	Net deposits[a]	% growth of net deposits
1964	19	—	14	—
1965	20	5.3	17	21.4
1966	25	25.0	21	23.5
1967	32	28.0	25	19.1
1968	46	43.8	34	36.0
1969	65	41.3	50	47.1
1970	86	32.3	65	30.0
1971	150	74.4	85	30.8
1972	210	40.0	110	29.4
1973	292	39.1	175	59.1
1974	459	57.2	230	31.4
1975	551	20.0	265	15.2
1976	672	22.0	340	28.3
1977	844	25.6	435	27.9
1978	1084	28.4	530	21.8
1979	1353	24.8	665	25.5
1980	1641	21.3	810	21.8
1981	1933	17.8	945	16.7
1982	2118	9.6	1020	7.9
1983	2193	3.5	1085	6.4
1984	2614	19.2	1265	16.6
1985	3269	25.1	1485	17.4
1986	4164	27.4	1775	19.5
1987	5309	27.5	2220	25.1
1988	5754	8.4	2545	14.6
1989	6522	13.4	2920	14.7
1990	7466	14.5	3535	21.1
1991	7497	0.4	3610	2.1

Note:
[a] Net of interbank deposits.
Source: BIS and other.

a very elastic supply schedule. The total size of the Eurocurrency banking markets has grown to some $7.5 trillion (see table 4.1). Monetary authorities can operate in these markets on much the same terms as any other market participant. The growth of deposit taking and lending in these markets depends on supply and demand, which are in turn dependent on the monetary conditions generated by the authorities of the countries issuing the currencies traded.

The growth and increasing integration of financial markets have been accompanied by developments in portfolio theory. This too has played its part in reducing the focus given to international reserve holdings in the transmission of economic conditions. Governments and central banks, like other economic agents, are viewed as allocating their portfolio of assets and liabilities so as to maximize a welfare function. The markets in which they deal have great depth and breadth, so that economic agents (including monetary authorities) can reallocate their portfolios without difficulty. What is determined exogenously is not the supply of international liquidity, but monetary conditions (i.e., short-term interest rates) in the major financial centres. Changes in these monetary conditions affect both international economic developments and, indirectly, reserve holding decisions by individual central banks. But it would not be accurate to say that the stock of reserves is the channel by which economic influences are transmitted. Rather, the stock of reserves is one among many factors that are the *consequence* of monetary decisions taken elsewhere.

4 The supply of international reserves 1945–92

As is apparent from the previous section, the analysis of reserve supply arrangements has undergone considerable evolution during the postwar period. For the purposes of this section, we identify five subperiods, during each of which the sources of reserve increases have been different. Naturally, the choice of subperiods is somewhat arbitrary, and the distinctions are not clear cut; nevertheless, such a division highlights the main milestones in the development of the various liquidity sources through time.

1945–58: gold as the primary liquidity source

Following the end of the World War II, there was a chronic shortage of international liquidity which delayed the reintroduction of currency convertibility and a multilateral payments system. Gold was the primary source of liquidity, but it was very unevenly distributed, with the great bulk of the world's monetary gold being held by the United States. Many people had expected that the creation of the IMF would provide usable liquidity either through the creation of a new asset (such as Keynes' Bancor) or at least the provision of generous drawing rights to deficit countries. In the event, that did not occur, and it was only with the establishment of the Marshall Plan in 1948 that the United States in effect made dollar liquidity available to the European countries to begin the process of creating a multilateral settlement system.

The restoration of convertibility owed relatively little to the growth of

Table 4.2. *Sources of reserve growth 1948–58 (US$ billions)*

	Foreign exchange	Of which US official external liabilities	Reserve positions in the fund	Gold	Total
1948	—	—	1.6	32.5	—
1949	—	—	1.7	33.0	—
1950	13.3	4.9	1.7	33.4	48.4
1951	13.5	4.2	1.7	33.6	48.8
1952	14.0	5.6	1.8	33.6	49.4
1953	15.3	6.5	1.9	34.1	51.3
1954	16.5	7.5	1.8	34.7	53.0
1955	16.7	8.3	1.9	35.2	53.8
1956	17.8	9.2	2.3	35.9	56.0
1957	17.1	9.1	2.3	37.1	56.5
1958	17.1	9.6	2.6	37.8	57.5

Sources: US official external liabilities and gold – IFS Yearbook. Foreign exchange, reserve positions, and SDR – IMF Annual Report.

total world liquidity. As may be seen from table 4.2, world reserves rose by less than 20 per cent between 1950 and 1958, an annual rate of growth of just over 2 per cent. However, regional settlement systems (particularly the European Payments Union, but also the sterling area) provided important sources of additional liquidity. The strengthening of the European economies, together with a redistribution of liquidity away from the United States, provided the basis for the move to *de facto* convertibility in 1958. There were grounds for satisfaction in the overall economic management of the postwar years. Unlike previous periods following major wars, the growth of output and trade was well sustained, and the global price level established itself on a gradual upward path. However, with world output increasing at a rate of perhaps 6 per cent in nominal terms, and world trade growing even more rapidly, it seemed likely that the slow growth of primary liquidity could pose a threat to the sustainability of economic expansion.

1958–67: the growth of dollar holdings

A prospective shortage of international liquidity was forestalled for a time by the emergence, in the early 1960s, of a sizeable US balance of payments deficit. Initially, surplus countries were happy to add dollars to their reserves, easing their international liquidity position. As early as 1960,

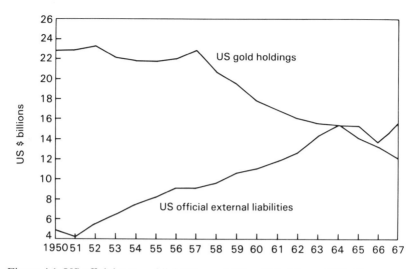

Figure 4.1 US official external liabilities and US gold holdings, 1950–67.
Source: IFS Yearbook.

however, Triffin pointed out the unsustainability of this trend (Triffin 1960). Countries were willing to hold dollars because they provided an interest return and were unconditionally convertible into gold. However, the larger the stock of dollars became relative to the United States' holding of gold, the more problematic was dollar convertibility. As may be seen from figure 4.1, US external liabilities were growing and gold reserves were shrinking throughout the postwar period. This problem became more acute as the structure of the US balance of payments changed from the late 1950s onwards. In the earlier postwar years, the United States had run persistent surpluses on current account, so that any deficit on official settlements simply reflected the acquisition of assets overseas by the US private sector. In this situation, as Despres, Kindleberger, and Salant later pointed out, the United States was performing a banking type function of maturity transformation, that need not necessarily be regarded as unsustainable (Despres, Kindleberger, and Salant 1966). Once the US current account moved into deficit, however, there was a more serious problem of sustainability. Either the US balance of payments deficit would continue, in which case there might at some stage occur a loss of confidence in the gold convertibility of the dollar and an exchange crisis; or else the United States would correct its balance of payments deficit, in which case world liquidity would stop growing. This would pose a threat of deflationary policies or payments restrictions.

The general recognition of the 'Triffin dilemma' produced a plethora of

Table 4.3. *Sources of reserve growth 1958–67 (US$ billions)*

	Foreign exchange	Of which US official external liabilities	Reserve positions in the fund	Gold	Total
1958	17.1	9.6	2.6	37.8	57.5
1959	16.1	10.7	3.3	37.8	57.2
1960	18.5	11.1	3.6	38.0	60.1
1961	19.1	11.8	4.2	38.8	62.1
1962	19.9	12.7	3.8	39.2	62.9
1963	22.7	14.4	3.9	40.2	66.8
1964	24.2	15.4	4.2	40.7	69.1
1965	24.0	15.4	5.4	41.8	71.2
1966	25.7	13.7	6.3	40.8	72.8
1967	29.4	15.6	5.7	39.4	74.5

Sources: US official external liabilities and gold – IFS Yearbook. Foreign exchange, reserve positions, and SDR – IMF Annual Report.

plans to develop official sources of liquidity that could replace dollar balances and allow the correction of the US payments deficit without stifling liquidity growth. The search for an official source of reserve creation acquired urgency as the rate of increase of monetary gold tailed off and then went into reverse (see table 4.3). Eventually, as is well known, agreement was reached, at the Rio de Janeiro Meeting of the IMF in 1967, to establish the SDR mechanism. At that time, most projections were for the elimination of the US balance of payments deficit, and a gradual increase of the newly created SDRs in the stock of international reserves.

1967–73: the explosion of liquidity and the collapse of Bretton Woods

The establishment of the SDR facility required a decision to amend the IMF's Articles. Following the Rio de Janeiro Agreement, it was not until 1969 that the actual decision to make an allocation was taken. A total of SDRs 9.5 billion[2] was allocated during the three years 1970–2. This figure represented over 10 per cent of the stock of reserves in 1969. There should, therefore, have been an increase in the relative importance of primary liquidity and a decline in the role of national currencies. In fact, the reverse occurred. With the escalation of the Vietnam War, the US balance of payments deficit, far from contracting as had been foreseen, expanded by a very large amount. The attempt to maintain fixed exchange rates in the face

Table 4.4. *Sources of reserve growth 1967–73 (US$ billions)*

	Foreign exchange	Of which US dollars	Reserve positions in the fund	Gold	SDR	Total
1967	29.4	20.0	5.7	39.4	—	74.5
1968	32.5	19.8	6.5	38.8	—	77.8
1969	33.0	19.5	6.7	39.0	—	78.7
1970	45.3	35.0	7.7	37.1	3.1	93.2
1971	81.3	62.9	6.9	39.2	6.4	133.8
1972	104.1	81.8	6.9	38.8	9.4	159.2
1973	122.9	93.5	7.4	43.2	10.6	184.1

Sources: US official external liabilities and gold – IFS Yearbook. Foreign exchange, reserve positions, and SDR – IMF Annual Report.

of a growing US balance of payments deficit, and increasing speculation against the dollar, required large-scale official intervention by countries outside the United States. As may be seen from table 4.4, the upsurge in national currencies coincided, paradoxically, with the allocation of SDRs that was intended to reduce the role of national currencies.

By the time the Bretton Woods system broke down irretrievably in 1973, international holdings of US dollars in reserves had increased more than fourfold from their level of five years earlier. This increase in reserves went far beyond the desire of the countries concerned to acquire liquidity for balance of payments management purposes. It was, rather, a reflection of the inadequacy in the international adjustment process and an important contributory factor to the upsurge in inflation that characterized the 1970s.

1973–82: attempts to reassert official control over liquidity creation

Following the move to floating exchange rates in 1973, some extreme academic opinion considered that there would no longer be any need to hold official international reserves. Instead, these observers believed exchange rate movements could be relied upon continuously to balance private supply and demand for foreign exchange, with relatively minor movements in exchange rates. The official view, as reflected, *inter alia*, in the report of the Committee of Twenty (C-20), was that there would continue to be a demand for international reserves, even though the change of exchange regime might lead to a step change in the reserve demand function (C-20 1973). It was noted that countries would continue to have objectives

in the exchange rate field (for example to avoid unnecessary or damaging volatility in exchange markets), while a large number of countries continued to operate a pegged exchange rate regime.

In the aftermath of the oil price increases of 1973–4, the need to facilitate the recycling of petrodollars was seen as another reason for official reserve holding. For one thing, the oil-exporting countries would have to hold a substantial part of their new wealth in the form of liquid holdings of national currency, as well as in official loans (e.g., through the IMF's oil facility). Beyond this, oil-importing countries would wish to have adequate reserves to counteract the impact of speculation against their currencies in the wake of changes in their current account positions. Over time, however, there were grounds for believing that the role of national currencies in reserves might decline. With the demise of the fixed exchange rate system, monetary authorities would no longer be obliged to acquire reserves in order to defend fixed parities. So there was unlikely to be any repetition of the upsurge in US dollar holdings that had characterized the later years of the Bretton Woods system. At the same time, the United States itself was keen to strengthen its international competitive position and move towards eliminating its external payments deficit. Other potential reserve centres, such as Germany and Japan, were extremely reluctant to see an increase in the international use of their currencies. They feared that this would curtail their freedom of monetary management, much as it had for the United Kingdom when sterling was a secondary reserve currency. In the years immediately following the move to floating, therefore, there was quite a widespread belief that official reserve creation could continue to play an important role in international economic management. In the event, however, countries found the international capital markets to be a convenient source for meeting their need for international liquidity, and, despite the absence of SDR allocations for most of the 1970s, there was no obvious evidence of reserve stringency. Table 4.5 shows that holdings of non-gold reserves increased at an annual average rate of some 12 per cent during the period 1973–82.

The case for using the mechanism of SDR creation during this period relied on two basic arguments. First, not all countries had access to international capital markets. The poorer and less creditworthy members of the international community had to generate balance of payments surpluses in order to acquire their immediate liquidity, while better-off countries could simply use the financial markets. Second, the accumulation of reserves in national currency form could lead to instability if asset holders tried collectively to shift from one currency to another. Neither of these arguments was sufficiently persuasive to change the opposition of several major countries to further SDR allocations. These countries

Table 4.5. *Sources of growth of non-gold reserves 1973–82 (US\$ billions)*

	Foreign exchange	Of which US dollars	Reserve position in the fund	SDR	Total non-gold reserves
1973	122.9	93.5	7.4	10.6	140.9
1974	154.6	120.3	10.8	10.8	176.2
1975	160.7	127.8	14.8	10.3	185.8
1976	186.1	148.3	20.6	10.1	216.8
1977	245.7	195.1	22.0	9.9	277.6
1978	289.9	222.9	19.3	10.6	319.8
1979	327.5	241.4	15.5	16.4	359.4
1980	373.2	256.4	21.5	15.1	409.8
1981	339.8	242.6	24.8	19.1	383.7
1982	314.0	221.4	28.1	19.6	361.7

Sources: US official external liabilities and gold – IFS Yearbook. Foreign exchange, reserve positions, and SDR – IMF Annual Report.

generally felt that the main problem confronting the world economy was that of inflation. Even if SDR allocations would change only the *composition* of reserves rather than the quantum, it would seem strange to be creating liquidity at a time when monetary restraint was required. As far as the problem of the poorer countries was concerned, it was noted that these represented a relatively small share of the world economy (and therefore of potential SDR allocations) and that it was more appropriate to help them through increases in concessional aid. The period after 1973 can therefore be considered the beginning of the time in which increases in international liquidity were essentially market determined. It is true that there was an SDR allocation in 1979–81 but this was small in size. Virtually the whole of the increase in foreign exchange holdings that occurred can be considered demand determined. Even to the extent that it represented the counterpart of deficits by reserve currency countries, it was voluntarily held.

1982–92: a two-tier world

Since 1982, there have been no allocations of SDRs, and the only increases in officially created liquidity have come through quota-related increases in access to the IMF, much of it conditional. Increases in reserves have been essentially demand determined. Nevertheless, there has been an increasingly stark distinction between those countries (largely OECD members)

Table 4.6. *Sources of growth of non-gold reserves 1982–90 (US$ billions)*

	Foreign exchange	Of which US dollars	Reserve positions in the fund	SDR	Total
1982	314.0	221.4	28.1	19.6	361.7
1983	323.3	230.8	40.9	15.1	379.3
1984	342.5	240.1	40.7	16.1	399.3
1985	382.6	248.7	42.5	20.0	445.1
1986	445.4	298.9	43.2	23.8	512.4
1987	647.1	440.4	44.6	28.7	720.4
1988	665.5	430.6	38.0	27.1	730.6
1989	716.4	432.0	33.5	26.9	776.8
1990	831.2	468.8	33.2	28.5	892.9

Sources: US official external liabilities and gold – IFS Yearbook. Foreign exchange, reserve positions, and SDR – IMF Annual Report.

that have access to international capital markets, and that can satisfy their reserve needs by asset transformation in these markets, and those whose access to financial markets is restricted and which have to acquire reserves either by forgoing imports, or by conditional borrowing from the IMF. Within this latter group, there are of course important differences. Whereas very few developing countries could attract capital flows of any sort in the immediate aftermath of the debt crisis, more recently several countries (e.g., Mexico) have demonstrated that prudent domestic policies can generate substantial reflows of capital.

5 Is there a reserve supply problem?

The simple paradigm in which reserves are wholly demand determined, and held mainly in foreign currency form, suggests that the stock of international liquidity is no longer a major issue for international economic management. However, there remain a number of potential shortcomings in an international economic system where the global reserves stock is the passive consequence of decentralized decisions by individual countries:

(i) Changes in perceptions about the prospects of currencies held in reserves can lead to attempts to change reserve portfolios, with potentially damaging effects on exchange rate stability, relative to most industrial countries.

(ii) The inability of less creditworthy countries to access international capital markets puts them at a costly disadvantage.

(iii) The absence of effective control over international reserves means that there is no mechanism for influencing international developments at the global level or for assigning adjustment responsibilities.

(iv) The determination of world economic conditions is dependent upon monetary conditions of the major financial powers.

Concern about the destabilizing effects of currency substitution in reserves has surfaced on several occasions, notably at the time of the C-20's discussions on reform of the international monetary system (C-20 1973), and during the second oil crisis (G-30 1980). The argument is that the greater the share of national currencies in reserves, the greater the scope for exchange market pressures, as reserve-holding central banks reassess the relative prospects of different reserve currencies. If the overall quantum of desired reserves is given, deliberate creation of SDRs would allow countries to hold fewer reserves in the form of national currencies, thus limiting the scope for currency switching. This was the rationale for the proposed creation of a substitution account in the IMF. A substitution account would allow countries to deposit national currencies in a special account at the IMF and receive SDR-denominated claims in return. These SDR-denominated claims, being protected against the risks of changes in the relative value of individual reserve currencies, would be less vulnerable to asset switching decisions.

Although concerns about asset switching have force, it is not clear that they can be met by the mechanism of a substitution account. So long as substitution is only partial, marginal holdings of reserves will be in national currency form and therefore just as vulnerable to asset switching. It is difficult to see how switching between currencies can be prevented without major interference in the working of international capital markets. A more fruitful way of ensuring that central bank activity does not adversely affect market stability would seem to lie in avoiding policies that provoke asset switching, and in informal understandings among central banks to cooperate in matters of market management.

Developing countries have, understandably, been concerned about the effects of present reserve supply arrangements on the costs of acquiring the reserves they need. The least-developed countries have never been able to borrow on international markets. Middle-income countries have had intermittent access, borrowing heavily in the 1970s but being abruptly cut off following the emergence of the debt crisis. Of course, lack of access to international capital markets is a function of creditworthiness, rather than of income levels *per se*. But whatever the reason, for most of the last decade, all but a handful of developing countries have had to satisfy their reserve needs through import compression. The cost of reserve acquisition to them has been the difference between the yield on real resources invested in the domestic economy and the return on liquid financial assets held in reserves.

Amelioration of the reserve constraints of developing countries has therefore been the main focus in recent discussion of international liquidity arrangements. The main objection to using SDRs to meet developing countries' reserve needs is that an allocation would have to be uniform across countries, and the bulk of any allocation would therefore go to the richer countries that had no reserve needs. To attempt to address this point, various proposals have sought to 'skew' SDR allocations, perhaps through a prior agreement among the richer countries to use their allocations for the benefit of developing Fund members. However, it has to be recognized that these proposals *compensate* countries for their loss of creditworthiness, rather than providing incentives to reestablish creditworthiness.

A more general objection to the present system of reserve creation is that it deprives the international financial system of an instrument of discipline in the adjustment process. Unlike the Bretton Woods system when countries had to respond to loss of reserves with corrective measures, current arrangements allow inappropriate domestic policies to persist for a considerable period. It is doubtful, however, whether management of reserve supply could be a particularly effective tool for controlling the world economy, even if market-determined sources of liquidity did not exist. And it is even more doubtful that the benefits of improved reserve control would outweigh the costs of the restrictions that would have to be imposed on international capital markets. The argument for controlling international liquidity is that there exists a relationship between the level of international reserves and the macroeconomic policies pursued by national authorities. However, this relationship is so tenuous that it seems more effective to find ways of operating directly on national monetary conditions. This could be done formally, for example, through the adoption of world monetary growth targets as proposed by McKinnon (1984); or it could be done more informally, through the intensification of policy coordination discussions among the major countries. As a practical matter, the informal route seems the more likely to be used. This is, indeed, what has happened in recent years in the process of the Group of Seven (G-7). The objections to the G-7 process lie in its exclusivity (most countries have no say in the discussions) and in the *ad hoc* nature of the decisions. Despite attempts in the late 1980s to develop the 'indicators exercise' (G-7 1986), there is no model underlying the process of policy coordination, and therefore no mechanism for producing welfare-enhancing outcomes when the participants in the process are unable to agree. The search for a more robust basis for international economic cooperation is likely to continue for some time to come. It is important that it be taken seriously, for there can be no assurance that the relatively benign coordination of recent years will persist. But it is unlikely that the answer will be found in fundamental changes in the reserve supply mechanism.

Notes

The views expressed are not necessarily those of the Bank of England. Helpful comments on an earlier draft were provided by T. de Vries, L. Price, O. Page, M. Foot, T. Coleby, I. Plenderleith, C. Taylor, D. Green, and J. Bulloch.

1 Although some central banks (e.g., Belgium) with very large gold holdings have made sales for reserve diversification purposes.

2 Initially SDR 1 = $1; following the devaluation of the US dollar in December 1971, the SDR was worth $1.086. Following the introduction of generalized floating and the second amendment to the IMF Article, the SDR became defined as a basket of currencies (initially sixteen, later five).

References

Britto, R. and Heller, H.R. 1973. 'International Adjustment and Optimal Reserves', *International Economic Review*, March.

Committee of Twenty 1973. *Documents of the Committee of Twenty*, Washington DC, IMF.

Despres, E., Kindleberger, C.P., and Salant, W.S. 1966. 'The Dollar and World Liquidity: A Minority View', *The Economist*, 2 February.

Frenkel, J.A. 1974. 'The Demand for Reserves by Developed and Less Developed Countries', in R.Z. Aliber (ed.), *National Monetary Policies and the International Monetary System*, Chicago, University of Chicago.

Group of Seven 1986. *Tokyo Economic Declaration*, May 6.

Group of Ten 1965. *Report of the Study Group on the Creation of Reserve Assets* (Ossola Report).

Group of Thirty 1980. *Towards a Less Unstable International Monetary System*, Group of Thirty.

Heller, H.R. and Khan, M.S. 1978. 'The Demand for International Reserves under Fixed and Floating Exchange Rates', *IMF Staff Papers*.

International Monetary Fund 1970. *International Reserves: Needs and Availability*, Washington DC, IMF.

Machlup, F. 1966. 'The Need for Monetary Reserves', *Banca Nazionale del Lavoro Quarterly Review*, vol. 19.

McKinnon, R.I. 1984. *An International Standard for Monetary Stabilisation*, Washington DC, Institute for International Economics.

Triffin, R. 1960. *Gold and the Dollar Crisis*, New Haven, Yale University Press.

Williamson, J. 1973. 'Surveys in Applied Economics – International Liquidity', *Economic Journal*, September.

Discussion

ROBERT D. HORMATS

Crockett's chapter provides a very thoughtful and thorough assessment of one of the more interesting issues that has been at the centre of the international monetary debate for a number of years. He examines the issue in the context of the past debate and then tries to relate it to the problems we are facing today.

I will elaborate on some of the points that Crockett has underscored. First is the question that he closed with: can control over reserve or liquidity creation have an effect on international monetary discipline? The answer is a general, and definitive, 'no', for all the reasons mentioned in the chapter. Masera made the point in his discussion that, in the world monetary system and in international capital markets, deregulation and globalization have given rise to a whole plethora of new financing techniques. These widen the scope for central banks and governments that want to borrow additional liquidity on open markets and include derivatives, swaps, and a wide range of 'new products'. A reflection of the new possibilities offered by the markets is shown in the chart that Crockett has on the change in the currency composition of reserves: in 1982 they were predominantly, two thirds, in US dollars; in 1990 that ratio switched rather dramatically. This says something about the range of currencies in which countries are holding reserves and their ability to have access to markets in which to accumulate reserves. Currencies that were local ten years ago have today become international, even against the wish of the countries that issue them. The financing options available are vastly different, both in scope and in size, from ten years ago; at the same time, borrowers are now subject to what one might call the discipline of the 'green screen brigade', that is the discipline of the operators of the international capital markets. Anyone familiar with the way markets perform knows how they evaluate a currency, a bond market, a country. The ability of a country to borrow as well as the terms on which it borrows are being judged every day in international capital and currency markets. And that is a day-to-day rating system and a way of disciplining countries probably better than any centralized mechanism that the Inter-

national Monetary Fund (IMF) could put together or any scheme to provide conditional liquidity. The discipline really is in the market rather than in decisions collectively made by an international institution.

However, the question of utilizing liquidity and reserves as a macroeconomic management instrument becomes particularly relevant when the situation of individual countries is considered. In the long run, one still has to find ways of providing large countries that wish to get into the global market with a chance to do so in a reasonable way. And it is not fair or effective, as Williamson has pointed out, to have a system that penalizes countries which, like Russia, have been poorly managed for fifty or sixty years, and which are trying to get into the system but cannot do so because they cannot get an effective launching pad. And if the objective is to enhance global growth in the 1990s, one way of pursuing it is to bring into the global market the countries that have been on the periphery of the system: Russia, Eastern Europe, India, just to mention some. This implies finding a solution to the question of reserves or liquidity shortage for these countries.

I agree with Mundell's point that it is not a particularly useful approach to create Special Drawing Rights (SDR) as a way of boosting the reserves of countries. A more focused creation of reserves through, for instance, a currency stabilization scheme as was done for Poland and as might be put into practice for Russia, is a more interesting proposition. With regard to Poland, it worked reasonably well: it was not utilized. My worry regarding such an arrangement in Russia is that it may be seen as the answer to every problem. If they could get a few billion dollars and stabilize the rouble, some argue, everything else would follow. But it is more important that the Russians do other things, like privatization, creating corporate law and making a whole range of internal reforms, and particularly freeing up prices. On the other hand, stabilizing the currency is important for psychological reasons and to avoid the inflationary impact of a rouble that is constantly spiralling down. However, I do not think it is possible to fix a currency like the rouble in any rigid way. Therefore, a well-organized and well-managed stabilization fund, applied in the context of other structural reforms and other policy changes, could be useful psychologically and economically, provided it is used to support an adjustable peg, or something of that sort.

A final comment is on the question in Crockett's chapter about the relationship between liquidity creation and exchange rate stability. He is absolutely right that one cannot simply put forward a substitution account, or a partial substitution account, and think that it will deal with the problem of exchange rate stability. If the perception of currencies changes, if there are fundamental changes in national policies, then the markets

themselves are going to move the currency. The central banks may, or may not, have an influence on such movements, but there is a broader game being played out there by many other players other than central banks. Therefore, I think the notion that one can put up a substitution account and that it will dramatically improve prospects of stability misses the point: most of the currency trading is by the private sector, by the green screen people, and not by central banks.

Discussion

STEFANO MICOSSI

Crockett provides a clear and complete account of developments in the area of international liquidity over the past forty years as regards both ideas and facts. I basically agree with his reading; in my comments, therefore, I will only put a slightly different emphasis on certain features of the present system, and move from there to discuss some implications of the changing nature of the demand for official reserves, and the specific issue of how to cope with 'local' liquidity problems.

The main features of the present system can be summed up as follows:

(a) The supply of international liquidity (a broader concept than official liquidity, as it is well explained by Crockett) is very, or even perfectly, elastic, which is a desirable feature, since the demand for international liquidity is highly unstable (to this latter point I will come back shortly); most liquidity is borrowed, rather than 'owned', liquidity.

(b) The system is based on a multiplicity of currencies; this, however, has not been *per se* a source of instability, except when policy conflicts developed between reserve currency countries and their central banks tried to resist the exchange rate implications of that pattern of national (fiscal) policies with foreign exchange interventions.

(c) There is no 'liquidity-forced' international adjustment mechanism: however, if large countries 'behave' in their domestic policies, notably monetary policies, the system will remain fairly stable and financial market incentives will also encourage stable behaviour by non-reserve currency countries; to the extent that reserve currency countries 'behave', notably in the sense of avoiding sharply expansionary or restrictive monetary policies, symmetry will also be less of a problem.

(d) There is no need to restore myths of the old days, such as an asset settlement rule; any such rule would be difficult to define and justify (with reference to what external imbalances would it be introduced, and why?), and impossible to implement in practice.

(e) Instability can arise both because the system is unable to prevent

reckless behaviour by individual participants, who can borrow beyond their ability to service their external debt, and because it may not satisfy the demand for liquidity by countries that do not have access to international markets (to this last issue I will also come back).

(f) Finally, there is no aggregate rationale for keeping the Special Drawing Rights (SDR) – as it is now – alive: its existence is either irrelevant, if kept to the present negligible share of total liquidity, or potentially destabilizing, if that share is increased to a meaningful number; the SDR also is not a very efficient tool for providing liquidity selectively to Fund members or country groups, since the Fund allocates the burden of such financing in an unpredictable way (through its operational budget); the experience with the SDR should convince everyone that a bureaucratically administered money, managed by politically selected country representatives (the IMF Board) has no future in the international monetary system.

Let me turn briefly to the issue of the instability of the function of demand for reserves/liquidity and its systemic implications. Reserve assets always suffered from the following paradox: when you have plenty you don't need them, so that there is unnecessary hoarding (welfare loss); when you start using them, however, the rate of depletion will be increased by the markets' reaction to the fact that you are using them. In other words, the more you need reserves, the less you have.

Capital market development and financial integration have strengthened the paradox, since:

(i) A greater share of reserves is borrowed and credit lines are typically curtailed when used intensively; this phenomenon, for instance, has aggravated financing problems of Latin American countries, after the Mexican debt crisis of 1982, and is making it more difficult today to arrange adequate support of countries in transition to a market economy.

(ii) Capital flows have become very large and respond very rapidly to a changing perception of (country) risk.

As a result, the room for using reserves and interventions in foreign exchange markets to any large extent or for prolonged periods has been much reduced. The evidence of a country making large use of reserves is like a bell calling speculators to attack, since large-scale intervention usually is sterilized, to reconcile inconsistent domestic and external monetary objectives, thus creating a systematic opportunity for profit for private agents.

The implication of this is that a country may still need to hold large reserves, or have large standby credit facilities, for reasons of confidence, but it will not be able to use them extensively. The European Monetary System offers a good example of this with the Basle-Nyborg Agreement

that improved remarkably the functioning of its exchange rate mechanism: the *form* of the agreement is an expanded use of reserve facilities (for intramarginal intervention); its *substance* is more active use of interest rates and exchange rate flexibility in meeting pressure in foreign exchange markets; intervention is to be confined to only a subsidiary role, for short periods and small amounts. These considerations would also imply that much of the recent literature on foreign exchange crises, based as it is on the notion that crises are triggered by a low level of reserves, may be misguided, to the extent that the rate of change, rather than the level of reserves, may be the relevant signal variable to financial markets. This is also relevant for the analysis of 'localized' liquidity problems that arise when countries do not have access to international capital markets, and for the identification of correct solutions. I have in mind the specific difficulties of Central and Eastern European countries.

The issue is clear enough. Convertibility, and (reasonably) stable exchange rates, have been identified as an effective anchor for macropolicies as well as a way of importing quickly the 'right' prices as part of price reform. Establishing convertibility, however, requires foreign financing to stabilize the exchange rate, that could otherwise fall out of control; but if foreign financing is used to retard the adoption of the 'right' policies, the objectives of convertibility will not be attained, a lot of money will be wasted, and the exchange rate (and domestic inflation) will end up out of control. The only way to approach this intricate moral hazard problem is conditional financing, strictly linked to the pursuit of sound policies. There is no such thing as sufficient money to stabilize the rouble if the money-printing press is not halted; stabilizing the rouble can only be an element of a broader package.

5   High world interest rates: shortage of saving or liquidity?

WILLIAM H. BRANSON

1 Introduction

World interest rates have stayed unusually high during the slowdown in Europe and Japan and the recession in the United States that began in 1990. This may prompt us to ask the following question: 'Is the problem a shortage of saving or of liquidity?' The answer to the question has potentially important implications for monetary and fiscal policy at the international level. If the reason for high rates is an unexpected increase in investment demand, due to the reconstruction in Eastern Europe for example, optimal fiscal policies might tighten in a coordinated way to accommodate it. If the reason is an upward shift in world money demand, due, for example, to a move towards hard currencies in Eastern Europe, monetary policies might accommodate it leading in a coordinated way. If the reason is simply a shift in time preference leading to a reduction of saving, no policy response may be called for.

In order to formulate an analytically operational approach to the problem, I will restate the above question as: 'What explains the behaviour of interest rates since 1989?' This is an analytical question that can be approached by asking what pattern of exogenous events is consistent with the recent behaviour of interest rates and exchange rates.

The stylized facts that we are attempting to explain are the following:

(1) Real Gross Domestic Product (GDP) growth slowed markedly in the European Community (EC) and Japan, and North America experienced a recession beginning in early 1990.
(2) German long-term interest rates rose sharply beginning in late 1989, going above US rates in early 1990.
(3) The German term structure inverted in 1990, while us short-term rates moved well below long-term rates.
(4) The Deutsche mark appreciated against the dollar from late 1989 to early 1991, and then reversed.

Presumably, these facts can be explained by some (perhaps more than one) combination of anticipated or unanticipated shifts in the behaviour of

107

excess saving in the economy or of excess demand for liquidity (that is, money). The first would be a change in the economy's flow relations and a shift in some kind of IS curve. The second would be a change in financial stock relations and a shift in some kind of LM curve. The IS shifts that the chapter discusses are essentially increases in fiscal spending or investment demand related to the reunification of Germany and reform in Central and Eastern Europe. The LM shifts are monetary policy changes and an increase in demand for hard currency reserves to back convertible currencies in Central and possibly Eastern Europe. The approach of the chapter is to develop models that can discriminate among the effects of anticipated or unanticipated versions of these shifts on interest rates and exchange rates, and then to ask what combinations are consistent with the facts.

Two fairly simple dynamic models are developed and used below. The first is a world IS–LM model with a term structure equation that can discriminate among the effects of disturbances on the path of output and the term structure over time. The second is a two-country model that can discriminate among the effects on the real exchange rate and long-term interest differentials. The combination of the two will at least permit us to narrow down the range of possible answers to the restated question. The models developed below both have the same basic structure. They can be reduced to two endogenous variables, for ease of graphical exposition. One of these, the financial market variable, can jump discontinuously in anticipation of future events. The other, a goods market variable, adjusts gradually over time; it is 'sticky'. Adjustment following unanticipated exogenous disturbances to policy variables or private-sector behaviour, which represent the market 'fundamentals', follows a unique 'saddle path' into a long-run equilibrium. This is essentially the analysis of exchange rate behaviour proposed by Dornbusch (1976). This solution assumes that any speculative bubble path eventually collapses to the relevant saddle path. With an anticipated disturbance, the market searches for a path that will put it on the saddle path when the disturbance occurs. This is the solution to the analysis of anticipated events proposed by Wilson (1979, pp. 639–47). The models exhibit financial market overshooting in reaction to monetary disturbances, consistent with excess volatility in financial markets. But they also exhibit a form of undershooting with respect to goods market disturbances, so that the excess volatility result may not be general.

We begin with an integrated world model in section 2 that is a version of an Aoki's average model (Aoki 1981). Here the financial variables are short-term and long-term interest rates, and output adjusts gradually. This is a dynamic version of a world IS–LM model discussed in Branson, Fraga, and Johnson (1986). The model illustrates the overshooting of short-term and long-term interest rates with an unanticipated monetary shock (a shift

in the excess demand for liquidity), but undershooting with respect to a goods market disturbance such as a change in government spending or excess private saving. It also illustrates the possibility that an anticipated fiscal expansion can cause a recession by driving up long-term rates. This may be happening in Germany in 1992 in anticipation of expenditures for rebuilding Eastern Germany.

A two-country real model is introduced in section 5. Here the financial variables are long-term real interest rates and the real exchange rate; the current account gradually changes the countries' debt positions. In this model, a fiscal or saving shock in one country leads to an overshoot of the real exchange rate between the two countries and of the real interest rate in the other country, and an undershoot of the real interest rate in the first country. The model illustrates the path of the dollar and US long-term interest rates during the 1980s, following the fiscal shift that began in 1981. It also illustrates the movement of the Deutsche mark and German long-term interest rates since anticipations of unification began to affect the bond and foreign exchange markets in early 1990.

The main events we have in mind in setting out the models in sections 2 and 5 are (a) the fiscal and investment aspects of the transformation in Central and Eastern Europe, (b) the tightening of monetary policy in Germany in response to (or anticipation of?) inflationary pressure from the latter, and (c) the possible increase in demand for hard currency reserves in the Central and Eastern European countries as they move to convertibility at fixed exchange rates. The first would shift an IS curve, and the second and third would shift an LM curve. The bottom line to the chapter in section 6 is that we have seen an anticipated shift in fiscal spending and investment and an unanticipated tightening of monetary policy in Europe. Thus the policy indication is a coordinated programme of tightening of fiscal positions to help accommodate the increase in investment demand. An increase in the demand for liquidity in the form of demand for hard currency reserves may be still to come.

2 A world model with the term structure of interest rates

In looking at the data on interest rates and the movement of output, changes in the slope of the term structure of interest rates will help to distinguish between exogenous shocks to liquidity demand or to excess saving. Thus we begin by developing a simple dynamic macromodel that focuses on the term structure and its relationships to expectations and these exogenous shocks. The main purposes here are (a) to describe the link from shifts in saving or liquidity demand to long-term rates *via* expectations, and (b) to introduce the general form of dynamic model that will be used

throughout the chapter. Thus we are interested in both the structure of the analysis and in the particular results. The exposition begins with the simplest fixed price IS–LM model of a closed economy. This is sufficient to describe the link from fundamentals to expectations dynamics in financial markets. We will add on price dynamics at the end of this section.

IS–LM with short- and long-term interest rates

The basic model can be stated in four equations:

$$d = ay + b - \delta(I - h) \qquad \text{(IS curve)} \tag{1}$$

$$i = (\tau y - m)/\lambda \qquad \text{(LM curve)} \tag{2}$$

$$\dot{y} = \psi(d - y) \qquad \text{(gradual output adjustment)} \tag{3}$$

$$E\hat{I} = I - i \qquad \text{(path of long rate or term structure)} \tag{4}$$

Variable definitions are given in table 5.1. Equation (1) gives aggregate demand d as a function of output y, an exogenous component of demand b, and the real long-term (actually consol) interest rate. Expenditure is assumed to be at least partly a function of current income, in Keynesian fashion. This is clearly an important assumption for an analysis of the effects of shifts in fiscal policy on excess saving, represented by changes in b. If infinitely lived consumers take into account fully all future tax liabilities, including those related to debt service, then a shift from tax financing to debt financing of government spending will have no effect on aggregate demand (see Barro 1974, pp. 1095–117, for a discussion of this case). For a variety of reasons such as liquidity constraints, the difficulty of increasing investment demand and supply quickly as expected returns increase, and uncertainty regarding remaining years of life (Blanchard 1984), the neutrality assumption is too strong. The expected, or 'core' inflation rate h is given exogenously in equation (1), and set at zero for the time being. It will be endogenized later. A reduction in excess saving by the private sector will be represented below as an increase in b in equation (1).

Equation (2) is the LM curve normalized on the short-term interest rate i. The short rate is assumed to clear the money market at all times. In the LM curve m is real balances M/P, and λ is the semielasticity of the demand for money with respect to i. An exogenous increase in the demand for liquidity (or reduction in supply) will be represented as a decrease in m. Equation (3) gives the change in output over time as a gradual adjustment to the excess of demand over output. A more complete model would include inventory dynamics, but the specification here is sufficient to maintain a focus on the fundamentals of exogenous shifts in saving or liquidity demand and expectations dynamics.

Table 5.1. *Variable definitions*

d	aggregate demand
y	output
b	budget deficit
I	long-term nominal interest rate
i	short-term nominal interest rate
r	short-term real interest rate
h	expected or 'core' inflation
x	trade balance
m	real money balances
p	prices level
B	stock or real bonds
E	nominal exchange rate
e	real exchange rate

Note:
A hat over (^) a variable denotes its
proportional rate of change, a dot its
time derivative, and a star a foreign
variable.

Equation (4) specifies the term structure of interest rates, providing one link with the future, and thus bringing expectations dynamics into the model. Aside from a risk premium, which we set equal to zero, any differential between the long and short rates must be equal to the expected rate of change of the long rate. If $I - i > 0$ in equation (4), the long rate must be expected to rise (i.e., consol price to fall) to generate a capital loss that offsets the rate differential for the bond market to be in equilibrium.

The dynamics of the model are described in the IS-LM diagram of figure 5.1. The short-term rate i and the long-term rate I are measured on the vertical axis; output and demand are on the horizontal axis. The stationary equilibrium is at point A, where $I = i$ and $d = y$. Away from equilibrium, demand is on the IS curve, y and I move along the 'saddle path' II, and i moves along the LM curve. Output adjusts towards the IS curve, following equation (3). This gives the horizontal arrows in figure 5.1. The short-term rate clears the money market, so it moves along the LM curve following output. The innovation in figure 5.1 is the II saddle path. This comes from the combination of equation (4) and the assumption of rational expectations in financial markets. (In this non-stochastic model, rational expectations is the same as perfect foresight.) The II saddle path can be derived as follows. If the long rate I were to adjust along the LM curve, $E\hat{I}$ would be zero throughout, from equation (4) with $I = i$. This is inconsistent with

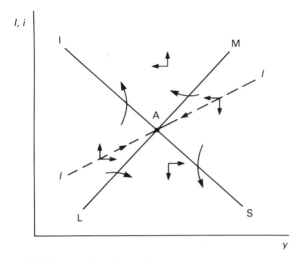

Figure 5.1 Expectations dynamics

rational expectations. If the long rate I is above the LM curve, then $I > i$ and $E\hat{I}$ is positive, and *vice versa* if I is below the LM curve. This gives the vertical arrows that show the motion of I in figure 5.1. If I is above LM, $I > i$ and $E\hat{I}$ must be positive for equilibrium between short and long rates; *vice versa* below LM. This gives us the stable adjustment branch, the saddle path II that is consistent with rational expectations equilibrium. It is positively sloped but flatter than LM. A negative slope can be ruled out because then with $I > i$ to the left of equilibrium, $E\hat{I}$ would be inconsistently negative. A steeper slope than LM can be ruled out because then to the left of equilibrium $E\hat{I}$ is positive but $I < i$. Along the II path, to the left of point A, $E\hat{I} = I - i > 0$ and, to the right of A, it is negative. The II path has two essential properties. It leads to the equilibrium, and along it the expected movements of long rates are realized. All other paths are unstable branches that explode away from the equilibrium. They are 'bubble' paths that cross IS vertically ($\dot{y} = 0$) or LM horizontally ($E\hat{I} = 0$) and explode to the northwest or southeast. The assumption that the market seeks out the stable II path is equivalent to assuming that these speculative bubbles are unsustainable. Eventually they collapse, and the market moves back to the stable II path. In the analysis below, these unstable branches will play an important role in the analysis of anticipated policy changes.

Price dynamics

It is easy to add price dynamics to the model. We adopt a model of 'core inflation', in which inflation adjusts gradually to monetary disturbances

and is also sensitive to output disturbances. We use this model to reflect the idea that inflationary expectations are adaptive, rather than forward-looking. In our specification, the inflation rate is a geometric average of past money growth rates. This can be taken to represent a credibility effect, where a policy change is not immediately assumed to be permanent, as well as an element of stickiness on the supply side, such as would be implied by staggered wage contracts. People tend to believe that inflation is coming down only when they see it come down.

There are two inflation equations:

$$\dot{h} = \pi(\hat{M} - h) \qquad \text{(adjustment of core inflation)} \tag{5}$$

$$\dot{p} = h + \phi(y - \bar{y}) \quad \text{(Phillips curve)} \tag{6}$$

Equation (5) has the core inflation rate, $\dot{h}$, adapting to deviations of money growth from h. Equation (6) says the actual inflation rate is the core rate plus a Phillips curve term for deviations of output from its natural level, $\bar{y}$. The solution algorithm for this dynamic world model is clear. The IS–LM equilibrium is on a trend inflation rate given by $\hat{M}$. Core inflation is $\hat{M}$, so $\dot{h}$ in equation (5) is zero. Equilibrium output is $\bar{y}$, so $\dot{p}$ in (6) is equal to h. Demand and output are equal, so $\dot{y}$ in equation (3) is also zero. With $I = i$ from equation (4), we can solve equation (1) for I and then (2) for P. The saddle path into this solution gives the motion of the real long-term interest rate $I - h$.

3 Unanticipated shifts in liquidity demand or excess saving

The diagram of figure 5.1 can be used to characterize the effects of unanticipated monetary or fiscal policy on demand and the term structure of interest rates. This is the usual textbook case. The effects of exogenous shifts in liquidity demand or excess private saving are qualitatively the same as changes in the policy variables m and b that are usually analysed. Consider first the effects of a contractionary monetary policy or increase in liquidity demand ($dM < 0$), illustrated in figure 5.2. The LM curve shifts up, so the equilibrium moves from point A to point B. At the initial level of income y_a, the two interest rates rise to i_1, I_1 with the short rate above the long rate. As y falls, the two interest rates also fall, converging to point B. Figure 5.2 illustrates the well-known overshooting effect on financial market prices with a monetary disturbance. The unanticipated tightening raises both short and long rates immediately, with bond prices falling. This movement is then reversed as both rates fall. In anticipation of the decrease, the long rate initially rises less than the short rate, so $E\hat{I} = I - i < 0$. The effect of an unanticipated fiscal expansion or reduction in saving ($db > 0$) is shown in figure 5.3. Again the equilibrium point moves from A to B. With y

There are two inflation equations:

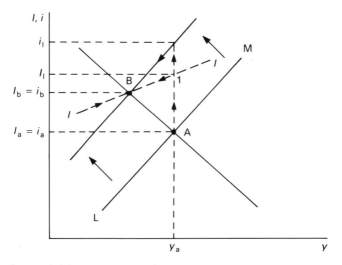

Figure 5.2 Monetary contraction

at y_a, initially the short rate remains at i_a. But in anticipation of the future rise in both rates, the long rate jumps to I_1. As output then rises to y_b, both interest rates rise to i_b, I_b. Figure 5.3 shows how the expectation of the effect of the unanticipated fiscal expansion or reduction in saving on *future* output moves *current* long-term interest rates and bond prices. The financial markets bring the future into the present. It also illustrates the undershooting of financial market prices with real disturbances. There is no reversal of movement in figure 5.3.

Let us summarize the results from this analysis of unanticipated shifts in saving or the demand for liquidity that are relevant for distinguishing between the two. The unanticipated increase in liquidity demand in figure 5.2 yields a slowdown in growth or recession with short-term rates rising above long-term, and then both falling. The unanticipated reduction in saving in figure 5.3 yields an expansion in output with long rates rising above short, and then both rising. The data to be reviewed below show at least a slowdown in Europe and Japan, and a recession in the United States, but long-term rates above short-term, with the possible exception of Germany. Thus neither figure 5.2 nor 5.3 fits the facts particularly well, and we move on to the cases of anticipated shifts in saving or liquidity demand.

4 Anticipated shifts in excess saving or liquidity demand

The effects of German reunification, reform in Eastern Europe and the former Soviet Union, and rebuilding Kuwait and Iraq, on government

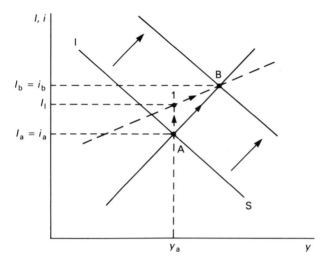

Figure 5.3 Fiscal expansion

budgets and investment demand can all be interpreted as an announcement of a *future* outward shift in the IS curve, as saving is reduced or investment is increased. This is illustrated in figure 5.4. With the economy at point A, a future autonomous demand expansion ($db > 0$) is announced. The financial markets come to understand that the future equilibrium is at point C, with higher interest rates. This means the long rate will jump immediately. But on to what path? The *future* saddle path will be II at the time of the *actual* demand expansion. The long rate will rise seeking an unstable branch relative to the existing equilibrium A that has the following property: as the economy moves along that unstable branch, it will reach the new saddle path at the time the announced fiscal expansion actually takes place, i.e., when equilibrium C comes into existence. This solution was first proposed by Charles Wilson (1979). Thus the long rate jumps to I_1 in figure 5.4 with output at y_a. This depresses investment and sends the economy into recession along the unstable branch from point 1 to point B. Output and the short rate fall to y_b, i_b, while the long rate rises to I_b. When the actual demand expansion occurs, the recovery begins. Output increases from y_b to y_c, with the short and long rates rising to converge to C. The financial market's anticipation of the *future* demand expansion raises the *present* long-term interest rate and throws the economy into an *anticipatory recession*. Branson, Fraga, and Johnson argued that this anticipation contributed to the recession of 1982 in the United States. This effect may also have appeared in 1990–1, as the expectation of future demand expansion raised real long-term interest rates and depressed bond prices.

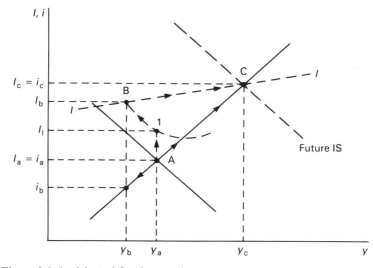

Figure 5.4 Anticipated fiscal expansion

Here the financial market's anticipation of future changes in fundamentals actually drives the economy in the opposite direction in the short run.

The effects of an anticipated increase in the demand for liquidity (or tightening of monetary policy) are shown in figure 5.5. The world economy is initially in equilibrium at point A. When the expectation of the *future* increase in liquidity demand appears, the financial markets understand that the *future* equilibrium is at point C. The long rate again jumps immediately, seeking the unstable path relative to the existing point A that will reach the future dashed II saddle path at point B when the *actual* shift in liquidity demand occurs. The rise in the long rate to I_1 again generates an anticipatory recession along the path to point B, with output and the short rate falling and the long rate rising. When the actual shift in liquidity demand appears, the short rate jumps from i_b to i_b' on the new LM curve, and the recession continues to point C, with the long and short rate converging.

A comparison of figures 5.4 and 5.5 is instructive. The short-run anticipation effects are essentially the same. The long rate jumps, and the economy goes into recession (or slows relative to potential growth) with the term structure steepening. The pictures diverge when the actual events appear. The reduction in saving, or fiscal or investment boom, is expansionary and leads to recovery with the term structure still positively sloped, but flattening. The increase in liquidity demand leads to continued recession with a reversal in the slope of the term structure as the short rate jumps on to

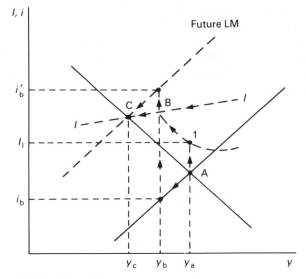

Figure 5.5 Anticipated monetary contraction

the new LM curve. Thus the anticipations effects of the two alternatives are similar, but the results when the actual events appear are much different. This can also be seen in the contrast between figures 5.2 and 5.3.

5 Two-country model: real exchange rate and the current account

The previous section discussed shifts in saving or liquidity demand as the exogenous shocks and focused on the resulting movements in output and the term structure in a world model. However, the events that we are characterizing as a reduction of excess saving are concentrated in Central and Eastern Europe, and differentially affect Europe and the United States and Japan. They should have predictable effects on European exchange rates against the dollar and the yen. Given the existence of the European Monetary System (EMS), it may be sensible to model these effects as movements in the mark/dollar exchange rate, with the reduction in excess saving coming in the area of the Deutsche mark. The analysis is the mirror image of that of the path of the dollar following the fiscal shift in the United States in the early 1980s, and draws heavily on the analysis of that case in Branson (1988). Thus in this section we split the world into two countries with different currencies, so that the exchange rate becomes relevant, and study the dynamics of the *real exchange rate* $e \equiv EP^*/P$ and the current

account, focusing on a shift in saving in one country as the exogenous event. Here we will characterize Europe as the home country and the exogenous event as an increase in the 'European' structural budget deficit or reduction in excess private saving. For simplicity, we will focus on an increase in the deficit, but the analysis is exactly the same if the exogenous event is a reduction in excess saving.

A two-country 'real' model

The model has four equations, representing the national accounts, or IS, equilibrium in the two countries, the arbitrage equilibrium between the two financial markets, and the accumulation of their net debt position *via* the current account. The national income equations are

$$b = s(r) - x(e, B) \qquad \text{(home IS)} \tag{7}$$

$$b^* = s^*(r^*) + x(e, B) \qquad \text{(foreign IS)} \tag{8}$$

Here b, b^* are the home and foreign country's 'structural' fiscal deficits, since we assume full employment in this section; s, s^* are the excesses of private saving over investment; x is the home country's current account surplus; r, r^* are the long-term real interest rates; e is the real exchange rate in terms of home currency per unit of foreign exchange (so an increase signifies a depreciation of the home currency); and B is the net debt of the home to the foreign country. If $B < 0$, the home country is a creditor. Since the home country here is Europe, B is negative, at least initially. We assume that s and s^* are increasing functions of r and r^*, and x is an increasing function of e and a decreasing function of B. Since we have only two countries, the same x enters both equations. To avoid problems in evaluation of B, we assume it is denominated in an average of the two currencies.

The arbitrage condition that links the financial markets is

$$r = r^* + \hat{e} + \rho(B) \qquad \text{(arbitrage condition)} \tag{9}$$

Here $\hat{e}$ is the expected rate of change of the real exchange rate, and ρ is a risk premium, increasing in B. This is a summary form of a portfolio model in which debt in both currencies is held in international portfolios. Equation (7) introduces real exchange rate dynamics into the picture. The other dynamic equation is the accumulation of the debt position, given by

$$\dot{B} = -x(e, B) \qquad \text{(current account dynamics)} \tag{10}$$

A home country current account surplus reduces its debt position.

Stationary equilibrium

In the stationary, or long-run equilibrium, the real exchange rate is expected to remain constant, or trendless in a stochastic version of the model, so $\hat{e}$ in equation (9) would be zero. The current account would be balanced, so x in equations (7), (8), and (9) would be zero. This would be the case even if the two economies were on a balanced growth path, with each accumulating the other's debt.

The stationary solution of the model is recursive and simple. Equations (7) and (8) with $x=0$ determine the real interest rates at which domestic private saving finances the budget deficit in each country. An increase in b or b^* eventually requires an increase in r or r^* to finance it domestically. Then equation (9) with $\hat{e}=0$ determines the debt position that yields the risk premium ρ that equals the difference between the two real interest rates. Finally, the requirement that $x=0$ gives the value of the real exchange rate that is consistent with the debt position. This is the value of the exchange rate that gives a trade balance that just finances the debt service.

An example will illustrate the movement of long-run equilibrium. Consider an increase in b, the home (European) structural budget deficit. From equation (7) with $x=0$, the home long-term real interest rate r must rise to stimulate the excess saving to finance the rise in b. From (9) with $\hat{e}=0$ and an increase in $r-r^*$, the home debt position must rise. This increases the debt service, requiring a real depreciation in the long run to generate the trade surplus to finance it. With $x=0$ in the long run, if B increases so must e.

Short-run equilibrium and dynamics

In the short run, neither $x=-\dot{B}$ nor $\hat{e}$ need be zero, so we need the entire model to locate the dynamic path to the long-run equilibrium. To locate that path, we find the separate loci in e, B space along which alternatively $\dot{B}=0$ and $\hat{e}=0$. The stationary equilibrium is at their intersection. Then we study graphically the dynamics around that point to locate the unique stable saddle path into it. This is the dynamic adjustment path of B and e. Finally, we can do comparative dynamics by seeing which locus is shifted by any given disturbance, and how the saddle path shifts.

The $\dot{B}=0$ line in figure 5.6 is the locus of points along which $x=0$. An increase in B reduces x by increasing debt service or reducing investment income (if $B<0$), and requires an increase in e to hold x to zero. So along the $\dot{B}=0$ line the current account is in balance. Above it, the home current account is in surplus, that is $x>0$, and B is decreasing. Below it, B is

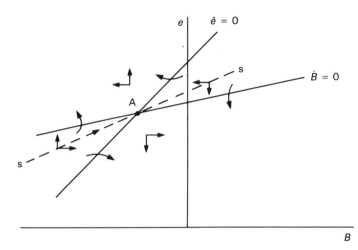

Figure 5.6 Two-country real dynamics

increasing. These dynamics of the debt position are given by the horizontal arrows in figure 5.6. Any exogenous event such as a change in tastes or technology that makes the home country more competitive, that is, would generate a current account surplus at the preexisting equilibrium real exchange rate, shifts the $\dot{B}=0$ line down. Any such event favouring the foreign country's competitiveness shifts it up.

Derivation of the $\hat{e}=0$ line is a little more complicated. From equation (9), an increase in B with $\hat{e}=0$ requires an increase in $r-r^*$. An increase in r increases s in equation (7), and a reduction in r^* reduces s^* in equation (8). Both require an increase in x to maintain equilibrium in (7) and (8). This requires an increase in e, and, since x has increased, the rise in e is greater than along the $\dot{B}=0$ line. So the $\hat{e}=0$ line in figure 5.6 is steeper than the $\dot{B}=0$ line. To obtain the dynamics of e around $\hat{e}=0$, begin with a point on the line, and then consider an increase in e for a given B. The increase in e increases x requiring an increase in r and a decrease in r^* to maintain equilibrium in (7) and (8). This increases $r-r^*$ in equation (9), so for a given B, $\hat{e}$ must become positive. For financial equilibrium to be maintained with the interest differential greater than the risk premium, the exchange rate must be expected to rise. Thus for financial market equilibrium, if the exchange rate is higher than is compatible with a zero expected increase, it must be expected to rise even more. If expectations are rational, the exchange rate will rise. Below the $\hat{e}=0$ line, the exchange rate falls. These unstable dynamics are shown by the vertical arrows in figure 5.6.

An increase in b or a decrease in b^* shifts the $\hat{e}=0$ line down. Consider an increase in b. For a given debt position, maintaining $\hat{e}=0$ in equation (9)

requires that r and r^* rise by the same amount. In equation (8), with b^* unchanged, the rise in r^* and therefore s^* requires a fall in x and therefore e. This is consistent with an increase in s in equation (7) that is smaller than the increase in b, so x goes down. Similarly, if b^* is reduced, both interest rates fall. In equation (7), the resulting reduction in s with b unchanged requires a reduction in x and therefore a reduction in e to maintain equilibrium. So an increase in b or reduction in b^* shifts $\hat{e} = 0$ down, and a reduction in b or increase in b^* shifts it up. Figure 5.6 is drawn with an initial equilibrium with a negative B, that is, a creditor position for the home country. Both equilibrium loci stretch across the vertical axis, however. A large enough downward or rightward shift in the $\hat{e} = 0$ locus could move the equilibrium to the right-hand quadrant where $B > 0$ in equilibrium. This would represent a shift from a creditor to a debtor position, as the United States experienced in the 1980s.

Putting the dynamics of e and B together in figure 5.6, we see the unique stable saddle path ss into the equilibrium, lying between the $\dot{B} = 0$ and $\hat{e} = 0$ lines. The ss path has the properties that it goes to the equilibrium point, and along it expectations are realized. All the other paths are speculative bubbles, heading off towards infinity along an asymptote that is perpendicular to ss. Following a disturbance, for the existing debt position B, the exchange market searches for the e value that is on the saddle path into the new equilibrium.

Unanticipated fiscal policy (or reduction in excess saving)

We can illustrate the dynamics by looking at the example of an unanticipated, but fully credible when announced, increase in the home (European) structural deficit b. This shifts the $\hat{e} = 0$ line down, creating a new ss path that runs into a new long-run equilibrium out along the $\dot{B} = 0$ line in figure 5.6. The situation is shown in figure 5.7, which is drawn with a positive B (a US debt position) in the new equilibrium at point B. The original equilibrium from figure 5.6 is point A, and the new equilibrium is point B. The new adjustment path is ss into B. The real exchange rate jumps down (Deutsche mark appreciates) to point 1 at the original debt position, creating a current account deficit. This then begins the adjustment towards B.

The example of an unanticipated shift in fiscal policy can be used to illustrate the expectations link from fundamentals, here the budget deficit or excess private saving, to interest rates. In figure 5.7, we see the downward jump of the exchange rate from point A to point 1, creating an expectation of a future increase along ss. The jump appreciation of the exchange rate creates a current account deficit in the home country, that is, x becomes

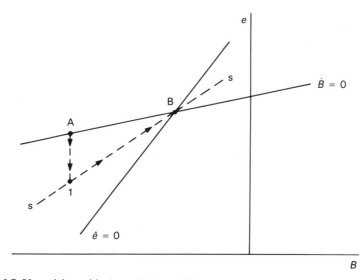

Figure 5.7 Unanticipated increase in home (German) structural deficit

negative. This requires an increase in r and a smaller increase in r^* to maintain balance in equations (7) and (8). The increase in $r - r^*$ must be consistent with the new expected rate of depreciation in equation (9). As the home currency depreciates gradually along the path from point 1 towards point B, the home long-term real interest rate r must rise further to increase s as x increases in equation (9), back towards zero at point B. The foreign interest rate falls as the reduction in the trade surplus in (9) reduces the crowding out of s^*. Eventually at point B, r^* is back where it was at point A, and r has risen enough to crowd out s to finance the entire increase in b.

The implications for our analysis of the consequences of a reduction in excess saving or an increase in the structural deficit in Europe (or, more precisely, Germany) are the following. The Deutsche mark initially appreciates against the dollar, from point A to point 1 in figure 5.7, and then gradually depreciates. German long-term interest rates move above US rates as both rise initially. Then German rates rise further while US rates fall. These movements roughly fit the events from 1989 to 1992, but we probably need to consider anticipated fiscal policy to obtain a better fit.

Anticipated fiscal policy

The analysis of an anticipated shift in fiscal policy in the two-country real model follows the same line as in the world model in figure 5.4. Suppose the home country, in the example to follow, Germany, credibly announces a

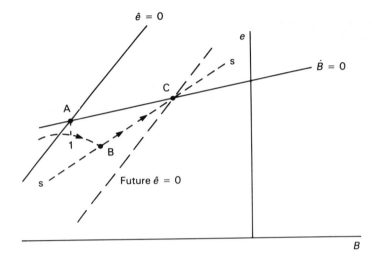

Figure 5.8 Anticipated increase in home (German) structural deficit

future expansion in the structural budget deficit, or in investment demand. In figure 5.8, the initial equilibrium is at point A, and the announcement establishes a future $\hat{e} = 0$ locus to the right of point A, with an ss saddle path into a new stationary equilibrium at point C. The real exchange rate jumps down to the unstable 'bubble' path relative to the existing equilibrium point A that will take the two economies to the new ss path at the time of the future expansion. Thus the real exchange rate jumps to point 1 at the time of the announcement, generating a current account deficit in the home country. The rate then falls further along the path from point 1 to point B, with a growing deficit. At point B the announced expansion is implemented, path ss comes into existence, and the real exchange rate begins to rise with a decreasing deficit towards the final equilibrium point C.

Real long-term interest rates rise in both countries along the path from point A to 1 to B. The home rate must be lower than the foreign rate, however, since the real exchange rate is expected to fall from 1 to B. At point B, the home rate moves above the foreign rate, and continues to rise to point C. At point C, the current account is back in balance, the foreign rate is back to its original level, and the home rate has increased relative to the foreign rate by the amount of the change in the risk premiun in equation (9). This scenario fits the process set off by the collapse of the Berlin Wall in late 1989. This led quickly to the anticipation of some form of reunification of Germany, and the likely expansion of both investment and the fiscal deficit as Eastern Germany would be rebuilt. During 1987–8, German long-term interest rates were about 2–3 percentage points below US rates. German

Table 5.2. *Growth of real GDP and non-residential fixed investment 1985–91*

(Percentage changes from previous period)

	1985	1986	1987	1988	1989	1990	1991
Real GDP							
US[a]	3.4	2.7	3.4	4.5	2.5	1.0	−0.7
Germany	1.8	2.2	1.5	3.7	3.8	4.5	3.1
OECD Europe	2.5	2.8	2.7	3.8	3.4	2.8	1.1
EC	2.4	2.7	2.7	4.0	3.5	2.9	1.4
Investment							
US	6.7	−3.3	2.6	8.3	2.2	1.2	−6.7
Germany	5.5	4.6	4.0	5.9	8.5	10.5	8.6
OECD Europe	6.1	5.5	8.1	10.0	8.2	4.1	−0.5
EC	6.3	5.0	8.4	10.5	8.3	5.0	0.2

Note:
[a] GNP for the US.
Source: OECD *Economic Outlook*, 51, June 1992.

rates began to rise in 1989, and moved up sharply in early 1990, as the market began to see more clearly the financial implications of reunification. By mid 1990 German long-term interest rates were above US rates. The Deutsche mark appreciated gradually against the dollar (*e* falling from point A to point B in figure 5.8) from late 1989 until early 1991, and then reversed with a gradual depreciation. The German current account moved from a surplus of nearly 5 per cent of Gross National Product (GNP) in 1989 to a small deficit in 1991. The German reunification thus provides an example of the financial markets anticipating the consequences of reasonably clear future events, bringing the future into the present. In this case German long-term bond rates rose and prices fell sharply, and the Deutsche mark first appreciated against the dollar, and then reversed itself. Shifting expectations of future real fundamentals created substantial movements in current financial variables.

6 Interpretation of macro events 1989–92

The macroeconomic data that represent our stylized facts are summarized in table 5.2, taken from the *OECD Economic Outlook* of December 1991 (see OECD 1992), and figures 5.9 and 5.10, taken from the *IMF World Economic Outlook* of May 1992 (see IMF 1992). Let us begin with table 5.2.

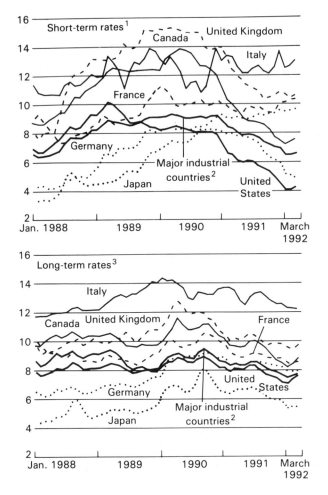

Figure 5.9 Interest rates
Notes: 1 Three-month certificate of deposit rates for the United States and Japan; three-month treasury bill rate for Italy; rate on three-month prime corporate paper for Canada; and three-month interbank deposit rates for other countries. Monthly averages of daily observations are plotted for all countries other than Italy and Canada. Monthly averages of fortnightly treasury bill auctions are shown for Italy, and monthly averages of weekly observations for Canada.
2 1987 GDP weights.
3 Yields on government bonds with residual maturities of ten years for the United States and the United Kingdom; nine–ten years for Germany; seven–ten years for France; over ten years for Canada; and two–four years for Italy. For Japan, the yield on ten-year government bonds with longest residual maturity is shown. Monthly averages of daily observations are plotted for the United States and Japan; for the other countries, they are monthly averages of weekly data.
Source: IMF, WEO, May 1992.

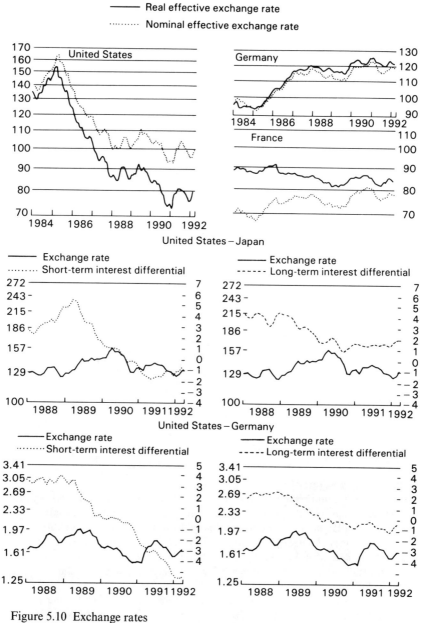

Figure 5.10 Exchange rates
Source: IMF, WEO, May 1992.

There we see the slowdown in investment and GDP growth in Europe except Germany since 1988, and the recession in the United States. Thus the growth data rule out an unanticipated fiscal or investment expansion. This would have generated an increase in growth, not a reduction.

However, the lower panel of figure 5.9 (chart 26 from the *IMF World Economic Outlook*) shows the rise in German long-term interest rates from late 1989 to early 1990. This coincided with the collapse of the Berlin Wall and the spread of expectations of German reunification. These events would raise real long-term interest rates in anticipation of expenditures associated with social support and rebuilding in Eastern Germany. Long-term rates also rose in the rest of Europe, following German rates. This contributed to (or even caused) the European slowdown. This anticipation of expansion in Germany is also consistent with the path of the mark/dollar exchange rate in the lower panel of figure 5.10, and the effective Deutsche mark rate in the top right-hand panel. The Deutsche mark appreciated against the dollar from late 1989 to early 1991, following approximately the path from point A to 1 to B in figure 5.8. Then, when the actual expenditures begin in 1991, the Deutsche mark began to depreciate. Thus the combination of the rise in the German long-term rates and the path of the mark/dollar exchange rate are consistent with an anticipated fiscal and investment expansion that began to be realized in 1991.

The upper panel of figure 5.9 shows German short-term rates rising beginning in 1988, but flattening at around 8 per cent in 1990. Long-term rates were above short-term in 1990, consistent with the anticipated fiscal/investment expansion. Then, in late 1990, short rates moved above long rates. This is consistent with a shift in the LM curve, due either to an increase in money demand or a tightening of monetary policy. Since the convertibility of the central and Eastern European currencies is still prospective, while it is known that the Bundesbank has tightened monetary policy, we conclude that the effects of an increase in the demand for liquidity are still to come.

Thus the answer to the original question posed at the outset is: the problem so far is an anticipated reduction in excess private saving due to an increase in investment demand based on Eastern Europe (including Eastern Germany). An appropriate policy response would be a coordinated programme of tightening fiscal policies.

References

Aoki, M. 1981. *Dynamic Analysis of Open Economies*, New York, Academic Press.
Barro, R.J. 1974. 'Are Government Bonds Net Wealth?', *Journal of Political Economy*, 82.

Blanchard, O.J., 1984. 'The Lucas Critique and the Volker Deflation', *American Economic Review – Papers and Proceedings*, vol. 74 (May).

  1991. 'Output, the Stock Market, and Interest Rates', *American Economic Review*, 71.

Branson, W.H. 1988. 'International Adjustment and the Dollar: Policy Illusions and Economic Constraints', in W. Guth (ed.), *Economic Policy Coordination*, Washington DC, IMF.

Branson, W.H., Fraga, A., and Johnson, R.A. 1986. 'Expected Fiscal Policy and the Recession of 1982', in M.H. Peston and R.E. Quandt (eds.), *Prices, Competition, and Equilibrium*, New York, Barnes & Noble Books.

Dornbusch, R. 1976. 'Expectations and Exchange Rate Dynamics', *Journal of Political Economy*, 84, 6.

International Monetary Fund 1992. *World Economic Outlook*, Washington DC, IMF.

Organization for Economic Cooperation and Development (OECD) 1992. *Economic Outlook*, 51, June.

Wilson, C.A. 1979. 'Anticipated Shocks and Exchange Rate Dynamics', *Journal of Political Economy*, 87.

Discussion

MARCELLO DE CECCO

Starting from the consideration that world interest rates have stayed unusually high during the slowdown in Europe and Japan and the recession in the United States which began in 1990, Branson tries to determine whether the problem is a shortage of saving or of liquidity.

Branson sets up a two-step inquiry. The first is a world model based on the overshooting of financial variables compared to real variables. When a disturbance is anticipated, financial variables overshoot, and this induces a counterintuitive first adjustment followed by the intuitive one, based on the different adjustment velocity of financial and real markets. Branson examines how an anticipated fiscal expansion works itself through the model. He makes the assumption that the fiscal expansion takes place in Germany. The second step is the construction of a two-country model. The fiscal expansion takes place in Germany and works itself through, causing the increase in long rates of interest in Germany, followed by propagation to the rest of the world, and by a subsequent tightening of monetary policy in Germany which induces short rates to rise and eventually an inverse yield curve to appear in Germany. In both steps the primum mobile is a fiscal expansion occurring in Germany, being anticipated by world financial markets, with rising long rates, and being followed by a tightening of monetary policy in Germany and long rates staying high not only in Germany but also in countries where a recession is taking place.

I will not take issue with the two models used by Branson. What I intend to focus my comments upon is the stylization of facts which Branson chooses to draw. His reflections are based on a couple of graphs he appends to his chapter, which show the dynamics of interest rates, both short and long, in several countries and in particular in Germany, the United States and Japan, since 1987. It is true that the long rate started climbing very fast in Germany in 1989. But it is also true that the long rate was already very high in the United States in the years preceding 1989. Those were years when the US economy had boomed and Germany and Europe were having a recession. But long-term interest rate differentials were, before 1989, quite

large between Germany and the United States. The US rate was very high, about 9 per cent, the German rate was low, about 6 per cent. The remarkable thing is that this differential has disappeared after German rates climbed in 1989. The long rates of the United States just did not follow US prices and output when its economy fell into a recession. This is an interesting asymmetry, but not one which Branson seems to have found fit to consider and explain.

The question then could become, starting from a slightly different stylization of facts: is it certain that the savings deficit occurs only in Germany? Could it not be that it is at its most serious in the United States, so serious that it prevents the US long-term rate from falling in nominal as well as in real terms when the economy goes into recession? That something is worrying with US savings is indicated by several pointers. First of all let us repeat that the German long rate was low when the German economy was in recession. It rose when investment and output picked up, after 1987. But US long rates failed to fall with investment and output, after 1990. Branson's graphs also show that US short rates fell to extremely low levels after they peaked in 1988, and are at present about 3.5 per cent. This makes the US yield curve an extremely steep one with a differential of nearly 4 per cent between short and long rates. Long rates have remained high unlike German long rates in the years of the German slump, in the mid 1980s, and until 1989.

The matter must therefore be with US long rates. Why do they show hysteresis while German ones did not? Indeed, hysteresis of long rates is not shown by any other financial system. All long rates go up from the very low levels they had reached in the early 1980s. Only US long rates hover at about 8 to 10 per cent no matter what phase of the cycle one is considering in the late 1980s and early 1990s. We can therefore advance a reasonable modification of Branson's stylized facts. German reunification certainly caused an anticipated fiscal expansion which induced the Bundesbank to adopt a restrictive monetary policy. Short rates have climbed everywhere in Europe, following the Bundesbank's policy, even in countries where cyclical requirements might have asked for the opposite treatment. And long rates have been sent high by intermediaries anticipating a mounting German fiscal deficit. There is however, another important reason why rates have been kept high in the United States in spite of recession, and this is the extremely deep decrease in bank credit which has been experienced in that country in 1990 and 1991. In those years banks contributed negatively to the financing of firms' capital expenditure, in 1991 to the tune of 15 per cent. It is then no wonder that firms have been sent to the bond market, where they have borrowed about 20 per cent of their capital outlays. And new issues of shares have also taken place, after seven years of net and heavy

share repurchases by firms. The disappearance of banks as lenders, which has been noticed in the United States, has concentrated firms and other borrowers at the long end of the bond market. This, added to the permanent US budget deficit, has meant that long-term rates have remained high in the United States. Lastly, but very importantly, US banks have been compelled to rebuild their capital base by the ratios established at the Bank for International Settlements by the Banking Supervision Committee. They have therefore been themselves absorbing large amounts of capital, and have to a large extent replaced foreigners as buyers of US Treasury Paper.

In conclusion, I suggest that Branson should also take financial markets into account when drawing his stylized facts. The hysteresis of US long rates bears witness to a financial crunch in the United States which is probably as important as the German fiscal expansion in explaining why long-term rates are so high in the United States in spite of recession.

Discussion

ALEXANDRE SWOBODA

Branson's primary concern in this interesting and topical chapter is to explain the persistence of high real interest rates at a time of falling growth rates, and to seek clues in the recent evolution of macroeconomic variables as to whether a shortage of saving or of liquidity can be held responsible. He starts with four stylized facts and presents some models and 'exogenous' shocks that might explain them. His main conclusion is that the persistence of high interest rates is a consequence of a saving and not a liquidity shock.

On the whole, I have much sympathy both with his interpretation of recent events and with the types of models he uses. In the comments that follow I will therefore confine myself to raising a few notes of caution about the type of analysis in which Branson engages, on the one hand, and to broadening the discussion to the general theme of the management of international liquidity, on the other hand.

Some caveats

According to Branson's world IS–LM model, an anticipated fiscal expansion should create an anticipatory recession. I have some difficulty in attributing the slowing of growth in the world economy since 1989 exclusively to the 'reunification fiscal shock'; nor can the model explain why Germany should escape the recession or through what channels an anticipated fiscal tightening should produce beggar-thy-neighbour effects on the rest of the world. There are at least three reasons why Branson's analysis (and most analyses of that type, whatever their merit) needs to be taken with a grain of salt.

In the first place, there are alternative patterns of shocks and/or different models that could generate a time path of interest rates, outputs, and so on compatible with Branson's stylized facts. This being said, it must be stated that Branson's explanation has the virtue of being economical in terms of choice of both models and shocks. Second, and related, Branson's approach is in the single event/single cause tradition. To be truly convinc-

ing, it would need to be inserted in a fully specified econometric model: this would allow it to be checked both against alternative patterns of shocks and for compatibility with longer-term trends, notably in real rates of interests. Third, and this is more specific to Branson's analysis, the models he presents need to be completed in two directions, especially if they are to be used for policy prescription. Branson presents two models that are not really integrated; what would be required is to combine the IS–LM model with the real exchange rate one to produce a two-country macroeconomic model which determines simultaneously the real exchange rate, the current account, national outputs, and interest rates. This is not too difficult to do for the static case; dynamics would be more difficult to establish. Moreover, Branson's IS–LM model does not incorporate long-run dynamics. True, Branson does provide us with two equations that specify how 'core' inflation adjusts to changes in money growth and how prices adjust to deviations of output from its natural level; but these two equations are not integrated into the IS–LM model, the scenarios that he describes, or the diagrams he presents. As a result, the output changes that follow monetary and fiscal shocks appear, misleadingly, as permanent. Incorporating the longer-run dynamics into the IS-LM model would be important because it would produce much richer dynamics than those outlined by Branson. It would, however, also make interpretation of current patterns of economic variables much more difficult, for instance, in terms of the particular point of a real exchange rate or relative output cycle at which the world economy currently is and, as a consequence, in terms of the appropriate policy remedy.

International liquidity

In addressing the question of whether high interest rates are due to a shortage of international liquidity or a shortage of savings, Branson's choice was to focus on national (and even more specifically on German) rather than international liquidity and to ask himself: are the four stylized facts referred to in his paper consistent with either a specific shock to saving or to liquidity? This is quite a legitimate way of making the question manageable. It may nevertheless be worthwhile to comment briefly on the broader theme.

In the situation of high real interest rates that has prevailed since the 1980s, there can be little doubt that a shortage of saving relative to desired investment at lower real rates of interest is, almost by definition in any standard macroeconomic model, the source of the problem. There is no lack of recent studies documenting the fall in household saving rates and the rise in public deficits over the past ten years or more. As for explanations of

real interest rate changes, empirical studies such as those of Barro and Sala-i-Martin (1990) and Barro (1992, pp. 323–42) provide a good starting point for understanding the determinants of world interest rates (or the world component of such rates) as proxied by the Group of Ten (G-10) industrialized countries treated as making up a single 'world' capital market. In a fundamental sense, high real interest rates are not a problem but the symptom of a problem. Similarly, simply to ascertain that there is a 'shortage' of saving does not get at the root of the problem: one must also ask why there is such a shortage.

In that context, it is worthwhile asking whether there is a possible connection between the supply of international liquidity and the real interest rate (or the saving investment balance). More broadly speaking, is there a connection between the level of real interest rates and the international monetary regime? In a long run where the institutional framework is firmly set and money is neutral (perhaps even superneutral), the answer must be negative. In such a regime, whether exchange rates are fixed or flexible and whether the nominal quantity of money, credit or liquidity is x or twice x, it will be the basic determinants of thrift and productivity that determine real interest rates. In the short or medium run and/or with uncertainty as to the coming shape of the international monetary, including exchange rate, regime, there are a number of possible connections between international liquidity and the level of real interest rates. Among these, let me suggest a few to provide a basis for discussion.

First, under fixed or heavily managed exchange rates, there is a clear and well-documented positive link between the quantity of international liquidity (defined as the stock of international reserves) and the levels of national money stocks. To the extent that there is a negative link in the short run between national money stocks and real interest rates, a similar negative connection between the supply of international liquidity and real interest rates would exist. That connection, however, is unlikely to provide much of an explanation for the high level of real rates of interest in the recent past. For one thing, the growth of recorded international reserves has remained strong over the past decade. For another, with the important exception of the European Monetary System (EMS) about which more follows below, exchange rates among major currencies have by and large been floating, cutting the systematic link between national money stocks and international reserves or liquidity, and depriving the latter concept of some of its meaning. One may still argue for a connection by attributing the current high level of real interest rates to a level of expected inflation remaining stubbornly above actual inflation in spite of recent monetary tightening. The stickiness of expected inflation could be attributed, at least partly, to the fact that past high inflation was facilitated by a permissive international

monetary regime and that expected inflation will remain high as long as no credible discipline is imposed on national monetary policies by a reformed international monetary regime. Second, it has been argued, to my mind convincingly, that, within the EMS, uncertainty about the future of the Exchange Rate Mechanism (ERM) and about the prospects of an irrevocable fixing of parities has raised a number of national interest rates above what they would have needed to be if full confidence in the implementation of monetary union at prevailing exchange rates ruled. As a result, a country such as France with a lower rate of inflation than Germany has had to have higher nominal, and hence realized real, interest rates than the latter. More generally, uncertainty about the international monetary regime can create risk premia that make for higher real rates of interest. Finally, changes in the structure of the supply and demand for international liquidity, or more generally of credit both nationally and internationally, can lead to higher levels of real interest rates. The decreasing role of banks in national and international financial intermediation may provide one example of a structural cause of changes in the level of real rates of interest.

These considerations suggest that it is appropriate to look beyond or behind shocks to the saving investment balance within a standard macroeconomic model with given behavioural parameters when trying to ascertain the causes of changes, especially relatively durable ones, in real rates of interest. There are many causes for changes in thrift, productivity, and the preferences of investors. A period of increased uncertainty, political as well as economic, accompanied or not by international monetary disorder, is likely to be accompanied by a heightened degree of 'impatience' and, hence, by a higher level of real rates of interest.

References

Barro, R.J. 1992. 'World Interest Rates and Investment', *The Scandinavian Journal of Economics*, 94, 2.
Barro, R.J. and Sala-i-Martin, X. 1990. 'World Interest Rates', in G.J. Blanchard and S. Fischer (eds.), *NBER Macroeconomics Annual*, Cambridge Mass., MIT Press.

III

Exchange rates

6   Floating exchange rates reconsidered: the influence of new ideas, priorities, and problems

PETER B. KENEN

1 Introduction

Before trying once more to detect and appraise trends in exchange rate arrangements and the way we think about them, I should perhaps review my remarkable record. In 1979, I said that the European Monetary System (EMS) was bound to collapse, just like the Bretton Woods system, because 'stable but adjustable exchange rates' cannot go together. Ten years later, in 1987, I said that the informal methods of exchange rate management introduced by the Louvre Accord were also unviable; the countries of the Group of Seven (G-7) would have to adopt more formal arrangements or retreat to freer floating. On that occasion, moreover, I sought to retrieve my earlier mistake by citing the EMS as an attractive model for more formal G-7 arrangements, because the EMS had shown that adjustability was not incompatible with systemic stability. At that very time, however, the EMS countries started to migrate from adjustability to more rigid fixity (see Kenen 1979 and 1988 for proof of my fallibility). Events are less likely to overtake me this time, because I will take a different tack. Rather than proposing or forecasting reform, I will focus on the way we *evaluate* exchange rate arrangements, to shed light on a fundamental change in the approach adopted by economists and governments.

For the last fifty years, economists have sought to understand how the exchange rate regime affects the transmission of policies and shocks, given the structures and policy preferences of the countries involved and the sorts of shocks to which they are exposed. In other words, we have been chiefly concerned with the effects of exchange rate arrangements on economic interdependence. Recently, however, we have begun to ask how the exchange rate regime can affect the *quality* of national policies, especially the quality of monetary policies. In other words, we have returned to an older issue – the quest for an appropriate monetary standard.

I draw this distinction boldly to make the reader take notice. There are many ways in which the two approaches overlap. Economists have given a great deal of attention to the ways in which fixed and floating exchange

139

rates affect the functioning of national policies. Recall the large body of work begun by Fleming (1962) and Mundell (1963) on the effectiveness of monetary and fiscal policies under fixed and floating rates. Recall that we blamed the Bretton Woods system for letting the US 'export' inflation to the rest of the world, even before it had much inflation to export, and that the final collapse of the Bretton Woods system in 1973 was triggered by the impact of capital inflows on monetary aggregates in Germany (Emminger 1977). Furthermore, economists have long been engaged in the quest for a better monetary standard. The debate about 'rules *versus* discretion' goes directly to that issue. For the most part, however, that debate has been conducted in a closed economy context, although an occasional voice has been raised on behalf of the old gold standard, the quintessential monetary rule.[1] Interest in basing the monetary standard on an exchange rate rule did not emerge strongly until the 1980s. Moreover, one must give much credit to Italian economists for their contribution to our thinking on this subject. Giavazzi and Pagano (1988) were perhaps the first to articulate fully the view that Germany's benign hegemony in the EMS has helped the fight against inflation in other European countries. Nevertheless, their contribution must be seen to reflect basic changes in the way economists think about two issues.

First, economists have come to understand that fighting inflation is very important. Some of us have reservations about the common corollary to that proposition – that monetary policy should have no other aim. Even those who have such reservations, however, would be gravely concerned if policies aimed at combating a recession were likely to ignite inflationary pressures. Second, economists have become quite pessimistic about the ability of democratic governments to fight inflation vigorously. Economists have never been very respectful of politicians, but this familiar disdain has turned into something else: contempt for the democratic process itself. Few of us dare to display it boldly. We rely on arcane notions, such as time inconsistency, to convey our belief that democratic governments are doomed to behave deplorably and have to be saved from themselves.[2] Two ways to save them have gained popularity: using an exchange rate rule to enhance the quality of monetary policy, and granting independence to 'conservative' central bankers, whose role in many economists' ideal polity evokes the role of the philosopher king in Plato's Republic.[3]

2 The taxonomic ordering of exchange rate arrangements

Until the recent revival of interest in a policy-improving role for the exchange rate regime, it was hard to stage an interesting debate between the advocates of pegged rates and floating rates. Once we had begun to analyse

exchange rate arrangements in theoretical models bearing some resemblance to the real world, we were obliged to acknowledge that the ranking of exchange rate regimes involved damage limitation rather than optimization. A regime that appeared to have clear advantages in simple theoretical models looked far less attractive in more realistic models, and no regime worked very well in a world of imperfect policies and imperfect foresight.

The exchange rate is a price, of course, and economists rightly believe that markets are better than governments at setting and altering prices. The exchange rate, however, is nearly unique and may be too important to be left to market forces. Three considerations are relevant here.

Exchange rate responses to real shocks

The exchange rate, like the wage rate, affects many other prices. That is why changes in the nominal exchange rate are often viewed as substitutes for changes in the nominal wage rate. The pervasive effects of exchange rate changes would not be worrisome if all other prices were perfectly flexible. Prices could adjust individually to product-specific and asset-specific shocks, and they could also adjust individually to the market-specific manifestations of macroeconomic shocks. There would be no strong reason for wanting exchange rates to change or wanting to keep them from changing, and no clear basis for choosing between the tendency of markets to change rates too often and the tendency of governments to change them too rarely. Prices are not perfectly flexible, however, and the degree of flexibility varies from market to market. Hence, exchange rate changes have real effects, which likewise vary from market to market.[4]

Exchange rate responses to nominal shocks

The exchange rate affects the general price level, i.e., the real value of the money supply. That was all it did, indeed, in simple monetary models. Any small open economy, then, faces the risk that frequent and large changes in the nominal exchange rate will undermine the usefulness of the domestic currency. The currency may cease to serve as an adequate store of value and thus cease to serve as a medium of exchange. This was McKinnon's (1963) contribution to the theory of optimum currency areas. But its relevance depends on the nature of the shocks that cause the exchange rate changes. McKinnon's concern is very relevant for countries that experience real goods market shocks that require real depreciation of the domestic currency. When the nominal exchange rate is pegged, real depreciation can be achieved only by cutting home currency prices, the prices of non-traded goods relative to traded goods in one class of models, and the prices of

exports relative to imports in another class. Therefore, adjustment depresses the whole price level: it is deflationary rather than inflationary. (Furthermore, it will depress output and employment when home currency prices are sticky.) When the nominal exchange rate floats, by contrast, real depreciation will be achieved by nominal depreciation, which raises home currency prices. Hence, adjustment tends to be inflationary, which was McKinnon's point.

When shocks are monetary, however, their effects depend on their origins. When they originate abroad, a floating exchange rate can stabilize domestic prices and thus enhance the usefulness of the domestic currency; when they originate at home, it can destabilize domestic prices. Yet market structure matters, even here. The extent to which exchange rate changes can destabilize domestic prices depends on the stickiness of the real wage rate.

Finally, exchange rate arrangements have vital consequences for the way in which goods markets are affected by asset market shocks. Under a pegged exchange rate, asset market shocks affect goods markets indirectly, by way of their influence on money stocks and interest rates, and they do so gradually. Under a floating rate, asset market shocks affect goods markets directly, because of the pervasive price-changing effects of the exchange rate change induced by a capital outflow or inflow, and they are likely to do so abruptly. Therefore, I have argued elsewhere that floating exchange rates, rather than reducing interdependence, affect the form of interdependence in peculiarly painful ways (Kenen 1988).

Expectations, errors, and misalignments

The exchange rate is an asset price, and the foreign exchange market is forward looking. At one time, these incontrovertible statements were deemed to be decisive arguments in favour of floating exchange rates. To argue in favour of pegging or, indeed, any form of exchange rate management, one had to claim that governments have 'private' information, unavailable to others. They do, of course, have private information about their own policy plans and may have private information about other governments' plans. But that fact, by itself, does not settle the matter. It merely leads one to ask why governments should not disclose their policy plans and allow the market to interpret them.[5] Or does it perhaps lead one to ask whether the foreign exchange market makes good use of information, including information provided by governments?

Some economists have trouble with this question; it casts doubt on the value of *our* own private information – our superior understanding of the way that markets work. Nevertheless, a number of economists have begun to entertain the subversive notion that markets may not process infor-

mation judiciously. Mussa (1990, p. 7) puts it vividly: 'I have long been sympathetic to the view that the behaviour of asset prices, including exchange rates, is afflicted by some degree of craziness. Many aspects of human behaviour impress me as being not entirely sane, and I see no reason why the behaviour of asset prices should be a virtually unique exception.' Mussa goes on to suggest, however, that economists must take the blame for some of this craziness, because we have been unable to produce a theory of exchange rate determination capable of helping the foreign exchange market interpret the relevant information. And others have gone further, suggesting that the market does not even try. It has turned to black box methods for forecasting exchange rates (see, e.g., Frankel and Froot 1986 and Taylor and Allen 1992). It is thus possible for floating exchange rates to lead lives of their own, detached from so-called fundamentals, and affect the real economy in unpredictable ways.

Discussions of this possibility usually cite the huge swing in dollar exchange rates that took place in the 1980s, and Krugman (1988) was probably right to say that the last part of the upswing, in 1984–5, was a trip that the dollar took on its own, not due to any basic change in the fundamentals. But no one would blame 'irrational' traders for the whole episode, which began when US fiscal and monetary policies began to move in opposite directions.

3 Exchange rate arrangements and the quality of policies

No one has ever adduced any reason for me to believe that an exchange rate constraint would have prevented the Reagan administration from pursuing the outlandish fiscal policy it adopted in the early 1980s. It is equally hard for me to believe that the monetary side-effects of intervention aimed at pegging the dollar would have forced the administration to reverse or modify its fiscal policy. Institutional arrangements in the United States sterilize automatically the main monetary consequences of intervention. Had the monetary problem proved serious, moreover, Washington would have given more weight to the vindication of supply-side economics than to the integrity of the exchange rate constraint. The dollar would have been revalued step by step or, in the end, allowed to float freely.

Hard on the heels of that episode, however, economists and others began to examine the policy-improving potential of a pegged exchange rate. To be sure, they were not thinking about the United States, let alone the policies of the early Reagan years. Furthermore, they focused chiefly on monetary policy, not fiscal policy. Some sought to make it more credible by replacing tarnished commitments to price stability with bright new commitments to exchange rate stability. Others sought to make it more potent by relying on

goods market arbitrage to stabilize the prices of traded goods. And others sought to make it less fallible by relying on asset market arbitrage to maintain equilibrium in the domestic money market.

Making monetary policy more credible

Belief that an exchange rate peg can make monetary policy more credible has been the central theme of the recent literature on the EMS.[6] It has likewise been important in transforming the EMS from a system of adjustably pegged exchange rates into a system of virtually fixed rates. Nevertheless, debate continues on the actual contribution of the EMS to the reduction of inflation rates in Europe, because inflation was subsiding elsewhere too.[7]

Why should a commitment to a pegged exchange rate be more credible than a straightforward commitment to price stability? It is, of course, far more transparent and easier to monitor. An exchange rate can fluctuate within the band around its peg, but a change in the peg itself is easily detected; it is harder to detect a change in the commitment to bring down the inflation rate.[8] Furthermore, it is easier to fix responsibility for a change in the exchange rate. The actual rate is endogenous, but the exchange rate peg is policy determined; the inflation rate, by contrast, is totally endogenous, even though it is affected by monetary policy. But these considerations bear on accountability rather than credibility. A commitment to a pegged exchange rate will not be more credible than a commitment to price stability unless it is more costly to abandon a pegged rate than to abandon a promise to fight inflation.

Years ago, Cooper (1971) found that devaluation under the Bretton Woods system shortened the political life expectancy of a finance minister. That may not be true today, however, because of the great freedom governments enjoy to choose, change, and customize their exchange rate arrangements. The pegged rate arrangements of the EMS are unique in this respect. In fact, they represent an exchange rate constraint stronger than the one imposed by the Bretton Woods system. A change in EMS exchange rates can be initiated by a single government, but it requires collective consent. Furthermore, EMS membership derives from the membership of the European Community (EC) and a government that violates the rules of the EMS puts at risk its standing in the EC as a whole.[9] A pegged rate adopted unilaterally is bound to be less credible.

Yet pegging to acquire credibility is a high risk strategy. When a government ties down its exchange rate, it deprives itself of recourse to the instrument most useful for offsetting the effects of previous inflation and, more importantly, for offsetting the additional increase in prices that

typically occurs before exchange rate pegging can impart credibility to monetary policy and thus help to stabilize the price level. Worse yet, a government may try to cling to a pegged exchange rate even after it has failed to impart credibility. Remember the charge made most often against the Bretton Woods system: that governments tried too hard to keep exchange rates fixed, having staked their reputations on promises not to devalue. Having broken those promises, moreover, they tried even harder to keep the next ones, frequently by using trade and capital controls. Concerns of this sort have led Corden (1992) to conclude that the policy commitment to price stability 'must be direct, rather than brought about *via* an exchange rate commitment'.

Tying domestic prices to world prices

A second version of the case for using the exchange rate as a nominal anchor argues that goods market arbitrage can slow down inflation by tying domestic prices to world prices. The argument has been advanced in two quite different contexts. The 'heterodox' approach to stabilization in Latin America said that the inflation rates could be reduced abruptly by freezing prices and wages temporarily and by anchoring domestic prices to world prices by exchange rate pegging.[10] Many writers on reform in Central and Eastern Europe have recommended a speedy move to current account convertibility combined with exchange rate pegging as the most expeditious way of attaching sensible prices to domestic goods and factors (see Kenen 1991, Polak 1991, and Williamson 1991).

Advocates of 'heterodox' stabilization concede that price controls and pegged exchange rates cannot halt inflation permanently. But they can affect expectations temporarily, thus buying the time required for strict monetary and fiscal policies to have orthodox effects on credit creation and excess demand. Once this is acknowledged, however, something else must be conceded. Although a pegged exchange rate can help goods market arbitrage hold down the home currency prices of traded goods, it cannot stabilize the prices of non-traded goods. When those prices rise, moreover, the domestic currency appreciates in real terms, causing the current account to deteriorate and depressing output in the traded goods sector. Higher prices for non-traded goods will also drive up wage rates, making matters worse. This is, of course, another way to state a point made earlier. The use of exchange rate pegging to confer credibility on domestic monetary policy makes it hard to change the exchange rate later and thus hard to offset the increase in prices that occurs *en route* to stabilization. A colleague put it nicely in a recent conversation: no sensible sailor throws out an anchor before the boat stops moving.

Exchange rates and money market equilibrium

The third version of the case for exchange rate pegging to improve the quality of monetary policy would combine asset market arbitrage with goods market arbitrage to neutralize the errors made by central bankers. This is proposed pragmatically by those who believe that many central banks lack the skills and instruments to manage money properly, especially in periods of rapid change in economic and financial conditions. Rather than trying to pursue an interest rate or money supply target and thus trying to detect and offset shifts in the demand for money, they should target the exchange rate and make no attempt whatsoever to sterilize the money supply effects of their operations in the foreign exchange market.

The same argument is made more dogmatically by those who believe that central banks should be constrained – or should constrain themselves – to defend them from profligate governments and minimize the damage done by their own fallibility. Thus, Bofinger (1991) maintains that exchange rate pegging should be combined with *full* currency convertibility, so as to facilitate asset market arbitrage as well as goods market arbitrage. And because he identifies asset market arbitrage with the maintenance of open interest parity, we can regard his recommendation as a device to keep central banks from engaging in sterilized intervention and thus to prevent them from pursuing any policy goal other than exchange rate pegging.[11]

The flaw in this argument resides in the identification of asset market arbitrage with open interest parity. For the latter to obtain, foreign currency assets must be perfect substitutes for domestic currency assets. When they are perfect substitutes, in turn, there can be no shifts in investors' preferences and thus no exogenous changes in the size or direction of capital movements. Capital flows can serve merely to reflect and offset shocks occurring in the money market. They cannot disrupt the real economy. It must be pointed out, moreover, that the underlying economic model holds only for countries small enough to export money without affecting the money supply in the outside world. Hence, it depends on the dubious premise that small countries' central banks are fallible or vulnerable to political pressure and large countries' central banks are governed by philosopher kings.

4 Trends in exchange rate arrangements

Interest in using exchange rate arrangements to improve the quality of monetary policy was inspired largely by developments in Europe and has, in turn, affected them. The last major realignment of EMS exchange rates took place in 1987, and three more EC countries have joined the system

since that time: Spain, Portugal, and the United Kingdom. Other European countries have pegged their currencies to the ECU, directly in the cases of the Nordic currencies and indirectly in the case of the Austrian schilling, which is pegged to the Deutsche mark. In Central Europe, moreover, several stabilization programmes, most notably those adopted in 1990, attached a great deal of weight to exchange rate stability; the Polish zloty was pegged to the dollar, and the Yugoslav dinar was pegged to the Deutsche mark.

This tendency, however, has not been confined to Europe. Although the governments of the G-7 have given less attention to exchange rate management than they did right after the Louvre Accord of 1987 (see Frankel 1990 for a detailed account), they are not indifferent to exchange rate movements and have intervened on many occasions with a view to limiting them. They can presumably claim some credit for the relative stability of the mark-dollar and yen-dollar exchange rates in 1988–91. Finally, exchange rate pegging played a key role in the heterodox stabilization programmes adopted by Argentina in 1985 and by Brazil in 1986 and in the more orthodox Argentine programme adopted in 1991.

A somewhat different picture emerges, however, from the tabulations of exchange rate arrangements published by the International Monetary Fund (IMF). The Fund classifies its members' currencies under these broad rubrics.

Currencies with pegged rates:
    pegged to another national currency
    pegged to the SDR or some other composite
Currencies with limited flexibility:
    in terms of another national currency
    belonging to a cooperative arrangement
Currencies with more flexible arrangements:
    adjusted according to a set of indicators
    other managed floating rates
    independently floating rates

Table 6.1 summarizes the Fund's tabulations for the ten years since the Fund began to use these rubrics (but treats the middle groups of countries as having pegged exchange rates).

The numbers in this table have to be used cautiously. Member governments are supposed to inform the Fund of any change in their arrangements, but some have not done so consistently, and the prevalence of multiple exchange rates makes it hard to classify some countries' arrangements. Pegged rates, moreover, are not always fixed rates, and some rates have been altered more frequently than others. Most importantly, no country can peg its exchange rate completely when other countries' rates

Table 6.1. *Classification of IMF members' exchange rate arrangements (ends of calendar years)*

Arrangement	1982	1983	1984	1985	1986	1987	1988	1989	1990	1991
Pegged[a]	111	107	108	105	103	103	105	103	100	96
of which EMS	*8*	*8*	*8*	*8*	*8*	*8*	*9*	*9*	*10*	*10*
Based on indicators	5	5	6	5	6	5	5	5	5	5
Other managed	20	23	21	20	21	23	22	22	23	27
Independent float	8	9	11	17	19	18	17	20	25	27
Total[b]	144	144	146	147	149	149	149	150	153	155

Notes:
[a] Includes rates limited in terms of a single currency.   [b] Yemen Arab Republic and People's Democratic Republic of Yemen treated as a single country throughout (with its currency pegged to the US dollar); Cambodia omitted; Kiribati treated throughout as pegging to the Australian dollar and Namibia as pegging to the South African rand.
Source: International Monetary Fund, *International Financial Statistics* (various issues).

are allowed to float. Nevertheless, tests reported in the appendix to this chapter suggest that table 6.1 provides a reliable guide to major trends in exchange rate policies. What, then, does the table show? There has been a moderate decline in the number of countries with pegged exchange rates and a larger increase in the number with independently floating rates. A close look at the numbers, however, shows that the shift from pegged to floating rates was concentrated in 1983–5 and 1989–91. There were fewer changes in 1986–9, when, in fact, some countries went the other way. These variations show up clearly in table 6.2.

In the first three-year period, eleven countries moved from pegged exchange rates to more flexible arrangements, and six of the eleven to independent floating. Furthermore, most of the twelve countries that shifted between pegged rate arrangements moved from single currency or Special Drawing Rights (SDR) pegs to pegging in terms of a customized basket,[12] while most of those that shifted between flexible rate arrangements took to independent floating. In the next three-year period, ten countries moved from pegged exchange rates to more flexible arrangements, but only three of those countries moved to independent floating. Furthermore, eight countries went in the opposite direction, compared with

Table 6.2. *Changes in exchange rate arrangements, 1983–91*

Nature of change	1983–5	1986–8	1989–91
Between pegged rate arrangements	12	9	3
From US$ or SDR to other composite	*5*	*3*	*2*
From limited flexibility to other pegs	*4*	*1*	*0*
From flexible rate to pegged rate	2	8	5
To exchange rate mechanism of EMS	*0*	*0*	*2*
Plus new with pegged rate	3	2	5
From pegged rate to flexible rate	11	10	18
To independent floating	*6*	*3*	*8*
Plus new with flexible rate	0	0	1
Between flexible-rate arrangements	5	5	3
To independent floating	*4*	*2*	*1*
Reversing arrangements within period	0	1	4

Source: See the appendix.

only two in the previous period. This time, moreover, most of the countries that shifted between pegged rate arrangements went from customized baskets to single currency or SDR pegs,[13] and only two of the five countries that shifted between flexible rate arrangements took to independent floating. The third three-year period was more like the first one. A total of eighteen countries moved from pegged to flexible rates, and eight of them took to independent floating. Only five countries moved the other way (and two of them were EC countries that entered the exchange rate mechanism of the EMS). Very few countries moved from one type of pegging to another or from one type of flexibility to another. It should be noted, moreover, that five of the eight countries which had moved from flexible to pegged rates in 1986–8 returned again to flexible rates in 1989–91. Finally, new members of the Fund have usually adopted pegged exchange rates initially, but some have moved on to more flexible arrangements.[14]

It would seem, then, that the quality-improving case for exchange rate pegging had some effect on exchange rate arrangements in the mid 1980s. But its appeal was not strong enough to halt or reverse the long-term trend towards more flexible rates. The notion still holds sway in Europe, but its influence there will be short lived if European and Monetary Union (EMU) replaces the EMS. The independent central banker will take over from the exchange rate anchor.

I will not undertake to explain why exchange rate flexibility continues to

appeal to so many countries (including some very small countries with close economic ties to one large trading partner), apart from noting that many of them have been unable to reduce their inflation rates and thus have had to change their nominal exchange rates repeatedly in order to keep their real rates from appreciating.[15] I will venture to suggest that the appeal of exchange rate flexibility is probably strong enough to keep currency blocs from forming, even among countries that seem likely to form trading blocs. Canada and Mexico are far from ready to peg their currencies to the dollar, let alone become the thirteenth and fourteenth Federal Reserve Districts.[16]

Turning finally to the question of exchange rate arrangements among the major industrial countries, the question to which Rinaldo Ossola devoted much of his talent, there is, I fear, not much new to be said and even less reason to predict that something new will happen. In fact, events and attitudes are moving in directions that will probably reduce the willingness of governments to contemplate improvements in the monetary system. On the one hand, the regionalization of world trade makes it easier and more appropriate for the major industrial countries to tolerate floating exchange rates, an outcome predicted by Ossola (1971) in a remarkable paper written two decades ago. On the other hand, the closer integration of financial markets makes exchange rate management far more difficult. Bayoumi and Sterne (1992, pp. 27–8) provide evidence and sum up this way:

As far as trade in goods goes, there does appear to be substance in the widely-held view that the world is evolving into three major regional trading blocs, with decreasing trade between these blocs ... Looking to the future, it seems probable that these trends will continue. Moves to EMU imply steadily greater European integration. In North America, the probable success of a North American Free Trade Agreement (NAFTA) is likely to exacerbate the existing trend toward intraregional trade, while the increasing importance of East Asia in overall trade is likely to increase regional trade insularity, even in the absence of moves towards a free trade zone. In short ... trade outside of these regional blocs will continue to decline, and hence inter-bloc exchange rates will matter less for activity. At the same time, the trend toward greater integration in international capital markets seems likely to continue... Greater capital market integration in turn implies a decreasing ability to separate exchange rate policy from domestic monetary policy ... In these circumstances, it appears unlikely that bilateral exchange rates will be an important focus for international policy coordination in the 1990s.

The likelihood grows even dimmer when we look inside Europe and the United States. Both are absorbed by domestic challenges, Europe with deepening and widening and all of their ramifications; the United States with the need to reorder priorities and reallocate resources within and between the public and private sectors. And both are increasingly worried about the challenge from Japan, which has problems of its own. Finally, there is still a distinct difference between the macroeconomic policy

preferences of Americans and Europeans. The size of the difference is underscored by the concern expressed so frequently in Washington about the costs of meeting the requirements for EMU set out in the Maastricht Treaty and about the possible costs of making price stability the primary objective of monetary policy. Despite widespread agreement on the importance of fighting inflation, Americans appear to be less tolerant of the costs of doing so and to have far more affection for old-fashioned contracyclical policy. Americans find it hard to understand why the EC countries, particularly those with deep recessions, such as the United Kingdom, tolerate the interest rates imposed by the Bundesbank. Differences in national policy preferences do not preclude beneficial policy coordination but can prevent cooperation aimed at exchange rate stabilization.

I am nevertheless impressed by the orderly way in which foreign exchange markets have dealt with big policy differences during the last few years. It may not be too costly to let exchange rates 'take the strain' until they start to misbehave and thus produce the political will to design a better monetary system.

Appendix: The classification of exchange rate arrangements

Under the Articles of Agreement of the IMF, member countries may adopt 'exchange arrangements of their choice' but must notify the Fund of any change (Article IV, section 2). The rubrics used by the Fund to classify its members' exchange rate arrangements were listed in the text and reappear in table 6.A, which shows the situation at the end of 1991. Asterisks identify the eighty-three countries that did not change their exchange rate arrangements after 1982, when the present classification was adopted; double asterisks identify fifteen other countries that did not change them after 1985. The countries listed by the Fund as belonging to a cooperative exchange rate arrangement appear in table 6.A beneath under a more familiar rubric – as participants in the exchange rate mechanism of the EMS.

Formal arrangements and actual experience

The classification reproduced in table 6.A must be interpreted cautiously, for the reasons indicated in the text. A number of countries switched *de facto* to exchange rate pegging when they introduced new currencies, Argentina in 1985, when it introduced the austral, and Brazil in 1986, when it introduced the cruzado, but there is no trace of these episodes in the Fund's tabulation, presumably because the governments involved did not notify the Fund of formal changes in their exchange rate arrangements. Similarly, Poland pegged the zloty to the US dollar at the start of 1990, but

Table 6.A. *Exchange rate arrangements of member countries, end-1991*

Pegged to US dollar	*Pegged to French franc*	*Pegged to other composite*
Angola	*Benin	Albania
*Antigua and Barbuda	*Burkina Faso	*Algeria
Argentina	*Cameroon	*Austria
*Bahamas	*Cent. African Rep.	*Bangladesh
*Barbados	*Chad	*Botswana
*Belize	*Comoros	*Cape Verde
*Djibouti	*Congo	*Cyprus
*Dominica	*Cote d'Ivoire	Czechoslovakia
*Ethiopia	**Equatorial Guinea	*Fiji
*Grenada	*Gabon	*Finland
*Iraq	*Mali	*Hungary
*Liberia	*Niger	Iceland
Mongolia	*Senegal	Jordan
Nicaragua	*Togo	Kenya
*Oman		*Kuwait
*Panama	*Pegged to other currency*	**Malawi
**St Kitts & Nevis	*Bhutan	*Malaysia
*St Lucia	*Lesotho	*Malta
*St Vincent	*Swaziland	**Mauritius
Sudan	Yugoslavia	Morocco
*Suriname		**Nepal
*Syrian Arab Rep.	*Pegged to special drawing right*	*Norway
*Trinidad & Tobago	**Burundi	*Papua New Guinea
*Yemen	*Iran	*Solomon Islands
	Libya	*Sweden
	*Myanmar	*Tanzania
	**Rwanda	**Thailand
	*Seychelles	Tonga
		Uganda
		Vanuatu
		Western Samoa
		*Zimbabwe

Flexibility limited in terms of single currency	*European Monetary System*	*Adjusted according to set of indicators*
*Bahrain	*Belgium	*Chile
*Qatar	*Denmark	*Colombia
*Saudi Arabia	*France	Madagascar
*United Arab Emirates	*Germany	Mozambique
	*Ireland	Zambia
	*Italy	
	*Luxembourg	
	*Netherlands	
	Spain	
	United Kingdom	

Table 6.A. (*cont.*)

Other managed	Independent float
China	Afghanistan
*Costa Rica	**Australia
Ecuador	**Bolivia
Egypt	Brazil
*Greece	Bulgaria
Guinea	*Canada
**Guinea Bissau	Dominican Republic
Honduras	El Salvador
*India	Gambia
**Indonesia	Ghana
Israel	Guatemala
*Korea	Guyana
Lao P.D. Rep.	Haiti
Maldives	Jamaica
Mauritania	*Japan
*Mexico	Kiribati
*Pakistan	*Lebanon
Poland	Namibia
Portugal	**New Zealand
Romania	Nigeria
Sao Tome & Principe	Paraguay
Singapore	Peru
Somalia	**Philippines
*Sri Lanka	Sierre Leone
Tunisia	*South Africa
*Turkey	*United States
Viet Nam	*Uruguay
	Venezuela
	**Zaire

Notes:
* No change in 1983–91.   **No change in 1986–91.
Source: International Monetary Fund, *International Financial Statistics* (various issues). As the currency of Kiribati is the Australian dollar, Kiribati is treated in tables 6.1 and 6.2 of the text as pegging to the Australian dollar; as the currency of Namibia is the South African rand, because Namibia has not yet introduced its own currency, Namibia is treated in tables 6.1 and 6.2 of the text as pegging to the South African rand.

the Fund was not notified officially until 1991 and had to change its table retroactively in 1992. There have been other, less dramatic cases. The Austrian schilling, for example, is listed by the Fund as being pegged to a 'currency composite' but has been pegged *de facto* to the Deutsche mark for several years.

Several countries have separate exchange rates for different types of transactions, and some of those multiple rates may be pegged while others float more or less freely in legal, grey, or black markets. Some countries that peg their exchange rates change the pegs from time to time. And no country can peg its exchange rate completely when other countries' rates are floating. It can, of course, peg to a basket of foreign currencies, which has become very common, but the domestic currency will still vary in value in terms of every other individual currency. (The same problem arises in classifying members of the EMS. Their currencies are tightly pegged to each other but float against all other major currencies. The Fund treats them as partaking of 'limited flexibility', which does not describe the situation adequately.)

If the Fund's classification has any operational significance, one would expect to find that pegged rates are more stable than flexible rates, and this is broadly true. The staff of the Fund has measured the short-term variability of trade-weighted effective exchange rates in 1989–90, using the average of absolute monthly percentage changes during those two years, adjusted for the frequency of large exchange rate changes.[17] Its calculations can be used to classify countries by the amount of short-term variability in their effective rates, which is done below for eighty-five countries (the ninety-eight shown in table 6.A that did not change their exchange rate arrangements after 1985 less eight participating in the Exchange Rate Mechanism (ERM) of the EMS, four with limited flexibility in terms of a single foreign currency, and one for which the requisite measure of variability was not available).

Degree of variability	Single currency peg	Composite peg	More flexible
Low	16	14	2
Medium	12	8	10
High	7	4	12

Countries with adjusted measures of short-term variability no larger than 1.25 per cent are listed as having low variability; those with measures no smaller than 2.50 per cent are listed as having high variability; and the rest are listed as having medium variability.

These results are broadly consistent with what one would forecast. The effective exchange rates of countries that peg to currency composites are

less variable than those of other countries; more than half the countries pegging to composites have 'low' variability. (If their currency baskets employed the same trade weights that were used to define their effective exchange rates, they would show no variability whatsoever unless they devalued or revalued in terms of their currency baskets.) A similar outcome obtains for countries that peg to another country's currency, even though single currency pegging should not be expected to stabilize an effective exchange rate completely. (The low variability shown for the countries in this group reflects their tendency to peg to the foreign currency that dominates the country's trade; the group includes US dollar peggers in Central America and the Caribbean having close trade ties to the United States and French franc peggers in Africa having close trade ties to France.) The story is different, however, for countries having more flexible rates; only two countries in this group have low variability.

Treated as a contingency table, this tabulation yields a chi-squared statistic large enough to reject at the 0.01 level the null hypothesis that there is no significant difference among the three country groups. That is likewise true when the first and second columns are combined (and the result is even stronger when the eight EMS countries are added to the group of pegged rate countries, because they all display low variability).

The countries excluded from the previous tabulation, i.e., those that changed their exchange rate arrangements after 1985, showed much more variability in 1989–90. There were eighteen such countries with pegged exchange rates at the end of 1990, and seventeen had medium or high variability; there were twenty-eight such countries with flexible rates, and twenty-five had medium or high variability.

What can be said about longer-term exchange rate behaviour? Table A lists thirty-nine countries as pegging continuously to another currency or to the SDR in 1986–91.[18] Only five changed their pegs in that nine-year period. (Oman, the Syrian Arab Republic, and Trinidad changed their US dollar pegs; Burundi and Rwanda changed their SDR pegs.) The table lists twenty-two countries that pegged to other composites and twenty-one that had more flexible arrangements.[19] The Fund does not publish effective exchange rates for all of these countries, and it was not worth constructing them for this exercise. The SDR values of their currencies are readily available, however, and can serve as crude measures of long-term variability. Cross-country averages of cumulative percentage changes in SDR rates are shown below for the two groups of countries.

	Other composite	Flexible rate
All countries in group	151.5	646.4
Excluding extreme causes	75.5	197.0

The average percentage depreciation in terms of the SDR was more than four times as large for countries with flexible rates than for countries pegging to composites, and it remained almost three times as large when three countries with very large depreciations were dropped from the two groups.[20]

These comparisons do not speak to the merits of various exchange rate arrangements. They say merely that the Fund's tabulations provide useful information about actual exchange rate behaviour, although they will always contain anomalies.

The variability of exchange rate arrangements

Table 6.2 of the text summarizes the changes in exchange rate arrangements that occurred in 1983–5, 1986–8, and 1989–91. Five rules were used to prepare it:

(1) Countries with limited exchange rate flexibility, including the EMS countries, are treated as having pegged rates.
(2) Countries that moved between different pegged rate arrangements but also moved to flexible rates within a period under study are treated as moving to flexible rates.
(3) Countries that moved between different flexible rate arrangements but also moved to pegged rates within a period under study are treated as moving to pegged rates.
(4) Countries newly listed within a particular period (mainly those that joined the Fund during that period) are listed separately.
(5) The changes themselves were identified by comparing successive end-year tables in *International Financial Statistics*. Hence, they omit exchange rate arrangements that lasted less than a year, including some short-lived attempts at exchange rate pegging. But a quarter-by-quarter study of 1990 and 1991 turned up only two such cases.

The discussion in the text focuses on changes between pegged rate and flexible rate arrangements. Some other regularities are noted here. In 1983–5, many changes between pegged rate arrangements involved the 'customizing' of pegged rates; of the thirteen countries making changes of this sort, nine moved to their own composites, six from single currency or SDR pegs and three from limited flexibility in terms of a single currency.[21] (Note, however, that four of the five countries which went from flexible to pegged rates adopted single currency or SDR pegs). In 1986–8, by contrast, shifts to single currency or SDR pegs were more common than shifts in the opposite direction; only three of the nine countries making such shifts adopted their own composites. In 1989–91, all five countries shifting between pegged rate arrangements moved to their own composites, but the

countries adopting pegged rate arrangements were more evenly divided between those choosing single currency or SDR pegs and those choosing their own composites.[22]

In 1983–5, most countries moving between flexible rate arrangements went to independent floating, and half of those moving to flexible rates did so too; of sixteen countries in those two groups together, ten had independently floating rates by the end of 1985. In 1986–8, the trend went the other way; once again, fifteen countries made changes of this sort, one adopted indicators and nine adopted other forms of managed floating. In 1989–91, there was more diversity; twenty-two countries adopted flexible rates or moved from one sort to another, and ten of them wound up with independent floating.[23]

Notes

1　There has been useful work on the effects of using rules to coordinate national policies (see, e.g., Frenkel *et al.* 1989). Most of that work, however, has focused on the benefits and costs of using rules as second-best substitutes for fully optimal coordination.

2　The model proposed by Barro and Gordon (1983) is widely cited in this context. Although it is compatible with two views of government, both are pessimistic. The government may be machiavellian, in that it deliberately misleads firms and workers, leading them to base wage bargains on promises about monetary policy the government does not plan to keep. Alternatively, the government may be myopic, in that it plans to keep its promises but cannot resist the temptation to exploit the short-run wage rigidity produced by the decision-making sequence in the model. On either view, however, politicians and the public must be protected from the harmful effects of their own behaviour.

3　Cooper (1992) uses the same metaphor to describe and criticize the way that the Maastricht Treaty would protect the European Central Bank (ECB) from political meddling; it confuses operating independence with immunity from democratic accountability. I make the same objection in Kenen (1992). Goodhart (1992) is also concerned about accountability but frames the issue differently; the ECB will not be fully accountable because its statute does not define price stability operationally. Giovannini (1992) takes the opposite view, saying that the Maastricht Treaty fails to give the ECB enough independence; Article 109 would allow the Council (Ecofin) to make exchange rate agreements that would force the ECB to intervene on foreign exchange markets even when such intervention would interfere with pursuing price stability, and Article 105 could subordinate the ECB to the agencies responsible for prudential supervision. He is right about Article 109 but may misinterpret Article 105.

4　This point has been stressed by Melitz (1992) in his reformulation of the theory of optimum currency areas. It was implicit in Kenen (1969), where I took issue with Mundell (1961) on the equivalence between exchange rate flexibility and labour mobility when nominal wages are rigid and economies are subject to

goods market shocks; I went on to suggest that when those shocks are independent, supply-side diversification is a partial substitute for exchange rate flexibility.

5 The currently popular treatment of official intervention as a form of 'signalling' extends this argument; it says that sterilized intervention can influence exchange rates by disclosing information about future policies. The classic statement of this view is provided by Mussa (1981); for empirical work on intervention as a form of signalling, see Dominguez (1989), Dominguez and Frankel (1990), and Ghosh (1992).

6 A useful survey is provided by Haldane (1991).

7 Compare Collins (1988) and De Grauwe (1990) with Ungerer et al. (1986) and Artis and Nachane (1990). But empirical work on the early years of the EMS may not measure clearly the contribution of the EMS to the credibility of monetary policies; Frankel and Phillips (1991) show that it took a long time for EMS exchange rates to gain credibility.

8 A single currency peg may be superior for this reason to a basket peg but may be harder to sustain when other exchange rates are changing. Poland pegged the zloty to the dollar in 1990 but switched to a basket peg in 1991, when the dollar was appreciating against the Deutsche mark, dragging the zloty with it, and threatening Poland's competitive position in EC markets.

9 This point is stressed by Giavazzi and Giovannini (1989) when arguing that the EMS would be hard to copy outside Europe (see also Kenen 1988).

10 Dornbusch (1986) provides an incisive statement of the 'heterodox' view; Kiguel and Liviatan (1992) provide a retrospective critique.

11 The proposal by Hanke and Schuler (1990) to convert central banks into currency boards aims at the same result, but at a higher opportunity cost, because the whole money supply must be backed by hard currency assets.

12 These include three of the four that moved from limited flexibility to a stricter form of pegging, making for eight of the twelve in this group.

13 These include one that went from limited flexibility to a stricter form of pegging, making for five of the nine in this group. (The remaining country moved from a dollar peg to an SDR peg.)

14 Poland began with basket pegging, moved to dollar pegging in 1990, but went to basket pegging in 1991 and then to an 'other managed' rate; Mozambique followed the same path. Bulgaria began with basket pegging in 1990 but moved to independent floating in 1991, while Albania, Angola, Czechoslovakia, and Mongolia began and stayed with pegged rates.

15 The same point is stressed by Aghevli et al. (1991), who show that developing countries with flexible exchange rates have had higher inflation rates than those with pegged rates but have not experienced much larger changes in their real rates.

16 Mexico's central bank Governor (Mancera 1991, p. 95) makes this very clear: 'Mexico's possible participation in one or more free trade zones does not imply that we anticipate the formation of monetary unions in these zones. Furthermore, currency areas are not necessarily essential to a free trade zone's good performance, nor are the benefits from the formation of such areas self-evident.'

17 The adjusted measure is equal to $v(1 + n/24)$, where v is the simple average of monthly changes and n is the number of months in which the effective exchange rate changed by more than 0.7 per cent. Hence, a country whose effective rate did not change by more than 0.7 per cent in any single month will have an adjusted measure equal to v, while a country whose effective rate changed by more than 0.7 per cent in every single month will have an adjusted measure equal to $2v$.

18 This count omits Yemen (and does not add Kiribati).

19 The last group omits Guinea Bissau and Zaire because of gaps in the data.

20 These were countries with cumulative depreciations exceeding 1,500 per cent; Tanzania was removed from the group with composite pegs, while Lebanon and Uruguay were removed from the group with flexible rates. No other country in the group with composite pegs showed a cumulative depreciation larger than 500 per cent; two other countries, Mexico and Turkey, had cumulative rates between 500 per cent and 1,000 per cent. (If those countries were likewise removed from the flexible rate group, the average rate of depreciation would fall to 104.0 per cent, but it is hard to make a case for going further in this manner.)

21 These thirteen countries include Zambia, which moved to its own composite before moving to an independent float. One of the four other countries moved from one single currency peg to another.

22 The first five countries include Bulgaria and Mozambique, which adopted their own composites before moving to more flexible rates.

23 These numbers exclude Kiribati and Namibia, for reasons given in the source note to table 6.A.

References

Aghevli, B.B., Khan, M.S., and Montiel, P.J. 1991. 'Exchange Rate Policy in Developing Countries: Some Analytical Issues', *Occasional Paper*, 78, Washington DC, IMF.

Artis, M.J. and Nachane, D. 1990. 'Wages and Prices in Europe: A Test of the German Leadership Thesis', *Weltwirtschaftliches Archiv*, 126.

Barro, R.J. and Gordon, D. 1983. 'A Positive Theory of Monetary Policy in a Natural Rate Model', *Journal of Political Economy*, 91.

Bayoumi, T. and Sterne, G. 1992. *Regional Trading Blocs, Mobile Capital and Exchange Rate Coordination* (processed).

Bofinger, P. 1991. 'The Transition to Convertibility in Eastern Europe: A Monetary View', in *Currency Convertibility in Eastern Europe*, J. Williamson (ed.), Washington DC, Institute for International Economics.

Collins, S.M. 1988. 'Inflation and the European Monetary System', in *The European Monetary System*, F. Giavazzi, S. Micossi, and M. Miller (eds.), Cambridge, London, and New York, Cambridge University Press.

Cooper, R.N. 1971. 'Currency Devaluation in Developing Countries', *Essays in International Finance*, 86, Princeton, International Finance Section, Princeton University.

1992. 'The 'Eurofed' Needs Accountability', *Economic Insights*, Washington DC, Institute for International Economics.

Corden, W.M. 1992. 'Integration and Trade Policy Issues in the Ex-Soviet Union' (mimeo).

De Grauwe, P. 1990. 'The Costs of Disinflation and the European Monetary System', *Open Economics Review*, 1, 2.

Dominguez, K.M. 1989. 'Market Response to Coordinated Central Bank Intervention', *Working Paper*, 3192, Cambridge, National Bureau of Economic Research.

Dominguez, K.M. and Frankel, J.A. 1990. 'Does Foreign Exchange Intervention Matter? Disentangling the Portfolio and Expectation Effects for the Mark', *Working Paper*, 3299, Cambridge, National Bureau of Economic Research.

Dornbusch, R. 1986. 'Inflation, Exchange Rates, and Stabilization', *Essays in International Finance*, 165, Princeton, International Finance Section, Princeton University.

Emminger, O. 1977. 'The D-Mark in the Conflict between Internal and External Equilibrium', *Essays in International Finance*, 122, Princeton, International Finance Section, Princeton University.

Fleming, J.M. 1962. 'Domestic Financial Policies under Fixed and under Floating Exchange Rates', *IMF Staff Papers*, 9.

Frankel, J.A. 1990. 'The Making of Exchange Rate Policy in the 1980s', *Working Paper*, 3539, Cambridge, National Bureau of Economic Research.

Frankel, J.A. and Froot, K.A. 1986. 'Understanding the Dollar in the 1980s: The Expectations of Chartists and Fundamentalists', *Economic Record*, Supplement.

Frankel, J.A. and Phillips, S. 1991. 'The European Monetary System: Credible at Last?', *Working Paper*, 3819, Cambridge, National Bureau of Economic Research.

Frenkel, J.A., Goldstein, M. and Masson, P.R. 1989. 'Simulating the Effects of Some Simple Coordinated Versus Uncoordinated Policy Rules', in *Macroeconomic Policies in an Interdependent World*, R. Bryant et al. (eds.), Washington DC, IMF.

Last?', *Working Paper*, 3819, Cambridge, National Bureau of Economic Research.

Ghosh, A.R. 1992. 'Is It Signalling? Exchange Intervention and the Dollar Deutschemark Rate', *Journal of International Economics*, 32.

Giavazzi, F. and Giovannini, A. 1989. *Limiting Exchange Rate Flexibility*, Cambridge, London, and New York, Cambridge University Press.

Giavazzi, F. and Pagano, M. 1988. 'The Advantages of Tying One's Hands: EMS Discipline and Central Bank Credibility', *European Economic Review*, 32.

Giovannini, A. 1992. 'Central Banking in a Monetary Union: Reflections on the Proposed Statute of the European Central Bank' (mimeo).

Goodhart, C.A.E. 1992. 'The ESCB After Maastricht' (mimeo).

Haldane, A.G. 1991. 'The Exchange Rate Mechanism of the European Monetary System', *Bank of England Quarterly Bulletin*, 31, 1, February.

Hanke, S. and Schuler, K. 1990. 'Keynes and Currency Reform: Some Lessons for Eastern Europe', *Journal of Economic Growth*, 4.

Kenen, P.B. 1969. 'The Optimum Currency Area' in *Monetary Problems of the International Economy*, R.A. Mundell and A.K. Swoboda (eds.), Chicago, University of Chicago Press.

1979. 'Comment', in *EMS: The Emerging European Monetary System*, R. Triffin (ed.), Brussels, National Bank of Belgium.

1988. *Managing Exchange Rates*, London, Royal Institute of International Affairs, and New York, Council on Foreign Relations.

1991, 'Transitional Arrangements for Trade and Payments among the CMEA Countries', *IMF Staff Papers*, 38.

1992. *EMU After Maastricht*, Washington DC, Group of Thirty.

Kiguel, M.A. and Liviatan, N. 1992. 'When Do Heterodox Stabilization Programs Work?', *World Bank Research Observer*, 7.

Krugman, P.R. 1988. *Exchange Rate Instability*, Cambridge Mass., MIT.

Mancera, M. 1991. 'Characteristics and Implications of Different Types of Currency Areas', in *Policy Implications of Trade and Currency Zones*, Kansas City, Federal Reserve Bank of Kansas City.

McKinnon, R.I. 1963. 'Optimum Currency Areas', *American Economic Review*, 53.

Melitz, J. 1992. 'A Multilateral Approach to the Theory of Optimal Currency Areas' (mimeo).

Mundell, R.A. 1961. 'A Theory of Optimum Currency Areas', *American Economic Review*, 51.

1963. 'Capital Mobility and Stabilization Policy under Fixed and Flexible Exchange Rates', *Canadian Journal of Economics and Political Science*, 29.

Mussa, M.L. 1981. 'The Role of Official Intervention', *Occasional Paper*, 6, New York, Group of Thirty.

1990. 'Exchange Rates in Theory and Reality', *Essays in International Finance*, 179, Princeton, International Finance Section, Princeton University.

Ossola, R. 1971. 'Towards New Monetary Relationships', *Essays in International Finance*, 87, Princeton, International Finance Section, Princeton University.

Polak, J.J. 1991. 'Convertibility: An Indispensable Element in the Transition Process in Eastern Europe', in *Currency Convertibility in Eastern Europe*, J. Williamson (ed.), Washington DC, Institute for International Economics.

Taylor, M.P. and Allen, H.L. 1992. 'The Use of Technical Analysis in the Foreign Exchange Market', *Journal of International Money and Finance*, 11.

Ungerer, H., Evans, O., Mayer, T. and Young, P. 1986. 'The European Monetary System: Recent Developments', *Occasional Paper*, 48, Washington DC, IMF.

Williamson, J. 1991. 'The Economic Opening of Eastern Europe', in *Currency Convertibility in Eastern Europe*, J. Williamson (ed.), Washington DC, Institute for International Economics.

Discussion

GIANCARLO GANDOLFO

The chapter tries to give new insights in the debate on the appropriate exchange rate regime for the international monetary system by taking a different perspective in comparing fixed versus flexible exchange rates. That is to say, the two regimes are evaluated according to their capability to affect the quality of monetary policies rather than by considering their influence on economic interdependence. In my opinion, these two methods of comparison are closely related since the existence of very interdependent economies makes it very difficult – whatever the exchange rate regime – to insulate one country from the shocks that occur in the other, and as a result the achievement of an appropriate monetary standard becomes very difficult.

After considering the effects of exchange rate movements on real and nominal macroeconomic variables (which depend considerably on the flexibility of wages and prices), the chapter deals specifically with the relationship between the exchange rate regime and the quality of monetary policies. In particular, exchange rate pegging is related to some characteristics of monetary policy, i.e., its degree of credibility, its power in stabilizing prices, and its capability of maintaining the equilibrium in the money market. The author shows that exchange rate pegging is not able to improve the quality of monetary policies according to all three criteria. First, exchange rate pegging can enhance monetary policy credibility only when the exchange rate agreement is credible in itself. The European Monetary System (EMS) is exactly an example of this kind, since the credibility is given to the exchange rate agreement, according to the author, by the fact that EMS membership implies membership of the European Community (EC), so that commitments entered into in the EMS framework are in fact commitments *vis-à-vis* the other EC governments. Hence any government failing to honour them undermines its standing in the Community, a point already stressed by Giavazzi and Giovannini. Otherwise, governments are generally free to choose the exchange rate system they prefer; unilateral pegging is not reckoned to be so highly credible and will not enhance the

credibility of monetary policy. Second, exchange rate pegging can improve the power of monetary policy only for the stabilization of traded goods prices, but not for wages and non-traded goods prices, as the author notices. Finally, exchange rate pegging can be viewed as the monetary rule only if central bankers are deemed completely unable to manage policy instruments properly, which is certainly not the case as regards industrialized countries.

This chapter can be considered as background material for any kind of exchange rate arrangement, since it is full of factual and descriptive material, but lacks any indication of the author's own ideas, priorities, and suggestions for solving the problems. For this one must turn to other works by the author (for example Kenen 1988). It would have been preferable to have developed this instance further, as a contribution to the design of a better international monetary system.

One of the main facts that require explanation is why huge variations in the real exchange rate have had so small an effect on the trade balance. The sections of the chapter that deal with the exchange rate response to real and nominal shocks and the feedback effect of exchange rate changes do not mention this fact. And I feel that the sunk costs hysteresis hypothesis should be taken into account when examining the real effects of exchange rate changes (Baldwin 1988, pp. 773–85).

My final comment concerns the section on expectations, errors, and misalignments. By now many of us agree with the 'subversive notion' that foreign exchange markets may not process information judiciously, as Mussa pointed out already in 1990, and as a few of us and all central bankers have always known. But from this it would be incorrect to jump to the conclusion (attributed to Frankel and Froot 1986 and to Taylor and Allen 1992) that the participants in the foreign exchange market no longer try to interpret it, and have turned to black box methods for making money. I find more sensible and realistic the idea that in this market both chartists and fundamentalists are present, as the same authors have suggested (of course this is a functional distinction: the same agent can be a chartist or a fundamentalist according to the circumstances). It is then easy to see that the dynamic stability of the market depends on the relative weight of the two categories. Hence I would like to suggest and stress the idea that an important concern of both economists and central bankers should be that of increasing the weight of fundamentalists. I fully agree with the author when he says that economists should take the blame for the prevalence of chartists, because 'we have not produced a theory of exchange rate determination capable of helping the foreign exchange market interpret the relevant information'. Hence economists should try and build and test better exchange rate models, which is indeed being done (Gandolfo *et al.*

1990, pp. 963–92). And central bankers should carry out official intervention taking account of the fact that fundamentalists must make profits to remain in the market and help in stabilizing it, as was already suggested some thirty years ago (Cutilli and Gandolfo 1963, pp. 216–31 and 1972, pp. 111–24).

References

Baldwin, R. 1988. 'Hysteresis in Import Prices: The Beachhead Effect', *American Economic Review*, 78.

Cutilli, B. and Gandolfo, G. 1963. 'The Role of Commercial Banks in Foreign Exchange Speculation', *Banca Nazionale del Lavoro Quarterly Review*, 65.

1972. 'Wider Band and "Oscillating Exchange Rates"', *Economic Notes*, 1.

Frankel, J.A. and Froot, K.A. 1986. 'Understanding the Dollar in the 1980s: The Expectations of Chartists and Fundamentalists' *Economic Record*, Supplement.

Gandolfo, G., Padoan, P.C., and Paladino, G. 1990. 'Exchange Rate Determination: Single Equation or Economy-Wide Models?', *Journal of Banking and Finance*, 14.

Kenen, P.B. 1988. *Managing Exchange Rates*, Royal Institute of International Affairs.

Taylor, M.P. and Allen, H.L. 1992. 'The Use of Technical Analysis in the Foreign Exchange Market', *Journal of International Money and Finance*, 11.

Discussion

RONALD McKINNON

Kenen begins with confessions worthy of St Francis, or even St Augustine! In 1979, he underestimated the ability of the European Monetary System (EMS) to maintain stable par values for exchange rates down to the present day. Subsequently he underestimated the ability of the less formal Louvre Accord of February 1987 to create and maintain informal target zones for the mark/dollar and yen/dollar exchange rates. Yet, under the auspices of the Banca d'Italia, remarkable new data[1] show that informal target zones for the dollar have been maintained since 1986; concerted intervention by the principal central banks have succeeded in reversing trends in the dollar exchange rate which threatened to pierce the unannounced zonal boundaries. Remarkably, this intervention seems to have succeeded without short-run monetary adjustment, i.e., it was largely sterilized. For example, twelve central banks intervened massively and in concert to support the dollar on 20 July 1992. Despite the fact that US short-term interest rates remained very low and unchanged, that the Bundesbank actually raised its discount rate shortly thereafter, and that the central banks did not continue to intervene, this sharp concerted intervention was successful in stopping the dollar's sharp downward trend that had developed in the first months of 1992.

However, Kenen remains forthrightly ambivalent regarding whether the industrial countries should strive towards reestablishing fixed exchange rates. His honest ambivalence reflects the slowly changing attitudes of an economics profession that is still torn between two conflicting views of the exchange rate. The first is what I shall call the *international adjustment* approach, which is not only the dominant view of 'the economist in the street',[2] but also that of many economists specializing in international economics. Harping back to the venerable elasticities model of the balance of trade, this approach treats the exchange rate as a useful instrumental or adjustment variable for balancing – with minimal stress – international trade and capital flows across countries with (implicitly) differing monetary policies. The second is what I shall call the *monetary standard* approach,

which is more the province of specialists in monetary economics. In order to improve the efficiency of international trade and investment, agreements to limit exchange fluctuations – as under a par value system – are seen as devices for securing greater monetary harmonization across countries while reducing investment risk.

In the postwar period, the dominant academic influence favoured exchange flexibility and the international adjustment approach. Coming from Keynes and Keynesians like James Meade, on the one hand, or from Milton Friedman and a host of other monetarists, on the other, both had the objective of securing national monetary autonomy with as little disruption in foreign trade as possible. Of course, Keynesians and monetarists differed dramatically on how national monetary autonomy should best be exercised. But in the 1950s and 1960s they were united in believing that (greater) exchange rate flexibility was desirable. The fixed rate dollar standard, under which they lived until 1971, was by most measures (price stability, the reduction in trade barriers, and extraordinary growth in real output) the most successful international monetary system the world had ever seen (Madison 1989). Nevertheless, so strong was the intellectual pull of the international adjustment approach that, by the end of the 1960s, most economists were demanding greater exchange flexibility in order to escape the straight jacket of having to live with a common monetary policy.[3]

Perhaps the most concrete evidence of the then prevailing mores of a broad spectrum of economists – who were not government officials – is encapsulated in the proceedings of the conference on *Approaches to the Greater Flexibility of Exchange Rates* held in Burgenstock, Switzerland, on 30 June 1969. From ten different countries, there were thirty-eight experts in international finance: twenty practitioners from banking and business firms and eighteen academic economists. As the title implies, the conference studied virtually all methods by which exchange rates could be made more flexible: (1) widened bands around a central parity, (2) a crawling or slowly gliding central parity, (3) some combination of (1) and (2), and (4) a free float where each government had no specific exchange rate objectives or obligations. As indicated in the proceedings,

The answers to a questionnaire ... taken near the end of the conference ... showed that a large majority of the participants favoured a move toward greater flexibility in exchange rates. The participants were asked what changes, if any, they would like to see in the present exchange rate system. It was further agreed that advocates of fully flexible rates could vote in favour of limited flexibility if they felt that the former was politically unrealistic at the present time. Of the thirty-four participants who replied, only three favoured making no change in the present exchange rate system. Six favoured a modest widening of the band by amounts ranging up to (plus

or minus) 2.5 per cent; these were all practitioners, i.e. officials of banking or business firms. Eighteen participants voted for versions of the band-and-crawl system with a width of the band up to (plus or minus) 3 per cent. Within this group, which was evenly split between practitioners and academics, there were different views as to whether the gliding parity arrangements should be automatic, presumptive, or discretionary. The seven remaining respondents – all academics – favoured even more flexibility in one form or another, and generally expressed a personal preference for freely floating rates (as did one or two of the previous group) (Bergsten *et al.* 1970, pp. vi–vii).

Quite a remarkable convergence of opinion in a profession not noted for its concord! And such virtual unanimity on the gains from making exchange rates more flexible could hardly fail to impress government officials and policymakers – particularly President Nixon when he was trying to decide in 1969–71 whether to disinflate the American economy to preserve the fixed rate dollar standard, or to devalue and continue to inflate. By 1992, however, economists had shifted towards the monetary standard approach, although this is not yet the majority view. Kenen helps us identify those empirical and theoretical considerations responsible for the shift. On the empirical side, the benign hegemony of Germany in the EMS helped the Europeans set up a common – and less inflation prone – monetary standard (although in 1991–3, high German interest rates were not viewed so benignly). In addition, the extraordinary volatility in exchange rates experienced by the world at large, once the commitment to the par value system broke down after 1971–3, was much greater than the advocates of floating had anticipated. Rather than a smoothly adjusting variable for 'balancing' international trade flows, floating exchange rates behaved like volatile asset prices that were highly sensitive to 'news' about future monetary events and then overshot any 'reasonable' equilibrium defined with respect to current commodity flows. And the resulting exchange risk proved difficult if not impossible to hedge fully. Further, I would argue that the upsurge in protectionism in the world economy since the early 1970s in the form of quantitative restrictions – import quotas, 'voluntary' export restraints, market sharing agreements, and so on – can be interpreted as an attempt to shield politically sensitive producer groups from exchange risk (McKinnon and Fung 1993). In contrast, modest tariffs are ineffective in reducing the investment risk associated with exchange fluctuations. Indeed, from the 1970s into the 1990s, successive rounds of the General Agreement on Tariffs and Trade (GATT) continued to achieve modest reductions in statutory tariffs even as interbloc quantitative restrictions proliferated.

The main point of Kenen's chapter, however, is to note a major doctrinal change in economists' views on the proper conduct of national macroeco-

nomic policy. The earlier advocates of floating – whether monetarist or Keynesian – viewed unfettered national monetary autonomy positively. Keynesians wanted to fine-tune the macroeconomy, and monetarists wanted each national central bank to exercise absolute control over its national money supply. But new developments in macroeconomic theory emphasize the problem of 'time consistency' in monetary policy: how can we effectively bind the central bank to keep the price level stable when the national government is under ongoing pressure to surprise the populace with a sudden monetary stimulus (leading eventually to price inflation), before elections or other periods of political stress? Given the lags between undue monetary expansion undertaken now and inflation in the future, monetarists have advocated binding the national central bank to a constant rate of growth in some monetary aggregate – where observation lags are somewhat less long. But this domestic monetarist approach has been undermined by unpredictable shifts in the velocity of money – whether measured by M1, M2, or M3 – in virtually all the industrial countries.

Thus, in line with the modern view of achieving time consistency in macroeconomic policy, the idea of binding national monetary authorities to an exchange rate rule based on an external monetary standard becomes a more attractive alternative. If a stable external monetary standard with stable prices for tradable goods can be established – a big if – and if the domestic financial system is open, the exchange rate commitment is easily monitored and would effectively prevent the national central bank from engaging in a surprise monetary expansion. As Kenen notes, this implies a major doctrinal reversal in the advantages perceived in the 1950s and 1960s of unfettered monetary autonomy based on exchange rate flexibility. Instead, an exchange rate commitment is now seen as a way of reducing national monetary autonomy in order to improve the 'quality' of national macroeconomic policy. Thus, ideologically, we are now in better shape to return to an international monetary standard – with narrow exchange rate bands – than we were in trying to defend the (highly successful) fixed rate dollar standard of the 1950s and 1960s.

But the enormous problem of building on the 1987 Louvre Accord to establish an international standard anchored by a stable common price level which is comparable to, but nevertheless more symmetrical than, the dollar standard still remains. However, suppose the big three – Europe, Japan, and the United States – succeeded in setting up such a standard, then this would go a long way towards resolving another problem which Kenen examined in some detail: the enormous state of flux in exchange rate relationships among smaller industrial countries and Less Developed Countries (LDCs). Kenen examines the continual movement from countries pegging their exchange rates, to greater flexibility, to floating, and then

back to pegging. Other authors (notably Edwards 1989) have noted the great upsurge in the variance of real exchange rates and domestic price levels in LDCs after the fixed rate dollar standard broke down in the 1970s. If a stable international monetary standard among the major industrial economies was again established, then smaller industrial countries and LDCs (and perhaps now transitional socialist economies) would again rush to join. As with the late nineteenth-century gold standard or the fixed rate dollar standard of the 1950s and 1960s, they would again seek to permanently fix their exchange rates to the new standard as means of better anchoring their own national monetary policies while reducing risks in their foreign trade and investment.

Notes

1 'Concerted Interventions and the Dollar: An Analysis of Daily Data' by P. Catte, G. Galli, and S. Rebecchini in Part III of this volume.
2 Judging from the remarkable recent spate of letters in *The Economist* supporting Martin Feldstein's essay (13 June 1992) attacking exchange rigidity within the EMS and questioning the whole idea of bending national monetary policy to support exchange stability.
3 The advent of the fixed rate dollar standard was itself an historical accident arising out of the exigencies of the Marshall Plan in 1948–52 and was not at all what the negotiators in 1943–5 at Bretton Woods had in mind. For the postwar, they imagined that the Bretton Woods par value system would be much more flexible with fairly full national monetary autonomy. After the disastrous collapse of the gold standard in the 1930s, Keynes in particular was adamant that no new international monetary standard should be imposed on the domestic monetary processes of member countries (McKinnon 1993).

References

Bergsten, C.F., Halm, G.N., Machlup, F., and Roosa, R. 1970. *Approaches to Greater Flexibility of Exchange Rates: The Bürgenstock Paper*, Princeton.
Edwards, S. 1989. *Real Exchange Rates, Devaluation, and Adjustment: Exchange Rate Policies in Developing Countries*, Cambridge Mass., MIT Press.
Madison, A. 1989. *The World Economy in the 20th Century*, Paris, OECD.
McKinnon, R.I. 1993. 'The Rules of the Game: International Money in Historical Perspective', *Journal of Economic Literature*, March, 31 .
McKinnon, R.I. and Fung, K.C. 1993. 'Floating Exchange Rates and the New Interbloc Protectionism' in Protectionism and World Welfare, Dominick Salvatore (ed.), Cambridge University Press.

7 The credibility of adjustable parities: the experience of the European Monetary System

ZHAOHUI CHEN and ALBERTO GIOVANNINI

1 Introduction

One of the central questions in the theory of international monetary regimes is: are fixed but adjustable exchange rates a contradiction in terms? In other words, can a system of adjustable parities survive? Is it, in some sense, stable? This question is an important key to interpret the experience of the Bretton Woods regime, and its eventual collapse. Did the Bretton Woods system collapse because of 'structural' reasons, apparent from the Articles of Agreement of the International Monetary Fund (IMF), or was it brought down by shocks whose importance could not, and should not, have been forecast by the drafters of the Bretton Woods charter? In other words, was the Bretton Woods regime doomed from the start?

This question is also central in the debate on the European Monetary System (EMS). Dissatisfaction with the adjustable rates system and the failure of an early attempt – the Snake – to limit bilateral exchange rate fluctuations among the countries in the European Community (EC) prompted observers to give a very cool reception to the newly created EMS in 1978–9. Yet, those who were quick at dismissing the chances of the EMS in its inception have been forced to catch up with it, though suspicion is still maintained by many who view the EMS as fundamentally unstable. The EMS is now widely regarded as the most significant international monetary reform in the post-Bretton Woods era. Does the EMS disprove the view that adjustable rates systems are unstable? More importantly, the initiative to transform the EMS into Economic and Monetary Union (EMU) was inspired by a very strong view on the question of the stability of adjustable rates systems. The Delors Report proposed a gradual transition to a single currency among EC countries. It justified this momentous reform not with an optimum currency area analysis of the costs and benefits of a single currency. Instead, it based it on the consideration that with increased financial market integration and the completion of the internal market, even small deviations of national monetary policies from the rest of the EC would bring down the EMS. Hence, the Delors Report implicitly subscribed to the instability view of fixed but adjustable exchange rates.

Critics of EMU pointed out that the EMS had held out for a long time,

proving its resilience and effectiveness, and did not need any further reform. Proponents of EMU claimed that the EMS was made credible by the very announcement of EMU, and the initiative that preceded it – the Single Market programme. They claimed that, during the first eight years of the EMS, without the prospect of EMU only the presence of capital controls avoided its collapse; and that significant deviations from the policies set out in the Maastricht Treaty would bring about changes in EMS parities, and worse things later. The EMS crisis of the Fall of 1992 seems to have confirmed these concerns.

Recent research in international finance, in particular the work of Flood and Garber (1984) and the empirical research in the vein of Lizondo (1983) has clearly and convincingly established the linkage between the collapse of a fixed exchange rate and expectations held by actors in financial markets. In addition, the analysis of the stabilizing properties of monetary policy rules (Simons 1936; Friedman 1968; Barro and Gordon 1983) has shown that the crucial channel through which such rules can stabilize inflation and economic activity is the behaviour of the private sector's expectations. Hence the 'strength' or 'weakness' of an adjustable rate system is directly related to the behaviour of expectations under such a regime.

This chapter is an exploration of the expectations of the French franc/ Deutsche mark and Italian lira/Deutsche mark parity changes. Such an exploration should, in our view, be the first step of a broader analysis of the stability properties of a fixed but adjustable rate system. More precisely, the question that we ask in this chapter is the following: 'What determines expectations of parity changes?' In order to answer this question we need to obtain reliable estimates of such expectations, and then attempt to relate them to economic variables. The methodology we follow is essentially an extension of the line of research started by Collins (1984 and 1986). Our chapter extends the work of Collins and others (see, for example, Cetorelli 1992) by paying the proper attention to the dynamics of exchange rates within fluctuations bands, and its effects on expectations of realignments. Section 2 describes how to filter out expectations of exchange rate changes within EMS fluctuation bands to obtain estimates of expected changes of EMS central parities. Section 3 presents a model that helps interpret expected changes of central parities. Section 4 describes the empirical methodology and the results. Section 5 contains a few concluding remarks.

2 Measuring expected parity changes

The measurement of expected parity changes has to take into account two problems. The first is the measurement of expected changes in exchange rates. That is possible if interest rate differentials reflect expectations of exchange rate changes and risk premia, or other sources of differences

between *ex ante* returns in different currencies, are insignificant. Svensson (1990) argues that in a managed exchange rate regime with target zones, given realistic distributional assumptions about fundamentals, the exchange rate risk premium should be insignificant. The second problem in measuring parity changes is the presence of exchange rate bands, or target zones. Since exchange rates are flexible within these target zones, in order to estimate the expected change in a central parity it is necessary to separate the expected changes within the band and the expected shift of the central parity.

To fix ideas, we decompose the log exchange rate s into the log central parity c and the log percentage deviation from the central parity x

$$s_t = c_t + x_t \tag{1}$$

It follows that the one-period expected change (devaluation) of the exchange rate can be decomposed into the expected central parity shift and the expected change in the percentage deviation from the central parity

$$E[\Delta s_t | I_t] = E[\Delta c_t | I_t] + E[\Delta x_t | I_t] \tag{2}$$

All expectations are conditional upon information available at time t, denoted by I_t. Under interest rate parity the left-hand side can be replaced by the interest rate differential between the home country and foreign country. Denoting the differential of interest of deposits of maturity j by δ^j, the expected devaluation can be written as

$$E[C_{t+j} - C_t | I_t] = \delta_t^j - E[(x_{t+j} - x_t) | I_t] \tag{3}$$

With δ_t^j observed in the interest rate data, the task of measuring expected devaluation is reduced to measuring expected changes in x. It should be noted that the expectation is a *full information* expectation in the sense that the information set I_t should contain the possibility of both a realignment and no realignment in the next j periods; in other words, the observations on x should reflect the markets assessment of future realignment possibilities.

Rose and Svensson (1991) develops an alternative measure of expected devaluation associated with realignment expectations. It is formulated as follows

$$\hat{c}^e = \delta_t^j - E[(x_{t+j} - x_t) | \text{no realignment}] \tag{4}$$

where $\hat{c}^e$ denotes the expected devaluation. We refer the reader to Rose and Svensson for the derivation and the intuition of the above measure. The key feature of this measure is that the second term on the right-hand side of the above equation is a conditional expectation, conditional on an information set that is generally smaller than the full set I_t, with the realignment events excluded from the latter.

To obtain the measures in (3) and (4) empirically requires the estimation

of the second terms on the right-hand side of the two equations. The common practice is to construct an *ex ante* measure of x using the *ex post* observation of x. The *ex ante* measure is usually estimated by projecting future realized exchange rates on the current information set. We note, however, that there may be an observational equivalence problem with the *ex ante* measures – a point that has not been properly addressed in the current literature. We consider first the extreme case in which all realignment events are fully anticipated with perfect foresight, and the market is rational and free of imperfections. Then the effect of a future realignment will show up in the current exchange rates, in other words, it should be 'priced' by the current market. Thus the data consisting of the *ex post* realizations of exchange rates, or x, should reflect fully anticipated realignments. Using this data set will not lead to a proper estimation of expected exchange rate changes that is *conditional on no realignments*. Even when realignments are removed from the data, the resulting estimates are still consistent with (3), but not with (4). We then consider the opposite case in which the realignment is entirely unanticipated, or is anticipated but has no effect on the current market due to either irrationality or market imperfections.[1] In this case, the market prices (exchange rates) during periods of no realignments do not reflect realignment expectations at all, and a data set that excludes realignment observations can be used to estimate the *ex ante* exchange rate changes conditional on no realignment, as defined in (4). But the trimmed data set is not proper for estimating the measures defined in (3). The observational equivalence problem arises when we have few realignment sample observations and no prior knowledge about the market rationality and imperfections. In other words, when we obtain an estimate of *ex ante* exchange rate changes, we are not sure whether it fits in the definition described in (3) or the definition in (4).

The more general, and perhaps practically more important, cases are the intermediate cases in which the market assigns a probability of realignment that is between 0 and 1. A projection of future realized exchange rates on current information set should yield an estimate of the full information expectation as defined in (3), provided that sufficient sample observations on realignment events are included in the information set. Since realignment under the EMS is not a frequent event, the sample we have usually contains only a few realignment observations. The small realignment sample relative to the larger sample from the no-realignment periods tends to yield biased estimates of expectations. This is because the market expectation is a probability weighted average of future exchange rates under realignment and under fixed parity. With small samples, the probability of realignment cannot be properly identified without imposing further identifying assumptions, such as distributional assumptions under a jump diffusion model.

Instead of resorting to more complicated econometric models and further identifying restrictions, we try in this chapter to obtain a simple approximation of conditional expectations defined in (4). The reasoning is as follows: as mentioned above, given that realignments are less frequent and the data are dominated by observations from the no-realignment periods, the estimated expectation is biased towards the conditional expectation measure in (4). If we further exclude the observations in the data prior to and at realignments, the bias goes even further towards the conditional expectation measure, as is suggested by the 'peso problem' literature. Therefore the 'unintended' econometric biases actually lead to a close approximation of the conditional expectations as defined in (4). Therefore we follow the usual projection equation methodology to obtain the estimates of expectations, with realignment observations removed from the sample, and interpret our result as an approximate measure of the Svensson definition of expected devaluation.

3 Interpreting expected parity changes

We now present a way to interpret expected parity changes following and extending the model originally developed by Barro and Gordon (1983). The basic assumption is that exchange rate changes have real effects, and that the monetary authorities wish to induce a level of economic activity systematically different from the natural rate. The discrepancy between the authorities' objective and equilibrium can be due to a number of distortions, including monopoly power of trade unions (which could induce too high real wages and too low a level of economic activity); the presence of tax distortions like income taxes and unemployment insurance (which could provide disincentives to labour supply and induce too low a level of economic activity); 'excessive' demands on the monetary authorities (myopic politicians could believe that monetary policy could, and should, be systematically devoted to the increase of economic activity and well being, and could put pressure on the monetary authority to do so); and the presence of a large stock of government debt, requiring a heavier use of the inflation tax or of political pressures to systematically lower real interest rates.

A model

We start from the benchmark case, whereby central banks set the exchange rate in a discretionary way. This regime could be labelled managed floating. The authorities choose $\hat{c}$ which is the percentage change in the central parity, to maximize their objective function, after observing the stochastic shock ϵ. The public chooses $\hat{c}^e$ before observing the stochastic disturbance.

This gives an informational advantage to the monetary authorities allowing them to affect real variables with the use of a monetary instrument. The maximization problem of the monetary authorities is

$$\min[\hat{c}^2 + \phi(y - K)^2] \tag{5}$$

subject to the supply function

$$y = (\hat{c} - \hat{c}^e) - \epsilon \tag{6}$$

The first-order condition of this maximization problem is

$$\hat{c} + \phi[(\hat{c} - \hat{c}^e) - \epsilon - K] = 0 \tag{7}$$

Under rational expectations, the public uses knowledge of the monetary authorities' first-order condition to form its expectations

$$E\{\hat{c} + \phi[(\hat{c} - \hat{c}^e) - \epsilon - K]\} = 0 \tag{8}$$

which leads to

$$\hat{c}^e = \phi K \tag{9}$$

and

$$\hat{c} = \phi K + \frac{\phi}{1 + \phi}\epsilon \tag{10}$$

The level of economic activity in this case becomes

$$y = -\frac{1}{1 + \phi}\epsilon \tag{11}$$

An alternative regime involves a credibly fixed exchange rate. In this case the monetary authorities follow the simple rule $\hat{c} = 0$ and this rule is credible to the public, i.e., $\hat{c}^e = 0$. Under credibly fixed exchange rates output becomes

$$y = -\epsilon \tag{12}$$

It is well known that under managed exchange rates there is a depreciation bias associated with the incentive of the monetary authorities to devalue the currency to increase economic activity – for any of the reasons discussed above.[2]

The third regime is one where the central parity is changed only when certain realizations of ϵ occur. Denote q as the probability that a critical value of ϵ is reached whereby the authorities change the central parity in a discretionary fashion. Then the expected devaluation is

$$\hat{c}^e = q\hat{c}^{e,d} + (1 - q) \times 0 \tag{13}$$

where $\hat{c}^{e,d}$ is the expected devaluation when the authorities follow a discretionary policy. As pointed out by Lohmann (1990) and Flood and Isard (1990), there exist conditions on the distributions of the exogenous shocks under which this escape clause regime is superior to either a credibly fixed parity or to the discretionary regime. The intuition is the following. When the 'extraordinary' shock occurs the exchange rate realignment can be more effective than under discretion, to the extent that it comes as a bigger surprise and has larger real effects. At the same time, the escape clause gives some extra flexibility to the monetary authorities, and therefore – under certain parameter values – can be superior to a fixed rule.

Before proceeding, we observe that a basic simplifying assumption behind the models presented above is violated in practice: the exogenous disturbance does not follow an identically and independently distributed process. However, as Cassard (1992) shows, the heuristic value of these models is preserved under more general specifications of the exogenous disturbances and more general assumptions on the nature of nominal rigidities. Essentially, under a more general setting the probability of the escape clause being resorted to becomes time varying. However, under a more general setting it is not possible to compare the 'welfare' properties of the different regimes by comparing the period objective function of the monetary authorities. Of course, our objectives here are much more limited, having to do with the interpretation of expected parity changes.

So far, we have shown that expected parity changes are related to the probability that the authorities will invoke an escape clause, and we have argued that this probability is in general time varying. In the case of the EMS, however, we think there exists an additional element of uncertainty that the public faces when forming expectations about parity changes. This is due to the presence of imperfect information about the real intentions of monetary authorities. As Giovannini (1990) argues, the observed high *ex post* excess returns on certain EMS currencies are suggestive of the importance of learning about the exchange rate regime. We wish here to combine the presence of an escape clause with uncertainty about the objectives of the monetary authorities. There are different ways of doing this.

The one we prefer assumes that the monetary authorities follow a fixed exchange rate rule with probability $(1-p)$ and an escape clause rule with probability p, with p defined as the public's subjective probability. In this case,

$$\hat{c}^e = (1-q) \times 0 + q[p\hat{c}^{e,d} + (1-p) \times 0] = pq\hat{c}^{e,d} \tag{14}$$

In equilibrium, the expected parity change is

$$\hat{c}^e = \frac{pq}{1+\phi(1-pq)}\phi K \tag{15}$$

We thus put forward the proposition that the expected devaluation increases with p and q. It is easy to show that

$$\frac{\partial \hat{c}^e}{\partial p} = \frac{(1+\phi)q}{[1+\phi(1-pq)]^2} \phi K > 0$$

$$\frac{\partial \hat{c}^e}{\partial q} = \frac{(1+\phi)p}{[1+\phi(1-pq)]^2} \phi K > 0$$

It is important to note that $(1 - p)$ is the probability that, *in the future*, the monetary authority will follow a fixed rule. The probability is perceived by the public based on all available information. Thus at a given point in time, p should be independent of the forecasting horizon. In other words, the public's assessment on the monetary authority's policy stance is the same for all future periods. Of course, p can change period by period, for the same forecasting horizon, as new information arrives. The constance of p across forecasting horizon allows, in principle, identification of p and q.

4 Empirical evidence

A projection equation

In the previous sections we have argued that the estimation of the expected change in the central parity requires an estimation of the expected change in the exchange rate within the band. Our task is to explore the determinants of expectations of parity changes. To do this, we estimate the following equation

$$\delta_t^j - (x_{t+j} - x_t) = Z_t' \beta + u_{t+j} \tag{16}$$

where Z_t' is a vector of variables in agents' information set at time t. The disturbance term u_{t+j} has two components. One is the expectation error $(x_{t+j} - Ex_{t+j})$, the other is an error due to the imprecise measurement of expectations, or the existence of variables affecting expectations that are left out from the vector Z. The former is, under the assumption of rational expectations, orthogonal to any variable included in Z, depending on the severity of specification errors. In general, the expectation error always swamps the error due to mismeasurement, because, as is well known, the variance of the unpredictable component of exchange rates is very high. When $j > 1$ the expectation error follows a moving average process of order $j - 1$.

Consider the linear projection

$$\delta_t^j - E[(x_{t+j} - x_t)|\text{no realignment}] = Z_t'\hat{\beta} \qquad (17)$$

where $\hat{\beta}$ is a consistent estimate of β. Equation (17) shows that the projection of the interest rate differential net of the realized exchange rate changes within the band on information provides an estimate of the expected change in the central parity. The coefficient vector β will indicate the relation of the expected change in the central parity to fundamentals. The basic strategy of this regression is inspired by the following observation. Under the assumption of linear rational expectations, the best estimate of the expectations of any economic variable is its projection on variables in agents' information set at the time such expectation is formed. The property of this estimate is that the estimated residuals, which represent the 'surprises', are orthogonal to the variables used to form expectations. In this sense, information cannot be used more efficiently to form expectations, and therefore expectations are rational.

Two problems remain to be tackled before estimating equation (16). The first is the estimation of the expected change in the position of the exchange rate within the band. We follow the strategy discussed earlier by excluding realignment observations to arrive at an estimate close to the expected change of x within the band. More precisely, we eliminate the observations at each realignment, and one (three) observation prior to a realignment to estimate the one-month (three-month) expected changes of the exchange rate within the band (conditional on no realignment). The second problem is the fact that an unrestricted projection usually fails to explicitly specify the restrictions implied by the presence of the target zone band, which is a part of the public's information set and non-linearly related to, and correlated with, many other information variables. This may result in incorrect estimates of expectations. This problem is discussed by Chen and Giovannini (1992), who propose a type of Box–Cox transformation which recovers the good properties of projection equations. This transformation cannot be used in the equation we estimate in this chapter, because it would not allow the simple joint estimation of expectations of realignments and exchange rate movements within the band. However, we have verified that, in the case of the EMS, the errors that arise from not exploiting the information on exchange rate bands are likely to be negligible (see also Svensson 1991).

Data and estimation

The frequency of the data used in our regressions is monthly, and the horizons we study are one month and three months, but only the one-month results are fully reported.[3] We look at the Italian lira/Deutsche mark

and French franc/Deutsche mark exchange rates since the beginning of the EMS. The data included in the information set Z are:

$C1, C2,...$: Constant dummies corresponding to each central parity regime. Ten regimes for Italian lira and seven for French franc.

$X1$: Log relative foreign exchange reserve position measured in terms of the Deutsche mark.

$X2$: The per cent change in budget surplus on a cash basis (Italy or France minus Germany).

$X3$: The difference of the trade balance surpluses (Italy or France minus Germany).

$X4$: Relative industrial production indices, e.g.,

$$\ln\left(\frac{IP^{IT}}{IP^{GER}}\right) \tag{18}$$

$X5$: The position of the exchange rate within the band (x).

$X6$: The log of one plus the number of months since the last realignment.

$X7$: An index of relative CPIs, e.g.,

$$\ln\left(\frac{CPI^{IT}}{CPI^{GER} \cdot \underset{DM}{IL}}\right) \tag{19}$$

$X8$: An index of relative wages, e.g.,

$$\ln\left(\frac{W^{IT}}{W^{GER} \cdot \underset{DM}{IL}}\right) \tag{20}$$

$X9$: Relative liquidity, e.g,

$$\ln\left(\frac{L^{IT}}{L^{GER} \cdot \underset{DM}{IL}}\right) \tag{21}$$

$X10$: Deutsche mark/US dollar exchange rate.

$X11$: Jump dummy that takes the value 1 at the first month of realignment and zero otherwise.

$X12$: $X1$ multiplied by the slope dummy that equals 1 before the Basle-Nyborg Agreement and zero afterwards.

$X13$: $X5$ multiplied by the same slope dummy as in $X12$.

Results

Tables 7.1 and 7.2 contain the estimates of the projection equation over the one-month horizon, respectively for the Italian lira and the French franc,

Table 7.1. *One-month IL/DM expected devaluation: full-sample regression (March 1979–January 1992)*

Variable	Coefficient	t-value	p-value
C1	− 1929.3645	− 5.5425	0.0000
C2	− 1912.1711	− 5.5399	0.0000
C3	− 1900.8901	− 5.5236	0.0000
C4	− 1906.7471	− 5.5354	0.0000
C5	− 1887.5780	− 5.5008	0.0000
C6	− 1879.4571	− 5.5013	0.0000
C7	− 1881.0074	− 5.5254	0.0000
C8	− 1864.6947	− 5.5119	0.0000
C9	− 1866.5002	− 5.5303	0.0000
C10	− 1854.8213	− 5.5242	0.0000
X1	17.1363	3.3791	0.0010
X2	0.3142	1.6451	0.1024
X3	− 10.0859	− 0.0434	0.9655
X4	− 36.3762	− 1.2165	0.2261
X5	0.3175	6.8399	0.0000
X6	− 2.2852	− 2.0026	0.0474
X7	− 132.2719	− 1.6203	0.1077
X8	− 137.7111	− 2.1060	0.0372
X9	− 15.0322	− 1.5994	0.1123
X10	35.9178	2.3162	0.0222
X11	− 16.7238	− 4.6778	0.0000

Diagnostics

Number of observations	146	
Standard error	8.276	
R-squared	0.600	
$F(21, 125)$	10.952	
Durbin–Watson	1.365	

for the full sample period (March 1979 to January 1992); tables 7.1A and 7.2A contain the estimates over the period from March 1979 to August 1987, while tables 7.1B and 7.2B contain the estimates over the period from September 1987 to January 1992. The breakpoint is the date of the Basle-Nyborg Agreement (12 September 1987), which strengthened the Exchange Rate Mechanism (ERM) of the EMS by adopting a number of measures, including in particular an extension of the use of the Very Short-Term Facility (VSTF) to finance intramarginal intervention.

In the case of Italy, the variables whose coefficients tend to be consis-

Table 7.1A. *One-month IL/DM expected devaluation: subsample regression (March 1979–August 1987)*

Variable	Coefficient	t-value	p-value
C1	− 14.4028	− 1.3763	0.1728
C2	− 15.3171	− 2.2129	0.0299
C3	0.9421	0.1200	0.9048
C4	− 4.4453	− 0.5250	0.6011
C5	10.3016	1.0627	0.2913
C6	16.3915	1.6141	0.1107
C7	8.5724	0.9726	0.3339
C8	8.3708	1.4444	0.1528
X1	− 2.5826	− 0.3716	0.7113
X2	0.2476	1.1476	0.2548
X3	− 84.0405	− 0.2773	0.7823
X4	− 25.2136	− 0.5963	0.5528
X5	0.2575	3.7955	0.0003
X6	− 2.3368	− 1.5094	0.1354
X7	168.4982	1.9147	0.0593
X8	− 134.8374	− 1.5890	0.1163
X9	− 36.6214	− 2.5416	0.0131
X10	− 15.0362	− 0.6736	0.5027
X11	− 23.6028	− 5.0019	0.0000

Diagnostics	
Number of observations	94
Standard error	9.021
R-squared	0.660
$F(19, 75)$	9.025
Durbin–Watson	1.926

tently significant are $X5$ (the position of the exchange rate within the band), and $X11$ (the jump dummy). The coefficient of $X5$ is always positive, indicating that a wider deviation from a central parity increases expectations of exchange rate changes; interestingly, it is not significant in the period since the Basle-Nyborg Agreement. The jump dummy has a large negative coefficient: it indicates that the occurrence of a realignment induces sharp revisions of realignment expectations. The fact that $X11$ is not significant after Basle-Nyborg is not surprising: the realignment of the lira of January 1990 was only due to the narrowing of the fluctuation band of that currency *vis-à-vis* the ERM partners. The coefficient of $X6$, a variable meant to capture learning or reputation effects, while having the

Table 7.1B. *One-month IL/DM expected devaluation: subsample regression (September 1987–January 1992)*

Variable	Coefficient	t-value	p-value
C1	−2461.9933	−2.3181	0.0258
C2	−2450.3973	−2.3079	0.0264
X1	23.7820	1.9628	0.0568
X2	0.8447	0.9837	0.3313
X3	578.5895	1.1309	0.2650
X4	−47.0880	−0.9334	0.3564
X5	0.1773	1.3932	0.1714
X6	−0.4164	−0.1946	0.8467
X7	−437.5687	−1.8085	0.0782
X8	60.1427	0.4709	0.6404
X9	−1.5152	−0.1195	0.9055
X10	37.1790	1.3993	0.1696
X11	−0.6841	−0.0736	0.9417
Diagnostics			
Number of observations	52		
Standard error	7.327		
R-squared	0.389		
$F(13, 39)$	3.097		
Durbin–Watson	1.606		

Notes:
Chow test: $F(11, 104) = 0.42$.
(Not significant at 10% level.)

sign consistent with our prediction, is significant in the full sample, but not in the subsample. The significance and the negative sign of the coefficient of $X6$ imply that a tough exchange rate stance – represented by the lack of recourse to realignment for a long period – seems to improve, other things equal, the reputation of central bankers (that is the credibility of the exchange rate). The two relative price variables ($X7$ and $X8$) are not consistently significant, and not because of a multicollinearity problem (we have also tried to include them separately). Similarly, the relative trade balances, the relative balance of payments, and news about the government borrowing requirements do not appear to have a consistently significant effect on expected devaluations. Table 7.1B reports also the result of a Chow test of stability of all coefficients in the regression. The null hypothesis (no change in coefficients) cannot be rejected at the 10 per cent level.

Table 7.2. *One-month FF/DM expected devaluation: full-sample regression (March 1979–January 1992)*

Variable	Coefficient	t-value	p-value
C1	− 94.9703	− 2.1313	0.0349
C2	− 82.3655	− 1.9334	0.0553
C3	− 89.7503	− 2.1087	0.0369
C4	− 90.3979	− 2.0278	0.0446
C5	− 85.3425	− 1.9027	0.0593
C6	− 95.2443	− 2.1124	0.0365
C7	− 92.7362	− 2.1082	0.0369
X1	4.8058	1.7867	0.0763
X2	− 0.0669	− 0.7473	0.4562
X3	− 42.5179	− 0.4708	0.6385
X4	− 37.0348	− 1.2005	0.2321
X5	0.4033	7.8570	0.0000
X6	− 2.3092	− 2.3581	0.0198
X7	− 89.7591	− 1.4472	0.1502
X8	− 0.5302	− 0.0121	0.9903
X9	− 14.4472	− 1.7393	0.0843
X10	6.2472	0.7804	0.4366
X11	− 16.7481	− 4.1714	0.0000
Diagnostics			
Number of observations	149		
Standard error	6.556		
R-squared	0.727		
$F(18, 131)$	19.832		
Durbin–Watson	1.704		

The results for the case of France are broadly similar to Italy's, with $X5$ and $X11$ being the most significant variables, i.e., the position of the exchange rate within the band and the occurrence of a recent realignment are the most powerful source of revision of expectations. However, the Chow test result reported in table 7.2B suggests a change in parameters (at the 10 per cent significance level) associated with the Basle-Nyborg Agreement.

Tables 7.3 and 7.4 report regression results for one month projections over the whole sample for Italy and France, with slope dummies on $X1$ and $X5$ to capture the effects of Basle-Nyborg. The slope dummies $X12$ and $X13$ are obtained by multiplying $X1$ and $X5$, respectively, by a series that equals zero up to August 1987, and one thereafter. For the one-month horizon,

Table 7.2A. *One-month FF/DM expected devaluation: subsample regression (March 1979–August 1987)*

Variable	Coefficient	t-value	p-value
C1	− 131.0036	− 2.4320	0.0173
C2	− 118.2900	− 2.2938	0.0245
C3	− 119.0431	− 2.3102	0.0235
C4	− 115.7943	− 2.1599	0.0338
C5	− 111.6120	− 2.0643	0.0423
C6	− 121.9509	− 2.2354	0.0282
C7	− 116.1597	− 2.1912	0.0314
X1	4.8840	1.4675	0.1462
X2	0.0480	0.4339	0.6655
X3	− 105.5685	− 0.9619	0.3390
X4	− 17.3126	− 0.4194	0.6760
X5	0.4890	8.2036	0.0000
X6	− 0.4435	− 0.3785	0.7061
X7	− 34.3494	− 0.3766	0.7075
X8	− 76.5843	− 1.0321	0.3052
X9	− 11.3451	− 1.0392	0.3019
X10	3.0994	0.3018	0.7636
X11	− 12.5947	− 2.8750	0.0052
	Diagnostics		
	Number of observations	97	
	Standard error	6.660	
	R-squared	0.815	
	$F(18, 79)$	19.549	
	Durbin–Watson	1.709	

$X12$, the slope dummy on the budget variable is not significant for both Italy and France, while $X13$ is significant and negative for both countries, suggesting that the Basle-Nyborg Agreement on the VSTF may have strengthened central banks' ability to defend the announced parity.

To visualize the projected devaluations arising from the equations we estimated, we plot the predicted values of the regressions, together with the dates of the actual EMS realignments (indicated by the tip of the triangle). Figures 7.1 and 7.2 plot the predicted one-month realignment (expressed in per cent per annum) for the lira/Deutsche mark and the French franc/ Deutsche mark, respectively (the predictions are based on equations whose estimates are in tables 7.3 and 7.4). Interpreting the figures in terms of the

Table 7.2B. *One-month FF/DM expected devaluation: subsample regression (September 1987–January 1992)*

Variable	Coefficient	t-value	p-value
X1	− 5.2332	− 0.8223	0.4153
X2	− 0.2134	− 2.0981	0.0415
X3	31.0167	0.2222	0.8251
X4	− 29.1455	− 0.6056	0.5478
X5	0.2486	1.9240	0.0607
X6	1.9294	0.4337	0.6665
X7	4.4488	0.0753	0.9403
X8	3.1691	0.0541	0.9571
X9	− 11.4794	− 1.0224	0.3120
X10	6.7050	0.4622	0.6462
	Diagnostics		
	Number of observations	55	
	Standard error	5.461	
	R-squared	0.280	
	$F(10, 45)$	2.320	
	Durbin–Watson	1.696	

Notes:
Chow test: $F(10, 111) = 1.7953$
(Significant at 10% level.)

model in section 3, we observe that they imply unambiguously a positive p (perceived probability that the government follows an escape clause policy and does not credibly peg the currency). The figures also show that the market tends to anticipate a realignment in the one-month horizon at all times, though the timing of realignment is not clear. The figures also highlight the importance of the information about the occurrence of the realignment: after the realignment the expected devaluation of the lira and of the franc turn sharply negative.

Another interesting feature of the estimated model – displayed in the figures – is the suggestion that markets do not appear to anticipate parity realignments with great precision for the case of the lira. We observe a variable, but uniformly high, expected rate of devaluation, like a *plateau* without clearly distinguishable spikes prior to actual realignment dates. The case of the franc is a little better, with visible increase of expected devaluation prior to most actual realignment dates.

Table 7.3. *Final regression results with regime dummies: expected one-month IL/DM devaluation (March 1979–January 1992)*

Variable	Coefficient	t-value	p-value
C1	− 2234.6193	− 5.9099	0.0000
C2	− 2220.4165	− 5.9036	0.0000
C3	− 2205.7212	− 5.8850	0.0000
C4	− 2211.7202	− 5.8960	0.0000
C5	− 2188.1945	− 5.8661	0.0000
C6	− 2178.3502	− 5.8622	0.0000
C7	− 2180.4443	− 5.8858	0.0000
C8	− 2163.6365	− 5.8735	0.0000
C9	− 2163.4252	− 5.8960	0.0000
C10	− 2155.2886	− 5.8945	0.0000
X1	24.9478	3.0986	0.0024
X2	0.3161	1.6642	0.0986
X3	105.7217	0.4475	0.6553
X4	− 29.8348	− 0.9982	0.3202
X5	0.4028	6.4406	0.0000
X6	− 1.6284	− 1.3928	0.1662
X7	− 184.0180	− 2.1808	0.0311
X8	− 130.3749	− 2.0043	0.0472
X9	− 17.8441	− 1.8932	0.0607
X10	25.9283	1.6177	0.1083
X11	− 12.7760	− 3.1744	0.0019
X12	− 5.9188	− 0.9048	0.3673
X13	− 0.2374	− 2.0278	0.0447

Diagnostics	
Number of observations	146
Standard error	8.188
R-squared	0.614
$F(23, 123)$	10.419
Durbin–Watson	1.367

For comparison, figures 7.1A and 7.2A report the observed one-month interest rate differentials. While there are more visible spikes, the timing does not seem to be precise. Another noteworthy feature of figures 7.1A and 7.2A is the familiar evidence on interest rate convergence for both countries (relative to Germany) over time. This evidence, however, is not accompanied by drastic decline of realignment expectations in figures 7.1 and 7.2, although the variability of the expected devaluation has decreased over time.

Table 7.4. *Final regression results with regime dummies: expected one-month FF/DM devaluation (March 1979–January 1992)*

Variable	Coefficient	t-value	p-value
C1	− 110.3343	− 2.3281	0.0215
C2	− 97.2834	− 2.1475	0.0336
C3	− 103.2564	− 2.2860	0.0239
C4	− 105.0443	− 2.2409	0.0267
C5	− 101.6565	− 2.1525	0.0332
C6	− 110.2595	− 2.3015	0.0230
C7	− 107.0765	− 2.2802	0.0242
X1	4.2407	1.4416	0.1518
X2	− 0.0239	− 0.2673	0.7896
X3	− 37.8129	− 0.4283	0.6692
X4	− 29.7435	− 0.9654	0.3361
X5	0.4608	8.5177	0.0000
X6	− 1.4389	− 1.4185	0.1585
X7	− 109.3822	− 1.7864	0.0764
X8	5.9590	0.1362	0.8919
X9	− 13.6811	− 1.6844	0.0945
X10	4.8161	0.6003	0.5493
X11	− 13.0836	− 3.1401	0.0021
X12	0.0154	0.0048	0.9962
X13	− 0.3485	− 2.7126	0.0076

	Diagnostics		
	Number of observations	149	
	Standard error	6.404	
	R-squared	0.744	
	$F(20, 129)$	19.123	
	Durbin–Watson	1.716	

5 Concluding remarks

In this chapter we have presented a methodology to explore the relation between expectations of parity changes and economic variables. This methodology accounts for the expectation of exchange rate changes within fluctuation bands, and therefore should in principle yield more precise estimates of expected parity changes. In order to evaluate the performance of an adjustable parity system like the EMS it is tempting to assess whether the expectations of parity changes which we estimate in this chapter appear, according to various different criteria, to be rational. Some of our observations in the previous section were indeed motivated by that question.

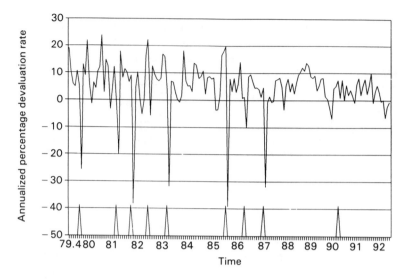

Figure 7.1 One-month expected devaluation: IL/DM

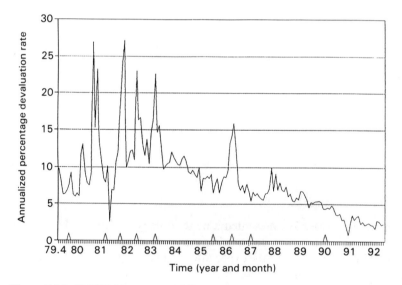

Figure 7.1A IL/DM interest rate differential (1 month)

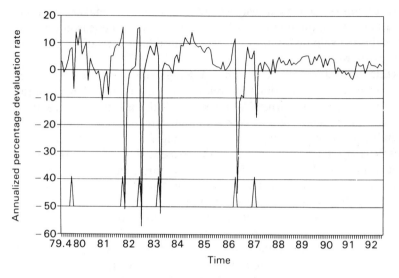

Figure 7.2 One-month expected devaluation: FF/DM

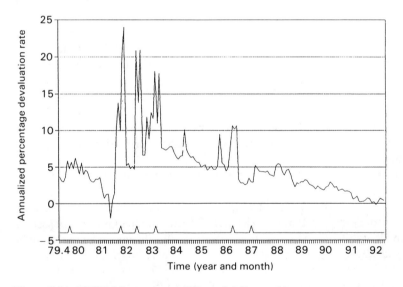

Figure 7.2A FF/DM interest rate differential (1 month)

However, one of the reasons why we did not assume rational expectations of parity changes, the small size of our sample, is also the reason why it is impossible to evaluate formally the proposition that expectations of parity changes are rational.

In this concluding section we want to highlight a couple of characteristics of our estimates that we think are relevant for the current debate on the viability of adjustable parities' systems. In this discussion we concentrate on one-month data, since they presumably are the best indicators of impending realignments: expected parity changes over longer horizons are necessarily affected by more variables than expectations of short-run parity changes, because the passage of time allows more things to happen (that more variables explain expectations of parity changes over longer horizons is borne out by the empirical results in this chapter).

The two most important results of our regressions are the significance of the variable representing the per cent deviation of the exchange rate from the centre of the band, and the large turnaround of expected parity changes after realignments. According to the widely held view that the band has a stabilizing effect, we should find a negative coefficient, but we find the opposite. This could be consistent with herd-like behaviour in the foreign exchange markets, which however is not necessarily inconsistent with rational expectations. The size and significance of the dummy variable representing the recent occurrence of a realignment is also not inconsistent with the presence of a sort of 'overspeculation' in the European foreign exchange markets. The estimates of expected parity changes after realignments are always negative – the Deutsche mark is to be devalued relative to the lira and the franc – and large. Since the event of a devaluation of the mark relative to the other two currencies does not, in our opinion, belong to the state space, we are tempted to interpret the large negative expectations of realignment after realignments as another form of overreaction by financial markets.

In general, the data at our disposal do not seem to provide evidence in support of the theory that adjustable parity systems are 'stable'. Indeed, two of the most consistent empirical facts we uncovered – discussed heretofore – suggest that the existence of fluctuation bands does not seem to provide stabilization of private expectations. While our evidence cannot be considered conclusive, it adds to other empirical regularities that characterize adjustable parity systems, the most prominent of which is perhaps the so-called 'capital inflow problem'. Our results, and the capital inflow problem all indicate inherent instabilities of adjustable parity systems. Two extensions of the present study are, in our view, possible and worthwhile. The first is a study of higher frequency data, which rather than published economic series uses announcements of all the variables that might belong

to agents' information sets. A second extension would be a structural estimation of a model, like the one we have sketched in section 3. We regard the results of this chapter encouraging, and hence we view these two extensions as promising.

Notes

1 Giovannini (1992) found evidence of market inaction to nearly fully anticipated events in the short-term Euro-Swiss interest rate data.
2 If the exogenous shock is identically and independently distributed, it is easy to evaluate the indirect objective function of the authorities, and quantify the loss due to the phenomenon of 'dynamic inconsistency'.
3 The sources of the data are the following:
Exchange rates: *Financial Times*. End of month observation.
Interest rates: *Financial Times*. Eurodeposit rates. End of month observation.
Interest rates:
External position:
> Germany: Bundesbank external position. *Monthly Report*, table 12. Measured in millions of Deutsche mark.
> France: Banque de France, *Quarterly Bulletin*, table 10, Counterparties of M3. Measured in billions of French franc.
> Italy: Banca d'Italia net external position, *Economic Bulletin*. Measured in billions of Italian lira.

Budget surplus/deficit:
> Italy: Treasury borrowing requirement. Banca d'Italia.
> Germany: Federal finance on a cash basis. Data Resources, Inc.
> France: Public authority financial deficit (national accounts). INSEE Comptes et Indicateurs Economiques.

Trade balance: OECD.
Industrial production: OECD. Index 1985 = 100.
Consumer prices: OECD. Index 1985 = 100.
Wages:
> Italy: Contract wages. International Financial Statistics.
> Germany: Monthly wage and salary rate in the overall economy. Datastream International, Inc.
> France: Labour costs. International Financial Statistics.

Liquidity:
> Germany and Italy: Liquidity of deposit banks line 20, IFS.
> France: M1, IFS.

References

Barro, R. J. and D.B. Gordon 1983. 'A Positive Theory of Monetary Policy in a Natural Rate Model', *Journal of Political Economy*, 91.

Cassard, M. 1992. 'A Positive Theory of Monetary and Exchange-Rate Policy with Overlapping Wages', mimeo, Columbia University.

Cetorelli, N. 1992. 'La speculazione sulla lira e le attese di un riallineamento delle parità nello SME', in *Ricerche applicate e modelli per la politica economica*, Roma, Banca d'Italia.

Chen, Z. and Giovannini A. 1992. 'Estimating Expected Exchange Rates under Target Zones', mimeo, Columbia University.

Collins, S.M. 1984. 'Exchange Rate Expectations and Interest Parity During Credibility Crises. The French Franc, March 1983', *Discussion Paper*, 1080, Harvard Institute of Economic Research.

1986. *The Expected Timing of Devaluation: A Model of Realignment in the European Monetary System*, Harvard University Press.

Flood, R.P. and Garber P. 1984. 'Collapsing Exchange Rate Regimes. Some Linear Examples', *Journal of International Economics*, 17.

Flood, R.P. and Isard P. 1990. 'Monetary Policy Strategies – A Correction: Reply to Lohmann', *IMF Staff Papers*, 37.

Friedman, M. 1968. 'The Role of Monetary Policy', *American Economic Review*, 58.

Giovannini, A. 1990. 'European Monetary Reform: Progress and Prospects', *Brookings Papers on Economic Activity*, 2.

1992. 'Monetary Policy, Liquidity and Foreign Exchange Markets: an Exploration', mimeo, Columbia University.

Lizondo, J.S. 1983. 'Foreign Exchange Futures Prices under Fixed Exchange Rates', *Journal of International Economics*, 14.

Lohmann, S. 1990. 'Monetary Policy Strategies – A Correction', *IMF Staff Papers*, 37.

Rose, A.K. and Svensson, L.E.O. 1991. 'Expected and Predicted Realignments: The FF/DM Exchange Rate During the EMS', *IIES Seminar Paper*, 485, University of Stockholm.

Simons, H.C. 1936. 'Rules versus Authorities in Monetary Policy', *Journal of Political Economy*, 44.

Svensson, L.E.O. 1990. 'The Foreign Exchange Risk Premium in a Target Zone With Devaluation Risk', mimeo, Stockholm, IIES.

1991. 'Assessing Target-Zone Credibility: Mean Reversion and Devaluation Expectations in the EMS', *IIES Seminar Paper*, 493, University of Stockholm.

Discussion

LUIGI SPAVENTA

This chapter provides a relevant and interesting contribution to a crucial problem of economic theory and policy. Consider that popular oxymoron of international economics: fixed but adjustable parities. Is such a regime stable or is it destined to end up in uncontrolled convulsions? For orderly adjustments to be an exception, compatible with the rule of peaceful and reasonably long intervals of fixity, they should be the outcome of timely discretion, undisturbed by market pressures and not affecting market sentiments. But this, as shown by a bulk of literature in related fields, is not possible if agents, on the one hand, anticipate the reasons for a dis- cretionary change of parities, while, on the other, regard any such change as a precedent pointing to further moves in the same direction. What are then the factors affecting agents' expectations? The authors make a bold attempt to provide a quantitative answer to this latter question, considering the exchange rate experience of the Italian lira and the French franc with respect to the Deutsche mark in the Exchange Rate Mechanism (ERM).

Before setting down to this relevant task, the authors feel compelled – more by convention, one suspects, than by conviction – to present an exchange rate change version of the overfamiliar Barro–Gordon model, with the usual slightly maniac authorities wanting to fool the market and take a short-lived trip along a short-run Phillips curve. They only add to the picture a probability, q, that a shock occurs, and a probability, p, that the authorities react to the shock with a parity change. It seems to me that, in view of the more important analysis in the rest of the chapter, the exercise is needless and may even be misleading. One does not need that model to conclude, as the authors do, that the expectations of a realignment increase with p and q. Moreover, the experience of the ERM is one of growing convergence of monetary policies and of countries being compelled to devalue rather than wanting to devalue. Finally, and more importantly, the variables considered in the empirical part as potentially affecting expec- tations have nothing to do with the model which is supposed to interpret parity changes: it is hard to see how the empirical results presented by the

authors can be made compatible with the particular piece of theory they illustrate.

The strategy followed in the empirical part is conceptually simple and convincing. From interest rate parity, the expected parity change must equal the interest rate differential minus the expectation of movements of the exchange rate within the band, conditional on no realignment occurring in the period. A vector of variables that may conceivably enter in the agents' information set is then regressed on this measure of expected devaluation to see which of them is relevant for explaining the latter. The problem of course is how to measure expected changes within the band which are independent of expected parity changes. The authors take the observed changes in the relevant time interval (one month and three months), eliminating the observation corresponding to each realignment and that prior to the realignment. Under rational expectations, the expectation error will be orthogonal to the explanatory variables entering the information set. This procedure has its drawbacks: first, movements within the band may reflect a change in market sentiments regarding the parity; second, floating within the band is often managed, as witnessed by frequent and often sizable intramarginal interventions. The error due to mismeasurement of expectations may thus be quite large. It is, on the other hand, difficult to see how to improve upon the method used in the chapter. A tentative suggestion may be to use Svensson's 'simple test' of credibility, according to which expected changes of the central parity are measured by the excess of the interest rate differential over the difference between the band's limit and the spot rate – the presumption being that, if the parity is credible, a depreciation within the band should narrow the interest rate differential.

I now turn to the variables which, in the authors' view, are candidates for entering the agents' information set. Among such variables there are those somehow reflecting fundamentals and those proxying credibility. There is a rather odd assortment in the first group. While it is plausible to presume that agents should consider relative wage and price inflation, or relative liquidity, or the mark/dollar exchange rate, why – and how – should their expectations be affected by the differences (Italy or France minus Germany) of foreign exchange reserves, or of budget surpluses, or of trade surpluses? First, what is the economic rationale behind taking the differences with respect to Germany, rather than the individual country's level? Second, in the case of the budget variable, one would expect that it matters less or more according to whether the level of debt is low or high. Third, there is no reason to consider the trade rather than the current account position, as it is on the latter and not on the former that a country's net foreign indebtedness depends.

These queries are however of little relevance, as the tests show that practically none of these fundamental variables is significant, while the signs are often the opposite of those one would expect and change inexplicably in the different experiments (one month without regime dummies, full sample and two subsamples, one month and three months full sample with regime dummies). Relative liquidity appears to be significant for the three-month expected lira devaluation: but in this case (as in the other experiments) it appears with a negative sign, meaning that when liquidity increases in Italy relative to Germany the expectation of a devaluation of the lira central parity decreases. In the end, the stage is occupied almost entirely by three 'credibility' variables: the position of the exchange rate within the band, by itself or multiplied by a slope dummy, taking the value one before the Basle-Nyborg Agreement and zero afterwards; the time elapsed since the last realignment: and a jump dummy, taking the value one at the first month of realignment and zero otherwise.

The authors' evidence seems to indicate that, in general, a wider deviation from the central parity increases expectations of parity changes: after Basle-Nyborg however the variable becomes not significant and changes its sign when multiplied by the slope dummy in the one-month case. These results raise some interesting problems. First, one wonders whether the authors have somehow controlled for the fact that the lira, unlike the franc, was allowed to float in a wider band until the beginning of 1990: with a different band's width, a meaningful comparison should consider the distance from the band's limit rather than from the central parity. Second, with the increase in credibility after 1987, both in Italy and in France the position of the exchange rate within the band was often used as an auxiliary instrument of monetary policy. With a credible central parity an appreciation (depreciation) within the band induces expectations of an opposite movement, thus allowing higher (lower) interest rates. The relatively long period in which the franc was at the bottom and the lira in the upper part of the band probably reflects the authorities' intention to keep interest rates at a relatively low level in France and at a relatively high level in Italy, for domestic purposes. But when, as also noted earlier, the position of the exchange rate in the band is itself a policy variable, its use as an explanatory variable may be subject to qualifications. The jump dummy is almost always significantly negative and with a high value. Why the authors attribute this to 'overspeculation' in, and 'overreaction' by, foreign exchange markets is not clear. After a devaluation, as speculative positions are closed, the exchange rate usually appreciates sensibly within the new band while the interest rate differential falls: expectations, if measured by the difference between the interest differential and the actual movement within the band, may thus improve dramatically relative to earlier obser-

vations. One final query. The authors plot the projected parity changes arising from the estimated equations. Their graphs display extremely high values of expected devaluations (even in the range of 10–20 per cent for the lira and sometimes above 10 per cent for the franc) and great volatility. To know how plausible these projections are, however, it would be helpful to have some information on the residuals, or at least to have the values of the adopted measure of expected devaluation plotted along the projected values.

In conclusion, the chapter by Chen and Giovannini is a valuable and stimulating contribution to the knowledge of the working of the ERM – as it was. Though it leaves many problems unsolved, it points to new directions of research. In view of what has happened in the Fall of 1992, one wonders whether further research can be of more than historical interest.

Discussion

NIELS THYGESEN

Can fixed but adjustable exchange rates be made credible? This is the general question addressed by the authors in the very specific format of the European Monetary System (EMS). And along with others I take their main conclusion to be yes. Other investigators have confined themselves initially to looking at what can be inferred from simple observations of exchange rates and interest rate differentials. If we look for example at the April 1992 report of the Committee of Central Bank Governors covering the first eighteen months of the first stage of European Monetary Union (EMU), we find some charts that suggest that the forward exchange rates of several currencies *vis-à-vis* the Deutsche mark, had moved inside the bands in recent years. For the Dutch guilder this has been the case for a number of years, for the Belgian franc it occurred from mid 1990, for certain other currencies more recently. This simple measure suggests an increased credibility that the exchange rate bands will remain around existing central rates.

One can go beyond this kind of simple illustration in a number of ways; one would be to include in the calculations of credibility mean reversion (to the central rate) as suggested by Svensson (and quoted by Chen and Giovannini) in a series of papers and discussed already by Spaventa. That would be particularly relevant if one has a longer time horizon, going all the way to the time – 1996 or 1998 – when exchange rates would become fully fixed, presumably at the present central rates. One could also try to introduce direct measures of exchange rate expectations, following the lead of Frankel, and more specifically of Frankel and Phillips (1992). A third and more ambitious possibility is taken up by the authors: they try to explain the implicit expected devaluation in the EMS with the help of a number of macroeconomic variables and here the authors have done an admirable job in beginning this analysis with their study of France and Italy. I shall skip going through the variables where I think the authors have used considerable ingenuity, though I share the reservations of Spaventa about using differences between say national budget deficits rather than strictly national variables. Of course, from an empirical point of view, the

197

results are somewhat disappointing because few of the variables are anywhere near being significant in explaining the implied devaluation expectations. Maybe they could have used a more aggregate approach. Taking up a suggestion by Williamson, the departure of an exchange rate in the EMS from its fundamental equilibrium value could have comprised several of the macroeconomic indicators used in the Chen–Giovannini paper. The authors set up a number of variables that indicate symptoms of overvaluation of a currency, relative cost levels, trade balances, relative output levels, relative public deficits, etc. I share the surprise of Spaventa that no monetary variables have been used, except the position of the currency in the band. The data are well presented, though I have one small reservation: the two subperiods identified may not be quite enough to give due emphasis to the evolution of the EMS. The long period from 1979 to 1987 is not fully homogeneous; realignments became more infrequent after March 1983, so a break into two subperiods around that time might give further evidence of value to the authors.

I would like to focus on two subjects that are not addressed adequately in the chapter. The first is the link of the discussion in the chapter to the criteria in the Maastricht Treaty which will be used in the second half of the 1990s to assess whether a member state is ready for full economic and monetary union. The second is the discussion of the position of a currency in the band.

The Maastricht Treaty prescribes for the transition a number of criteria that will have to be met in order for countries to be admitted to the third stage; relative inflation measured by consumer price indices, the size of budget deficit, the level of debt, stability of the exchange rate over a period of two years prior to the decision to start stage three, and long-term interest rate convergence. If the two authors had published their chapter while the intergovernmental conference was working in 1991, I think they would have produced an interesting input, viz. to ask: What are the criteria that markets have watched in the past in assessing whether exchange rates are credible?

In that perspective it is interesting that the authors find that the only variable which has some significance in some periods in explaining devaluation expectations is relative output levels. I have a third rationalization for the inclusion of this variable beyond the two that Spaventa suggested: if there is a relative decline in output, say in France or Italy, it is an indication that the political will to sustain the present parities may be fading. This is in fact a feature of the domestic political debate in several member states: a decline in relative output is in that sense the symptom of an overvalued currency as policymakers normally perceive it. The Maastricht Treaty did not include among its criteria any reference to the output or the employment level. Personally I regret that because I think it would have conveyed

information about the sustainability of an exchange rate structure to determine whether convergence with respect to the other indicators has been achieved by means of a temporary (or longer-drawn out) recession, as appears to be the case in some countries of the European Community (EC). Hence Chen and Giovannini supply an argument for saying that the Maastricht convergence criteria are not as comprehensive as they should have been. Be that as it may, the Treaty was signed in its present form. Assuming the criteria will be applied, they are what the markets will watch in the future. Policymakers have essentially said to the markets: this is what we will look at in 1996 or at some other date when we are to decide on the entry into the third stage. Though these criteria may also reflect what markets have been concerned about in the past there is now a new element because these criteria have been singled out. They should therefore be the focus of any subsequent extension of the chapter by the two authors.

My second point relates to the importance of the position of a currency in the band. The two authors, of course, give due importance to the Basle-Nyborg Agreement of 1987. The Agreement was a judicious compromise: it did include larger financial facilities – that is the one point the authors mention – but the EC Central Bank Governors' Report of April 1992 gives a different flavour: the Agreement implies, first, more active and coordinated use of interest rates; second, availability of the Very Short-Term Facility (VSTF) also for intramarginal interventions; and, third, more active use also of the fluctuation band as an absorption mechanism. This last point would appear important for the authors to discuss, because of the inclusion in the Agreement of the principle derived from the observation that, prior to the January 1987 realignment, there had been discontinuities in market exchange rates surrounding realignments. Jumps in market exchange rates were felt to have increased the speculative build-up prior to realignments, by creating one-way speculative options similar to what existed under the Bretton Woods system. One consequence of countries using the greater flexibility within the bands is that countries that allow their currencies to drift towards the floor, risk that this may be taken as a signal that they are preparing for a realignment. They gain, however, if they succeed in minimizing that risk, because as long as market participants expect on average that the currency will appreciate, this anticipated mean reversion back to the centre of the band will permit a lower interest rate than otherwise. If so, that would be a recipe not only for eliminating interest differentials relative to Germany but even for driving non-German rates below German levels.

There have been interesting developments and contrasts in the EMS in this respect. The Dutch and Belgian currencies have been managed close to the centre of the band for some time, the Danish and French currencies

more towards the bottom of the band. In the French case, however, there was an undeclared revision of that policy in recent months, back to the centre of the bands presumably in the belief that this was the best way of assuring that complete interest rate convergence with Germany could take place. The subject of the narrowing of the bands and the different strategies followed by different countries in the so-called hard core of the EMS would be an excellent topic to take up in an extended version of the chapter. In this regard I would like to make two simple points: the first is that among the possible extensions a study of other currencies in the EMS would come high on my list. Secondly, the emphasis on different strategies inside the band might be more productive than use of daily or other high-frequency data.

As a final point I would say that I expected the authors to mention what lessons for the international monetary system could be drawn from the experience of the EMS. I had in mind the excellent final chapter of the book by Giavazzi and Giovannini (1989) which looks at this broader question. There the two authors discuss to what extent the EMS is exportable to the rest of the world, as asymmetry was apparently fading in the EMS, and I looked forward to an update of that interesting discussion, obviously with much less weight on capital controls and asymmetry than in 1989 when that chapter was written. With more symmetry and hardly any capital controls, the EMS countries have found the system to be potentially unstable. Chen and Giovannini may go too far in saying that the Delors Report implicitly accepted this instability of a fixed-but-adjustable exchange rate system and justified economic and monetary union with this argument. The Delors Committee was not asked to justify economic and monetary union; that was an objective that was handed to the Committee while asking it to study how it could be achieved. You could not expect by any stretch of imagination the central bankers who manage the EMS to suggest that it was really unstable, though there was a recognition that it would become more stable as one moved to fully fixed rates and soon thereafter to a single currency.

References

Frankel, J.A. and Phillips, S. 1992. 'The European Monetary System: Credible at Last?', in F. Torres and F. Giavazzi (eds.), *The Transition to Economic and Monetary Union in Europe*, Cambridge, Cambridge University Press.

Giavazzi, F. and Giovannini A. 1989. *Limiting Exchange Rate Flexibility – The European Monetary System*, Cambridge Mass., MIT Press.

8   Concerted interventions and the dollar: an analysis of daily data

PIETRO CATTE, GIAMPAOLO GALLI, and SALVATORE
REBECCHINI

1 Introduction

A decade ago several studies of the scope and effectiveness of foreign exchange intervention were undertaken within a working group of the major industrial countries chaired by Ph. Jurgensen (1983). The final report's conclusions were very cautiously stated. Overall, (sterilized) intervention was not viewed as an independent instrument of economic policy, in the sense in which this term is usually applied to monetary or fiscal policy; it was nonetheless seen as a useful complement to more fundamental policy tools, especially in the very short run.[1]

In the years following the publication of the Jurgensen Report, important changes have taken place in the international monetary system. Starting in 1985, coordinated efforts were made first to reverse and later (with the Louvre Agreement of February 1987) to stabilize the value of the dollar. Broadly speaking, 1985 marks a shift from a system of almost complete flexibility to a managed float. Intervention has played an important role; indeed, it has been argued that, in view of the authorities' greater control over this instrument, the commitments of the Group of Seven (G-7) in the area of foreign exchange intervention have been much more specific than in the domain of macro or structural policies (Dobson 1991). In view of these developments, it is important to determine the circumstances in which intervention is likely to be effective and how it can affect the functioning of the international monetary system. This chapter uses daily data from 1985 on the interventions of sixteen central banks participating in the 'concertation procedure'.[2] The focus is on the exchange rate of the dollar *vis-à-vis* the Deutsche mark and the yen. Using the methodology explained in section 2, we identify nineteen episodes in which there is evidence that intervention was coordinated among at least two of the three major countries. We then look at the behaviour of exchange rates, interest rates, and other potentially relevant variables in each of these episodes to assess whether intervention was effective.

The chapter is organized as follows. In section 2 we explain the methodology and the definition of intervention; in particular, we clarify the criteria adopted to identify episodes of coordinated intervention. In section 3 we summarize the main findings and in section 4 we assess the role of intervention in determining the major turning points in dollar rates. In section 5 we pool the evidence and assess the relative effectiveness of intervention and other policy tools in a variety of circumstances. Section 6 concludes with a view that is rather different from that of the Jurgensen Report.

2 Methodology: selection of the episodes and measurement of intervention

In principle, it should be possible to use econometrics to identify the effects of intervention on exchange rates by defining a model in which the exchange rate depends on a set of 'fundamental' variables as well as on intervention. It is well known, however, that such a model does not exist, or at any rate has not yet been found. The simple random walk model of Meese and Rogoff (1983) predicts exchange rates very poorly, but no worse than models which include contemporaneous variables, as well as measures of expectations, on the right-hand side. Simultaneity, measurement errors and other more fundamental problems (which we examine later) give rise to incorrectly signed or insignificant coefficients, low R-squared, and poor out of sample performance. As noted by Dornbusch and Frankel (1987), 'econometrically, all the action is in the error term'; even measures of actual or anticipated monetary policy do not improve regression results. For these reasons, which have been widely recognized in earlier studies of intervention (see, for instance, Dominguez 1989), we adopt a different approach and identify episodes in which interventions appear to have been coordinated among the largest countries and assess their impact on the exchange rate of the dollar (against the Deutsche mark and the yen) on a case by case basis. Though the focus is on sterilized intervention, no attempt is made to select episodes on the (statistically rather shaky) basis of whether offsetting operation were undertaken on the domestic market;[3] we prefer to look at the behaviour of interest rates in each of the selected episodes.

Our selection procedure is based on three important facts concerning the intervention policies of the United States, Japan, and Germany (Group of Three) (see figure 8.1).:

(1) Interventions by the Group of Three (G-3) are rare and concentrated in time. Between 1985 and 1991, each G-3 central bank was on the market for less than one out of six trading days, though with very different quantities; the average daily gross intervention ranged between $130 million and $300 million.

(2) The three countries never pursued conflicting intervention policies *vis-à-vis* the dollar.[4] Whenever one of the three was in the market, the other two were doing either the same thing or nothing. This can be seen clearly in figure 8.1 which shows that when, for example, the intervention figures of the Federal Reserve are positive (purchases of foreign assets), the other two central banks have either negative figures or zero.

(3) The timing of the clusters almost always coincides for at least two of the three countries. The major exceptions are in 1986, when there was considerable intervention by Japan or Germany alone, and in 1990 and 1991, when there were also some cases of non-simultaneous intervention by these two countries.

Given these features, it would be easy to identify the episodes of concerted intervention by inspection. However, we use the following quantitative criteria, which in fact give very similar results, but are more precise: (i) at least two of the G-3 central banks start to intervene together; (ii) at least one of these three central banks continues to intervene with interruptions lasting no more than five working days. Moreover, to avoid dealing with insignificant episodes, we have utilized a *de minimis* rule whereby daily interventions of 20 million dollars and less are disregarded, as are episodes that do not include at least two (not necessarily consecutive) days of simultaneous intervention or that do not last more than four working days. Criterion (i) defines the opening date of an episode. There are cases in which one central bank was in the market in the preceding days, but we consider that intervention becomes concerted when at least one other G-3 bank joins in. Criterion (ii) defines the closing date of the episode. This occurs when all G-3 central banks abstain from intervening for more than five working days.[5] All told, nineteen episodes (shown in figure 8.1) have been identified covering a total of 461 days; as can be seen, there is little intervention by the G-3 taking place outside these episodes (about 20 per cent for Germany and Japan and 5 per cent for the United States).

Clearly, our procedure is based on a minimal criterion for coordination. It leaves open a large number of issues concerning the degree of coordination among both G-3 and non-G-3 central banks. In the analysis of the episodes, we report whether all G-3 central banks (rather than just two of them) took action, what non-G-3 central banks did, and the amounts of each currency that were put on the market. We also try to assess the extent to which intervention was supported by domestic policies and/or by consistent statements by the authorities.[6]

In eighteen of the nineteen episodes the authorities countered the trend of the dollar ('leaning against the wind'). It is therefore relatively easy to judge whether the action was successful simply by looking at the exchange rate in the weeks following the intervention. If the trend was reversed, we label the

episode as successful.[7] There were however different degrees of success, depending on whether the trend was temporarily or definitely reversed. Here again, we adopt a simple criterion to discriminate between these two possibilities. We label an episode as definitely successful if it reversed the trend and, in the next episode, intervention was in the opposite direction.[8] This is a rather restrictive criterion since an episode may have been definitely successful, but followed by events that reversed the trend and induced central banks to intervene again in the same direction. Such an occurrence is difficult to evaluate on objective grounds, so we treat it informally, on a judgmental basis, in the description of the episodes.[9]

To take account of the fact that interventions may involve one or both of the currencies whose relative price we are interested in, we construct a synthetic variable that is reported in all the figures, except figure 8.1. In the case of the dollar/mark rate, the variable is defined as

$$Y = \frac{(\text{purchases of dollars} - \text{purchases of marks})}{2}$$

where the purchases are on a net basis and refer to either the entire universe of sixteen central banks in our sample or to the G-3.[10] The key assumption underlying this definition is that interventions in third currencies have the same effect (on the mark/dollar rate) whether they are done against dollars or against Deutsche marks; by implication, a direct exchange of dollars against Deutsche marks is worth twice as much as an exchange of either dollars or Deutsche marks against a third currency. When the Y variable is defined over the entire sample of central banks, the implicit assumption is that, given the currency composition and amounts of interventions, operations by third countries have the same effect as those of the United States or Germany.

3 The results

The nineteen episodes identified with the methodology described in the previous section are summarized in table 8.1, in figures 8.2 and 8.3 (which show weekly data for the periods 1984–6 and 1987–91), and figures 8.1 and 8.6 (daily data for each year after 1985). All the episodes were public knowledge in the sense that the interventions were reported in the financial press at the time.

The main findings of our analysis can be summarized as follows:
(a) The amount of intervention during the episodes varied considerably; the total dollar equivalent operations undertaken by all central banks (column 11 of table 8.1) ranged from less than $2 billion in episode 5 to over $35 billion in episode 4 (which followed the Louvre Agreement of

Table 8.1. *Summary of intervention episodes*

Episode	Start	End	Dollar purch. (+) or sale (−)	Number of working days	Percentage of days with simultaneous interventions by		Total G-3 purchases of			All central banks		Results	
					G-3	2 of G-3	$	DM	Yen	Total $ purchases (1)	Net/gross (2)	(3)	(4)
1	850201	850307	−	25	0.16	0.48	−4,039	3,464	560	−8,728	0.96	TS	139
2	850924	851108	−	33	0.36	0.67	−7,754	3,171	4,583	−11,901	0.87	DS	288
3	870107	870126	+	14	0.00	0.29	8,785	−3,900	−8,287	10,550	0.80	TS	41
4	870324	870505	+	29	0.17	0.59	20,723	−594	−20,129	38,511	0.85	DS	67
5	870806	870811	−	4	0.00	0.75	−869	869	0	−1,979	0.62	DS	13
6	870828	870909	+	9	0.11	0.56	1,538	−340	−1,198	2,908	0.89	TS	35
7	871028	871111	+	11	0.55	0.73	8,078	−2,595	−5,483	10,542	0.79	TS	13
8	871130	880121	+	35	0.31	0.43	8,970	−3,248	−5,722	19,223	0.82	TS	46
9	880325	880420	+	18	0.06	0.33	2,267	−390	−1,877	4,939	0.70	DS	47
10	880627	880825	−	43	0.00	0.49	−11,366	11,365	0	−21,311	0.87	DS	47
11	881031	881202	+	24	0.08	0.38	5,722	−988	−4,734	8,175	0.67	DS	22
12	890105	890206	−	21	0.00	0.52	−3,355	3,355	0	−5,898	0.79	TS	29
13	890317	890411	−	18	0.00	0.22	−1,453	1,238	130	−1,987	0.44	TS	13
14	890502	890721	−	59	0.10	0.53	−26,659	6,124	20,534	−35,230	0.82	TS	15
15	890811	891012	−	44	0.27	0.57	−13,079	3,579	9,420	−19,424	0.73	TS	53
16	900102	900119	−	14	0.00	0.29	−3,507	50	3,457	−4,040	0.57	TS	25
17	900223	900419	−	39	0.10	0.31	−12,627	890	11,738	−12,535	0.67	DS	200
18	910204	910212	+	7	0.00	0.57	1,612	−6,612	0	3,211	0.97	DS	19
19	910311	910328	−	14	0.14	0.43	−2,944	1,684	1,260	−6,555	0.90	DS	n.a.

Notes:

(1) Millions of dollars.

(2) Ratio of net interventions to sum of interventions in absolute value.

(3) TS = Temporarily successful (next episode is of the same sign); DS = Definitely successful (next episode is of opposite sign).

(4) Number of working days before next episode.

February 1987). The length of the episodes also varied significantly (from one week to three months); however, no clear relationship has been found between the effectiveness of episodes and their size or length.

(b) In most episodes the bulk of interventions was carried out by two of the G-3 central banks, one of which was the Federal Reserve (except for episode 3 in January 1987); of the 461 days covered by the nineteen episodes only sixty-six saw all the G-3 intervene simultaneously; non-G-3 central banks were generally cooperative, but in several cases (episodes 5, 11, 13, 16, 17) some of them acted at cross-purposes (see column 12 of table 8.1).

(c) All of the episodes were successful in the sense that interventions inverted the trend of the dollar and, in the case of the post-Plaza episode (episode 2), caused its fall to resume; in nine cases they were definitely successful, in the sense that in the next episode intervention was in the opposite direction (see column 13 of table 8.1). Figure 8.6 shows that of the remaining ten episodes (which we have labelled as temporarily successful) three had very short-lived effects lasting no more than three weeks (episodes 7, 13, and 14), while the remaining episodes (1, 3, 6, 8, 12, 15, and 16) should probably be considered as successful *tout court* because their effects either lasted for several months or were interrupted by minor rebounds that induced central banks to intervene again in the same direction (see section 4).

(d) All the major turning points of the dollar (except for that in July 1991)[11] coincided exactly with episodes of concerted intervention. This finding will be examined in more detail in section 4.

(e) In the majority of the episodes very short-term interest rate differentials (those that are most directly affected by short-run liquidity conditions and, therefore, by intervention – if not sterilized) moved according to the exchange rate objective pursued by the authorities (i.e., helped the interventions); however, in several cases they did not change or even moved in the wrong direction; there were five such occurrences in the case of the United States–Germany differential and five in the case of the United States–Japan differential (table 8.2). This is also true for differentials at longer maturities, which also moved in the wrong direction on several occasions (table 8.2; see in particular episodes 1, 6, 8, 10, 12, 13, 17, and 18).[12]

All things considered, the degree of coordination was probably higher than is usually perceived: almost all G-3 interventions took place during the nineteen concerted episodes and were never at cross-purposes; non-G-3 central banks were usually cooperative. However, coordination was clearly partial: in no less than eleven episodes one of the G-3 was either absent or intervened for token amounts.

Table 8.2. *Movement of interest rate differentials during intervention episodes (in per cent)*

Episode	Start	End	Dollar purch. (+) or sale (−)	Particip. central banks	Changes in discount rates		Δ Overnight rate differential (1)		Δ Short-term differentials (2)		Δ Long-term differentials (3)	
							US–Ger.	US–Jap.	US–Ger.	US–Jap.	US–Ger.	US–Jap.
1	850201	850307	−	US, G, J			−0.72	−0.44	0.82	1.12	0.30	0.12
2	850924	851108	−	US, G, J.			0.17	−0.68	−0.31	−1.37	−0.67	−1.39
3	870107	870126	+	G, J.	G−0.5		−2.30	−3.04	0.49	0.31	0.18	0.28
4	870324	870505	+	US, G, J.			0.91	1.51	1.01	1.13	1.34	1.68
5	870806	870811	−	US, G,			−0.28	−0.11	−0.18	−0.18	−0.01	0.37
6	870828	870909	+	US, G, J.			0.09	0.06	0.57	0.56	0.26	−0.27
7	871028	871111	+	US, G, J.			−0.23	−0.29	0.12	0.06	0.16	0.54
8	871130	880121	+	US, G, J.	G−0.5		0.21	0.19	−0.06	−0.25	−0.73	0.43
9	880325	880420	+	US, (G), J.			0.45	0.74	0.38	0.69	0.25	0.36
10	880627	880825	−	US, G	US+0.5 G+0.5		−0.60	0.14	−0.13	0.43	0.41	−0.45
11	881031	881202	+	US, (G), J.			−0.09	0.41	0.50	0.75	0.30	0.78
12	890105	890206	−	US, G	G+0.5		−0.59	0.06	−0.55	0.07	−0.42	−0.44
13	890317	890411	−	US, G			−0.02	−0.09	0.13	0.26	−0.03	−0.01
14	890502	890721	−	US, (G), J.	G+0.5 J+0.75		−2.03	−1.62	−1.50	−1.62	−0.81	−0.61
15	890811	891012	−	US, G, J.	G+1 J+0.5		−0.98	−0.43	−1.06	−1.13	−0.44	−0.35
16	900102	900119	−	US, J.			−0.24	−0.69	0	−0.25	−0.04	−0.87
17	900223	900419	−	US, (G), J	J+1		−0.08	−0.47	0.44	0.07	0.34	0.20
18	910204	910212	+	US, G			−0.91	−0.74	−0.38	−0.50	0.09	−0.02
19	910311	910328	−	US, G, J.			−0.38	−0.25	−0.57	−0.07	−0.32	−0.07

Notes:

(1) Federal funds rate (US), day-to-day money market rate (Germany), call money rate (Japan).

(2) 3-month Euro-market rates.

(3) 10-year government bond rates.

4 Concerted interventions and the turning points of the dollar

The following displays the major turning points of the dollar (obtained by inspection from figures 8.2 and 8.3 and then checked, for exact timing, with figure 8.6).

Turning points	Date	Episode of concerted intervention
1	February 1985	1
2	April 1987	4
3	August 1987	5
4	January 1988	8
5	August 1988	10
6	November 1988	11
7	October 1989 for mark; April 1990 for yen	15–17
8	February 1991	18
9	July 1991	—

The first turning point occurs in February 1985 and marks the end of the extraordinary appreciation of the dollar in the period 1980–4. Looking at quarterly data on foreign exchange reserves for the United States and Japan and on asset acquisitions (net of capital gains) for Germany, Obstfeld (1989) concludes that 'all told, the (pre-Plaza) period shows no sustained, coordinated attempt to drive the dollar down'. He therefore looks at other possible reasons (basically interest rates) for the fall of the dollar that started in February. On the other hand, Dini (1988, p. 6) and Frankel (1990) give considerable importance to the role of intervention. According to the latter, 'the February intervention was reported in the newspapers, and by virtue of timing appears to be a likely candidate for the instrument that pricked the bubble'. Frankel also notes a change in attitude towards exchange rate policy and coordination when the new Reagan administration took office; the two key advocates of *laissez faire*, Regan and Sprinkel, had just been replaced at the Treasury Department by Baker and Darman. The latter attended the Group of Five (G-5) Meeting of 17 January where it was agreed to use foreign exchange intervention (Funabashi 1988, p. 10). The communiqué was unambiguous: 'the Ministers and Governors reaffirmed their commitment made at Williamsburg to undertake coordinated intervention in the markets as necessary'. Our analysis lends support to Frankel's reading of this episode. Though Germany did the lion's share, all the G-3 central banks intervened against the dollar; two of them intervened simultaneously (i.e., on the same day) 50 per cent of the time, and most of the non-G-3 central banks participated actively in the episode. All told, between 1 February and 7 March central banks sold an

unprecedented $8.7 billion; on both 27 February and 1 March about $1.5 billion were exchanged against the Deutsche mark.

Two years later, in April 1987, concerted intervention halted the fall of the dollar that had started in February 1985 and continued through 1986 in spite of sporadic uncoordinated purchases of dollars by Japan and, on a much smaller scale, by Germany. We take the end of April 1987, one month after the Louvre Accord, as the *second* major turning point. The importance of this episode (number 4), in terms of the amounts spent (more than $38 billion), its duration (more than a month), and the degree of coordination (especially between the Fed and the Bank of Japan) is well known. After this episode, the dollar appreciated rapidly until August, gaining about 7 per cent against the Deutsche mark and 10 per cent against the yen.

The *third* turning point in our chronology is in August 1987 when the dollar resumed a downward trend that continued, through the stock market crash, until February 1988; this is often seen as demonstrating the limited effectiveness of the Louvre Agreement and of the interventions undertaken in April (Bordo and Schwartz 1990). Obstfeld (1989) notes that the dollar fundamentals were weak throughout 1987, essentially because the trade balance was not improving, in spite of the depreciation of the preceding two years. This was the period in which pessimism prevailed regarding the prospects for US external adjustment and markets were nervously reacting to (very noisy and J-curve affected) monthly data on the US trade balance. It should be noted, however, that the August turning point coincided exactly with a short, highly concentrated episode of coordinated intervention (number 5). In this episode, the Fed played a major role, helped until 11 August by the Bundesbank and other central banks; non-G-3 countries continued to intervene until 18 August, the moment when the dollar started to fall (see figure 8.6c). Subsequently, there were sporadic interventions in the opposite direction. In less than ten working days, from 6 to 18 August, the sixteen central banks in the survey sold more than $4 billion.

The *fourth* turning point was in January 1988, when the decline in the dollar that had started in August 1987 halted and the US currency resumed an upward trend (episode 8). After the stock market crash of 22 October 1987 the dollar rebounded for a few days and then fell precipitously. Large-scale interventions by the G-3 central banks and all the others were initiated at the end of October. Obstfeld was to claim that: 'in spite of this heavy intervention, the dollar depreciated by 16.2 per cent against the mark, and by 18.5 per cent against the yen, between end-September and end-December 1987, before partially recovering and stabilizing in the last part of January'. With the benefit of daily data, we distinguish two distinct rounds of massive concerted intervention in the aftermath of the stock market crash: the first (episode 7) was very short (eleven working days), but

intense (more than $10 billion were purchased). This episode ended on 11 November, at the precise moment the dollar reversed its trend and started to appreciate. In the second half of November, however, the dollar weakened again following declarations by the United States and German authorities that seemed to welcome a decline of the dollar and because of mounting uncertainty about the prospects of an agreement between the US Administration and Congress on measures to reduce the budget deficit.

The second round lasted from 30 November until 21 January (episode 8); for almost two months, all the leading central banks intervened continuously purchasing about $20 billion. The dollar stabilized immediately at the beginning of the intervention episode, helped by a discount rate cut in Germany; nonetheless in mid December news of a record trade deficit in the United States sparked a new fall. On 22 December, G-7 representatives agreed over the phone on a communiqué that defined both a further decline and a rise in the dollar as counterproductive. The market reacted unfavourably to the G-7 statement, noting that it failed to announce concrete measures to support the dollar. On 28 December, however, interventions were stepped up and 'round-the-clock' continuous operations were undertaken for the first time and continued until the end of the episode (Gomel *et al.* 1990). Success was almost immediate, as the turnaround of the dollar occurred just a few days later, on 4 January. Thereafter, intervention continued until 21 January and underpinned a new phase of sustained appreciation of the dollar. According to Dobson (1991), the purpose of the coordinated interventions that followed the G-7 communiqué was to provide a bridge to the anticipated improvement of the US trade account, which indeed began to materialize in February 1988.

In the wake of the January episode, the dollar continued to appreciate until August 1988, with a minor interruption in April that was successfully countered by means of interventions that were coordinated mainly between the Fed and the Bank of Japan (episode 9). The rise of the dollar accelerated in June and in July, in spite of the renewed plea for stable exchange rates made at the Toronto Summit (19–21 June 1988). The perception of the state of health of the dollar had radically changed: both the budget and the trade balance were finally showing signs of adjustment and concern about the consequences of the October stock market crash for the real economy had vanished. The level of activity was rising and monetary policy was being tightened, after the loosening that had occurred in the period following the crash; markets came to be more impressed by the reputation of Fed Chairman Greenspan as an inflation fighter. As Frankel (1990, p. 32) recalls, there were also rumours that Japan favoured an appreciation of the dollar to help elect Bush in the following November, against more protectionist minded democrats. Why, then, did the upward trend of the dollar reverse in August? Concerted intervention again provides a plausible

explanation: episode 10 lasted from 27 June to 25 August and involved several central banks, though not the Bank of Japan. This action was reinforced by a discount rate rise in Germany on 26 August, though the dollar peaked against the Deutsche mark a few days before the German rate change and also began to fall against the yen, in spite of the United States–Japan interest differential moving in the wrong direction. We count this as the *fifth* turning point of the dollar.

The *sixth* occurred in November 1988 (episode 11), when intervention stopped the depreciation of the dollar (after it had fallen by about 10 per cent against the Deutsche mark and the yen since August) and started the rally of 1989. This episode has received little attention in the literature (though it was reported in the press, as were all the other episodes). The bulk of the interventions, carried out especially by the Bank of Japan, lasted until 25 November, the day on which both the dollar/yen and the dollar/mark rates started to recover from their troughs. The very short interest differential with Germany moved in the wrong direction during the episode. Finally, it is worth noting that the favourable US trade figures announced on 16 November did not break the downward fall of the dollar. The November episode marks the start of the dollar rally which was to last until October 1989 against the Deutsche mark and until April 1990 against the yen which defines the *seventh* turning point of our chronology. Two comments are in order. First, the interventions undertaken in the first half of 1989 to curb the dollar's rise were neither uncoordinated nor unsuccessful. On the other hand, Frankel (1990, p. 33) suggests that 'there is less evidence in 1989 that foreign exchange intervention succeeded in moving the market than there was in the 1985–8 period'. We basically agree with this statement. In fact, the first three episodes of the year (numbers 12, 13, and 14, respectively in January, March, and June) did not stop the rally, even though total intervention sales exceeded $40 billion. However, each episode was at least temporarily successful despite the first two having been accompanied by 'wrong' movements in interest differentials and non-G-3 central banks having intervened heavily at cross-purposes (especially during episode 13), as shown by the low ratio of net to gross interventions (see table 8.1). The second comment is that the definite end of the rally, against the Deutsche mark in October 1989 and the yen in April 1990, coincided with two major episodes of concerted intervention (numbers 15 and 17). Episode 15 was again very long, lasting from 11 August to 12 October. The dollar peaked on 11 September at DM 1.99 and yen 148. On Saturday 23 September the G-7 issued a communiqué stating that the value of the dollar was 'inconsistent with longer run fundamentals'. The following Monday a massive round of highly coordinated interventions was launched that lasted the whole week. All the major central banks conducted 'rolling intervention' around the clock, operating also on foreign financial

centres. The central banks sold a total $20 billion. When the episode ended, the dollar was set on a downward trend against the mark and well below its peak against the yen.

In the following months the dollar continued to fall against the Deutsche mark. On the other hand, it soon started to edge up again against the yen, in spite of the rapid narrowing of the interest differential. At the beginning of January 1990 concerted interventions were undertaken, mainly by the Bank of Japan, aimed at checking the dollar's appreciation against the yen (episode 16). At the end of February a new rally against the yen started (presumably linked to conflicts on monetary policy between the Bank of Japan, which favoured a tightening, and the Ministry of Finance, which opposed it on fears of financial fragility) and the yen fell almost to 160, reaching its lowest value since 1986. The intervention (episode 17) that stopped the weakening of the yen (and also a temporary fall of the Deutsche mark) was somewhat atypical, being perhaps the least coordinated in the whole 1985–91 period. The Fed and the Bank of Japan started to intervene on 23 February and were joined for just two days by the Bundesbank on 2 March. The dollar stopped rising with respect to the Deutsche mark on 7 March and started to fall on 28 March; thereafter, the Bank of Japan was left on its own to curb the continuing appreciation against the yen, which lasted until the end of the episode on 19 April. There was simultaneous intervention by at least two of the G-3 central banks only on one day in three; short-term interest differentials moved slightly in the wrong direction; several non-G-3 central banks acted at cross-purposes. Nonetheless, the episode was successful and marked the start of a sharp fall of the dollar from about 160 yen in April 1990 to 133 at the end of the year. In the same period, the dollar also fell against the Deutsche mark, from 1.71 to 1.48. The reasons for the subsequent fall of the dollar, which was especially rapid in the second half of 1990, are well known: the recession in the United States spurred expectations of lower interest rates, at a time when monetary policy was being tightened both in Germany, to counter the inflationary consequences of the unification, and in Japan, to correct the bubble in asset prices.

Episode 18 marks the *eighth* turning point of the dollar. It was very short, lasting from 4 to 12 February 1991, and closely coordinated among several central banks (with the exclusion, however, of the Bank of Japan). The episode started immediately after the outbreak of hostilities in Kuwait (which caused an immediate, precipitous fall of the dollar) and ended when the dollar was clearly set on an upward path. It is worth noting that the episode ended *before* the beginning of the land operations in the Persian Gulf (24 February), which rapidly demonstrated the military superiority of the allied forces and, together with optimistic forecasts regarding the American economy, underpinned the subsequent rise of the dollar.

The *ninth* and last turning point of the dollar occurred in July 1991, when it became clear that the long awaited US recovery was still not under way and the Fed accelerated the reduction of interest rates. This is the only turning point that does not coincide with an episode of concerted intervention.

5 Interpreting the evidence

Fundamentals or 'bouncing balls'?

The evidence examined in section 4 leaves little doubt about the importance of (even poorly) coordinated intervention. No satisfactory history of the dollar in the period 1985–91 can be written without reference to the episodes of concerted intervention. As we have seen they were all successful, though only temporarily in some cases; more importantly, all but one of the major turning points of the dollar coincided with one of the episodes. The evidence can be interpreted in various ways. At the least, concerted intervention can be seen as having determined the timing (say, within the year or the month) of the turning points, though these were the result of (actual or expected) fundamental changes in the economy or the stance of monetary policy. At the other extreme, the evidence suggests a sort of 'ping-pong' effect, with the exchange rate changing direction when hit by the central banks and continuing to move in that direction, almost without friction, until it is hit again in the opposite direction. It is not clear which is the right interpretation. The 'ping-pong' story is hard to justify on theoretical grounds; nonetheless, we believe that intervention did more than just determine the timing of the turning points. In this section we provide evidence supporting this claim; we also draw on some recent literature on asset prices to argue that exchange rates may deviate substantially from fundamentals, thereby leaving ample scope for intervention to operate as an expectations coordinating device.

Simplifying somewhat, the 'fundamentalist' interpretation of the broad trends of the dollar is more or less as follows.[13] The rise of the dollar from 1980 to 1984 is attributed to the combination of loose fiscal and tight monetary policies in the United States. The turning point at the beginning of 1985 is related to the sharp reduction in US interest rates in the second half of 1984 and to the growing awareness of the unsustainability of the US external position (Obstfeld 1989, p. 11). The subsequent weakness of the dollar through 1987 is explained by the large current account deficit, together with the turnaround of the budget that became apparent between 1986 and 1987. The dollar rallies of 1988–9 are attributed to the improvements in the US trade balance and the strong growth of domestic demand (in spite of the stock market crash), which induced a firming up of US

interest rates relative to Germany and Japan. In 1990, the dollar fell as the recession in the United States led markets to anticipate lower domestic interest rates; the weakness was accentuated between August 1990 and February 1991 by the crisis in the Persian Gulf. The US currency recovered in the spring, owing to expectations of a rapid recovery of the economy, and fell again in the summer with the second dip of the recession. This approach undoubtedly accounts for much of what happened in this period. It captures the factors that, in the end, were *perceived* by the markets as being the 'fundamental' determinants of the exchange rate. However, these perceptions changed over time as the emphasis shifted from one model of the economy to another,[14] a fact that is clearly brought out by the failure of econometricians to find statistical regularities linking the exchange rate to fundamentals.[15]

The scheme that is used to explain the 1980–4 rise of the dollar is probably an unnatural and imperfect blend of a short-run Dornbusch overshooting model and the Laffer curve (the latter serving to explain the belief that the budget deficit would redress itself automatically). In 1985 the emphasis shifted to the long-run sustainability of external deficits: the exchange rate was viewed as a key variable in the process leading to external equilibrium. This model had been largely abandoned by 1988, although the external debt of the United States was still growing at a very fast pace. Expectations about monetary policy, mainly determined by inflation and the level of activity, became the dominant paradigm.

Several objections have been raised with regard to this reconstruction (Dornbusch 1984, Krugman 1988, and Mussa 1990). Why, for example, did markets wait till 1985 to focus on sustainability, given that this issue was quite clear by the end of 1983, when the dollar was quoted at DM 2.72 and yen 232 and the trade balance had deteriorated by almost $50 billion in two years? And why has sustainability ceased to be an issue since 1988? Whatever answers are given to these questions, it has to be recognized that the sustainability of a given external position is very much an imponderable.[16] Writing in 1984, Dornbusch noted that his own explanation of the dollar's overvaluation (in terms of the US policy mix) took no account of the effects of current account imbalances on the exchange rate, for good reasons: 'the channel through which these effects operate and their quantitative magnitude make it empirically implausible that the market's belief that the current account does matter could lead to a collapse of the dollar'. But he then added for posterity: 'the uncomfortable part in this view is that the deficits have been so clearly predictable and predicted that the collapse should already have occurred' (Dornbusch 1984). As for the public debt or bank deposits, sustainability depends critically on strategic interactions between agents: a run on a currency occurs when agents believe that other agents will sell. The key task of each agent is thus to predict what other

agents will do, in order, at the very least, to avoid being the last to sell. Cass and Shell (1989) argue that we should expect indeterminacies and sunspot equilibria to be the rule rather than the exception in such circumstances.[17]

For the sake of concreteness, consider the situation of Japan and the United States today. Is the yen too strong or too weak relative to the dollar? It is much too weak for those who focus on the large, persistent, and recently increasing external surplus of Japan and worry about protectionist tendencies in the United States and elsewhere (see, for instance, Bergsten (1992), who would like to see the yen at 100). It is about right or too strong for those who look at a much longer time horizon and point to the reduction in private saving and the external surplus that is foreseen for the end of the century as a result of the rapid aging of the Japanese population (OECD 1991); it is definitely too strong for those who focus on financial fragility and falling real activity or look at Purchasing Power Parity and note that 200 yen are needed to buy the goods that can be bought with one dollar,[18] suggesting that, sooner or later, much cheaper US goods will beat Japanese competition. Given the scale of these uncertainties, it is hardly surprising that even weak signals, such as those provided by sterilized interventions, should be sufficient to coordinate agents' expectations, induce them to converge on a particular model of the economy, and pick a value of the exchange rate that is not too far from that targeted by the authorities. Likewise, wrong expectations may well be self-fulfilling, if not for ever, at least for very long periods, especially if noisy positive feedback traders (who buy when the market rises and *vice versa*) and chartists are present and prospering, as a wide literature has convincingly argued.[19] Perhaps the authorities were mistaken in 1987 when they concluded that the depreciation of the dollar had gone far enough. However, since they managed to convince the markets, dollar assets started to look attractive again and the exchange rate stopped falling; we can therefore say, but only *ex post*, that the external position of the United States was in fact sustainable (at least in the sense that it could be financed at the given exchange rate) and that the authorities' judgment was right.

To be sure, intervention is a much stronger signal than a pure sunspot. Agents know that when the authorities are determined, they have the option of moving the fundamentals, and in particular interest rates. If the threat is credible, the change in interest rates may subsequently prove unnecessary.[20]

Intervention and monetary policy

These considerations help overcome the 'substantial embarrassment' (to economic theory) stemming from the difficulty of demonstrating 'a consistent influence of monetary policy on the behaviour of exchange rates'

(Mussa 1990, p. 28). According to Dornbusch and Frankel (1987, p. 158), the fact that regression analysis can hardly beat a random walk 'tends to undermine any defense of exchange rate variability made on the ground that it is appropriate given changes in monetary policy'. In short, changes in the stance of monetary policy are seen as usually being motivated by domestic considerations, especially in the largest countries; they are not meant to be signals for the currency markets. Intervention is instead unambiguously aimed at the exchange rate.

In section 3, we noted that in several episodes intervention was successful despite interest differentials on short and long maturities having moved in the wrong direction (see table 8.2), a fact that contradicts the theory that intervention is effective only in so far as it signals monetary authorities' intentions. Looking at broader trends (figures 8.4 and 8.5), we find that changes in interest differentials played a minor role in determining the turning points of the dollar; the failures of monetary policy contrast sharply with the successes of interventions. A clear failure occurred in the second half of 1984, when fundamentals were hardly different from those of the following February. Short-term interest rates fell in the United States while remaining roughly unchanged in Germany and Japan; the US discount rate was cut twice by half a point, in November and December; as interest rates fell, the growth of M2, which had remained in the lower portion of the 6–9 per cent target range, jumped to the top at the end of the year. Nonetheless, until the turning point in February, the dollar rose at a record pace, gaining about 20 per cent against the mark and 10 per cent against the yen in less than four months. Strikingly, interest rates were firming in the United States from mid January to the end of the February episode, when the dollar finally turned.

Events between mid 1987 and 1989 are also of interest. Throughout the period, the United States–Germany short-term interest differential was stable or slowly drifting upwards, while the mark/dollar rate fluctuated widely. In spite of its 'fundamental' weakness, the dollar appreciated continuously after the post-Louvre April 1987 interventions (episode 5) until the following one in August. The subsequent fall, from August to the stock market crash, is not related to interest rate differentials, which were increasing (see figure 8.4b). Likewise, after the crash, the two spikes of the dollar from mid January 1988 to the end of February and from June to August occurred in spite of falling interest differentials with Germany and, in the first case, also with Japan. It is certainly true that optimism about the strength of the US economy and external adjustment was growing in this period, but this makes it all the more difficult to understand why the dollar kept on falling after the August episode (10) until the following November, when a new round of concerted intervention started the 1989 dollar rally (episode 11). In the analysis of the single episodes, we account for these

gyrations in terms of the standard *ex post* explanations that have been given (typically, news about the economy or the trade balance). It is nonetheless quite striking that neither interest differentials nor news about fundamentals were ever responsible for, or even coincident with, the main turning points (a fact that has been observed for stock prices by Cutler *et al.* 1989), while concerted interventions always were. It can be conjectured that *ex post* explanations suffer from selection bias: when the dollar falls, bad news is used as an explanation, while good news is neglected.

Another interesting case is the dollar's rally against the Deutsche mark in 1989 when German rates were increasing and the short-term differential in favour of the dollar was declining. After a temporary setback (coinciding with episode 14) the dollar climbed again in August and September, in spite of the interest differential having fallen by at least another percentage point since June.

Even more striking is the behaviour of the yen in 1989. At the time Japanese 'fundamentals' were perceived as being quite strong and residents appeared to be convinced that land and shares were not overpriced. Between February 1989 and April 1990, the Unite States–Japan short-term interest differential fell from 6 to 1 per cent, as the Bank of Japan started to worry about the economy overheating; nonetheless the dollar rose against the yen by over 17 per cent in this period. Only the April intervention (episode 17) finally stopped the US currency and started a precipitous fall, which lasted until October.

6 Conclusions

The evidence surveyed in this chapter leaves little doubt about the importance of concerted intervention in explaining the behaviour of the dollar from 1985 onwards. A few main facts stand out. First, interventions by the central banks of the G-3 were relatively infrequent and usually coordinated. The simultaneous presence in the markets of at least two of the three major central banks was therefore a notable event (and regularly reported by the financial press). Second, all nineteen episodes of concerted interventions were effective, though on four occasions their effects lasted only a few weeks. Third, during the episodes the behaviour of interest rates was not always consistent with the exchange rate objective; in several cases interest rate differentials did not change or changed in the wrong direction. Fourth, and most importantly, eight of the nine major turning points of the dollar between 1985 and 1991 coincided with an episode of concerted intervention. At the very least, concerted interventions appear to have determined the exact timing of the turning points, within the broad trends set by the development of fundamentals.

Econometrics should in principle be able to disentangle the separate

effects of interventions and fundamentals; we have not reported any results because, like all our predecessors, we failed to improve significantly on a simple random walk. With Dornbusch and Frankel (1987, p. 157), we argue that there may be something to learn from these failures; empirical regularities linking the exchange rate to fundamentals may be hard to find, precisely because the linkages are very weak. Markets may use different models at different times; the concept of the sustainability of an external deficit is hard to pin down empirically; strategic interactions, indeterminacies, and self-fulfilling expectations may be the norm rather than the exception; and positive feedback traders and chartists have been shown to prosper in very efficient markets. For any of the above reasons, which have been extensively studied in the literature, markets may deviate substantially and for long periods from fundamentals.[21] We see our chapter as providing further evidence in support of this proposition. In particular, we find it striking that major turning points should have coincided with episodes of intervention, while they appear to be unrelated to changes in interest rates (see section 5).

Overall, the evidence suggests that the traditional question (is intervention effective even when it is not accompanied by changes in domestic monetary conditions?) may need to be turned on its head: do changes in domestic monetary conditions affect the exchange rate, even when they are not accompanied by intervention? We suggest that changes in monetary conditions have usually been motivated by domestic considerations, especially in the largest countries; they were not meant to be signals for the currency markets. Intervention is instead unambiguously aimed at the exchange rate; it is effective when it helps to coordinate agents' expectations in an environment inevitably characterized by considerable uncertainty about the linkage between exchange rates and fundamentals. It is more than a pure sunspot or a conventional code of language between markets and central banks, because the latter can always threaten to resort to (possibly temporary) changes in interest rates and inflict losses on short-term speculators: if the threat is credible, the subsequent change in the interest rate need not take place.

Finally, a few words of caution. First, there are clearly limits to the effectiveness of even perfectly coordinated intervention. The following statement by Black (1986), a noted advocate of *laissez faire* and market efficiency, can perhaps serve as a benchmark: 'we might define an efficient market as one in which price is within a factor of two from value, i.e., the price is more than half the value and less than twice the value'. If, for instance, in February 1985 (at the peak of the bubble) the true (fundamental) value of $1 was DM 1.7, efficient markets could have produced pure 'noise' ranging anywhere from 3.4 (as in fact happened) to 0.85! Though we

are much colder on efficient markets than Black, we suspect that fundamentals put much tighter limits on exchange rates and, correspondingly, on the ability of central banks to affect them. Second, we do not believe that central banks can ever be successful if they act 'against' the markets; even very large interventions are tiny in comparison with the funds traded on the foreign exchange markets. Hence, the effectiveness of central banks' action hinges critically on their ability to persuade the markets that a given level or trend of the exchange rate is inconsistent with fundamentals; this is the sense in which we view intervention as an expectation coordination device. Thus, intervention is bound to fail if markets maintain that central banks are trying to defend 'unrealistic' parities. Ultimately, intervention is no substitute for appropriate domestic policies.

Likewise, intervention is likely to fail if different central banks are perceived as being imperfectly coordinated or pursuing different objectives. All the success stories discussed here involved some degree of coordination between at least two major central banks. The very few uncoordinated interventions that were undertaken in the 1985–91 period (mainly in 1986, 1990, and 1991) had hardly any effect on exchange rates. Intervention may fail because the authorities of one of the countries involved are perceived by markets as having 'second thoughts' about the objectives which have been set in an international agreement; their intentions or opinions may be revealed by words or movements of interest rates in a direction which is not consistent with the agreed objective. In these circumstances, interventions fail simply because no clear message is conveyed to the markets. Moreover, it is necessary to recognize the basic difference between intervening on an otherwise freely floating exchange rate and stabilizing it at a particular level or within very narrow margins. In almost all the cases we have analysed the objective of the authorities was to stabilize the dollar around current levels, not to reverse its trend, though intervention did in fact usually reverse the trend. While we leave the explanation of this fact for further research, we note an important implication: our findings cannot be mechanically extrapolated to suggest that coordinated intervention can be used to establish and defend a system of fixed exchange rates or even target zones.

In conclusion, intervention can be quite powerful when it helps to convey clear messages to the markets concerning the appropriate or sustainable level of the exchange rate. It has to be used very skilfully and in the right circumstances because its effectiveness depends critically on credibility, an asset that can easily evaporate. It is essential that intervention be used only when its objectives are truly shared by the authorities involved and there is a reasonable chance of persuading market participants that these objectives are consistent with the economic environment.

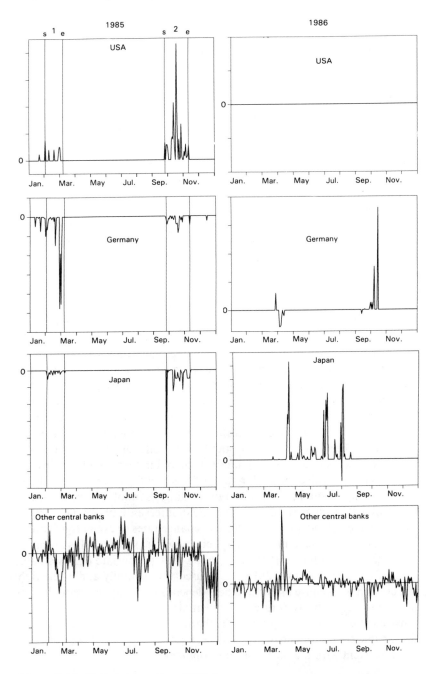

Figure 8.1A Daily intervention, 1985–6

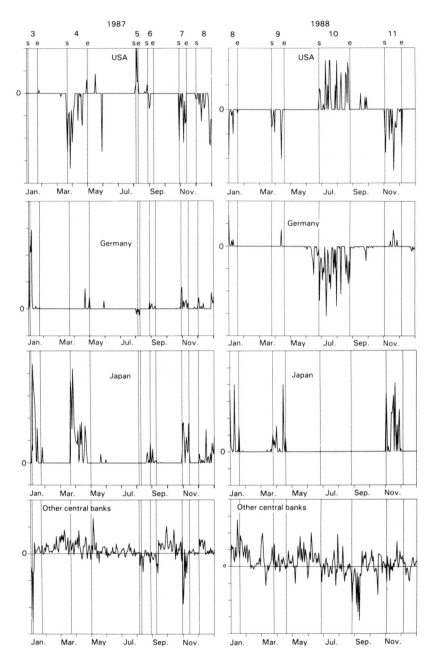

Figure 8.1B Daily intervention, 1987–8

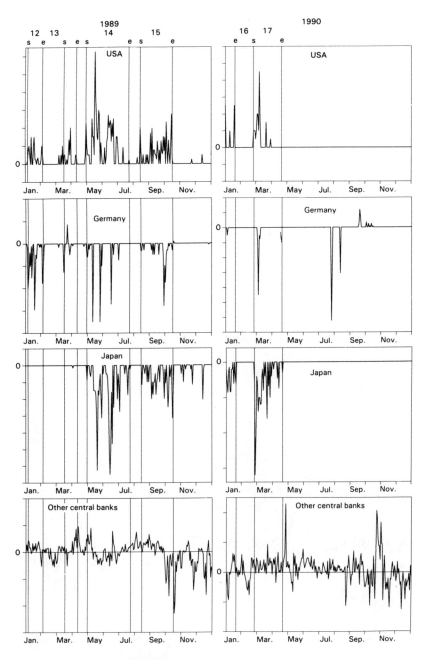

Figure 8.1C Daily intervention, 1989–90

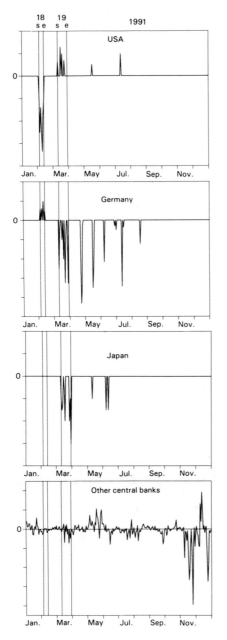

Figure 8.1D Daily intervention, 1991

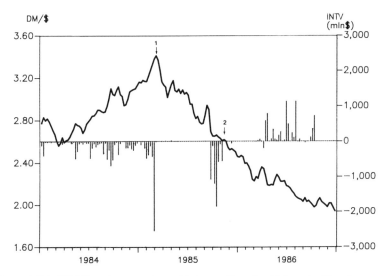

Figure 8.2A DM/$ exchange rate and interventions by G-3 central banks, 1984–6
Note: ($ purchases–DM purchases)/2. Weekly data.

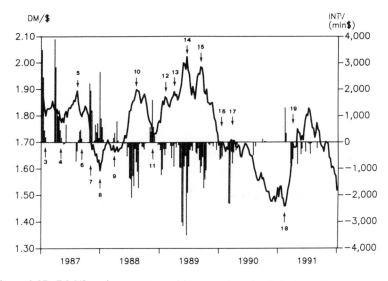

Figure 8.2B DM/$ exchange rate and interventions by G-3 central banks, 1987–91
Note: ($ purchases–DM purchases)/2. Weekly data.

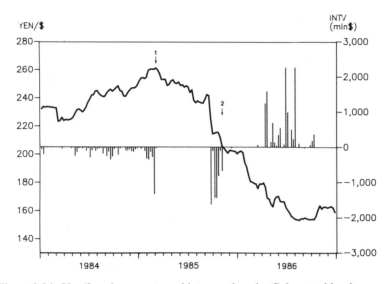

Figure 8.3A Yen/$ exchange rate and interventions by G-3 central banks, 1984–6
Note: ($ purchases–Yen purchases)/2. Weekly data.

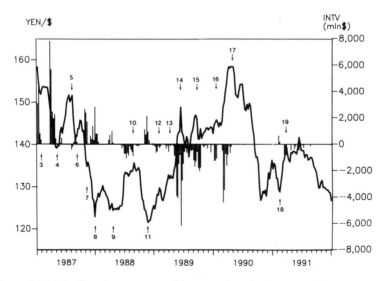

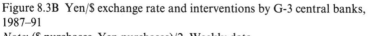

Figure 8.3B Yen/$ exchange rate and interventions by G-3 central banks, 1987–91
Note: ($ purchases–Yen purchases)/2. Weekly data.

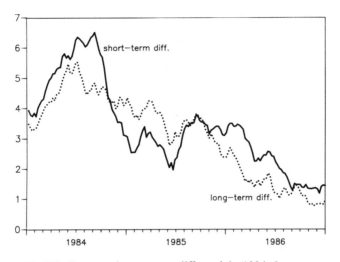

Figure 8.4A US–Germany interest rate differentials, 1984–6
Note: Short-term differentials are based on three-month Euro market interbank
rates. Long-term differentials are based on ten-year government bond yields.

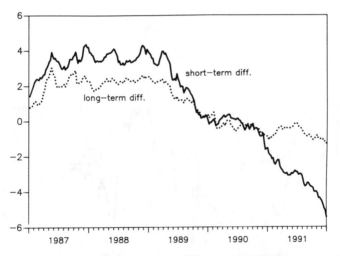

Figure 8.4B US–Germany interest rate differentials, 1987–91
Note: Short-term differentials are based on three-month Euro-market interbank
rates. Long-term differentials are based on ten-year government bond yields.

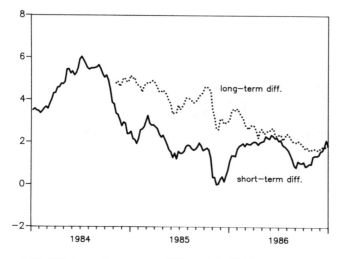

Figure 8.5A US–Japan interest rate differentials, 1984–6
Note: Short-term differentials are based on three-month Euro market interbank
rates. Long-term differentials are based on ten-year government bond yields.

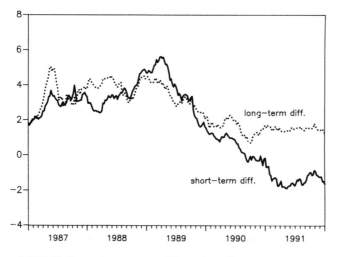

Figure 8.5B US–Japan interest rate differentials, 1987–91
Note: Short-term differentials are based on three-month Euro market interbank
rates. Long-term differentials are based on ten-year government bond yields.

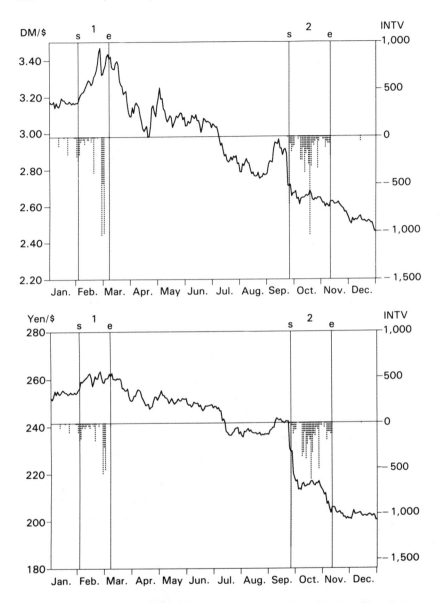

Figure 8.6A Exchange rate and daily interventions by G-3 central banks, 1985
Note: ($ purchases–DM or Yen purchases)/2.

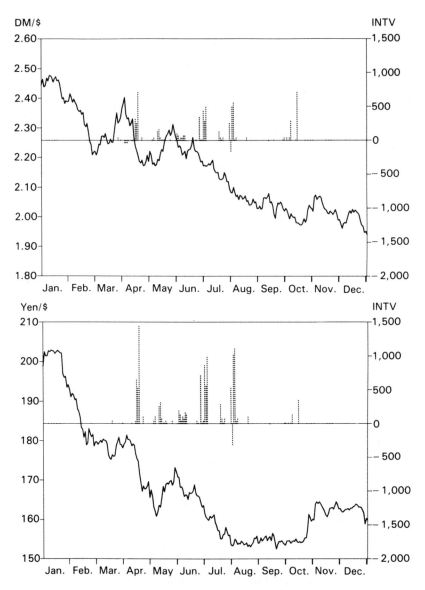

Figure 8.6B Exchange rate and daily interventions by G-3 central banks, 1986
Note: ($ purchases–DM or Yen purchases)/2.

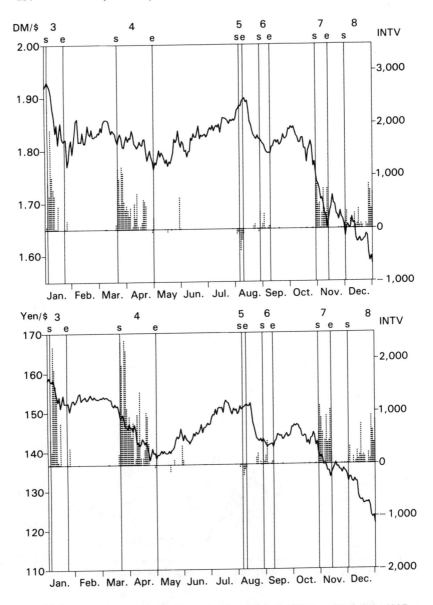

Figure 8.6C Exchange rate and daily interventions by G-3 central banks, 1987
Note: ($ purchases–DM or Yen purchases)/2.

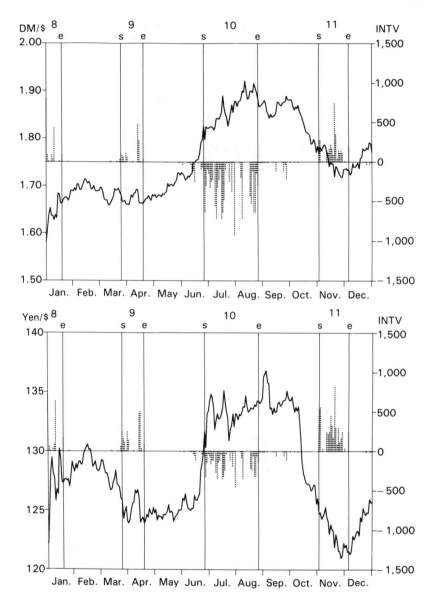

Figure 8.6D Exchange rate and daily interventions by G-3 central banks, 1988
Note: ($ purchases–DM or Yen purchases)/2.

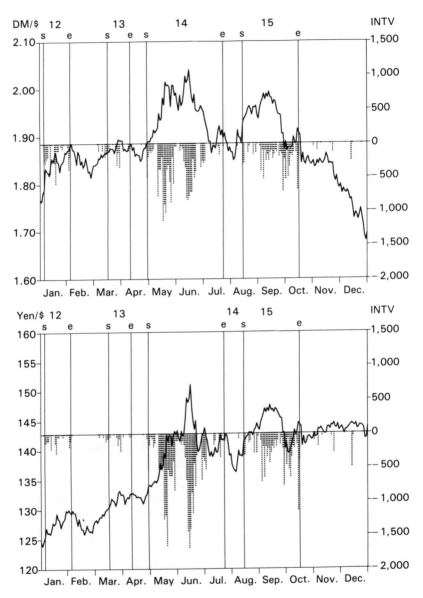

Figure 8.6E Exchange rate and daily interventions by G-3 central banks, 1989
Note: ($ purchases–DM or Yen purchases)/2.

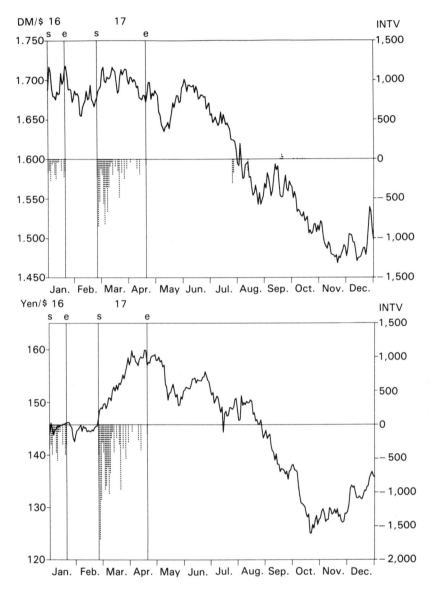

Figure 8.6F Exchange rate and daily interventions by G-3 central banks, 1990
Note: ($ purchases–DM or Yen purchases)/2.

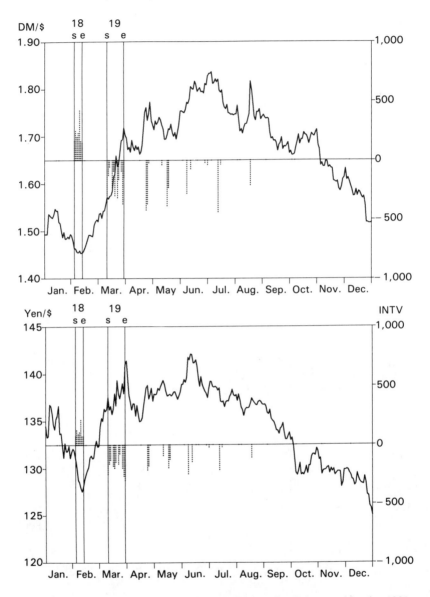

Figure 8.6G Exchange rate and daily interventions by G-3 central banks, 1991
Note: ($ purchases–DM or Yen purchases)/2.

Notes

The views expressed are those of the authors and do not involve the responsibility of the Banca d'Italia. We are particularly indebted to F. Saccomanni for prompting us into this endeavour and to A. Santorelli and F. Panfili for useful discussions on the technical aspects of foreign exchange intervention.

1 An extensive survey of the literature on foreign exchange intervention is contained in Edison (1990). See Giavazzi and Giovannini (1989), Gros and Thygesen (1992) for the role of intervention in the European Monetary System.

2 This is the procedure by which central banks exchange information on interventions four times a day. Our sample includes the central banks of the following countries: Belgium, Canada, Denmark, France, Germany, Greece, Ireland, Italy, Japan, the Netherlands, Portugal, Spain, Sweden, Switzerland, the United Kingdom, and the United States.

3 In some countries, there are procedures that normally call for immediate offsetting operations; however, this does not mean that intervention is sterilized over a full market day or over longer periods. To assess whether this is the case, one would have to distinguish empirically between demand and supply shocks and then judge whether the decision to intervene coincided with a decision to change the supply of the monetary base.

4 On only four days did two of the three central banks intervene simultaneously at cross-purposes, and only for very small amounts. This is in sharp contrast with the much higher frequency of such events in earlier periods, for instance in 1979–80.

5 In principle, this criterion does not include anomalous cases in which, for instance, two banks alternate in the market at weekly intervals. In practice this pattern is never observed, as intervention is usually sequential with interruptions of at most one or two days in each episode.

6 A detailed analysis of each episode is included as an appendix to the chapter, available on request from the authors.

7 The only episode that cannot easily be labelled as 'leaning against the wind' is the one that occurred after the Plaza Accord (episode 2). For this episode, and therefore for the preceding one, we use an evaluation criterion based on the objectives that were agreed at the meetings.

8 After a major sale of foreign currency, central banks sometimes intervene immediately in the opposite direction in order to accumulate reserves. However, this does not appear to be the case for the G-3.

9 The term 'successful' may not be completely appropriate. In most cases the target was stabilization around current levels, not trend reversal; however, the actual outcome of almost all episodes was a reversal of the trend.

10 The variable in brackets is divided by two in order to preserve the actual size interventions; an exchange of $100 against the Deutsche mark would otherwise be counted as being worth $200.

11 In June and July of 1991 intervention was small, discontinuous, and uncoordinated; only on one day (12 July) did two of the G-3 central banks intervene simultaneously.

12 For any given very short-term interest rates, the effects of intervention on longer-term differentials are ambiguous. A sale of dollars by the Fed may be taken by the market as signalling the intention of the US authorities to loosen monetary policy in the future; if, however, it gives rise to expectations of a devaluation of the dollar, it will lead agents to require a higher return on dollar assets. See section 5.2 for further discussion on the role of interest rates in the intervention episodes.

13 What follows is consistent with the writings of Blanchard and Dornbusch (1984), Dornbusch (1984), Sachs (1985), Feldstein (1986), Obstfeld (1989), De Grauwe (1989), Frankel (1990), though many of these authors cannot be labelled as 'fundamentalists'.

14 Goldberg and Frydman (1991) show that the actual, appropriately redefined, rational expectation paths of the exchange rate and of the economy depend on the distribution of agents across the different models of the economy adopted at any given moment and how this distribution changes over time.

15 MacDonald and Taylor (1992) manage to do slightly better than a random walk using an error correction monetary model of the exchange rate. We too have done a little better than a random walk by including broken trends between each pair of subsequent episodes; however, this is a rather obvious result given that virtually all the major turning points coincided with the episodes.

16 For a discussion of some of the definitions of sustainability see Krugman (1985 and 1987) and Marris (1985).

17 Blanchard and Fischer (1989, p. 261) see sunspots as interesting and disturbing, but implausible. However, they focus on models in which there is no uncertainty except about the realization of the sunspot. The idea put forward here is much less disturbing: essentially, markets may be virtually indifferent between different initial values of the exchange rate in the face of pronounced uncertainty, in the sense that different values may be viewed as being consistent with reaching equilibrium in the long run. The economy will then tend to behave as if there was a continuum of stable equilibria.

18 Based on consumption PPP data prepared by the Commission of the European Community in 1991.

19 See, among others, Summers and Summers (1989), Mussa (1990), De Long et al. (1990), Frankel and Froot (1986), MacDonald and Young (1986), Allen and Taylor (1990), and Taylor and Allen (1992).

20 According to Obstfeld (1991), if intervention has only a signalling value, it should not be viewed as an independent instrument of policy 'since it must be followed by concrete policy actions for signals to remain credible'. This argument, however, applies to a world in which there is a well-defined relationship between the exchange rate and fundamentals. Mussa (1981) provides a reason as to why intervention may prove a more credible signal than policy announcements by the authorities. He argues that intervention exposes a central bank to additional foreign exchange risk and enhances its incentive to pursue its objectives by other means in the future. Klein and Rosengren (1991) show that intervention was used, effectively, after the Louvre Accord to clarify imprecise policy announcements.

21 For a clear statement of this proposition see, among others, Krugman (1988, p. 117) and Kenen *Floating exchange rates reconsidered: the influence of new ideas, priorities, and problems* included in Part III of this volume).

References

Allen, H. and Taylor, M.P. 1990. 'Charts, Noise and Fundamentals in the London Foreign Exchange Market', *Economic Journal*, 100, supplement.

Bergsten, F. 1992. *Trade and Jobs: A Strategy for Export – Led Recovery*, Statement before the Committee on Banking, Housing and Urban Affairs, US Senate, January.

Black, F. 1986. 'Noise', *Journal of Finance*, 41, 3, July.

Blanchard, O.J. and Dornbusch R. 1984. 'U.S. Deficits, the Dollar and Europe', *Banca Nazionale del Lavoro Quarterly Review*, March.

Blanchard, O.J. and Fischer, S. 1989. *Lectures on Macroeconomics*, Cambridge Mass., MIT Press.

Bordo, M.D. and Schwartz, A.J. 1990. 'What Has Foreign Exchange Market Intervention Since the Plaza Agreement Accomplished?', *NBER Working Paper*, 3562.

Cass, D. and Shell, K. 1989. 'Sunspot Equilibrium in an Overlapping-Generations Economy with an Idealized Contingent-Commodity Market', in W.A. Barnett, J. Geweke, and H. Shell (eds.) *Economic Complexity. Chaos, Bubbles and Nonlinearity*, Cambridge, Cambridge University Press.

Cutler, H.D., Poterba, J.M., and Summers, L.H. 1989. 'What Moves Stock Prices?', *Journal of Portfolio Management*.

De Grauwe, P. 1989. *International Money. Postwar Trends and Theories*, Oxford, Clarendon Press.

De Long, J.B., Shleifer, A., Summers, L.H., and Waldman, R.J. 1990. 'Positive Feedback Strategies and Destabilizing Rational Speculation', *The Journal of Finance*, June.

Dini, L. 1988. 'Cooperation and Conflict in Monetary and Trade Policies', Address to the US–European Top Management Roundtable, *Economic Bulletin*, Banca d'Italia, 7, October.

Dobson, W. 1991. *Economic Policy Coordination: Requiem or First Step?*, Washington, Institute of International Economics.

Dominguez, K. 1989. 'Market Responses to Coordinated Central Bank Intervention', *NBER Working Paper*, 3192.

Dominguez, K. and Frankel, J. 1992, 'Does Foreign Exchange Intervention Matter? Disentangling the Portfolio and Expectations Effects', mimeo.

Dornbusch, R. 1984. 'The Overvalued Dollar', *Lloyds Bank Review*, April.

Dornbusch, R. and Frankel, J. 1987. 'The Flexible Exchange Rate System: Experience and Alternatives', *NBER Working Paper*, 2464.

Edison, H.J. 1990. 'Foreign Currency Operations, An Annotated Bibliography', Board of Governors of the Federal Reserve System, *International Finance Discussion Paper*, 380.

Feldstein, M. 1984. 'Why the Dollar is Strong', *Challenge*, January–February.

1986. 'New Evidence on the Effects of Exchange Rate Intervention', *NBER Working Paper*, 2052.

Frankel, J. 1985. 'The Dazzling Dollar', *Brookings Papers on Economic Activity*, 1.

1990. 'The Making of Exchange Rate Policy in the 1980s', *NBER Working Paper*, 3539.

Frankel, J. and Froot, K. 1986. 'Understanding the US Dollar in the Eighties: The Expectations of Chartists and Fundamentalists', *Economic Record*, 62, supplementary issue.

1987. 'Using Survey Data to Test Standard Propositions Regarding Exchange Rate Expectations', *American Economic Review*, March.

1990a, 'Chartists, Fundamentalists and the Demand for Dollars', in A.S. Courakis and M.P. Taylor (eds.), *Private Behaviour and Government Policy in Interdependent Economies*, Oxford, Clarendon Press.

1990b. 'Exchange Rate Forecasting Techniques, Survey Data, and Implications for the Foreign Exchange Market', *IMF Working Paper*, 43.

Funabashi, Y. 1988. *Managing the Dollar: From the Plaza to the Louvre*, Washington DC, Institute of International Economics.

Gaiotti, E., Giucca, P., and Micossi, S. 1989. 'Cooperation in Managing the Dollar (1985–87): Interventions in Foreign Exchange Markets and Interest Rates', *Temi di Discussione*, Banca d'Italia, 119.

Giavazzi, F. and Giovannini, A. 1989. 'Can the EMS Be Exported? Lessons from Ten Years of Monetary Policy Cooperation', *CEPR Working Paper*, 285.

Goldberg, M. and Frydman, R. 1991. 'Theories Consistent Expectations and Exchange Rate Dynamics', mimeo, New York University.

Gomel, G., Saccomanni, F., and Vona, S. 1990. 'The Experience with Economic Policy Coordination: The Tripolar and European Dimensions', *Temi di Discussione*, Banca d'Italia, 140.

Gros, D. and Thygesen, N. 1992. *European Monetary Integration: From the European Monetary System to Monetary Union*, London, Longman.

Klein, M. and Lewis H. 1991. 'Learning about Intervention Target Zones', *NBER Working Paper*, 3674.

Klein, M. and Rosengren, F. 1991. 'What Do We Learn from Foreign Exchange Intervention?', mimeo.

Krugman, P. 1985. 'Is the Strong Dollar Sustainable?', in *The US Dollar – Recent Developments, Outlook and Policy Options*, Symposium by the Federal Reserve Bank of Kansas City.

1987. 'Sustainability and the Decline of the Dollar', *Brookings Discussion Papers in International Economics*, March.

1988. *Exchange Rate Instability*, Cambridge Mass., MIT Press.

MacDonald, R. and Taylor, M.P. 1992. 'The Monetary Approach to the Exchange Rate: Rational Expectations, Long Run Equilibrium and Forecasting', *IMF Working Paper*, May.

MacDonald, R. and Young, R. 1986. 'Decision Rules, Expectations and Efficiency in Two Foreign Exchange Markets', *De Economist*, 134.

Marris, S. 1985. 'Deficits and the Dollar: the World Economy at Risk', Washington Institute for International Economics.

Meese, R. and Rogoff, K. 1983. 'Empirical Exchange Rate Models of the Seventies: Do They Fit Out of Sample?', *Journal of International Economics*, 2.

Mussa, M. 1981. 'The Role of Official Intervention', Group of Thirty, *Occasional Paper*, 6.

1990. 'Exchange Rates in Theory and in Reality', *Essays in International Finance*, 179, Princeton, International Finance Section, Princeton University.

Obstfeld, M. 1989. 'The Effectiveness of Foreign Exchange Intervention: Recent Experience, 1985–1988', *Harvard Discussion Paper*, 1452.

1991. 'Exchange Rates, Intervention and Sterilization', *NBER Reporter*, Winter 1991–2.

Organization for Economic Cooperation and Development 1991. *OECD Economic Surveys – Japan.*

Padoa-Schioppa, T. 1988. 'Towards a New Adjustable Peg?', Per Jacobsson Lecture on *The International Monetary System: the Next Twenty-Five Years.*

Sachs, I. 1985. 'The Dollar and the Policy Mix: 1985', *Brooking Papers on Economic Activity*, 1.

Stein, J. 1989. 'Cheap Talk and the Fed: A Theory of Imprecise Policy Announcements', *American Economic Review*, March.

Summers, L.H. and Summers, V.P. 1989. 'When Financial Markets Work Too Well: A Cautious Case for a Securities Transaction Tax', *Journal of Financial Services Research*, 3.

Taylor, M.P. 1991. 'Intervention, Interest Rates and Charts: Three Essays in International Finance', *IMF Working Paper*, 91/106.

Taylor, M.P. and H. Allen 1992. 'The Use of Technical Analysis in the Foreign Exchange Market', *Journal of International Money and Finance*, June.

Working Group on Exchange Market Intervention 1983. *Report on Exchange Market Intervention* (Jurgensen Report), March.

Discussion

GIORGIO BASEVI

This is a very interesting chapter both for the data it has access to and the use it makes of them, in order to evaluate the effectiveness of foreign exchange market intervention by central banks. In my comments I shall suggest that the main argument of the chapter could be further developed, and I will propose a model for this purpose.

The authors refer to two alternative and extreme possible interpretations in their reading of the evidence about the effectiveness of official intervention in the foreign exchange markets. According to the first, intervention is seen as an inducement for the market to react at the right time to changes in fundamentals. According to the second, intervention is seen as just introducing a 'ping-pong' or 'bouncing ball' process into exchange rate movements. Although not very explicitly, the authors seem to lean towards the second interpretation. If I am right in identifying where their sympathy lies, then I think that their positive evaluation of the episodes could be made more convincing if they were to go further along the line of analysis suggested in works to which they refer – for example that by Frankel and Froot (1987). Along this line, I think it should be possible to develop and extend a model recently devised by Kirman (1991).

In Kirman's model the market is characterized by switches from one type of stochastic process to another. In one process, fundamental elements dominate the forces that drive the exchange rate, while in the other process the market starts inflating a bubble away from fundamentals. The interesting issue raised in Kirman's model, then, is not so much whether bubbles exist and develop, but rather how far and for how long they can last and take the market away from the equilibrium based on fundamentals. In Kirman's model – as in Frankel and Froot – there are two groups of agents: fundamentalists and chartists. The novel aspect of Kirman's model, however, is that – given the population of agents made up of these two groups – individual agents change their opinion about the future exchange rate, from one based on fundamental factors, to one based on chartists elements, or *vice versa*, depending on the probability that individual agents from the two groups 'meet' each other; a probability that essentially

depends on their effective number. Thus, if there is a majority of fundamentalists at a given moment in time, the probability that a chartist is converted into a fundamentalist is higher than the probability of the opposite event. In this way the market gets stuck most of the time in either one of the two regimes, but, at certain points in time, there occur sudden reversals of regimes.

The novel element in Kirman's model is therefore that the weights attributed by the market to the two different types of expectations about the exchange rate, are not chosen through an exogenous mechanism – as in Frankel and Froot's model, where portfolio managers effectively choose the weights so as to make the actual outcome consistent with the market forecast. In Kirman, the weights are determined endogenously, in a probabilistic way, by the process that drives the numerical evolution of the two groups of agents. However, in Kirman's model there are only two groups of agents, i.e., there is no outside intervention in the foreign exchange market. My suggestion is that the model could be fruitfully extended by representing central banks intervention as an effective increase, at selected times, in the number of agents that belong to the group of fundamentalist. In other words, central banks intervene in the market with specified amounts and for a certain period of time and thus enlarge the weight of the fundamentalist group both directly (as they themselves belong to that group) and indirectly (as they increase the probability that chartists will change their opinion and shift to the group of fundamentalists). Clearly the idea is that central banks would do this whenever they feel that, without their intervention, the market would be shifting to a regime based on a majority of chartists and thus getting off into a bubble.

I submit that along this line of analysis the definition and measurement of successful intervention could be identified in a theoretically more satisfactory way. Moreover, it could be done in a way that, while preserving the idea that intervention is aimed at getting the exchange rate back to fundamentals and away from misalignments, it is also capable of generating swings of the 'bouncing ball' type, that in the authors' analysis would otherwise be inconsistent with what they state to be the basic objective of intervention.

References

Frankel, J.A. and Froot, K. 1987. 'Using Survey Data to Test Standard Propositions Regarding Exchange Rate Expectations', *American Economic Review*, March.
Kirman, A.P. 1991. 'Epidemics of opinion and speculative bubbles in financial markets', in M.P. Taylor (ed.), *Money and Financial Markets*, Cambridge Mass. and Oxford, Basil Blackwell.

Discussion

JEFFREY A. FRANKEL

The Onola Memorial Conference was held the same week as a meeting of the Group of Severn (G-7) in Munich. It was at another G-7 meeting, held precisely ten years earlier at Versailles, that the national leaders commissioned a study on the effects of foreign exchange intervention. At the time, the French were the most ardent supporters of intervention, and the Americans, under the first Reagan administration, were opposed. The results of the study, known as the Jurgensen Report, were submitted to the subsequent G-7 Summit at Williamsburg in 1983. The report said that the effects of sterilized intervention, that is intervention which is not allowed to affect money supplies, could at most be minor and transitory.

Econometric tests appeared to show that sterilized intervention was ineffective. The evident reason was that a typical investor treats bonds denominated in different currencies as perfect substitutes, so long as they pay the same expected rate of return, and thus is indifferent to the currency composition of his or her bond portfolio (e.g., Rogoff 1984 and Frankel 1980). The results of academic research happened to coincide with the views of many practitioners, particularly the view of policymakers in the 1981–4 US Treasury, that nothing needed to be done about the appreciating dollar. Thus there was a remarkable degree of consensus in the early 1980s that exchange market intervention did not offer a useful independent policy tool.

The US position changed in 1985, when James Baker and Richard Darman replaced Donald Regan and Beryl Sprinkel at the Treasury. Their policy of intervening to push the dollar down, and the subsequent policy adopted in 1987 of trying to stabilize the dollar, came to be widely perceived by practitioners to have been successful. Ever since 1985, when reports of intervention come out over Reuters, foreign exchange traders react by leaping for their terminals. Central bankers tend to be a bit more restrained than traders in their evaluations, but nevertheless share the view that intervention has often been effective. Only among academics does the consensus remain that sterilized intervention is ineffective. I think the time is ripe for research economists to reexamine this conventional wisdom in

light of the post-1985 experience, and I welcome the contribution of Catte, Galli, and Rebecchini to this effort. I found their chapter to be quite a persuasive accounting of the effects of intervention during this period, and I congratulate them for it.

Data and methodology

The use of true daily data on intervention operations is key to this study, as it is to any study that hopes to find effects in the foreign exchange market. Tests using quarterly or monthly data tend to find the wrong correlation between asset supply data and exchange rates. The explanation is probably the simultaneity created by the phenomenon of 'leaning against the wind': when the dollar falls in value, central banks buy dollars to support it, creating a negative correlation. It is very difficult to deal with such simultaneity bias with quarterly or monthly data.

One can get some idea of daily intervention by compiling reports in the financial press. But the true intervention series is not the same as the reported series. In a study that Dominguez and I wrote for the Institute for International Economics (IIE), we found that only 81 per cent of medium sized and large intervention operations by the US Federal Reserve are reported in the press, and only 71 per cent of smaller intervention operations (Dominguez and Frankel 1993b). Most central banks, while sharing their intervention data with each other, have long declined to make the data public, including until recently the Federal Reserve. The Banca d'Italia, like the Banque de France, Bank of England, and Bank of Japan, continues to keep its data confidential. Those who wish to learn about the implications of the data are thus obliged to read studies such as the one by Catte, Galli, and Rebecchini.

The authors start with the observation that intervention in the period 1985–91 was concentrated in nineteen episodes. Their approach is qualitative: they look at the direction of change of the exchange rate subsequent to the intervention episode. The approach and results are quite similar to a table of eight major episodes in our study for the IIE: we found that in each of the eight episodes, the exchange rate moved during the subsequent month in the same direction as the intervention.

The authors' criterion for judging when intervention is successful is that the subsequent change reverses the preceding trend in the dollar or, in one case (the Plaza episode of September 1985), pushes the dollar in the downward direction that it had already been moving. I agree that the central banks' goal most of the time is resisting the recent trend (the 'leaning against the wind' pattern already noted), and that the goal in September 1985 was to continue the recent trend. There are interesting questions in explaining the pattern of intervention. Fred Bergsten has called the Plaza

kind of policy 'leaning into the wind', and has suggested that it might be an especially potent way to intervene. I would suggest a characterization of intervention patterns that would encompass the Plaza episode at the same time as most of the others: central banks have tended to sell dollars when its value is above a medium-run moving average, and to buy dollars when it is below (the same strategy that one might wish private speculators to follow). But the proper criterion for judging whether the subsequent movement in the exchange rate is what was desired by the central banks is simple. One has only to ask whether the direction of the movement is the same as the direction in which they were intervening: does the value of the dollar increase after dollars are purchased? For this question, it is not necessary to know why the central banks were intervening.

Some episodes

I will discuss several of the authors' nineteen episodes that seem to me of particular interest, before moving on to broader lessons.

Episode 1 took place in February 1985. Almost everyone accepts the Plaza Accord of September 1985 as the big turning point in intervention policy. But January or February of that year seem to me more accurate, and I am glad to see the authors concurring. There are four reasons for dating the shift earlier in the year: (1) Baker and Darman took office in late January; (2) the communiqué from the January Meeting of the Group of Five (G-5) in Washington (which Baker attended in part) uses language that sounds at least as pro intervention as that in the later Plaza Accord; (3) substantial intervention took place, particularly by the Bundesbank in late February but also by the Federal Reserve (the magnitude of sales of dollars for marks was almost as great as in the Plaza episode); and (4) newspapers at the time reported both the view that the new Treasury officials might be more receptive to proposals to intervene to bring down the dollar, and the fact that dollar sales were taking place (Frankel 1985, pp. 199–217).

If one accepts the idea of dating the change in intervention policy from February rather than September, then a widely cited argument of Martin Feldstein's is turned on its head. Feldstein argues that, because the rate of dollar depreciation during the period after the Plaza (excluding the drop on the day of the announcement of 4 per cent or so) was no greater than the rate of depreciation from March to September, intervention must not have been effective. But if the policy shift is dated from February then, contrary to Feldstein, the timing is perfect to explain the reversal of the 1981–5 dollar appreciation. In this case one has to give more credit to the Germans, who were the strongest interveners in the earlier episode, than to the United States.

Episode 4, in March–April 1987, and *episodes 7 and 8*, both in the aftermath of the October 1987 stock market crash, illustrate the importance of using daily data. The authors find greater evidence that intervention had the desired effects, even if they were short lived, than have other observers using only publicly available data.

Episode 10, in the Summer of 1988, occurred in the midst of a US presidential election campaign. Rumours at the time had the Bank of Japan and other foreign central banks buying dollars to help President Bush. There is also a view, now held fairly widely in Japan, that the Japanese authorities were buying dollars throughout 1987–9 to help the United States, and that the effect of these dollar purchases on the Japanese money supply were a prime cause of the 1987–9 bubble in stock prices and land prices. But the actual intervention data show that the Bank of Japan was not intervening at all in the Summer of 1988, and that the Federal Reserve and Deutsche Bundesbank were actually selling dollars. *Episode 11*, November 1988, does show dollar purchases, but *episodes 12–15* in 1989 all show dollar sales again. How can these data be reconciled with the story of Japanese support for the dollar and the asset price bubble? One possible hypothesis, attributable to David Hale, is that the Japanese authorities did not so much intervene themselves as put pressure on Japanese institutional investors to buy dollar assets. Another – not inconsistent – hypothesis is that Japan undertook more rapid monetary growth in 1987–9 than it otherwise would have, in order to fulfil its obligations under the Louvre Agreement, but that the growth primarily took the form of domestic credit expansion rather than purchases of foreign currency. If these actions are still thought to have been motivated by a desire to help the United States, there remains the puzzle of why the United States itself would have been intervening to push the dollar down in mid 1988 and 1989.

Episode 18 took place in February 1991, when the authorities intervened to reverse a dollar depreciation. This is another occasion when the timing is crucial, and the authors' interpretation might be gainsaid by others, who have attributed the turnaround in the dollar to the success of Operation Desert Storm in Kuwait. The United States started to buy dollars on 4 February, and continued for seven days in conjunction with other central banks. The depreciation halted on February 11, intervention was ceased the next day, and a strong dollar appreciation then commenced. The authors attribute the exchange rate reversal to the intervention because Desert Storm did not end until later (24 February). But others would argue that the success of the military operations had become clear earlier, and that it explains the reversal.

Episode 20 does not exist in the authors' list, but I would add it. The authors show July 1991 as the only one of nine turning points in the

exchange rate that was not accompanied by coordinated intervention. I do not have the true daily intervention data for 1991. (The Federal Reserve and Bundesbank have agreed to release data only with a year lag.) But I know that intervention to cap the dollar appreciation was reported in July 1991. So I would add this dollar turning point to the list of successes.

Conclusions

The authors draw a number of conclusions from their analysis of the nineteen episodes. Three of the conclusions warrant particular comment. First, they find that all of these episodes were successful in achieving their goals. Second, they find that eight out of nine turning points coincide exactly with episodes of concerted intervention. (Their one exception is July 1991, the one that I would count as a success). Even a more skeptical view that judged some of their successes to be so short-lived as not to be successes at all, might still see the overall record as an impressive one. The authors' last conclusion regards contemporaneous monetary policy. It is that interest rate differentials moved so as to help pull the exchange rate in the desired direction in a majority of intervention episodes, but in many cases did not. This is not surprising. There are many ways to explain such episodes, where the value of the currency moves in the desired direction but the interest rate moves in the opposite direction. One explanation is simply that the dollar sales are sterilized (even if less than 100 per cent), implying that the supply of bonds increases, driving up interest rates, and thus moderating the resulting fall in the value of the dollar. As the authors note, these episodes are evidence that intervention potentially offers a tool distinct from monetary policy. The authors go so far as to reverse the conventional view that intervention is effective only to the extent that it constitutes a change in monetary policy; instead monetary policy seems effective only to the extent that it takes the form of intervention.

I am a fan of simple charts, tables, and recounting of historical events. These modes of analysis are useful, both when taking a first look at the data, and when presenting conclusions to a general audience. But in between, it is usually desirable to do some more complete econometrics. There are at least three reasons why this is called for in the context of intervention: first, to avoid *ex post* rationalization of exchange rate movements. The three authors are fairly careful about defining uniform criteria for central bank goals and success or failure. But the number of weeks over which subsequent performance is measured is arbitrary. Second, a number of studies (e.g., Loopesko 1984, pp. 257–77 and Dominguez 1990) have already found an effect from daily intervention data. One would like to disentangle the 'signalling effect' (and other varieties of effects *via* expec-

tations) from the 'portfolio effect'. One possibility is to use news reports to identify which interventions were known to the public, and to use survey data to measure the reactions of participants in the foreign exchange market.

Perhaps the most important reason for undertaking careful econometric analysis is the problem of simultaneity. Some readers are suspicious of results like those in the Catte, Galli, and Rebecchini paper and the IIE study, because they indicate that the effect on the exchange rate appears only after intervention stops. During the period of intervention, the exchange rate is almost always moving in the same direction as in the preceding period, the opposite of the direction desired. Some say demand for dollars appears to increase when the central bank is selling dollars; only when the authorities stop and the private market is left to clear on its own does the dollar fall. The change after intervention stops is often not enough to outweigh the change during the period of intervention. Some might claim that the total effect is zero. One would like to know what would have happened in the absence of intervention. Theory says the effect of intervention should be instantaneous (if not sooner). But then simultaneous equation techniques are called for. (In Dominguez and Frankel (1993a), we estimate two simultaneous equations, an expectations equation and a portfolio equation, and use news reports and survey data alongside the true daily intervention data).

References

Dominguez, K. 1990. 'Market Responses to Coordinated Central Bank Intervention', *Carnegie-Rochester Series on Public Policy*, North Holland, 32.

Dominguez, K. and Frankel, J.A. 1993a. 'Does Foreign Exchange Intervention Matter? Disentangling the Portfolio and Expectation Effects for the Mark', *NBER Working Paper*, abridged in *American Economic Review*, 83, 5, December.

1993b *Does Foreign Exchange Intervention Work?*, Washington DC, Institute for International Economies.

Frankel, J.A. 1980. 'A Test of Perfect Substitutability in the Foreign Exchange Market', *Southern Economic Journal*, 46, 4, April.

1985. 'The Dazzling Dollar', *Brookings Papers on Economic Activity*, 1.

Loopesko, B. 1984. 'Relationships Among Exchange Rates, Intervention and Interest Rates: An Empirical Investigation' *Journal of International Money and Finance*, 3.

Rogoff, K. 1984. 'On the Effects of Sterilized Intervention: An Analysis of Weekly Data', *Journal of Monetary Economics*, 14.

Discussion

EDWIN M. TRUMAN

The chapter by Catte, Galli, and Rebecchini on the effectiveness of concerted sterilized intervention is very interesting and revealing. It is interesting because it uses data on daily intervention operations along with other information to examine nineteen efforts over the past seven and a half years to influence the mark/dollar and yen/dollar exchange rates through intervention. As we found on the Jurgensen Report (1983), such case studies are illuminating because they tend to bring out the rich detail and complexity of individual episodes, details that tend to be homogenized in more formal analytical approaches. In addition, the authors use a common statistical framework to analyse and present the nineteen cases which is a useful organizational device.

However, the chapter's strengths also reveal some of its weaknesses. The statistical framework sometimes gets in the way of a more commonsense treatment of the episodes. With *ex post* case studies it is very difficult to prove anything up to the standards of academic scholars unless the hypotheses are very clearly stated at the start, there is general agreement on the criteria that are to be used to test the hypotheses and the facts are convincingly presented. While the authors try to satisfy us on the first two points, I am not persuaded that they are altogether successful. When it comes to the facts, other interpretations are equally plausible. To put this point more positively, these case studies conform to the old adage that where one stands depends on where one sits; the interpretation of case studies is often a matter of perspective.

In the United States, the Federal Reserve Bank of New York has the obligation to report to the Congress and the public at the end of every three-month period, with a lag of one month, on Treasury and Fed foreign exchange operations. These reports are subjected to careful review at the Treasury and the Federal Reserve Board, normally at a senior staff level. One advantage of these reports as raw material for case studies is that they are prepared with very little hindsight: one disadvantage, some might say, is that they in general do not attempt to reach firm judgments concerning the

success or failure of particular episodes of intervention. I reread the reports covering the nineteen episodes the authors of this paper selected, and I was struck by the lack of congruence with respect to (a) what motivated the operations, (b) how they unfolded, and (c) what brought them to a close. The consistency in these areas was, perhaps, 75 per cent. I should confess to my own biases in reading these materials. They have been formed from an experience in which I have found myself leaning against the wind of current US official fashion with respect to the effectiveness of foreign exchange market intervention. In the late 1970s, the wind was blowing very strongly and warmly. In the early 1980s, when the Working Group on Foreign Exchange Market Intervention did its work, the wind was very cold, and the instrument almost froze to death. More recently, the wind has been alternately hot and cold.

My reading of the economic literature over the past decade is that it has been difficult to prove that foreign exchange market intervention is effective in the sense that it has a lasting, quantitatively significant effect on exchange rates. Frankel is among the few who claim to have found otherwise, but he has not yet convinced the profession at large. On the other hand, paraphrasing Frankel, the market appears to take intervention seriously so there must be something to it. My view is that there is something to foreign exchange market intervention, but in a regime of floating exchange rates, foreign exchange market intervention is a limited tool, and when used alone its effects rather quickly wear off. Nevertheless, it can be a useful instrument. From this perspective, I am concerned about this chapter. It claims too much for intervention. As a consequence, it could be counterproductive to what I take to be the basic aim of central banks.

I first will deal with the narrower issue of the effectiveness of intervention. The chapter concludes 'all nineteen episodes of intervention were successful'. About half of them were successful in temporarily halting the course of the dollar; the other half were 'definitely successful' in reversing the course of the dollar. By my personal judgmental criteria, intervention was partially successful in about five of the episodes,[1] and I think this is a good enough record to support the continued judicious use of intervention as a supplementary policy instrument.

Let me illustrate some of my concerns with the chapter's analyses and conclusions.

In my view it can hardly be claimed that coordinated intervention was effective in influencing the course of the dollar in cases where the US monetary authorities were either not involved (episode 3, January 1987), when the monetary authority on the other side backed out and resorted to the use of monetary policy (the Bundesbank in episode 10, Summer of 1988), or when the US authorities were very reluctant

(episode 17, February–April, 1990) or minimal (episode 19, March 1991) participants.

Without detracting from the longer-run policy significance of the events of January through March of 1985, when the United States began to signal a shift in its position on the use of the intervention tool and more importantly its position about the dollar, intervention per se could not have had much to do with a turn in the dollar that was long overdue. The operations started in January, following the Meeting of the Group of Five (G-5) on 17 January in Washington, and the United States operated on a total of eight days following that meeting, selling a total of about $675 million spread over about a five-week period. This was hardly a massive operation, and if the intervention was effective, it took a long time to exert its influence.

I think it is difficult to sustain the argument that intervention had anything but very temporary effects during much of 1987. Repeated efforts to restrain the dollar's decline failed. If anything the intervention in August 1987 (episode number 5) to correct a temporary rebound of the dollar against the Deutsche mark was misguided. This having been said, I believe that the intervention operations in early January 1988 were quite effective in reversing the dollar's decline against the Deutsche mark at least, but not against the yen. Hence, the qualified success rating. The relative failure to reverse the decline against the yen, which the authors do not recognize,[2] gives rise to the March-April 1988 episode (number 9) which is recorded as a success even though on a monthly average basis the low for the dollar against the yen was in May 1988.

I think it is even more difficult to agree with the authors that the six efforts to push the dollar down in 1989 and 1990 can be chalked up as successes. In several cases the so-called success lasted less than a month before the effort had to be repeated, and several of the episodes spanned months with limited results. How can episode 15 (October 1989) be counted as a successful episode of concerted intervention when it involved intervention by all countries of the Group of Three (G-3), but only the mark/dollar rate by any reasonable standard stopped appreciating? Something else must have been going on if 'success' for the yen/dollar rate had to wait for episode 17 (April 1990). Calling the latter episode a success is questionable on other grounds.[3] In the end, in April 1990 (the last part of episode 17), the Bank of Japan was acting alone because the other members of the G-7 and G-3 had given up on the use of the intervention tool, and the Japanese declined to use monetary policy to curb the fall of the yen.

It is cases of prolonged intervention, such as the sixteen month period of frustration in 1989–90, that give intervention a bad name. They contrast

with briefer episodes, such as number eighteen in February 1991, where it is it more plausible that intervention helped to calm what was a very confused market and to reestablish a sense of two-way risk.

The authors claim that they find that intervention was always present when the dollar reached a turning point over the past seven and a half years. However, they find only one turning point when there was no intervention, July 1991. In fact, there was US and German intervention at that time; however, it did not pass the authors' tests for concerted intervention. The aftermath of episode 17 in April 1990 is an example of a turning point in the yen/dollar rate that cannot be associated with concerted intervention. The authors suggest two interpretations of their 'finding' with respect to turning points. The weaker interpretation is that concerted intervention has 'determined the exact timing of the turning points'. The stronger interpretation is that concerted intervention has been able to 'bounce' the exchange rate, 'when it is hit by the central banks, it changes direction and then continues to move in that direction, almost without friction, until it is again hit in the opposite direction'. The problem with the second interpretation is that the central banks often have to go through several 'episodes' before the currency, in fact, reverses direction again.

Let me suggest two alternative views of this notional success. First is a less kind interpretation.[4] Suppose the monetary authorities believe that foreign exchange market intervention can affect the weather; they sell dollars when the weather is nasty and refrain from doing so once the weather turns fair. Then it would appear that such operations are successful in turning nasty weather into fair. In fact, the authorities might not be concerned about a few rainy days or a few sunny days, but they might be concerned about severe flooding or severe drought. As a consequence, they may call upon concerted intervention when the weather reaches extremes, after a long series of rainy days or a long dry spell. Because concerted intervention only takes place after long periods of flooding or drought, it would appear to be associated with reversals of weather patterns.

A kinder view, one closer to my own, is that the monetary authorities are genuinely concerned about exchange rates; sometimes they may be concerned about them for the wrong reasons, but they are, nevertheless, concerned. Intervention provides a means of manifesting that concern, by either individual or collective action. The more extreme the perceived movements in the rates, the more the authorities may seek to influence them. Moreover, one should allow for the possibility that intervention is more likely to be concerted when those movements have been extreme, and the chances of 'success' are, therefore, increased. Sometimes interventions are successful, in the sense that they may cause market participants to think again about the fundamental determinants of exchange rates (what the authors refer to as 'expectations coordination'), and the currency does turn

– January 1988 may be an example. The dollar may have turned against the Deutsche mark without the intervention, but we cannot be sure of precisely when. Once the dollar turns, the intervention stops, and it appears to have 'caused' the turn. Who knows for sure? Sometimes the authorities through their intervention operations are able only to establish a bit of calm for a while. However, that achievement may be useful, as long as the scale of the intervention is not too large, because it serves to convince the authorities that if they want to affect the course of their currency they must use more fundamental policy instruments, in particular, monetary and fiscal policies.

The authors recognize the difficulties and ambiguities involved in assessing the effects of monetary policy on exchange rates especially when it comes to interpreting the movements of three-month or ten-year interest rates. It is reasonable, but not unambiguous, to focus on overnight rates. However, the authors' view of monetary policy, especially of US monetary policy, is too mechanical in the case of overnight rates. The federal funds rate is not manipulated by the Federal Reserve on a day-by-day basis to affect exchange rates. There are sometimes sharp, temporary movements in the funds rate, but those are most often associated with shortfalls or excesses in reserve availability on Wednesdays at the end of reserve maintenance periods.[5] More broadly, the profession has found it difficult to establish a systematic statistical relation between interest rates and exchange rates, nominal or real (Edison and Pauls 1991; Edison and Melick 1992). However, these results do not lead me to conclude that there is no connection between exchange rates and monetary policy. Instead, the relationship is more complex than has yet been captured by simple statistical exercises.

Intervention can be problematic for countries that have chosen to have floating exchange rates, which is the situation for each of the G-3 countries *vis-à-vis* the other two countries, because intervention, if effective, can be counterproductive, or if not effective, may confuse market participants. For a country with floating exchange rates, one of the channels of monetary policy is through changes in exchange rates. The authors appear not to recognize this dilemma situation. In fact, intervention was controversial for the United States during episode 10 (June–August, 1988) and episode 13 (March–April 1989). In both cases, US monetary policy – indexed by the federal funds rate – was tightening to deal with the building inflation pressures, and some observers and policymakers could not understand why the US authorities were trying to resist the dollar's appreciation which would have helped in this process.[6]

This brings me to my primary concern about this chapter: in claiming too much for intervention, the authors, despite their cautionary words at the end of the chapter, risk undermining the achievement of the fundamental

objective of monetary policy, what Paul Volcker calls stability, price stability. If the authorities believe that intervention is always effective, they will be inclined to believe that more is better. The next step is that they will believe that intervention and something called 'exchange rate policy' is a powerful, independent policy tool especially if it is coordinated or concerted. As a result the policymaker may be led to conclude, for example, that if a country has a large fiscal imbalance that is contributing to a large external imbalance, all that is necessary to correct the latter is to adjust exchange rates, while doing nothing about the former. As another example, if the central bank is running an overly expansionary monetary policy, inflation is rising, and the currency is depreciating, then this view of the effectiveness of intervention implies that all the authorities have to do is to use a bit of intervention to stabilize the currency, maybe even appreciate it a bit, without having to confront the difficult policy choices. I am concerned that the implicit message of this chapter turns on its head the traditional argument for stable exchange rates as a source of discipline over macroeconomic policies. While there are many who do not have much sympathy for the discipline argument, few, I hope, would argue today that flexible exchange rates realistically can be supported on the grounds that they permit the authorities to avoid discipline. This has been the lesson about floating exchange rates that was painfully learned in the 1970s and 1980s.

Notes

1 The Plaza (episode 2) September–November, 1985; August 1987 (episode 5) which in retrospect may have been a misuse of the instrument; January 1988 (end of episode 8); February 1991 (episode 18); and, perhaps, in small part, January–March 1985 (episode 1).
2 The chapter is a bit Deutsche mark-centred in its analysis.
3 The authors admit that intervention in this episode was very loosely concerted.
4 This interpretation is due to a colleague, Matt Pritsker, who is in fact a very kind fellow.
5 Thus, the authors obtain some spurious results by focusing on point-to-point comparisons.
6 In the first case, the net movement of the overnight interest differential was favourable to the Deutsche mark, but this was only because Deutsche mark interest rates moved more than dollar interest rates.

References

Edison, H.J. and Pauls B.D. 1991. 'Re-Assessment of the Relationship Between Real Exchange Rates and Real Interest Rates: 1974–90', *International Finance Discussion Papers*, 408, Board of Governors of the Federal Reserve System, August.

Edison, H.J. and Melick, W.R. 1992. 'Purchasing Power Parity and Uncovered Interest Rate Parity: The United States 1974–1990', *International Finance Discussion Papers*, 425. Board of Governors of the Federal Reserve System, March.

Working Group on Exchange Market Intervention 1983. *Report on Exchange Market Intervention* (Jurgensen Report), March.

IV

The international framework for national economic policies

9 Economic performance under alternative exchange rate regimes: some historical evidence

TAMIM BAYOUMI and BARRY EICHENGREEN

1 Introduction

The international monetary system has clearly passed through a succession of very different phases. The classical gold standard that prevailed before 1914 featured a remarkable degree of exchange rate stability throughout the industrialized world.[1] This contrasts with the international monetary turbulence of World War I and subsequent decades: exchange rate instability and controls during the war, free floating in its aftermath, and an abortive return to fixed rates in the second half of the 1920s followed by a period of unilateral devaluation and managed floating in the 1930s. World War II was succeeded by another period of comparative exchange rate stability in the advanced industrial countries.[2] Following the collapse of the Bretton Woods system in the early 1970s, international monetary instability resurfaced anew.

It is hard to think of another set of observations about whose causes there exists so little understanding, much less agreement. One can identify three generic explanations for this sequence of international monetary events. The first emphasizes differences over time in the willingness of policymakers to accept the discipline required for the maintenance of fixed rates. The classical gold standard and the Bretton Woods system survived for as long as they did, it is argued, because governments refrained from destabilizing them through the pursuit of inconsistent policies. If this explanation is correct, then the agenda for research is to understand why policymakers found the discipline of fixed rates more compelling in some periods than in others. The second potential explanation emphasizes instead differences in the stability of the underlying economic environment. Fixed rate regimes can be successfully maintained, this argument runs, when markets are not perturbed by real and financial disturbances, especially ones that affect different countries differently. When, however, the international economic environment is disturbed by (asymmetric) shocks exogenous to the exchange rate system, examples of which might arguably include the stock market crashes of 1929 and 1987 or the oil shocks of the 1970s, the costs of stabilizing exchange rates is increased and

fixed rate regimes break down. If this explanation is correct, then the agenda for research is to measure disturbances to the economic environment in ways that are not heavily contaminated by the exchange rate regime itself, and to understand why their magnitude has varied over time. The third potential explanation emphasizes not the stance of policy or the turbulence of the underlying environment but the economy's capacity to adjust to disturbances emanating from either source. If wages and prices are flexible, then markets will adjust smoothly. Disturbances will produce little unemployment. Policymakers have little incentive to sacrifice exchange rate stability in order to stabilize domestic economic conditions. Hence, fixed exchange rates can be painlessly maintained. For those who subscribe to this explanation, the agenda for research is to understand why speed of adjustment – of wages to unemployment, for example – has changed over time.

This is a trio of ambitious research agendas, which goes some way towards explaining why they have not been adequately pursued. Nor is it obvious which of these lines of inquiry is most relevant – in other words, which one or ones should be pursued first. In this chapter we therefore provide evidence on the incidence of disturbances and on adjustment to them during different phases in the history of the international monetary system. We apply a variant of the methodology developed by Blanchard and Quah (1989) to historical data. The appeal of this approach is that output fluctuations can be decomposed into disturbances to the economy and its subsequent response, thus speaking to the distinction between our first two and our third potential explanations. The Blanchard–Quah approach also distinguishes disturbances that affect the level of output permanently from those that affect it only temporarily. Previous papers have, not uncontroversially, interpreted these permanent and temporary disturbances as supply and demand shocks, and associated the former primarily with the instability of the underlying economic environment and the latter primarily with demand management policy.[3] This speaks to the distinction between our first and second explanations. The rest of the chapter is organized as follows. Section 2 describes the methodology in more detail. Section 3 applies it to a comparison of the Bretton Woods fixed exchange rate system and the post-Bretton Woods float. Section 4 extends the comparison to the interwar period and the classical gold standard years. Section 5 draws out the implications of our findings for research on alternative international monetary arrangements.

2 Methodology

Our methodological point of departure is the familiar aggregate demand and aggregate supply diagramme reproduced as the top panel in figure 9.1.

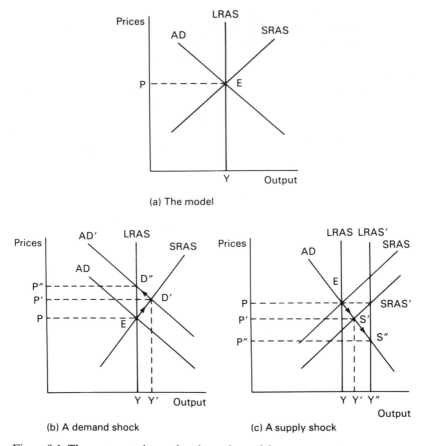

(a) The model

(b) A demand shock   (c) A supply shock

Figure 9.1 The aggregate demand and supply model

The aggregate demand curve (labelled AD) is downward sloping in price-output space, reflecting the fact that lower prices raise real money balances and therefore product demand. The short-run aggregate supply curve (SRAS) is upward sloping, reflecting the assumption that capacity utilization can be varied in the short run to capitalize on the profit opportunities afforded by changes in aggregate demand. The long-run aggregate supply curve (LRAS) is vertical, since capacity utilization eventually returns to its normal level, preventing demand shocks from permanently affecting the level of production.

The effect of a positive demand shock is shown in the left half of the lower panel. As the aggregate demand curve shifts from AD to AD', the short-run equilibrium moves from its initial point E to the intersection of SRAS with AD'. Both output and prices rise. As the aggregate supply curve becomes

increasingly vertical over time, the economy moves gradually from the short-run equilibrium D′ to the long-run equilibrium D″. As the economy traverses the new aggregate demand curve, output falls back to its initial level, while the price level continues to rise. Hence, the response to a permanent positive demand shock is a short-term rise in production followed by a gradual return to the initial level of output, and a permanent rise in prices.

The effects of a positive supply disturbance (a favourable technology shock that permanently raises potential output, for instance) is shown in the right-hand bottom panel. The short- and long-run aggregate supply curves shift to the right by the same amount, displacing the short-term equilibrium from E to S′. On impact, output rises but prices fall. As the supply curve becomes increasingly vertical over time, the economy moves from S′ to S″, leading to further increases in output and additional declines in prices. Whereas demand shocks affect output only temporarily, supply shocks affect it permanently. And whereas positive demand shocks raise prices, positive supply shocks reduce them.

We estimate this framework using a procedure proposed by Blanchard and Quah (1989) for extracting temporary and permanent shocks from a pair of time series variables, as extended to the present case by Bayoumi (1992). Consider a system where the true model can be represented by an infinite moving average representation of a (vector) of variables, X_t, and an equal number of shocks, ϵ_t. Formally, using the lag operator L, this can be written as

$$X_t = A_0\epsilon_t + A_1\epsilon_{t-1} + A_2\epsilon_{t-2} + A_3\epsilon_{t-3}\cdots$$
$$= \sum_{i=0}^{\infty} L^i A_i \epsilon_{t-i} \tag{2.1}$$

where the matrices A_i represent the impulse response functions of the shocks to the elements of X. Specifically, let X_t be made up of change in output and the change in prices, and let ϵ_t be demand and supply shocks. Then the model becomes

$$\begin{bmatrix} \Delta y_t \\ \Delta p_t \end{bmatrix} = \sum_{i=0}^{\infty} L^i \begin{bmatrix} a_{11i} & a_{12i} \\ a_{21i} & a_{22i} \end{bmatrix} \begin{bmatrix} \epsilon_{dt} \\ \epsilon_{st} \end{bmatrix} \tag{2.2}$$

where y_t and p_t represent the logarithm of output and prices, ϵ_{dt} and ϵ_{st} are independent supply and demand shocks, and a_{11i} represents element a_{11} in matrix A_i.

The framework implies that while supply shocks have permanent effects on the level of output, demand shocks only have temporary effects. (Both have permanent effects upon the level of prices.) Since output is written in first difference form, this implies that the cumulative effect of demand

shocks on the change in output (Δy_t) must be zero. This implies the restriction

$$\sum_{i=0}^{\infty} a_{11i} = 0 \qquad (2.3)$$

The model defined by equations (2.2) and (2.3) can be estimated using a vector autoregression. Each element of X_t can be regressed on lagged values of all the elements of X. Using B to represent these estimated coefficients, the estimating equation becomes

$$\begin{aligned}
X_t &= B_1 X_{t-1} + B_2 X_{t-2} + \ldots + B_n X_{t-n} + e_t \\
&= (I - B(L))^{-1} e_t \\
&= (I + B(L) + B(L)^2 + \ldots) e_t \\
&= e_t + D_1 e_{t-1} + D_2 e_{t-2} + D_3 e_{t-3} + \ldots
\end{aligned} \qquad (2.4)$$

where e_t represents the residuals from the equations in the vector autoregression. In the case being considered, e_t is comprised of the residuals of a regression of lagged values of Δy_t and Δp_t on current values of each in turn; these residuals are labelled e_{yt} and e_{pt}, respectively.

To convert equation (2.4) into the model defined by equations (2.2) and (2.3), the residuals from the VAR, e_t, must be transformed into demand and supply shocks, ϵ_t. Writing $e_t = C\epsilon_t$, it is clear that, in the two-by-two case considered, four restrictions are required to define the four elements of the matrix C. Two of these restrictions are simple normalizations, which define the variance of the shocks ϵ_{dt} and ϵ_{st}. A third restriction comes from assuming that demand and supply shocks are orthogonal.[4]

The final restriction, which allows the matrix C to be uniquely defined, is that demand shocks have only temporary effects on output.[5] As noted above, this implies equation (2.3). In terms of the VAR it implies

$$\sum_{i=0}^{\infty} \begin{bmatrix} d_{11i} & d_{12i} \\ d_{21i} & d_{22i} \end{bmatrix} \begin{bmatrix} c_{11} & c_{12} \\ c_{21} & c_{22} \end{bmatrix} = \begin{bmatrix} 0 & \cdot \\ \cdot & \cdot \end{bmatrix} \qquad (2.5)$$

This restriction allows the matrix C to be uniquely defined and the demand and supply shocks to be identified. Note that although the model is estimated in first differences, the restrictions are imposed on the level of output. Accordingly, we will report the estimation results in terms of the level of output and prices.

Interpreting shocks with a permanent impact on output as supply disturbances and shocks with only a temporary impact on output as demand disturbances is controversial. Doing so requires adopting the battery of restrictions incorporated into the aggregate supply–aggregate demand model of figure 9.1. One can think of frameworks other than the

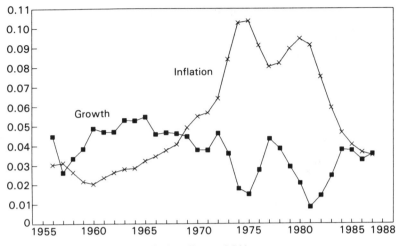

Figure 9.2A G-7 growth and inflation (3-year MA)

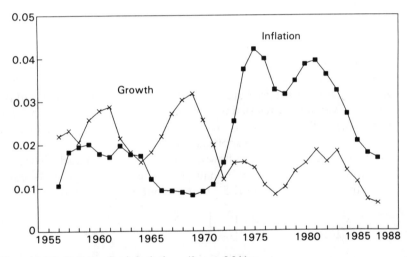

Figure 9.2B G-7 standard deviations (3-year MA)

standard aggregate supply–aggregate demand model in which that association might break down. Moreover, it is conceivable that temporary supply
shocks (for example, an oil price increase that is reversed subsequently) or
permanent demand shocks (for example, a permanent increase in government spending which affects real interest rates and related variables)
dominate our data. But here a critical feature of our methodology comes
into play. While restriction (2.5) affects the response of output to the two

shocks, it says nothing about their impact on prices. The aggregate supply–aggregate demand model implies that demand shocks should raise prices while supply shocks should lower them. Since these responses are not imposed, they are useful for testing our interpretation of permanent output disturbances in terms of supply and temporary ones in terms of demand[6].

3 Bretton Woods and the post-Bretton Woods float

Annual data on real and nominal Gross Domestic Product (GDP) for the countries of the Group of Seven (G-7) spanning the period 1953–88 were collected from OECD National Accounts volumes and their machine-readable counterparts. Growth and inflation were calculated as the first difference of the logarithm of real GDP and the implicit GDP deflator, respectively. We partitioned the series into the Bretton Woods period (1953–70) and the post-Bretton Woods float (1971–88). Allowing two observations for lags, this provided estimation periods of equal length: 1955–70 and 1973–88. In addition to analysing the individual country data, we considered the behaviour of aggregate G-7 output, computed using weights based on 1970 GDP converted into common currency using purchasing power parity exchange rates.

Table 9.1 displays these data for the Bretton Woods period, for the post-Bretton Woods float, and separately for the first and second halves of both periods. The first two rows in the growth and inflation panels summarize the aggregate G-7 series. The row labelled SD reports the standard deviation of the G-7 series, while SD* shows the GDP-weighted standard deviation of the individual country series around the G-7 aggregate. The first row thus summarizes aggregate variation, the second one variation around the aggregate. (Since the data are in logarithms, a value of 0.01 represents a variation of approximately 1 per cent). Comparing SD and SD* over the two regimes, a change in the aggregate behaviour of growth is apparent with the shift from fixed to floating rates. Between 1955 and 1970, the G-7 aggregate is stable compared to the amount of dispersion around the aggregate that is evident. Between 1973 and 1988, aggregate variation is essentially unchanged, but dispersion falls noticeably relative to the Bretton Woods period.[7]

To confirm that the change in behaviour is not an artefact of this particular statistic, we also computed the share of the variance of the individual country series explained by the first principal component, along with the number of negative factor loadings in this component (reported in parentheses).[8] The share of the variance explained by the first principal component rises from 33 to 63 per cent, confirming the increase in the cross-country coherence of output movements following the shift from fixed to

Table 9.1. *Basic data: Bretton Woods and post-Bretton Woods periods*

	1955–70	1955–62	1963–70	1973–88	1973–80	1981–88
GROWTH						
G7 SD	0.014	0.017	0.010	0.014	0.022	0.017
SD*	0.024	0.024	0.025	0.013	0.013	0.012
Per cent explained by						
first principal component	33(1)	45(0)	42(2)	63(1)	74(0)	62(0)
INFLATION						
G7 SD	0.011	0.006	0.011	0.028	0.016	0.022
SD*	0.014	0.016	0.012	0.031	0.036	0.026
Per cent explained by						
first principal component	41(1)	35(1)	44(1)	77(1)	50(0)	80(0)
CORRELATION OF GROWTH AND INFLATION						
G7	− 0.22	− 0.36	− 0.52	− 0.54	− 0.94	− 0.73

Notes:
G7 numbers derived from G7 data.
SD = standard deviation of series.
SD* = weighted standard deviation of variation around series.

floating rates. These summary statistics are at odds with conventional wisdom in which it is argued that the Bretton Woods period was one of output stability compared to the turbulent era of oil shocks and fiscal disturbances that followed, and where it is suggested that the shift from fixed to flexible rates after 1970 weakened the international synchronization of business cycles. The first and fourth columns of table 9.1 indicate that economic growth in the G-7 countries was no less volatile under Bretton Woods than under the post-Bretton Woods float, and that the international dispersion of growth rates was, if anything, greater under fixed than under floating rates. The other columns of table 9.1, which divide the data for each regime into halves, help to resolve this paradox. They show that G-7 growth was more volatile in the first half of the Bretton Woods sample than in the second. Similarly, growth was more volatile in the period of oil shocks (1973–80) than in subsequent years.[9]

Turning to inflation, there is an increase in both the variation of the G-7 aggregate and in the variation of individual countries around that average between the Bretton Woods and floating exchange rate periods. Industrial country inflation became more variable both over time and across nations with the switch from fixed to flexible exchange rates. Figures 9.2A and 9.2B show the behaviour of aggregate growth and inflation (in figure 9.2A) and

of country specific standard deviations around the aggregate (in figure 9.2B). For ease of interpretation, three-year moving averages are displayed. Figure 9.2B highlights the decline in the cross-country dispersion of growth rates after 1970, accompanied by a rise in the cross-country dispersion of inflation. An interpretation of these changes is that the shift from fixed to flexible exchange rates allowed countries to stabilize relative growth rates *vis-à-vis* one another at the expense of their relative inflation rates. This would be the case, for example, if countries experienced different shocks but were constrained under fixed rates in the policies that might be used to offset them, whereas under flexible rates they were able to use policies to stabilize output relative to the G-7 average, but at the expense of different rates of inflation that depended on the nature of domestic disturbances. The final row of table 9.1 therefore reports the correlation between growth rates and inflation rates for the G-7 aggregate and for each country. The negative correlation that dominates is suggestive of a predominance of supply shocks. Still, direct evidence on the incidence of shocks is required to substantiate this conjecture.

The magnitude and dispersion of shocks

To identify supply and demand disturbances we estimated bivariate VARs for each country and for the G-7 aggregate. In all cases, the number of lags was set to two to preserve the symmetry of specification across countries. The estimation and simulation results accord with the aggregate supply–aggregate demand framework discussed in section 2. Recall that the 'overidentifying restriction' that positive aggregate demand shocks should be associated with increases in prices while positive aggregate supply shocks should be associated with falls in prices was not imposed by the estimation procedure. In every case, it was an outcome of estimation and simulation using individual country data, supporting our interpretation of the results in terms of aggregate demand and aggregate supply. Figures 9.3A, 9.3B 9.4A and 9.4B display the impulse response functions for the G-7 aggre-gate. In figures 9.3A and 9.3B, supply disturbances raise output perma-nently, while demand disturbances have an output effect only in the short run. Both types of shocks alter prices permanently, but in different directions.

Table 9.2 summarizes the behaviour of individual country aggregate supply and aggregate demand disturbances in a format comparable to the analysis of output and inflation shown in table 9.1. Two different variants of the global aggregate are analysed: G-7 denotes supply and demand disturbances derived from the G-7 aggregate; while G-7' denotes distur-bances calculated using a GDP-weighted average of the residuals from the

individual country estimates. (Following table 9.1, when constructing the
weights, GDP was expressed in dollars using purchasing power parity
exchange rates.) Again, SD denotes the standard deviation of the aggregate, SD* is the standard deviation of individual country disturbances
relative to that aggregate.

Consider first the supply shocks. There is at most a slight rise in their
average magnitude following the shift from fixed to flexible rates. In
contrast, there is a pronounced increase – by a fraction on the order of one
half – in the dispersion of supply shocks around the aggregate with the shift
from fixed to flexible rates. SD* rises from 0.010 to 0.015 when G-7 is used,
and from 0.009 to 0.013 when G-7' is substituted. There is some evidence,
then, that while supply shocks have become no larger following the shift
from fixed to floating rates, they have become more diverse. The estimates
for demand shocks suggest a modest increase in both average magnitude
and dispersion whichever measure of the aggregate is used. In contrast to
the results for supply shocks, where the evidence of increased dispersion is
stronger than that of increased magnitude, for demand shocks the opposite
is the case. The two methods of constructing the G-7 aggregate make more
of a difference when the magnitude of shocks in various subperiods is
considered. For supply shocks the weighted average of individual shocks
(G-7') shows a large rise in aggregate variance in 1973–80. Aggregate
variance then falls back to Bretton Woods levels during the 1980s. In
comparison, disturbances derived from the G-7 aggregate show a smaller
rise in average magnitude. Neither measure of the aggregate indicates much
of a change in the cross-country dispersion of supply disturbances between
the first and second Bretton Woods subperiods or between the first and
second halves of the floating rate regime.

Turning to demand disturbances, both measures of the aggregate suggest
a fall in the magnitude of demand disturbances between the first and second
halves of Bretton Woods. In contrast, whereas the aggregate index suggests
no change in the average magnitude of demand disturbances between the
first and second halves of the floating period, the weighted average (G-7')
suggests that their average size fell by nearly a half between 1973–80 and
1981–8. Neither measure indicates a noticeable rise in cross-country
dispersion of demand disturbances between the first and second Bretton
Woods subperiods or between the first and second halves of floating.

Individual time series observations are useful for interpreting these
trends. Figures 9.5A and 9.5B plot three-year moving averages of the
underlying supply and demand disturbances for the G-7 (figure 9.5A),
along with the standard deviation of the individual country supply and
demand disturbances around these values (figure 9.5B), using the GDP-
weighted average of the shocks to individual countries. The break after

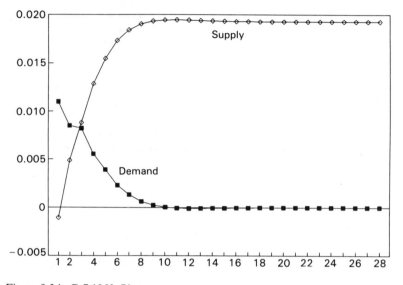

Figure 9.3A G-7 1953–70: output responses

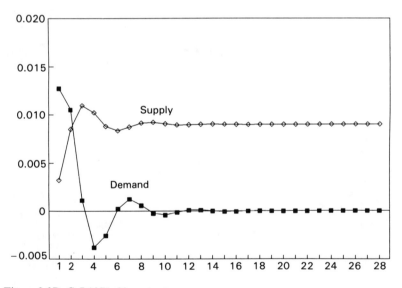

Figure 9.3B G-7 1971–88: output responses

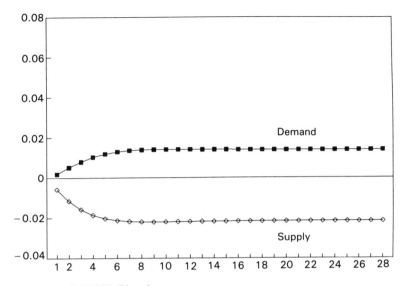

Figure 9.4A G-7 1953–70: price responses

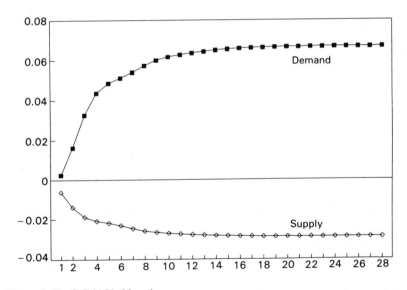

Figure 9.4B G-7 1971–88: price responses

Table 9.2. *Underlying disturbances: Bretton Woods and post-Bretton Woods periods*

		1955–70	1955–62	1963–70	1973–88	1973–80	1981–88
DEMAND							
G7	SD	0.012	0.013	0.007	0.014	0.013	0.013
	SD*	0.013	0.014	0.012	0.015	0.015	0.014
G7′	SD	0.008	0.008	0.006	0.011	0.013	0.007
	SD*	0.012	0.013	0.012	0.013	0.014	0.013
Per cent explained by first principal component		41(2)	44(1)	39(3)	31(3)	49(1)	53(3)
SUPPLY							
G7	SD	0.006	0.006	0.007	0.007	0.008	0.007
	SD*	0.010	0.010	0.011	0.015	0.015	0.014
G7′	SD	0.006	0.005	0.006	0.007	0.009	0.005
	SD*	0.009	0.009	0.010	0.013	0.013	0.013
Per cent explained by first principal component		24(2)	36(3)	30(2)	36(1)	44(2)	51(1)

Notes:
G7 numbers derived from G7 data. G7′ numbers derived from weighted average of individual country data.
SD = standard deviation of series.
SD* = weighted standard deviation of variation around series.

1969 reflects the fact that the VARs estimated separately for the (non-overlapping) Bretton Woods and post-Bretton Woods periods utilized two lagged values of each variable. Figure 9.5 paints a picture of increasing demand pressure as the Bretton Woods period progressed, matched by a decline in positive supply shocks. This shift from a predominance of positive supply shocks to a predominance of positive demand shocks may be relevant to the issue of why Bretton Woods collapsed, to which we return below.

The pattern traced out by supply and demand shocks since 1973 is readily interpreted in terms of historical events. Negative supply shocks are evident in 1974–5, coincident with the first oil price increase of the Organization of Petroleum Exporting Countries (OPEC). This is followed by a sequence of positive supply shocks as oil prices decline back towards pre-OPEC levels, and then by another series of negative supply shocks following the second OPEC price hike in 1979. The time profile of demand shocks in figure 9.5A resembles the time profile of inflation in figure 9.2A. The positive demand shocks of the mid 1970s reflect the G-7 countries' attempt to finance rather than adjust to the first OPEC hike and to the commodity price boom.

Demand disturbances then turn negative at the beginning of the 1980s, reflecting the shift to anti-inflationary policies in the United States, the United Kingdom, and other countries.

The dispersion of individual country supply and demand disturbances around disturbances to the aggregate is shown in figure 9.5B. The dispersion of both supply and demand disturbances falls to low levels during the first half of the 1960s, a period that might be called 'the heyday of Bretton Woods'. The dispersion of both series then rises in the second half of the 1960s, though not to historically unprecedented heights. Again, these trends may be relevant to the question of what prompted the collapse of Bretton Woods, a subject to which we return. Under the post-1971 float, the only obvious movement in the dispersion of supply and demand disturbances is their temporary increase at the beginning of the 1980s. The increased dispersion of demand disturbances can be accounted for by differences across countries in the timing of anti-inflationary initiatives, with countries like France lagging behind the United Kingdom and the United States. Also striking is the concurrent rise and fall in the cross-country dispersion of supply disturbances. This plausibly reflects differences across countries in the adoption of investment promoting policies, such as the US Congress' passage of accelerated depreciation provisions and the reduction of marginal tax rates on individual incomes.[10]

To recapitulate, then, while there is some indication of an increase in the average magnitude of supply shocks between 1973 and 1980 when we construct the G-7 aggregate using GDP weights and purchasing power parity exchange rates, in other respects (and using alternative measures) the magnitude of supply shocks is essentially unchanged. The same measure of the aggregate also suggests an increase in the average magnitude of demand shocks in 1973–80, but otherwise the picture is one of intertemporal stability. Perhaps the most important difference across periods is the increase in the dispersion of individual-country aggregate supply disturbances following the shift from fixed to floating rates. In contrast, there is little difference in the dispersion of demand disturbances across subperiods. Overall, then, unless increases in the dispersion of aggregate supply disturbances are responsible for them, it appears that the changes in the overall behaviour of growth and inflation evident in figure 9.2A are unlikely to flow exclusively from changes in the underlying aggregate supply and demand disturbances. The other principal factor that contributed, we will now suggest, was changes in the adjustment process.

The adjustment mechanism

Figures 9.3A, 9.3B, 9.4A and 9.4B suggest that both aggregate supply and aggregate demand shocks produced larger changes in prices as compared to

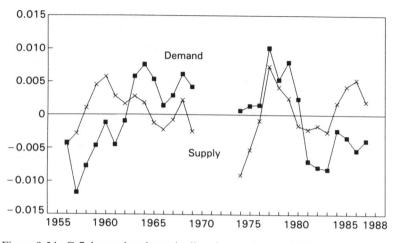

Figure 9.5A G-7 demand and supply disturbances (3-year MA)

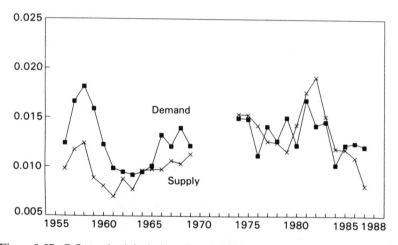

Figure 9.5B G-7 standard deviations (3-year MA)

changes in output under flexible than under fixed rates. For supply disturbances it is the size of the output response which falls, for demand disturbances it is the price response which rises. (To facilitate comparison, the figures for successive periods have been drawn to the same vertical scale.) Identically distributed supply shocks would produce this result – larger price responses and smaller output responses – if the aggregate demand curve was steeper under flexible than under fixed rates. In this section we first present evidence to this effect and then explain why this shift in the slope of the AD curve occurred.

Our impulse response functions can be used to plot the aggregate demand and short-run aggregate supply curves in price output-space. For the AD curve, this is simply the path traced out by prices and output in response to a supply shock. For the SRAS curve, it is the line segment marked off by the initial equilibrium, on one end, and by the level of output and prices that prevails in the first period following a demand shock, on the other end. (This is the impact effect of a shift in aggregate demand, which induces a movement up or down the SRAS curve.) The rest of the adjustment to a demand shock can be thought of as a movement along the AD curve. In response to a positive shock, we should expect to see a subsequent movement up the AD curve, with prices rising and demand falling; this can be thought of as another illustration of our 'overidentifying restriction'. These plots are shown in figure 9.6 for the G-7 aggregate. Consider first the impulse response functions for the Bretton Woods period, displayed in the upper half of the figure. The response to a positive demand shock appears in the upper right quadrant of the diagram on the left-hand side. In the first period, both output and prices rise, although the output response is large relative to the price response. This suggests a relatively flat SRAS curve. In all subsequent periods, output falls while prices continue to rise. Here the output responses are slightly smaller than the price responses. This suggests an AD curve slightly steeper in absolute value than a 45 degree line. The response to a positive supply shock (which should also trace out the AD curve) appears in the lower right-hand quadrant of the same diagram. Following a first period in which there is no output response, output rises and prices fall in response to the positive supply shock. The response of prices is slightly larger than the response of output, again suggesting an AD curve slightly steeper than a 45 degree line.

Stylized versions of these SRAS and AD curves are shown on the right-hand side of the upper row. The two parallel AD curves reflect the fact that we traced out the demand curve both by shifting the supply curve (in the lower right-hand quadrant of the first diagram) and without a supply shift (in the upper right-hand quadrant).

The bottom half of figure 9.6 displays analogous results for the post-Bretton Woods float. Although the slope of the SRAS curve is essentially the same, the AD curve is steeper than during the Bretton Woods period of fixed rates. This result emerges whether one compares the movement up the demand curve following the impact effect of a supply shock (the negatively sloped segment in the upper right-hand quadrant of the two diagrams) or the movement along the AD curve in response to a positive supply shock (the negatively sloped segment in the lower right-hand quadrant of the two diagrams). Figure 9.6 can also tell us something about the speed of adjustment to disturbances. Recall that the negatively sloping part of the

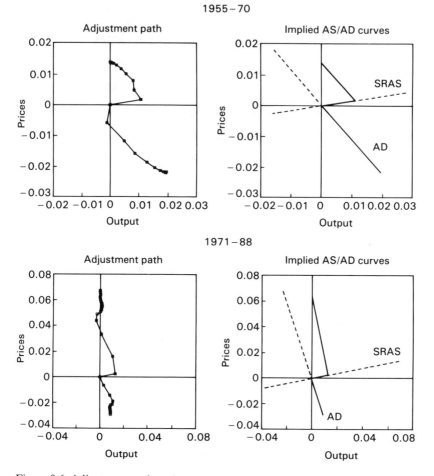

Figure 9.6 Adjustment path and curves, post-World War II periods

curve in the upper right-hand quadrant traces out the aggregate demand curve as the aggregate supply curve rotates from its relatively flat short-run slope to its vertical long-run position. Hence the speed of adjustment of the aggregate supply curve can be inferred from the rate at which the upper right segment of the curve returns to the initial level of output. Similarly, the speed of movement along the AD curve defined in the lower right-hand quadrant of the diagram also represents the rotation of the AS curve. In this case, neither period appears to have significantly faster adjustment than the other.

Why should the Bretton Woods period be characterized by a flatter AD

curve? The explanation, we suspect, lies in the monetary policy intervention rules used to stabilize exchange rates under Bretton Woods. Consider the following simple model of the economy, based on the AD/AS framework

$$y = -a(i - \Delta p) + G \qquad \text{(3.1) Product demand (IS)}$$

$$m - p = y - bi \qquad \text{(3.2) Money demand (LM)}$$

$$y - Y = d(p - w) \qquad \text{(3.3) Aggregate supply (AS)}$$

These three equations represent the IS, LM, and AS relationships. Demand depends upon the real interest rate $(i - \Delta p)$ and a shift parameter G. Money demand depends upon prices, output, and nominal interest rates in the standard manner; for simplicity we assume the output elasticity is unity. Level of output relative to potential (Y) depends negatively upon the real wage. (All variables except the interest rate are measured in logarithms.)

The model is completed by three additional equations

$$w = p_{-1} \qquad \text{(3.4) Wage adjustment}$$

$$e = p - p^* \qquad \text{(3.5) Exchange rate}$$

$$m = f(\hat{e} - e) \qquad \text{(3.6) Monetary intervention rule}$$

Equation (3.4) represents the assumption that wages are sticky. When combined with the aggregate supply relationship it defines the SRAS curve $(y - Y = dp)$ and provides a Phillips curve relationship which defines the price dynamics of the model $(y - Y = g\Delta p)$. Equations (3.5) and (3.6) define the exchange rate and monetary policy. The exchange rate e depends on the ratio of domestic to foreign prices $(p - p^*)$, while the intervention rule depends upon the deviation of $\hat{e}$, the target level of the exchange rate, from its actual level, defined as the domestic currency price of a unit of foreign currency. Thus, if e rises (depreciates) relative to its target level, the authorities reduce the money supply. The vigour of the response (f) is an increasing function of the fixity of the exchange rate.

Paths for output and prices for one set of 'reasonable' parameter values are shown in figures 9.7A and 9.7B.[11] The figure 9.7A shows the results when $f = 1$, which represents an exchange rate targeting regime, while figure 9.7B shows the results for $f = 0$, a floating exchange rate regime. The results generally accord with those shown in figure 9.6. The floating exchange rate period has a steeper AD curve (it is easy to show that the slope of the AD curve is given by $-(a + b)/\{a(1 + f)\}$ and hence that as f rises the AD curve becomes flatter for all parameter values). In addition, there is no clear difference in the speed of adjustment between the two exchange rate regimes. Finally, the path for the AD curve in the bottom right-hand quadrant is slightly curved due to the fact that the IS curve depends upon

real interest rates, a phenomenon which can be seen in the Bretton Woods period, although it does not show up under floating rates.

Thus, as f grows large, the AD curve becomes increasingly flat. There is little price response to an aggregate demand shock because the authorities intervene to stabilize the exchange rate and hence the price level. They increase the money supply in response to a positive supply shock which would lead otherwise to a fall in prices and an exchange rate appreciation; they reduce the money supply in response to a positive demand shock which would otherwise lead to price increases and exchange rate depreciation.

We can think of two independent checks on this interpretation. First, since monetary policy reactions affect output in the opposite direction from autonomous demand shocks (as can be seen in figures 9.7A and 9.7B), the output response to demand shocks should be smaller under fixed than flexible rates. Although difficult to discern due to the differences in scales between the panels of figure 9.6, this is indeed the case.[12] Second, one country in our sample, Canada, maintained a floating exchange rate for a good part of the first period as well as the second.[13] Since Canadian officials were not compelled to intervene to peg the nominal rate for much of the floating period, there should be little evidence of a shift in the slope of the Canadian aggregate demand curve. The Canadian responses, plotted in price-output space in figure 9.8, show little evidence of a steepening of the AD curve in the second period. Nor does it appear that the output response to demand shocks was smaller in the first than the second period.

Our results suggest that the increased cross-country dispersion of price variability relative to output variability following the shift from fixed to flexible rates (noted in the discussion of table 9.1) reflects not merely changes in the cross-country dispersion of supply shocks but the different opportunities for demand-side intervention to stabilize output (at the expense of destabilizing prices) afforded by the shift from fixed to floating rates. Under fixed rates, countries experienced different shocks but were constrained in the policies that might be pursued to offset them. Under flexible rates, in contrast, they had the freedom to use policy to stabilize domestic output relative to that of other countries, but at the expense of different rates of inflation that reflected the nature of local disturbances.[14] To the extent that supply shocks also grew more diverse in 1973–80, we would expect to see even greater dispersion across countries of price performance following the shift from fixed to floating rates, and some attenuation of the reduction in output dispersion.

Explaining the shift from fixed to floating rates
With these results in hand, it is logical to ask whether they can help one understand the collapse of the Bretton Woods system. The shift from fixed

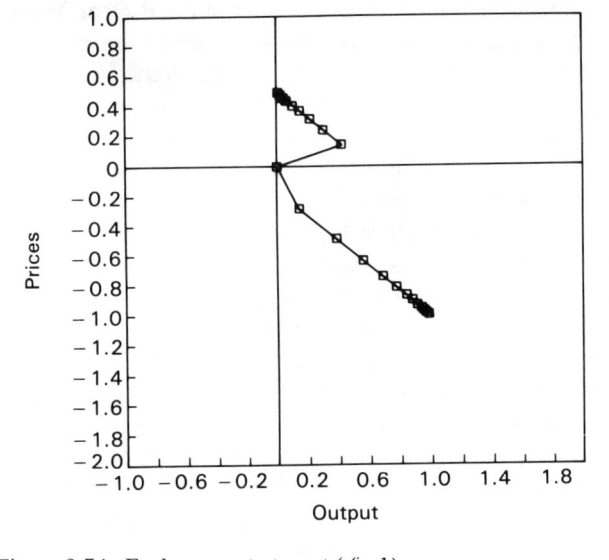

Figure 9.7A Exchange rate target ($f=1$)

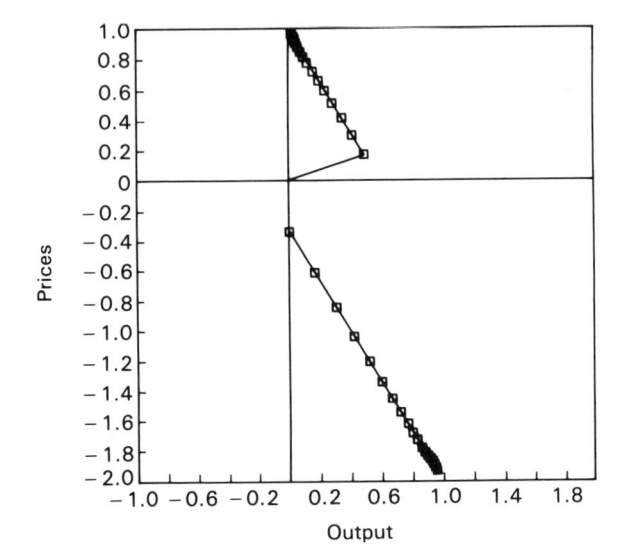

Figure 9.7B Floating exchange rate ($f=0$)

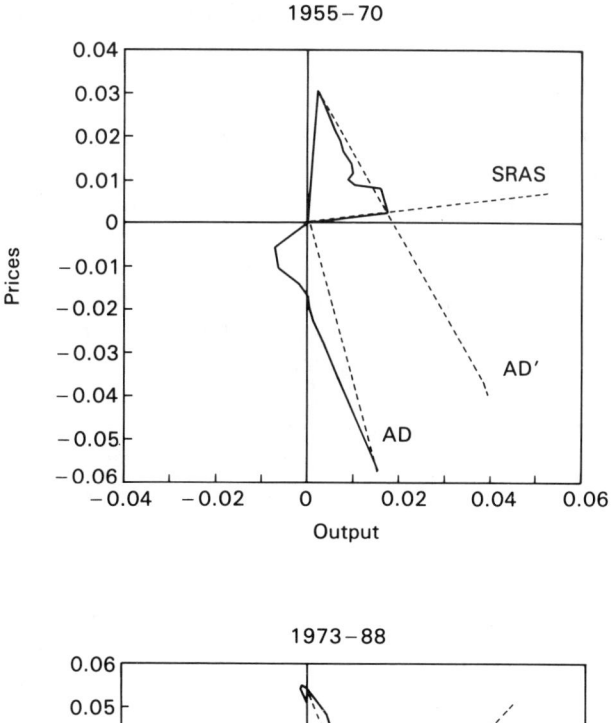

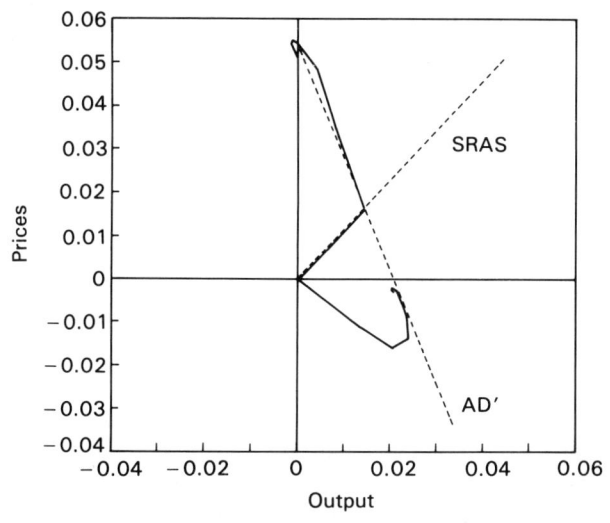

Figure 9.8 Canada: aggregate demand and supply curves

to flexible exchange rates occurred under duress. Governments may have found the maintenance of fixed rates increasingly difficult due to an increase in the 1960s in the magnitude of country-specific supply shocks which destabilized output and increased the cost of stabilizing prices and exchange rates. Alternatively, the collapse of the Bretton Woods parities may have been due to an increase in the magnitude of country-specific aggregate demand shocks that created inflation and pressure for exchange rate depreciation.

Some of our conclusions were foreshadowed above. Figures 9.5A and 9.5B indicate a slight rise in the average magnitude of positive aggregate demand disturbances in the second half of the Bretton Woods period, matched by a modest decline in the average magnitude of positive aggregate supply disturbances. However, there is no dramatic increase in the average size of supply and demand shocks or of a widening gap between concurrent supply and demand shocks at the end of the 1960s. Insofar as all that happened in the 1960s was that G-7 countries as a whole experienced accelerating inflation (see figure 9.1), it is not clear why this should have increased the difficulty of maintaining fixed exchange rates between them.[15] One possibility is that inflation increased the rate of growth of global monetary claims relative to international reserves of gold and dollars, thereby exacerbating the difficulty for countries like the United States of maintaining the convertibility of domestic currency into gold and heightening the fragility of the system.[16] Figure 9.5B indicates a modest rise in the dispersion of aggregate supply disturbances across countries, and a more noticeable increase in the international dispersion of aggregate demand disturbances after 1965. It could be that differences in supply shocks across countries and the different demand responses they elicited destabilized the fixed rate system. At the same time, the increase in the cross-country dispersion of shocks is relatively modest, and that dispersion – especially for demand shocks – remains low compared to that of the 1950s. This may indicate the importance of capital controls in the period of Bretton Woods' current account inconvertibility that ended in 1958.[17] Current account inconvertibility could have helped to reconcile different demand management policies across countries with the maintenance of stable exchange rates between them before 1958 but not after.

If demand management policies became increasingly constrained in the second half of the Bretton Woods period, we would expect to see an increase in the correlation of demand and supply shocks over the estimation period.[18] Governments would be forced to respond to a negative supply shock which raised prices and weakened the exchange rate, for example, by reducing demand (lowering prices and strengthening the exchange rate). As table 9.3 shows, there is precisely such an increase in the correlation of

demand and supply disturbances in the second Bretton Woods subperiod. Evidence of the increase is more striking when we aggregate the individual-country disturbances (in the line labelled G-7′) than when we analyse the behaviour of the G-7 aggregate (in the line labelled G-7), but it is apparent in both measures. An increase in the correlation is evident for all countries but Germany, the United Kingdom, and Italy.

Finally, a series of negative aggregate supply and/or positive demand disturbances in the United States could have undermined confidence in the dollar, and doubts about America's commitment to the dollar's Bretton Woods parity could have brought down the system. However, this interpretation finds relatively little support in the data. Our analysis suggests, then, that the collapse of the Bretton Woods system reflected a combination of factors.[19] Accelerating inflation increased the value of monetary liabilities relative to global gold reserves. This reflected an increase in (positive) aggregate demand disturbances relative to (positive) aggregate supply disturbances between the 1950s and 1960s. Supply and demand shocks also grew more diverse across countries, and more correlated with one another as if the impact of supply shocks on the exchange rate grew due to the removal of capital controls. Even if none of these effects is sufficient by itself to account for the collapse of the Bretton Woods system, together they would appear to provide a coherent explanation for the downfall of the pegged exchange rate regime.

4 The classical gold standard and the interwar period

We followed the same general approach to analysing the classical gold standard and the interwar years. For the pre-World War II period we analysed data for five economies for which it was possible to obtain consistent estimates of national income in both real and nominal terms: the United States, the United Kingdom, Italy, Sweden, and Australia. We refer to these countries as the Big Five (B5), as opposed to the G-7. Other countries which it would have been desirable to include, such as Germany and France, lack data for the beginning of the period or suffer from breaks in the series during World War I or the early 1920s; since our regression estimates are fit to data for the periods 1874–1913 and 1914–38, we were therefore forced to exclude them from the econometric analysis. Where possible, however, we report for comparative purposes summary measures of growth and inflation in selected subperiods for some of these countries as well. Data for the United Kingdom, Italy, and Sweden are taken from Mitchell (1976), Australian data from Butlin (1984).[20] Most of our analysis for the United States uses Romer's (1989) cyclically corrected estimates of real and nominal Gross National Product (GNP), although in some cases

Table 9.3. *Correlation of aggregate supply and aggregate demand disturbances*

	1955–62	1963–70	1973–80	1981–88
G7	−0.22	0.17	−0.13	0.28
United States	−0.23	0.43	0.78	−0.43
Japan	−0.31	0.11	0.09	−0.38
Germany	0.29	−0.33	0.67	−0.56
France	−0.30	0.54	0.28	−0.63
United Kingdom	0.38	−0.32	0.40	−0.34
Italy	0.05	0.03	−0.10	−0.77
Canada	−0.30	0.42	−0.53	0.49
G7′	0.12	0.74	0.80	0.11

Source: See text.

we also report findings based on the standard series in US Department of Commerce (1976). To construct the B5 aggregate, we converted national figures into common currency using 1900 gold parities as reported in the *1901 Bankers Almanac*. The behaviour of the aggregate is dominated by the United States and the United Kingdom, since they are far and away the largest economies in the sample.

A first look at the data

Table 9.4 reports the behaviour of growth and inflation for the classical gold standard and the interwar years in a format designed to facilitate comparison with table 9.1. In addition to reporting summary statistics for the entire classical gold standard period (1874–1913) and the World War I/ interwar years (1914–38), we provide them separately for four prewar decades (1874–83, 1884–93, 1894–1903, and 1904–13), for World War I (1914–18) and for the two interwar decades (1919–28 and 1929–38). The second set of statistics provided in parentheses shows the results of substituting the Commerce Department series for the Romer estimates. As in table 9.1, SD denotes the standard deviation of the B5 aggregate, SD* variability around that aggregate.

There is relatively little change in any of these measures over the different prewar decades. The volatility of the B5 aggregate, as measured by SD, is highest in 1874–83 and 1904–13. Figures 9.9A and 9.9B, where three-year moving averages are plotted, suggest that the unusual volatility of the first subperiod is concentrated towards its beginning, reflecting the 1873 finan-

cial crisis. The unusual volatility of the last prewar decade is similarly concentrated around 1907, mirroring the effects of the financial crisis in the United States and its European repercussions. The financial distress of 1907 was most severe in the United States; individual-country results for output variability (not reported) confirm that the proportionate rise in volatility between 1894–1903 and 1904–13 was largest in the United States.

Dispersion, as measured by SD*, is highest in 1874–83, when many of the countries in our sample had not yet joined the gold standard club, and lowest in 1904–13, when construction of the international gold standard was essentially complete, thus confirming the integrating properties of the gold standard system.[21] Similarly, both the variability of aggregate B5 inflation, as measured by SD, and the dispersion of national inflation rates around the B5 aggregate, as measured by SD*, were highest in 1873–83, before construction of the classical gold standard system was complete, and lowest in 1904–13.[22]

How does the classical gold standard compare in these respects with the other period of fixed exchange rates in our sample, the Bretton Woods years? The similarities are more striking than the differences, especially when we focus on the variability of aggregate output and inflation. One noteworthy difference is that the dispersion of national output and inflation movements around the aggregate appears to have been a quarter to a third higher under the classical gold standard than under Bretton Woods.[23] Overall, however, the two periods look quite similar. Contrasts with the 1914–38 period are more pronounced. Output variability (as measured by SD, the standard deviation of first differences in the B5 aggregate) is at least twice as high in 1914–38 as in 1874–1913. Breakdowns for different post-1913 subperiods indicate that output volatility was exceptionally high throughout, although the war years (1914–18) and the Depression decade (1929–38) stand out. The dispersion of output movements across countries, as measured by SD* (the standard deviation of the individual country series around the B5 aggregate), is also larger in 1914–38 than in 1874–1913, although the difference is less than dramatic. The variability and dispersion of inflation rates (as measured by SD and SD*, respectively) also rise markedly after 1913. In the case of dispersion, it is the 1920s rather than the preceding or succeeding periods that stand out (see Figure 9.9B), reflecting differences across countries in the speed with which postwar inflation was stabilized and countries' success or failure in deflating sufficiently to restore the prewar gold standard parity (Eichengreen 1986).

Finally, the bottom panel of table 9.4 shows the correlation between growth and inflation for the B5 aggregate. The correlation is positive for every subperiod but 1919–28, in contrast to the results for the post-World War II period, where the correlation was consistently negative. The positive

Table 9.4. *Basic data: prewar and interwar periods*

	1874–1913	1874–83	1884–93	1894–1903	1904–13	1914–38	1914–18	1919–28	1929–38
GROWTH									
B5 SD	0.018(0.031)	0.015(0.025)	0.013(0.024)	0.012(0.026)	0.028(0.046)	0.052(0.061)	0.032(0.040)	0.039(0.062)	0.071(0.071)
SD*	0.023(0.032)	0.025(0.035)	0.022(0.027)	0.026(0.035)	0.019(0.029)	0.034(0.036)	0.028(0.037)	0.035(0.037)	0.035(0.036)
Per cent explained by first principal component	29(1)	35(2)	40(2)	42(2)	47(0)	42(1)	59(1)	64(1)	
INFLATION									
B5 SD	0.027(0.034)	0.036(0.054)	0.019(0.017)	0.025(0.025)	0.014(0.016)	0.084(0.088)	0.087(0.083)	0.083(0.046)	0.045(0.045)
SD*	0.016(0.022)	0.021(0.037)	0.018(0.021)	0.014(0.014)	0.012(0.013)	0.036(0.034)	0.038(0.039)	0.095(0.042)	0.024(0.023)
Per cent explained by first principal component	53(0)	50(0)	43(0)	53(0)	57(0)	78(0)	70(1)	76(0)	82(1)
CORRELATION OF GROWTH AND INFLATION									
B5	0.34	0.67	0.20	0.04	0.51	0.24	0.05	−0.17	0.76

Note:
Values in parentheses refer to the Commerce Department series for US.

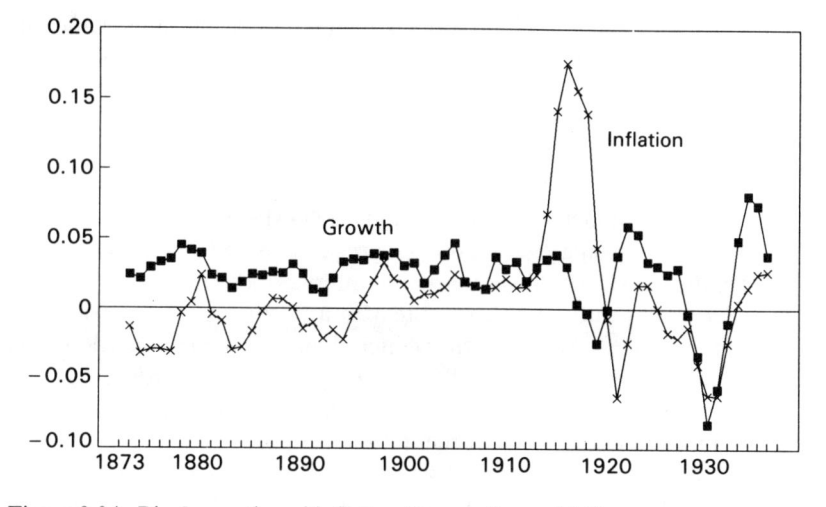

Figure 9.9A Big 5 growth and inflation (Romer 3-year MA)

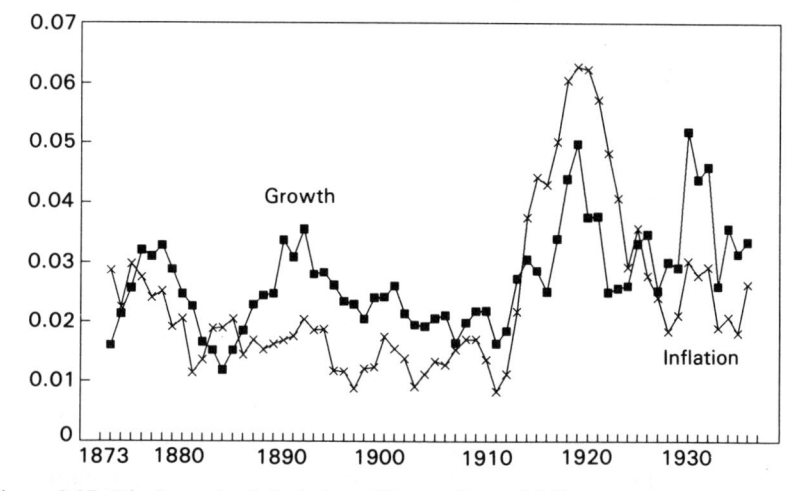

Figure 9.9B Big 5 standard deviations (Romer 3-year MA)

correlation of growth and inflation is suggestive of the importance of demand shocks, which is at odds with the way the classical gold standard period is conventionally portrayed.

Aggregate supply–aggregate demand analysis

Estimating the model over the periods 1874–1913 and 1914–38, we conducted the same aggregate supply-aggregate demand analysis as before. For both the classical gold standard and interwar periods, the B5's SRAS curve, derived by subjecting the system to a positive aggregate demand shock (shifting the AD curve to the right and thereby tracing out SRAS), is steeper than for the post-World War II period. In other words, a positive demand shock produces on impact a large price increase and only a small increase in output (as shown in the impulse response functions in figures 9.10A, 9.10B, 9.11A and 9.11B). For the classical gold standard years, the SRAS is almost vertical and therefore nearly indistinguishable from the long-run AS curve. For the interwar period, the SRAS curve is less steep than before World War I but still steeper than after World War II. Adjustment is very fast before World War I, less so between the wars. The SRAS curve will be steep in price output space when wages and other variable costs of production are very flexible in nominal terms. This result is suggestive, therefore, of greater wage flexibility before World War II, and especially before World War I.[24]

The price response to supply shocks is also of considerable interest. The data for both 1870–1913 and 1914–38 suggest, surprisingly, a positive price response to favourable aggregate supply shocks.[25] It could be that the gold standard itself, and the determinants of flow gold supplies in particular, were responsible for these peculiar dynamics.[26] The conventional gold standard specification relates flow gold supplies to the relative price of gold (Barro 1979). Increases in the overall price level reduce the relative price of gold and hence depress flow supplies of the metal. It is straightforward to show, however, that while this effect may reduce the price response to supply shocks, for essentially the same reasons as under other fixed exchange rate systems, it cannot reverse the sign of the effect. In any case, the evidence for a positive relative price elasticity of gold supply under the gold standard is mixed at best. Eichengreen and McLean (1991) show that time series and cross-section analysis suggests that price effects are dominated by non-price determinants of gold supply.

Table 9.5 summarizes the variability of aggregate supply and aggregate demand shocks for different countries and periods. Paralleling our previous procedure, we consider both estimated supply and demand shocks gleaned from our international aggregate and the measures constructed by first

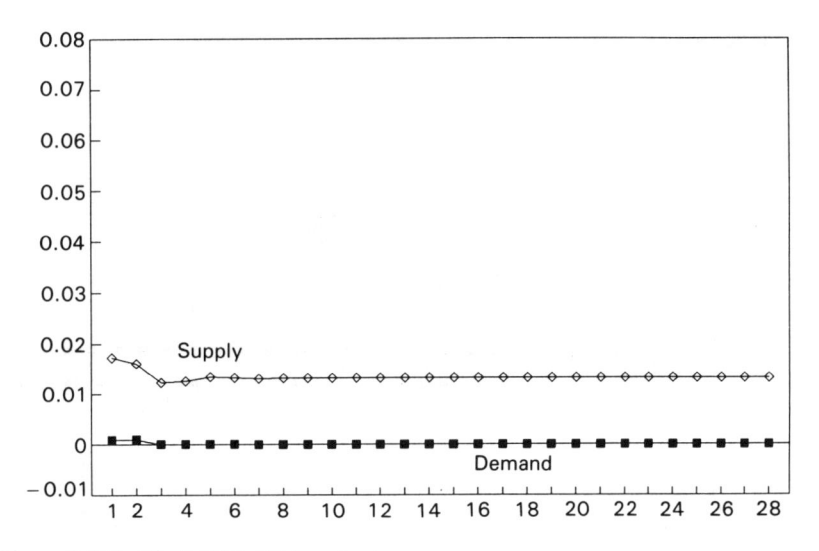

Figure 9.10A Big 5 1870–1913: output responses

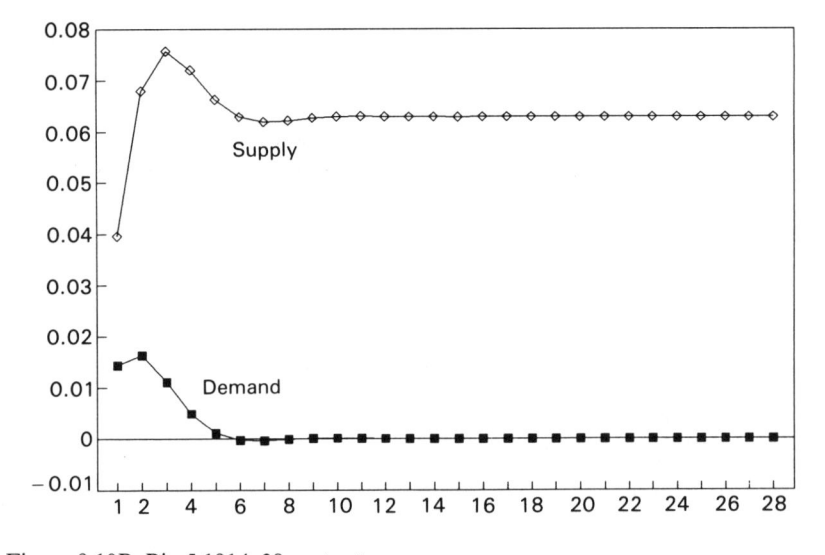

Figure 9.10B Big 5 1914–38: output responses

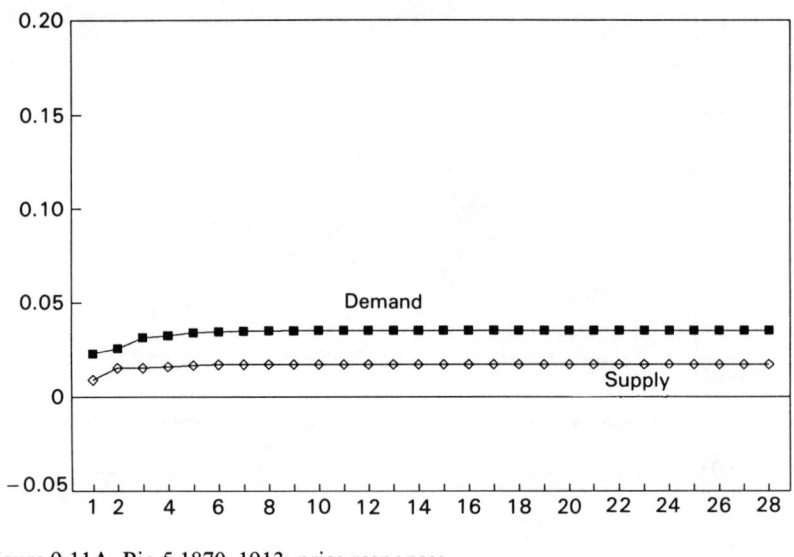

Figure 9.11A Big 5 1870–1913: price responses

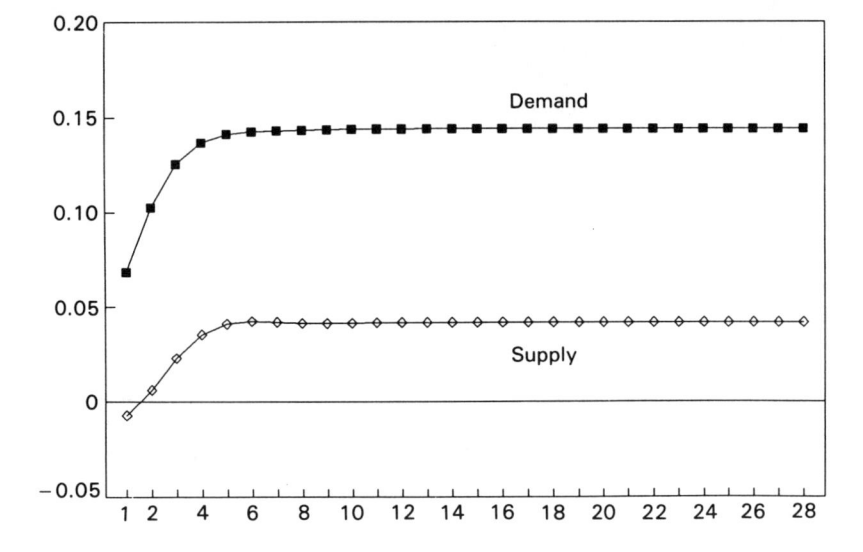

Figure 9.11B Big 5 1914–38: price responses

estimating supply and demand shocks on individual country data and then aggregating the results (B5 and B5', respectively). The standard deviation of demand shocks to the B5 aggregate is less than half as large during the classical gold standard period as between the wars (less than a third as large when the standard deviation of B5' is considered), supporting the notion that the gold standard disciplined policymakers.[27] The standard deviation of supply shocks was also less than half as large during the gold standard period as between the wars (again, less than a third as large when B5' is considered), suggesting that the smooth operation of the gold standard was further reinforced by the stability of the economic environment.[28] There are few obvious trends over time within the gold standard period in the magnitude of demand or supply shocks, other than some evidence of a decline over time in the size of demand shocks and an increase in the size of supply shocks after 1903. The interwar estimates suggest a predominance of demand shocks in the 1920s and of supply shocks in the 1930s, which is consistent with standard accounts of the period. The dispersion across countries of supply and demand disturbances is relatively stable during the gold standard years. During the interwar period, demand disturbances are more diverse in the 1920s than in the 1930s, reflecting the fact that countries differed in their policies towards postwar stabilization (Jack 1927). Supply shocks are more diverse in the 1930s, again reflecting the experience of the United States.

Figures 9.12A and 9.12B show the time profile of demand and supply shocks to the B5 aggregate (figure 9.12A) and the dispersion of individual-country shocks around that aggregate (figure 9.12B). The stability of the classical gold standard period compared to the interwar years is apparent. The 1893 and 1907 financial crises show up in figure 9.12A as negative supply shocks.[29] There is some evidence of a rise in the international dispersion of both supply and demand disturbances towards the end of the classical gold standard years, consistent with historical accounts of the growing strains experienced by the prewar system (de Cecco 1984; Eichengreen 1993a).

The aftermath of World War I is dominated by a series of negative demand shocks, as government spending was curtailed, but also by positive supply shocks associated with demobilization and unusually good harvests in the United States (Romer 1988). The deflation of the second half of the 1920s shows up as an increase in supply shocks relative to demand shocks. The onset of the Great Depression is marked by a series of negative demand shocks that commence before 1929; this is consistent with recent accounts of the Depression (Hamilton 1987; Eichengreen 1992) emphasizing the Federal Reserve System's shift to contractionary monetary policies in 1927 or 1928. Negative supply shocks, which peak in 1931 coincident with the US

Table 9.5. *Underlying disturbances: gold standard and interwar periods*

		1874–1913	1874–83	1884–93	1894–1903	1904–13	1919–38	1919–28	1929–38
DEMAND									
B5	SD	0.026	0.036	0.023	0.023	0.013	0.065	0.085	0.042
	SD*	0.030	0.042	0.024	0.028	0.025	0.038	0.046	0.030
B5'	SD	0.015	0.021	0.014	0.011	0.014	0.051	0.065	0.034
	SD*	0.023	0.032	0.018	0.022	0.018	0.031	0.039	0.023
Per cent explained by first principal component		47(0)	48(0)	35(0)	57(1)	55(0)	64(0)	67(0)	56(0)
SUPPLY									
B5	SD	0.018	0.013	0.013	0.012	0.025	0.045	0.029	0.057
	SD*	0.026	0.024	0.027	0.025	0.028	0.034	0.031	0.037
B5'	SD	0.018	0.015	0.021	0.020	0.011	0.043	0.033	0.053
	SD*	0.018	0.015	0.019	0.018	0.021	0.032	0.029	0.036
Per cent explained by first principal component		31(1)	38(2)	36(1)	42(2)	47(0)	35(0)	42(1)	51(0)
CORRELATION OF DEMAND AND SUPPLY									
B5	SD	—	0.68	−0.28	−0.15	−0.41	—	−0.30	0.50
B5'	SD	—	−0.58	−0.52	0.41	0.44	—	−0.28	0.20

Source: See text.

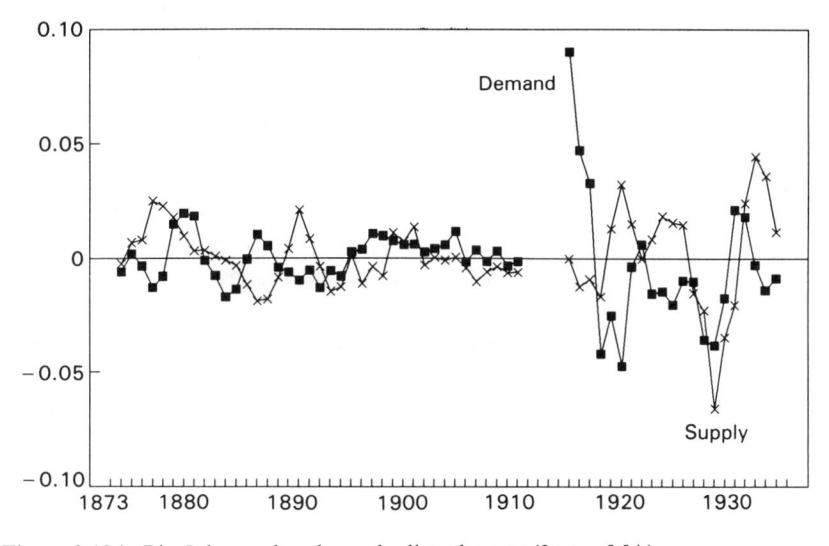

Figure 9.12A Big 5 demand and supply disturbances (3-year MA)

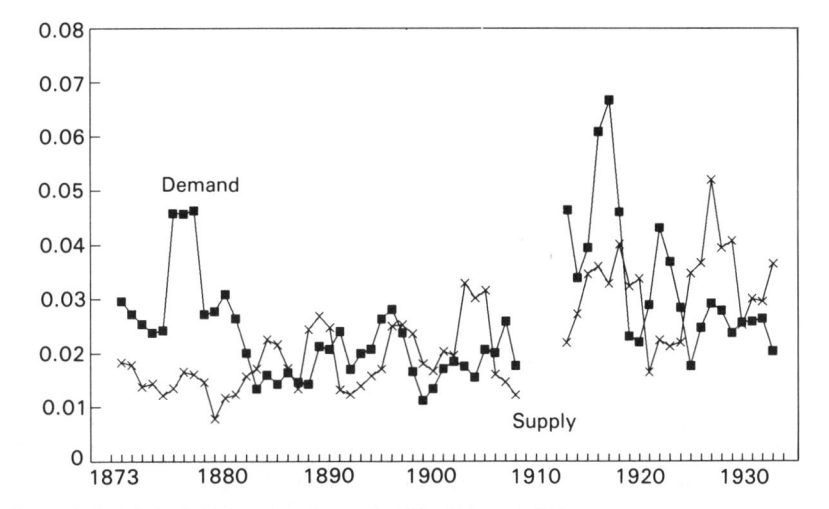

Figure 9.12B Big 5 demand and supply SDs (3-year MA)

financial crisis, then reinforce the downward spiral of output.[30] Our results thus suggest that recovery from the Depression was fuelled by both supply- and demand-side factors.[31] In figure 9.12B, we see a rise in the cross-country dispersion of demand shocks, auguring the collapse of the interwar gold standard system. The increased dispersion of aggregate supply shocks in the 1930s reflects their larger magnitude in America than elsewhere, itself reflecting the exceptional severity of the financial crisis in the United States.

The impulse response functions for the B5 for the pre-World War I and interwar periods suggest very fast adjustment of quantities to both supply and demand shocks, with output having essentially settled down to its long-run equilibrium level after two or three years. Adjustment is slower during the interwar period – output takes five years or so to settle down to its long-run level – but rapid compared to after World War II. The different scales of the two figures reflect the relatively small output response and large price response, especially to demand shocks, due to the existence of very steep SRAS curves under the gold standard.

What light is shed by these results on the patterns in the raw data in table 9.4? They suggest that the unusual magnitude and dispersion of output and price movements across countries in 1874–83 reflected primarily demand rather than supply shocks. The behaviour of prices and output indicated not only that the 1870s was marked by prominent supply disturbances (such as a financial crisis), which it was, but that demand shocks (reflecting the run up to convertibility in the US, among other factors) were unusually severe. Our results suggest that the rise in output and price volatility after World War I reflect neither supply- nor demand-side factors alone, but a simultaneous increase in the two, although demand disturbances were especially important in the 1920s, supply disturbances in the 1930s.

Comparisons with post-World War II experience

How do supply and demand disturbances in these earlier historical periods compare to those that obtained after World War II? Though the interwar years stand out as a period of exceptional turbulence and international divergence regardless of the period with which they are compared, the classical gold standard era was by no means characterized by an exceptionally stable underlying environment compared to Bretton Woods or the post-Bretton Woods float. The average supply shock was roughly three times as large under the classical gold standard as under Bretton Woods and the post-Bretton Woods float. Demand shocks, meanwhile, appear to have been about twice as large under the classical gold standard. Similarly, the dispersion of supply and demand shocks across countries, as captured by our SD* measures, was larger under the gold standard than under both

Bretton Woods and the post-Bretton Woods float. It hardly seems possible therefore to explain the smooth operation of the gold standard on the basis of the unusually small size or symmetrical distribution of shocks. There is little support here for the notion that the smooth operation of the gold standard, compared to modern international monetary arrangements, reflected the accommodating nature of the underlying environment or the exceptionally disciplined behaviour of policymakers.

What then can explain the successful operation of the pre-1914 gold standard? One factor identified by our results is the speed of adjustment. The gold standard was characterized by a very steep SRAS curve, implying flexible wages and fast adjustment to shocks. In a world where economies adjust quickly to disturbances, the costs associated with operating a fixed exchange rate regime are relatively low. This system was nevertheless unable to accommodate the strains imposed on monetary policy by World War I. The large shocks experienced by the international economy in the 1920s and 1930s, associated with the aftermath of the war and with the Great Depression, together with the slower adjustment to underlying disturbances then made it impossible to restore a stable fixed exchange rate system in the interwar years.

5 Conclusions

This chapter has addressed the question of what accounts for changes over time in the stability of the international monetary system. The goals of our analysis have been as much pedagogic as substantive. Pedagogically we have sought to distinguish three explanations for the successive phases of exchange rate stability and instability through which the international monetary system has seemingly passed – government policy, macroeconomic flexibility and the stability of the economic environment – and to show how it is possible to make headway in identifying their incidence and effects.

Substantively, our conclusions do not identify any one of these factors as the sole explanation for the maintenance of stable exchange rates in some periods but not in others. Under the gold standard, macroeconomic flexibility explains the successful maintenance of fixed rates, while the exchange rate instability of the interwar years seems to have been associated with both slower adjustment and larger shocks. The breakup of the Bretton Woods system in the early 1970s, in contrast, occurred despite no noticeable decline in the speed of adjustment and little rise in the average magnitude of disturbances relative to the early Bretton Woods years. There is a small but identifiable rise in the dispersion of supply shocks between the two periods, but this change does not appear sufficient to explain the

dramatic change in exchange rate regime. The loosening of capital controls and the shrinking of reserves as a ratio to liabilities, which made the regime more difficult to maintain, may also be part of the story. Our analysis suggests, then, that the breakup of Bretton Woods reflected a combination of these factors rather than any one.

In many ways the most interesting comparison is between the success of the pre-World War I gold standard, which survived intact until the coming of armageddon in 1914, and the breakup of Bretton Woods in 1971, at a time of no easily identifiable strains in the international system. The culprit appears to be the loss of macroeconomic flexibility over time.[32] Maintaining a fixed exchange rate entailed few costs during the gold standard years because of the speed with which economies adjusted to shocks. In the post-World War II period, on the other hand, slower adjustment resulted in strains which eventually destroyed the Bretton Woods system. Identifying the factors responsible for the decline over time in the speed of adjustment should be a central topic for future research.

Notes

Some of this research was completed during Eichengreen's visit to the Federal Reserve Board, whose hospitality is acknowledged with thanks. We are grateful to M. Bordo, W. Branson, F. Papadia, F. Saccomanni, and seminar participants at the Board for helpful comments, L. Lambertini for research assistance, and the Centers for German and European Studies and for International and Development Economics at the University of California at Berkeley for financial support. This chapter does not necessarily represent the views of the International Monetary Fund (IMF) or the Board of Governors of the Federal Reserve System.

1 Note that we are referring here to exchange rate or international monetary stability, not necessarily to the stability of output, unemployment, or financial markets. This important distinction runs throughout the chapter.

2 Cooper (1971) emphasizes the very different experience of developing countries.

3 Blanchard and Quah themselves originated the supply-demand interpretation. In previous work (Bayoumi and Eichengreen 1993), we have suggested that permanent and temporary disturbances to the European economy can be usefully interpreted in terms of supply and (policy-related) demand shocks.

4 The conventional normalization is that the two variances are set equal to unity, which together with the assumption of orthogonality implies $C'C = \sum$, where $\sum$ is the variance-covariance matrix of e_y and e_p. However, when we wish to calculate the variance of the shocks themselves, we report results using the normalization $C'C = \Gamma$, where Γ is the correlation matrix of e_y and e_p. These two normalizations gave almost identical paths for the shocks, except for a scaling factor, and hence are used interchangeably.

5 This is where our analysis, based on the work of Blanchard and Quah (1989), differs from other VAR models. The usual decomposition assumes that the variables in the VAR can be ordered such that all the effects which could be attributed to (say) either a_t or b_t are attributed to whichever comes first in the ordering. This is achieved by a Choleski decomposition.

6 We discuss alternative interpretations when introducing the evidence below.

7 This result differs from one reported by Bordo (1993). The explanation for the contrast appears to lie in the summary statistic used to measure dispersion; Bordo computes the absolute differences between each country's summary statistic and the grand means of the group of countries.

8 Negative factor loadings indicate the degree to which the underlying series are moving in different directions.

9 Authors like Baxter and Stockman (1989), who find that output growth was less variable under Bretton Woods than subsequently, limit their analysis of Bretton Woods to the years starting in 1960 and terminate their post-Bretton Woods sample in the mid 1980s.

10 For details on these policy initiatives and an attempt to measure empirically their impact on aggregate supply and aggregate demand, see Eichengreen and Goulder (1989).

11 The values were $a = 0.25$, $b = 0.25$, and $d = 3$.

12 The long-run output effect of a supply shock is actually smaller in the floating rate period than under Bretton Woods. This is further evidence that, on average, supply disturbances were no larger in the floating rate period than in the Bretton Woods years.

13 For details, see Johnson (1962).

14 This result is consistent with the evidence presented in Eichengreen (1993a) that policy was responsible for the decline in the cross-country dispersion of output movements following the transition from fixed to floating rates.

15 While figure 9.5A indicates a rise in the average inflation rate in the second Bretton Woods subperiod, figure 9.5B shows that the cross-country dispersion of inflation rates (as measured by the standard deviation) falls at the same time.

16 This relates to the debate over the possible inadequacy of international reserves in the 1960s and the Triffin Dilemma (the fact that the only way of significantly augmenting reserves was by acquiring US dollars, to the point where US monetary liabilities to foreigners came to exceed US gold reserves). For further discussion, see Garber (1993) and Genberg and Swoboda (1993).

17 For details on the importance of capital controls under Bretton Woods and the distinction between the periods of current account inconvertibility and convertibility, see Bordo (1993).

18 Since one of our identifying restrictions was that demand and supply responses are orthogonal over the entire estimation period, we are only able to compare behaviour within estimation periods, not between them.

19 This is the interpretation offered previously by one of the present authors (Eichengreen 1993b).

20 The German and Danish series are also taken from Mitchell.

21 Italy was not officially on the gold standard, but between 1903 and 1911 its exchange rate consistently remained within the gold points (see Fratianni and Spinelli 1984).

22 This is consistent with findings reported in Bordo (1993).

23 Using slightly different measures, samples of countries, and time periods, Bordo (1993) and Eichengreen (1993a) also conclude that output may have been more variable over time and across countries under the classical gold standard than under Bretton Woods.

24 This notion of secularly declining wage flexibility, supported by Sachs (1979) and Gordon (1982), has been questioned by Carter and Sutch (1990) and Allen (1992).

25 This result is also found in Keating and Nye (1991), who fit the Blanchard–Quah decomposition to historical data and find that temporary shocks to output produce falling prices for the majority of their countries.

26 Another possible explanation is that supply shocks were predominantly temporary in the nineteenth century because of the dominance of agricultural production. A bad harvest followed by the recovery of agricultural output to normal levels should be represented as a negative supply shock followed by a positive one but may be incorrectly categorized by our methodology as a single demand shock because of the output decline's temporary nature. For still another explanation, see Keating and Nye (1991).

27 A related interpretation is not merely that the gold standard constraints prevented policymakers from pursuing erratic demand management policies, but that discretionary monetary and fiscal measures were largely beyond the ken of governments prior to 1913 (Eichengreen 1992, chapters 1–2).

28 Below we provide evidence, however, that some of the largest supply shocks of the interwar period were policy induced, which complicates interpretations of the association between supply shocks and international monetary stability.

29 Bernanke (1983) highlighted the tendency for financial crises to have negative supply- as well as demand-side effects owing to the disruption of financial intermediation services. For evidence of relevance to the late nineteenth century US economy, see Grossman (1993).

30 To the extent that the financial crisis was caused by the ineptness of Federal Reserve policy, this is an example of the type of policy-induced supply shock described above.

31 These results are consistent with those of the one other attempt to apply this type of methodology to interwar data of which we are aware, Cecchetti and Karras (1991), who find that negative aggregate demand shocks were primarily responsible for the post-1929 downturn, but that negative aggregate supply shocks become important starting in 1931.

32 It is possible, of course, that speed of adjustment by private markets is regime dependent. One might conjecture, for example, that wage flexibility will be higher in periods when fixed rates prevent monetary policymakers from adjusting money supply and prices to reconcile the prevailing level of wages with

full employment. In fact, however, we find no evidence of a direct correlation between the flexibility of the exchange rate and the speed of adjustment; rather what we find is a steady tendency for flexibility to decline with time.

References

Allen, S. 1992. 'Changes in the Cyclical Sensitivity of Wages in the United States, 1891–1987', *American Economic Review*, 82.

Barro, R. 1979. 'Money and the Price Level Under the Gold Standard', *Economic Journal*, 89.

Baxter, M. and Stockman, A. 1989. 'Business Cycles and the Exchange Rate Regime: Some International Evidence', *Journal of Monetary Economics*, 23.

Bayoumi, T. 1992. 'The Effect of the ERM on Participating Economies', *IMF Staff Papers*, 39:2 (June).

Bayoumi, T. and Eichengreen, B. 1992a. 'Is There a Conflict Between EC Enlargement and European Monetary Unification?', *Greek Economic Review* (forthcoming).

1992b. 'Monetary and Exchange Rate Arrangements for the North American Free Trade Area', Journal of Development Economics (forthcoming).

1993. 'Shocking Aspects of European Monetary Unification', in F. Torres and F. Giavazzi (eds.), *Adjustment and Growth in the European Monetary Union*, Cambridge, Cambridge University Press.

Bernanke, B. 1983. 'Non-monetary Effects of the Financial Crisis in the Propagation of the Great Depression', *American Economic Review*, 73.

Blanchard, O. and Quah, D. 1989. 'The Dynamic Effects of Aggregate Demand and Supply Disturbances', *American Economic Review*, 79.

Bordo, M. 1993. 'The Bretton Woods International Monetary System: An Historical Overview', in M. Bordo and B. Eichengreen (eds.), *A Retrospective on the Bretton Woods System: Lessons for International Monetary Reform*, Chicago, University of Chicago Press.

Butlin, N.G. 1984. 'Select Comparative Economic Statistics 1900–1940', *Source Paper*, 4, Department of Economic History, RSSS, Australian National University.

Carter, S. and Sutch R. 1990. 'The Labour Market in the 1890s: Evidence from Connecticut Manufacturing', in E. Aerts and B. Eichengreen (eds.), *Unemployment and Underemployment in Historical Perspective*, Leuven, Leuven University Press.

Cecchetti, S.G. and Karras, G. 1991. 'Sources of Output Fluctuations during the Interwar Period: Further Evidence on the Causes of the Great Depression', unpublished manuscript, Ohio State University and University of Illinois at Chicago.

Cooper, R. 1971. 'Exchange Rate Devaluation in Developing Countries', *Princeton Essays in International Finance*, 86, Princeton, International Finance Section, Department of Economics.

de Cecco, M. 1984. *The International Gold Standard: Money and Empire*, London, Francis Pinter (2nd edn).

Eichengreen, B. 1986. 'Understanding 1921–1927: Inflation and Economic Recovery in the 1920s', *Rivista di Storia Economica*, sec. ser. 3.

1992. *Golden Fetters: The Gold Standard and the Great Depression, 1919–1939*, New York, Oxford University Press.

1993a. 'History of the International Monetary System: Implications for Research in International Macroeconomics and Finance', in F. van der Ploeg (ed.), *Handbook of International Macroeconomics*, Oxford, Blackwell.

1993b. 'Three Perspectives on the Bretton Woods System', in M. Bordo and B. Eichengreen (eds.), *A Retrospective on the Bretton Woods System: Lessons for International Monetary Reform*, Chicago, University of Chicago Press.

Eichengreen, B. and Goulder, L.H. 1989. 'The US Basic Industries in the 1980s: Can Fiscal Policies Explain Their Changing Competitive Position?' in S. Black (ed.), *Productivity Growth and the Competitiveness of the American Economy*, Norwell, Mass., Kluwer Academic Publishers.

Eichengreen, B. and McLean, I. forthcoming. 'The Supply of Gold Under the Pre 1914 Gold Standard', *Economic History Review*.

Fratianni, M. and Spinelli, F. 1984. 'Italy in the Gold Standard Period, 1861–1914', in M. Bordo and A.J. Schwartz (eds.), *A Retrospective on the Classical Gold Standard, 1821–1931*, Chicago, University of Chicago Press.

Garber, P. 1993. 'The Collapse of the Bretton Woods Fixed Exchange Rate System', in M. Bordo and B. Eichengreen (eds.), *A Retrospective on the Bretton Woods System: Lessons for International Monetary Reform*, Chicago, University of Chicago Press.

Genberg, H. and Swoboda A. 1993. 'The Provision of Liquidity in the Bretton Woods System', in M. Bordo and B. Eichengreen (eds.), *A Retrospective on the Bretton Woods System: Lessons for International Monetary Reform*, Chicago, University of Chicago Press.

Gordon, R.J. 1982. 'Why US Wage and Employment Behaviour Differs from that in Britain and Japan', *Economic Journal*, 92.

Grossman, R. 1993. 'The Macroeconomic Consequences of Bank Failures under the National Banking System', *Explorations in Economic History*, 30.

Hamilton, J. 1987. 'Monetary Factors in the Great Depression', *Journal of Monetary Economics*, 13.

Jack, D.T. 1927. *The Restoration of European Currencies*, London, P.S. King.

Johnson, H.G. 1962. *Canada in a Changing World Economy*, Toronto, University of Toronto Press.

Keating, J.W. and Nye J.V. 1991. 'Permanent and Transitory Shocks in Real Output: Estimates from Nineteenth Century and Postwar Economies', *Working Paper*, 160, St Louis, Department of Economics, Washington University.

Mitchell, B.R. 1976. *European Historical Statistics*, London, Macmillan.

Organization for European Economic Cooperation 1957. *Statistics of National Product and Expenditure*, Paris, OEEC.

Romer, C. 1988. 'World War I and the Postwar Recession', *Journal of Monetary Economics*, 22.

1989. 'The Prewar Business Cycle Reconsidered: New Estimates of Gross National Product, 1869–1908', *Journal of Political Economy*, 97.

Sachs, J.A. 1979. 'The Changing Cyclical Behaviour of Wages and Prices, 1890–1976', *American Economic Review*, 70.

United States Department of Commerce 1976. *Historical Statistics of the United States*, Washington DC, GPO.

10 Improving economic policy coordination: evaluating some new and some not-so-new proposals

MORRIS GOLDSTEIN

1 Introduction

The subject of my chapter – namely, evaluating proposals for improving the policy coordination process – is motivated by two considerations. First, while economic policy coordination is only one element of the international monetary system, the ways in which policy coordination is organized and implemented (e.g., rules versus discretion, exchange rate targets versus a broader orientation on macroeconomic and structural policies, etc.) will have a lot to do with how the international monetary system evolves over the next decade or two. Second, this may be a propitious time for examining where the policy coordination process has been and where it should be headed. Not only have we now had almost seven years of experience with the resurgence of economic policy coordination that began with the Plaza Agreement, but also the last few years have seen the publication of several studies (e.g., Dobson 1991 and Twentieth Century Fund Task Force 1991) that have made specific, new proposals for improving the coordination process. For the purposes of this chapter, it is convenient to regard economic policy coordination as 'a significant modification of national policies in recognition of international economic interdependence'.[1] Not much of what I have to say would be altered, however, if one thought of coordination more ambitiously as agreements among countries to adjust policies in light of shared objectives and/or to implement joint policy action. The perspective that I bring to these issues is neither that of a direct participant nor that of an independent outsider, but rather of something in-between.[2]

I have grouped the proposals for improving policy coordination under the following three headings: (i) adopting more explicit and more public exchange rate commitments; (ii) strengthening the analytical framework; and (iii) encouraging remedial action and better follow-up of policy recommendations. Lest the wrong impression be created at the onset, there is no grand plan or consistent blueprint for reform of the system underlying

the individual proposals. The emphasis is also on proposals that do not require major institutional changes. The plan for the rest of the chapter is as follows. Section 2 takes up the thorny issue of the 'effects' of policy coordination, with an eye towards assessing whether the resurgence of policy coordination should be regarded as a positive development. Section 3 initiates the discussion of proposals by considering the case for adoption of more ambitious exchange rate commitments by the largest industrial countries. In section 4, after summarizing current procedures, several proposals for strengthening the analytical framework underlying the policy coordination exercise of the Group of Seven (G-7) are examined. Section 5 turns to proposals aimed at delivering stronger remedial policy actions and more consistent follow-up of consensus policy recommendations. Conclusions are contained in each section.

2 What has economic policy coordination accomplished so far?

There is no shortage of assessments on what has, and what has not, been accomplished by past efforts at economic policy coordination. Feldstein (1990), for example, has characterized the G-7 coordination process as 'counterproductive' because it provides a political excuse for inaction, deflects attention from less glamorous areas (e.g., the debt problem of the Less Developed Countries (LDC), trade conflicts) where cooperation could be helpful, causes antagonisms with partner countries, and frightens business and portfolio investors into inappropriate actions. In contrast, US Treasury Secretary Brady (1990, p. 5) has argued that 'through the G-7 process, we and our partners have agreed to an overall policy approach which has been successful in maintaining growth, reducing trade and current account imbalances, containing inflation, and promoting exchange market stability'. Tobin (1987) has offered yet another perspective, concluding that while macroeconomic policy coordination is certainly not easy, it is in some sense inevitable because nationalistic solutions are apt to be so mutually destructive as to eventually evoke agitation for coordination. Clearly, all three of these wise persons cannot be right. In choosing among competing assessments, it would nice to have some 'harder' evidence on the effects of policy coordination. At least five approaches to estimating those effects are available.

One approach would be to do before–after comparisons of economic performance, where the results for coordination-on periods are matched against those for coordination-off periods. For example, a popular application of that approach is to compare the path of the US dollar after the Plaza Agreement with its path before it, and to attribute any difference to the influence of coordination. It is easy to see, however, that this approach

has several potentially serious shortcomings. For one thing, since it attributes all of the change in performance to the policy 'treatment', the true effects of the policy will be overstated or understated whenever 'other' (non-coordination) determinants of performance are also changing. This will often be the case; for example, a comparison of inflation performance as between 1973–85 and 1986–91 (i.e., pre- and post-Plaza) would need to take account of the two large, oil price shocks in the former period. The results are also apt to be sensitive to the choice of before–after periods; for example, the effect of Plaza on the path of the US dollar would be much smaller (perhaps zero) if we defined the 'before' period as six months prior to Plaza (when the dollar was already depreciating) than if we defined it as say, the three-year period preceding Plaza. In the case of G-7 policy coordination, there is the additional rub that defining a policy-off period is problematic since policy coordination surely was going on in other (non G-5 or G-7) fora – albeit probably not with the same intensity – well before Plaza.

A second tack would be to find a 'control group' of countries that were not affected by the policy treatment (i.e., by policy coordination), and then to compare their economic performance with that of the 'treatment group' (in this case, say, the G-7 countries); if the treatment group then performs better than the control group, the inference is that the treatment was the causal factor. Such an approach has been used with good effect, for instance, to test for the effect of membership in the European Monetary System (EMS) on the extent and cost of disinflation; in brief, the inflation and output performance of the EMS countries during the 1979–85 period was compared to that of a control group of non-EMS industrial countries (e.g., the United States, Japan, Canada, etc.) (Collins 1988; Giavazzi and Giovannini 1988). In the policy coordination case, however, prospects are less promising because it is hard to identify a suitable control group for the seven largest industrial countries.

Yet a third approach would be to infer the effects of policy coordination by comparing actual economic performance to the objectives or targets set out by the coordinating group itself. If the group then meets most of its objectives (e.g., to reduce current account imbalances, to improve economic growth), the presumption is that coordination was a success. Here, however, three problems arise. One is that achievement of the targets can be influenced by how ambitiously those targets are set; a government or group of countries that sets ambitious targets will find it harder to get a high score than those that set their sights much lower. A second difficulty is that, once again, non-coordination factors can impact on the target variables so that compliance with the targets may not reflect solely the influence of coordination; for example, if commodity prices were to unexpectedly decline in a

given period (they fell by almost 50 per cent in 1986), then countries might all overachieve their inflation targets for reasons that have little to do with policy coordination. And third, this approach must confront the reality that some objectives or targets are 'fuzzier' than others so that a scoring method has to be devised to determine if the targets were met.[3]

A fourth way to go would be to abandon observed performance altogether and instead attempt to infer the effects of coordination by simulation of economic models; more specifically, the effects of coordination are deduced by comparing the hypothetical performance of the economy under coordinated monetary and/or fiscal policy rules with that under less coordinated policy rules. With this approach, coordination is judged to be a good thing if the coordinated policy rules produced better average performance over the observation period – given the same pattern of exogenous shocks – than did the less coordinated policy rules. The development and increasing sophistication of multicountry econometric models has made these kind of exercises somewhat of a growth industry over the past five years. This approach has been used, for example, to compare the properties of fixed exchange rates (or target zones) for the three major currencies with those of floating rates with independent money targeting (see, for example, Frenkel *et al.* 1989); similarly, in its study *One Market, One Money*, the Commission of the European Community (EC 1990) used this approach to help gauge the costs and benefits of Economic and Monetary Union (EMU) versus those of both the current EMS and of more flexible exchange arrangements. To this point, neither coordinated nor decentralized policy-making emerges as the clear champion from such exercises. Also, the conclusions have tended to depend in good measure on whether exchange rate variability is assumed to be an independent public good, as well as on whether the existence of irrevocably fixed exchange rates is taken as sufficient to largely eliminate risk premia in interest rate differentials across countries. More to the point at hand, this comparison of policies approach may not tell us much about the effects of economic policy coordination as practised say, by the G-7 countries. That is because this method can be easily applied to alternative policy rules but not to *discretionary* policy regimes.

Still a fifth approach, pioneered by Oudiz and Sachs (1984) among others, is to compute the value of a welfare function (after assigning weights to various economic objectives in each country) under two different assumptions: one where each country maximizes welfare independently, and the other where the countries maximize a joint welfare function. The difference between the two calculations is then taken as a measure of the gains to coordination. Most applications of this approach have found that the gains to coordination were rather small. Again, however, interpretation

of the results is less than straightforward. Not only are such exercises sensitive to the choice of weights in the welfare function but also a comparison of optimal uncoordinated with optimal coordinated policies – which is what this kind of exercise produces – may not be very revealing about the more relevant comparison between *suboptimal* uncoordinated and suboptimal coordinated policies.[4] In that latter case, it becomes necessary to weigh the risks say, of beggar-thy-neighbour policies and adverse aggregation effects from synchronous policy actions under decentralized policy-making, against those arising from say, use of the wrong models or of weakening the potentially helpful disciplinary effects of markets under coordinated policy-making?[5]

What then to do – given that the empirical evidence is Janus-faced at best. My overall assessment is that the policy coordination process is helpful and worth improving. I do not regard it either as a 'new' international monetary system, or as antidote for all the ills that beset national policy-making in the industrial world. During those periods when countries are reluctant to propose and to implement corrective policy actions because they are unpopular with their electorates (or parts of it), neither decentralized nor coordinated policy-making will achieve much. Still, I believe coordination produces better macroeconomic and financial policies, on average, than we would get in its absence.

Specifically, I would give the revival of policy coordination some credit for averting a more pronounced tilt towards protectionism (particularly in the United States) in the wake of the large overvaluation of the dollar, for helping to engineer a soft landing for the dollar, for moving away from a benign neglect stance on major currency exchange rates, for pushing the ball forward on addressing structural rigidities in the largest industrial countries, and for achieving advances in the area of financial supervision and regulation (principally, the Basle Accord on common risk-weighted capital standards for international banks) that would not have been possible with a go-it-alone approach. The average 'bottom line' on growth and inflation has been much better – and that for current account imbalances, somewhat worse – in the 1986–92 period than during the preceding six years;[6] judging from Williamson's (1991) estimates of real equilibrium exchange rates, misalignments of key currencies were also smaller on average in the post-Plaza era. There were, however, clearly many factors at work in addition to policy coordination in generating these summary statistics and the counterfactual is not so easy to discern. My impression is that (contrary to the suggestion that emerges from before–after comparisons) policy coordination had perhaps the most potent, independent impact on current account imbalances, at least during the 1985–9 period when a concerted effort was made to encourage faster

growth of domestic demand than output in surplus countries, and the reverse for deficit ones. Under the heading of disappointments, I would point to the inability of peer pressure (and at least thus far, of everything else) to rein-in the medium-term course of fiscal policy in some large industrial countries with large deficits. Also, the track record on taking adequate account of aggregation effects from synchronous policy actions has, I think, been less impressive than might have been expected. There is also considerable scope for improvement in the credibility of exchange rate management (more on that below).[7]

3 Adopting louder and more explicit exchange rate commitments

As suggested above, one of the characteristics of the post-Plaza period has been greater activism in the management of major currency exchange rates. The change in attitude is evident from official appraisals of exchange market developments and from pledges to undertake concerted exchange market intervention, as revealed in communiqués of the G-7 and of the Interim Committee of the International Monetary Fund (IMF).[8] Both Funabashi (1988) and Dobson (1991) also report that reference ranges for key currency exchange rates were utilized from time to time. As for recourse to foreign exchange market intervention, both outside studies (e.g., Bordo and Schwartz 1990 and Obstfeld 1990) and insider accounts (Dobson 1991) indicate that it has been neither large nor persistent for the period as a whole. Instead, intervention has been concentrated in relatively short subperiods (e.g., the fall of 1985, early and late 1987) when it was heavy; at the same time, intervention has been carried out in a more concerted way than was the norm in the earlier days of managed floating. Coordinated adjustments in interest rates for exchange rate purposes have been the exception rather than the rule.

It has sometimes been suggested that the policy coordination process would be more effective if countries both shared their exchange rate objectives more openly with the public and gave stabilization of exchange rates more weight than they do now (Williamson 1985; Williamson and Miller 1987). Taken to its natural extension, this could of course be interpreted as a call for a return to fixed exchange rates for the major currencies, or even for viewing the world as an optimal currency area.[9] In the present context, however, something more limited – more in the nature of a target zone – is being proposed as a way both to give the market a sharper, stabilizing focus for its exchange rate expectations and to improve the public policy debate.

I am not persuaded that a move to 'loud' target zones would be helpful; in fact, I am inclined towards the view that it would be counterproductive in

present circumstances. As I have argued in earlier work (Frenkel and Goldstein 1989 and 1991; Goldstein and Isard 1992), I think it is preferable to have monetary policy in the largest industrial countries give the highest priority to price stability (or to nominal income), except in those unusual cases when there is evidence of large exchange rate misalignments. My argument can be summarized as follows. The (three) largest industrial countries have demonstrated that they are capable of achieving good inflation performance (relative to others) without relying on exchange rate targets. Their inflation (or internal balance) performance could well suffer if exchange rate commitments intruded unduly into the orientation of monetary policy, with unfavourable consequences not only for themselves but for countries that count on them to export stability. So long as the anchor countries give the highest priority to price stability – and this is to me the key point – tighter and louder exchange rate commitments will lack the credibility they need to be effective, since market participants quickly perceive that when push comes to shove, the interest rate increases needed to defend those exchange rate targets are not forthcoming. Sterilized exchange market intervention, concerted or not, will not be able to substitute for those policy adjustments other than possibly over the very short term.[10] Better therefore to have more limited but more credible commitments – i.e., monitor actual exchange rate movements, compare them to estimates of equilibrium real exchange rates, speak to the market when actual rates are moving away from fundamentals, and be prepared to intervene forcefully and adjust monetary policies in a coordinated manner only when there is evidence of large misalignments – than to wind up having the announced exchange rate targets chase market rates, with a loss in credibility.[11]

To be sure, when exchange rate objectives are not made very explicit by the authorities, you cannot get as much benefit from what Krugman (1987) has called the 'bias in the band'. This refers to the property of market expectations to keep the exchange rate within the band when market participants expect with *certainty* that the monetary authorities will intervene when the exchange rate hits the boundary of the band. This is indeed a most attractive property for managed exchange rates to possess. But such stabilizing behaviour is apt to be directly related to the demon-strated (not claimed) 'hardness' of exchange rate commitments. A target zone arrangement where the obligation to keep the exchange within the zone is hedged and where the zones themselves change over time, is unlikely to generate much of this bias-in-the-band.[12] For example, even in the EMS, where exchange rate commitments are much harder than what is being contemplated in a loud target zone for the three major currencies, empirical tests of the bias-in-the-band proposition produce results that are not supportive of the loud target zone proposal; see Flood *et al.* 1991 and the

literature cited therein. These tests look for a non-linearity in the relationship between the exchange rate and its fundamental determinants; such a non-linearity is consistent with the certain expectation of intervention by the authorities when the exchange rate reaches the boundaries of the band. This hypothesized kind of non-linearity does not seem to be there in the data for EMS currencies over the 1979–90 period. Whether this result reflects the number of realignments in the EMS, or the presence of significant intramarginal intervention (rather than just intervening at the boundaries),[13] or the inadequacies of the model used to describe the behaviour over time of the fundamentals, or some combination of all of the above, is not yet known. But what is more robust is the message that one should not count on market expectations being a strong enough ally to minimize the need for intervention and changes in monetary policy until relatively late in the game when the credibility of those exchange rate commitments has been tested and proven.[14]

It is also not obvious that more public exchange rate commitments are the preferred instrument to initiate a debate on the country's policies. The exchange rate has of course the virtue of being highly visible. It has, however, the disadvantage of sending an ambiguous signal about what's wrong (Frenkel and Goldstein 1988). For example, if the exchange rate is threatening to push through the top of the zone, it could mean, *inter alia*, either that monetary policy is too tight or that fiscal policy is too loose; also, since exchange rates are intrinsically two-sided, the exchange rate does not by itself tell you whose policies are at fault. Note also that, unlike monetary policy where the exchange rate might claim to serve as indicator of the stance of policy (when financial liberalization has muddied the meaning of the monetary aggregates), no such claim can be made for it as an indicator of fiscal policy. And if the aim is to generate a public debate on, say, fiscal policy, why not use a public deficit reduction commitment (e.g., along Gramm–Rudman lines, albeit hopefully with fewer loopholes) which does not have to go through the (imperfect) filter of the exchange rate? There have of course been cases when pressure on the exchange rate has served to initiate a policy debate that was instrumental in turning away from past policy excesses (France in 1983 is the classic example) but this is not sufficient to make the general case – especially when the political cost of changing the exchange rate (rather than underlying policies) is much lower in a target zone than with a harder exchange rate commitment.

4 Strengthening the analytical framework

One of the striking characteristics of the present international monetary system is the considerable diversity of exchange arrangements.[15] As suggested above, I do not regard that diversity as undesirable. This being said, I

do believe it is more difficult to write good codes of conduct for macroeconomic and exchange rate policies when there is wide diversity of exchange arrangements than when everyone is following the same regime; inevitably, there is a trade-off between being comprehensive and even handed across regimes, on the one hand, and being specific enough to make non-compliance transparent, on the other. In a similar vein, I would argue that it is easier to organize policy coordination when there is a dominant economic power with strong economic performance; then, there are strong incentives for countries to follow the leader. Again, this is not the world we now live in. Our world is one where the trend is clearly toward greater symmetry in economic size and influence among the United States, Europe, and Japan, and where, appropriately, economic leadership is increasingly shared.[16] All this, in combination with the dissatisfaction over the results of more decentralized policy-making in the first half of the 1980s, has resulted in a more discretionary, more informal, and probably more splintered, approach to policy coordination than existed in the Bretton Woods era. Following Crockett (1989), it is convenient to classify the existing framework for policy cooperation and coordination as taking place on three levels: a set of rules, institutional procedures for monitoring and evaluating policies, and development of guidelines on how policy should respond in particular circumstances. Since the existing framework has been recently described in detail elsewhere (e.g., Dobson 1991 and Twentieth Century Fund Task Force 1991), I will be selective. In addition, reflecting my comparative advantage, I will concentrate on the IMF and the G-7.

The existing set of rules, or codes of conduct, on macroeconomic and exchange rate policies are laid out in broad terms in Article IV of the Fund's Articles of Agreement. If it were written on stone rather than paper, Article IV might be summarized as saying to member countries: 'Thou Shalt Have Stable Domestic (Monetary and Fiscal) Policies, Thou Shalt Not Have The Wrong Exchange Rate, And Thou Shalt Consult With The Fund On Thy Exchange Rate Policies'. Article IV also instructed the Fund to develop specific principles for the guidance of members' exchange rate policies. In the event (1977), those principles did not emerge as very specific – with one exception. They do outline a set of 'pointers' that could be indicative of a wrong exchange rate. For fixers or highly managed floaters, these pointers include prolonged one-way exchange market intervention, an unsustainable level of official or quasi-official borrowing or lending, the introduction or intensification of payments restrictions, and policies that provide abnormal encouragement or discouragement to capital flows. For freer floaters, the key pointer is behaviour of the exchange rate that 'appears to be unrelated to underlying economic and financial conditions ...'. As a guiding framework for surveillance over members' policies, Article IV has,

at least, two strong attributes. First, it emphasizes that stability of the exchange rate system should not be artificially separated from the stability of monetary and fiscal policies. Stability of domestic policies is not a sufficient condition for exchange market stability but it comes close to being a necessary condition – regardless of the exchange rate regime. In more concrete terms, this has meant that in its Article IV consultations, as well as in discussions of the *World Economic Outlook* in the Fund's Executive Board and in G-7 meetings, it is accepted that exchange rate developments need to be appraised against the broader backdrop of the conduct of monetary and fiscal policies and the evolution of national saving and investment trends. Second, Article IV reinforces the simple but appealing points that the exchange rate, as a key relative price, is a legitimate international concern, and that certain types of behaviour are regarded as out of bounds. That being said, the fact is that there have been relatively few cases over the past sixteen years when the international community as a whole has singled out an industrial country (especially a large one) on charges of having the wrong exchange rate. How much this reflects genuine uncertainty or disagreement about what is the right exchange rate (particularly when the rate is floating), or sensitivities about potential market reactions to knowledge that such discussions are underway, or a desire to keep diagnoses and prescriptions (including recourse to exchange market intervention) in smaller groups, or even the lack of explicit penalties or sanctions for non-compliance, is hard to know.

Turning, next, to institutional procedures for monitoring and evaluating policies, let me focus on the use of economic indicators in the G-7 policy coordination exercise and of alternative medium-term scenarios in the context of the Fund's *World Economic Outlook*. Early in the year, G-7 authorities submit to the Fund their short-term projections for the current calendar year and for the following one. The variables covered include real Gross National Product (GNP), real total domestic demand, consumer price inflation, current accounts, and trade balances. They also furnish medium-term projections for a very similar set of variables, along with some indications of how fiscal balances and monetary conditions are expected to evolve over the coming three-year period. These official submissions are supplemented with the Fund staff's own projections for the same variables, defined over the same time horizons. Actual outturns are presented for the previous year so as to give a picture of the most recent forecast errors. In addition to these data for individual countries, various 'composite indicators' for the G-7 as a group are calculated, typically covering the most recent two- or three-year period. In brief, these composite indicators summarize recent developments in economic activity, in employment and unemployment, in commodity prices, and in monetary

conditions. Higher frequency data on exchange rates and interest rates also form part of the package. Later in the year, certain of the projections are updated, as are the actual outturns. These indicators are part of the background material for the meetings of finance deputies and of ministers and central bank governors that take place at least twice per year.

Neither too much nor too little should be made of these economic indicators. In one sense, they are similar in many ways to the tables and charts that have always been prepared for meetings of officials. No magic comes from numbers alone. On the other hand, the standardization and continuity of the indicator submissions, as well as the readiness they signal to discuss both official forecasts and some indications of future policy intentions, are suggestive of a serious effort to pave the way for a genuine policy dialogue. What the indicators do is to provide a common snapshot that participants can draw on to assess both the existing economic situation and the medium-term outlook under anticipated policies. But the substantive part of the exercise is the informal discussions where participants provide their own interpretations of the risks in the current and prospective outlook and, equally important, their recommendations about the macroeconomic, structural, and exchange rate policies that need to be implemented by each country; common policy actions may also be proposed. The Fund representative at these meetings also provides his own note evaluating the current and prospective situation and setting forth a view of the key policy priorities.

Starting in the mid 1980s, the Fund's *World Economic Outlook* began including, in addition to the baseline projection, alternative medium-term policy scenarios; since early 1987, these alternative scenarios have been model based, drawing on the Fund's global macroeconomic model, MULTIMOD. In brief, the baseline or central projection (which is judgmental rather than model based) makes the assumptions that present policies of national authorities will be maintained and that real effective exchange rates will remain constant throughout the projection period (except for members of the Exchange Rate Mechanism (ERM) where it is nominal rates that are assumed constant); likewise, the baseline makes technical assumptions about world oil prices and about interest rates. In the alternative medium-term scenarios, some elements of monetary, fiscal, structural, or exchange rate policies are changed from the course set out in the baseline scenario, and then the outcomes are compared. As illustrative of the kinds of policy changes that have been incorporated in such 'what if' scenarios, I might mention the following: a lower value of the dollar's real effective exchange rate; more rapid budget consolidation in the United States and Japan; more rapid fiscal consolidation in Germany following unification; easier monetary policies in the three largest economies; larger

cuts in military expenditure and in agricultural subsidies; increased lending to the developing countries; and larger demands on world saving stemming from reconstruction in the Middle East, German unification, and the transformation of Eastern Europe and the former Soviet Union.

The presentation of alternative medium-term scenarios is a good way to gauge how one set of possible policy actions compares to another, particularly in the context of policy coordination, where the options often involve simultaneous implementation of policy changes by several countries. True enough, the results of these exercises are sensitive to the models employed (Bryant 1990). But so too are the results sensitive when policy-makers have different conceptions about the how the world works. Moreover, in many cases, one does not need a precise estimate of the differences across policy options; a rough estimate or ordinal ranking of the differences will be adequate.

Finally, I come to the development of guidelines on how policy should respond in typical situations. Here, I agree with Polak (1988) that the guidelines for the 1980s underwent a significant change from those of the 1960s and 1970s: concerns about controlling inflation came to surpass those associated with high unemployment; real output targeting gave way to nominal (demand) targeting; a more eclectic view emerged on current account imbalances; fiscal policy came to be seen more and more in a medium-term context; monetary policy was set its own medium-term task, namely that of reducing inflation to low levels, but had to do it while being overburdened by several other subsidiary objectives;[17] and incomes policy was downgraded while structural policies (to remove rigidities and to improve the functioning of markets) moved up in importance. This medium-term strategy aimed at sustaining non-inflationary growth, at promoting national saving, and at eliminating structural rigidities still requires some tactical interpretation when applied to individual situations. Consider, for example, the recession/growth slowdown that hit the industrial world in the second half of 1990 and the recovery which is only just now beginning to take shape. Who should allow their automatic budgetary stabilizers to operate in a recession and who should not?[18] How rapidly should monetary policy proceed towards the longer-run goal of price stability? I am not sure that a consensus is yet fully in hand but nevertheless it is interesting to summarize the answers to these questions that have been put forward in the Fund's *1992 World Economic Outlook*. The scope for allowing automatic stabilizers to operate during a recession should depend on the sustainability of the longer-run fiscal position. For countries where that sustainability is very much in doubt, longer-run considerations need to take the upper hand. In contrast, where longer-run sustainability is not in question and where the track record on fiscal consolidation has been

relatively good, the automatic stabilizers should operate and should be viewed as symmetric to deficit reduction through rapid growth of tax revenue during phases of recovery. On monetary policy, permitting interest rates to decline during a period of sluggish activity, moderating inflation, and below target growth of monetary aggregates should be seen as symmetric to a non-accommodating monetary stance when output exceeds potential. But again, as in the fiscal policy case, in those countries where the longer-term inflation outlook is poor and/or the credibility of formal exchange rate commitments (in the ERM) needs to be reinforced, shorter-term cyclical considerations need to take a back seat to longer-term goals.

Bilateral nominal exchange rates versus effective real exchange rates

Both Funabashi (1988) and Dobson (1991) report that when reference ranges were used in the G-7 policy coordination exercise, they were centred on recent values of bilateral, nominal exchange rates – with no attempt to estimate the effective, equilibrium, real exchange rate. The proposal, which I support, is therefore that the latter replace the former in any kind of future reference rate or target zone analysis. If one is going to reject the view that the market rate is always the right rate, it is necessary to develop an estimate of what the 'right', or equilibrium exchange rate is. That estimate should be of the *real* exchange rate because it is the real rate that matters for competitiveness, for current account positions, and for resource allocation more generally. Changes in nominal rates are usually highly correlated with movements in real exchange rates (at least for the major currencies) because nominal wages and prices are stickier than nominal exchange rates (Mussa 1990). Nevertheless, targeting on nominal rates is clearly second best since differences in inflation rates across countries can mean that what was an equilibrium nominal and real rate, say, a year ago, is no longer the equilibrium nominal rate now. Bilateral exchange rates are also inferior to effective exchange rates as a target. This is because the former accounts for only part of a country's external transactions. Again, by restricting attention to bilateral rates with the other G-7 countries, one includes most of each country's external transactions but by no means all of them.[19] Also, as Williamson (1985 and 1991) and others have demonstrated, once you have an estimate of the equilibrium effective rate, it is possible to derive from it the estimates of equilibrium, key bilateral rates (e.g., the yen/dollar rate, the mark/dollar rate, etc.) that are needed for operational purposes.

Perhaps the largest potential source of error comes from picking a recent market observation as one's estimate of the equilibrium rate and from assuming that the equilibrium rate will stay constant over time. Even if markets do better, on average, than officials in finding the welfare-

maximizing value of the exchange rate, I believe that there are periods when markets push rates away from fundamentals. The only way to identify those periods is to go ahead and make the estimates of equilibrium rates and compare them to the actuals in that period. If the recent market rate is close to the calculated equilibrium rate, there is no problem in using it for the reference rate exercise; if the two are very far apart, it is better to consider which one is right. The real equilibrium rate can also be expected to change over time to reflect changes in real economic conditions. Permanent changes in the terms of trade, intercountry differences in labour productivity, changes in saving and investment propensities, and expected changes in the future course of these variables, all call for changes in the equilibrium rate. In general, one would expect these fundamentals to change rather gradually over time. Yet this need not always be the case: world oil prices can change markedly in a short period; financial sector failures can change almost overnight the medium-term fiscal outlook; and unexpected political changes can have large implications for the longer-term profitability of investing in one area versus another. Again, the only way to get a feel for how fast earlier estimates of the equilibrium rate become outdated is to review those estimates on a fairly regular basis.

Markets are not the only ones who get the equilibrium rate wrong. Official estimates of the equilibrium rate too are surely subject to large margins of error. On other occasions, I have discussed the various approaches to estimating equilibrium exchange rates, but none of them is immune from large uncertainties (Frenkel and Goldstein 1988). It is precisely because that margin of uncertainty is large that I share with Williamson (1985) the view that reference rates or target zones should be quite wide – especially at the early stages of the analytical exercise. Such wide ranges or zones would mean that only large misalignments (say, 20 per cent or more) could be detected. But that in itself would be a valuable contribution.

Current account imbalances

What should be the official attitude towards current account imbalances then? The Twentieth Century Fund Task Force (1991) recommends that they usually be given less importance as policy targets than economic and price stability, but also that they be targeted for reduction in certain situations. In short, their policy position is 'it all depends'. I agree.

It is not difficult to conceive of current account imbalances that would be not only benign but desirable.[20] These would include, for example, those arising from: different private-sector savings patterns attributable in turn to intercountry differences in demographic trends; consumption-smoothing of temporary terms of trade shocks; intercountry differences in cyclical

positions; and intercountry differences in investment opportunities. On the other hand, current account imbalances that reflect unsustainable fiscal deficits or serious distortions in the economy are legitimate cause for concern – all the more so in an environment where large imbalances (whatever their source) often incite pressures for protectionism. I do not believe there are simple rules of thumb that will allow one to short circuit this case-by-case approach to the evaluation of current account imbalances. One such rule or guideline, espoused by then UK Chancellor Lawson, is that any current account deficit that originates almost exclusively in the private sector is benign both because it reflects profit-maximizing behaviour and because it is self-correcting. I beg to differ, on four counts. First, deficits that start out in the private sector often do not stay there, particularly when the debtor is 'too big to fail'. Second, rates of return to saving and investment can be affected by market failures of various sorts, such as speculative bubbles in financial markets; in fact, some of the explanation for the recent recession in the industrial world was the correction of private-sector balance sheet positions, which had become unsustainable in part under the influence of speculative booms in asset prices (particularly in housing). Third, private incentives to save and to invest are affected by tax rates and by government regulations; hence, private-sector decisions may be distorted. And fourth, there is no guarantee that private-sector decisions will take adequate account of certain social-welfare considerations, such as the interests of future generations.

Aggregation effects

The rationale for policy coordination derives from the fact that national policy actions can have quantitatively significant spillover effects, or externalities, on other countries; reaching a global optimum requires that those externalities be taken into account in the decision-making calculus.[21] Policy coordination is a mechanism for internalizing those externalities. Of the many potential sources of externalities, one that often gets less attention than it deserves is synchronous policy actions – in either direction – by a number of large countries. Solomon (1991) documents, in fact, two episodes when countries underestimated the *aggregate* effects of their individual monetary and fiscal policy actions. The first episode occurred in 1972 when the larger industrial countries were seeking to get their economies moving again following the 1970–1 slowdown. As monetary and/or fiscal policies were loosened simultaneously, aggregate G-7 growth accelerated sharply (from 2.9 per cent in 1970–1 to 5.6 per cent in 1972–3). But so too did the import demand for raw materials and their world price – sowing some of the seeds of the subsequent inflation. If aggregation effects had been gauged better, it is conceivable either that the initiating expansion

would have been smaller or that the monetary/fiscal brakes could have been applied somewhat earlier. Solomon's second example is the simultaneous contraction of monetary policy in 1979–82, as most industrial countries sought to bring down the very high inflation rates that emerged in the wake of the second oil shock. Exports declined or slowed sharply in each of the G-7 countries and their aggregate growth rate in 1982 was less than 1 per cent. Elements of the same aggregation problem also surfaced in the most recent recession, as most industrial countries (as well as international agencies) underestimated the weakness of economic activity in partner countries. The point is not that countries should refrain from pointing policies in the same direction as their neighbours; after all, sometimes such a synchronous implementation of policies is called for by the common problem at hand. The point instead is that when this does occur, it is very helpful for each country to have a good picture of what is being prescribed elsewhere and its effects – lest the aggregate effects of individual policy dosages be beyond what was intended.

Conceptually, the aggregation issue is straightforward. Yet it has proved difficult to find a practical solution. Two obstacles stand out. First, even if it were accepted that decentralized adjustment does not guarantee the appropriate level of global demand, there are now no widely accepted criteria for deciding how national policy decisions ought to be adjusted to get closer to a global optimum. The IMF, the OECD, the G-7, and others try to work this out country by country, but that task is much harder without some agreed guidelines to rely on. For example, should only those countries whose economies are the healthiest adjust policies at the margin, or should others also participate? The second obstacle is that our tools for assessing whether – given intended policies – the existing and prospective levels of global demand will be reasonably satisfactory, are still developing. As noted earlier, some composite indicators (including a commodity price indicator) have been included in the policy coordination exercise to assist in the evaluation of potential aggregation effects. My impression, however, is that more is needed. Probably the best option would be to make greater use of simulation methods in global macroeconomic models. Their advantage over indicators is that they capture more of the essential, general equilibrium nature of the aggregation problem. They can be used to simulate the aggregate effects of varying degrees of policy synchronization, as well as to get a picture of how country A's efforts to reach its policy targets will be affected by what countries B and C are doing with their policies.

5 Remedial action and follow-up procedures

Mark Twain, the American author and humorist, had it right: 'you cannot build a reputation on what you're going to do'. You actually have to do it.

In this final section, two proposals are discussed that aim to increase countries' incentives to adopt remedial policy actions and/or to follow through on policy recommendations made by the international community.

Monitoring zones

As noted earlier, as part of the current use of economic indicators, the G-7 countries submit, *inter alia*, medium-term projections for such variables as real GNP, real domestic demand, inflation rates, current account and trade balances, fiscal balances, and monetary conditions. While differences between outcomes and projections are frequently discussed, the process is less intrusive than would be the case if these projections were regarded as official policy targets by all of the participating countries; if formal ranges or monitoring zones were set up for these variables; and if departures from these zones were linked either to consultations, or to the presumption of future policy actions, or to penalties and sanctions for prolonged deviation from the zones.

From time to time over the past twenty years, it has been proposed that something more structured – or automatic if you will – than the existing system is needed to enhance the working of the adjustment mechanism.[22] This idea was probably given its most intensive airing during the deliberations of the Committee of Twenty (C-20) (IMF 1974a) in the early 1970s. It will be recalled that the US Deputies were in favour of an objective indicator linked to convertibility and to the supply of primary reserves; this indicator would be used to induce consultations, policy actions by individual countries, and graduated pressures by the international community (I am told that the real aim was to make it easier to get changes in par values). Interestingly enough, Ossola himself was deeply involved in that debate on objective indicators in the C-20, and championed the case for a basic balance of payments indicator as the 'most satisfactory leading indicator for adjustment action' purposes (IMF 1974b, pp. 52–3). In its *Outline of Reform*, the Committee of Twenty proposed that 'the Fund gain further experience in the use of objective indicators, on an experimental basis, as an aid in assessing the need for adjustment, but will not use such indicators to establish any presumptive or automatic application of pressures'. In the end, the recommendations of the Committee were not implemented, as they were overtaken by events. The target zone proposal, as interpreted by Bergsten and Williamson (1983) and Williamson (1985), also is a variant of the monitoring zone concept; in this case, the deviation of the actual rate from the fundamental equilibrium, real exchange rate, is the single indicator that triggers consultation and, eventually, policy action. More

recently, former US Treasury Secretary Baker (1988) suggested that 'monitoring zones' be established for key indicators, so as to 'refine the means of assessing whether an economy's performance is significantly deviating from an appropriate path'.

At least three questions come up in evaluating the feasibility and desirability of implementing a system of monitoring zones for key macro-economic variables.

The first one is whether to have a single indicator or a set of indicators. The advantage of a single indicator is that it sends an unambiguous signal. When there are many indicators and very few policy instruments, there is the risk that those authorities that want to delay policy actions will point to the conflicting nature of the signal coming from different indicators as a rationale. The other side of the coin is that a single indicator runs the risk either of sending a false signal or at least of ignoring valuable information coming from other indicators. I have already mentioned how the exchange rate can give a false signal about the need for fiscal correction in a target zone where exchange rates are defended *via* alterations in monetary policy – but the problem is broader than that. In this connection, it is relevant to note that many central banks have over the past five years or so down-graded monetary aggregates as the intermediate target of monetary policy in favour of a more eclectic approach that utilizes a broader set of indicators; this example also highlights the point that structural change (in this case, financial liberalization) can reduce the reliability of any single indicator. On top of all this, the reason why the current list of economic indicators is so long is that it was apparently not possible to agree on a shorter list, i.e., different countries had different favourite indicators.

A second question is how to take account of the 'controllability' of the indicator. Of the indicators used in the current policy coordination exercise, some (growth, inflation) are closer to final targets, some are more in the nature of intermediate targets (monetary conditions, fiscal balances), and some lie in-between (trade and current accounts, exchange rates, total domestic demand). Any intermediate target strategy has to face the problem that those variables over which the authorities have the closest control may have the least reliable relationship to the ultimate targets of policy – and *vice versa*. Bryant (1990) has in fact gone so far as to suggest that this trade-off between controllability and reliability is inevitable and serious enough to tip the balance towards single stage strategies that forego intermediate targets. Would monitoring zones, therefore, only relate to those variables over which the authorities had reasonable control, or would they also include the ultimate targets of policy? A related issue is whether because of different degrees of controllability across variables and across countries, there should be wider monitoring zones for some variables than

for others, or even for the same variable across countries. In this latter connection, it might be recalled that some members of the ERM of the EMS have had, as a transitional arrangement, wider exchange rate margins than others. But allowing some countries to have wider monitoring zones on a permanent basis for the same variable than other countries raises issues of equal treatment.

Yet a third question is whether departures of variables from their monitoring zones would merely trigger policy consultations or would – perhaps when the deviation was larger and more persistent – also trigger remedial policy actions. If only consultations are triggered, then monitoring zones may not add much discipline to a system where economic indicators are already regularly discussed. At the same time, it has often been argued (Poehl 1987; Padoa-Schioppa 1988) that it is not desirable to 'robotize' economic policy making by simple policy rules: judgment and compromise are required to set priorities, make policy choices, and decide who should act; others have emphasized that the knowledge about the workings of the economy required to make multiple automatic policy triggers both consistent with one another and stabilizing, is beyond current capabilities.

So long as monitoring zones are regarded just as triggers for discussion and consultation, it is hard to see how they could do much harm. In fact, they may even do some good. I view them as operating much in the same spirit as announced money supply targets: they induce the authorities to be more specific about their policy objectives and about the intended course of policy; if policy departs from the earlier intended range, the authorities are under some obligation to explain both why such a departure has occurred and whether it is the target range rather than the policy itself that ought to be altered. Within the context of G-7 policy coordination, they could perhaps be tried on a quiet, experimental basis for either indicators of fiscal and monetary policy, or for, say, one ultimate target, such as nominal income. The objective should be to get an earlier indication of when and why policies and outcomes may be offtrack, and to mobilize some additional pressure to get them back on track. Some of this is done anyway but monitoring zones might give the indicator process some further structure. It might also help to provide better integration between any (quiet) exchange rate targets and underlying fiscal and monetary policies, as well as to focus attention more sharply on who has responsibility for what.

Follow-up procedures

At present, members of the IMF have at least three occasions each year to express their views on the policies of each of the larger industrial countries: once during the Executive Board's discussion of the Article IV consultation

for that country and twice during the biannual discussion of the *World Economic Outlook*.[23] In each case, the Managing Director makes a summing-up of the meeting which is distributed to all members; the summing-up of the *World Economic Outlook* discussion also forms part of the documentation for the twice yearly meetings of the Interim Committee. These summings-up typically provide a capsule evaluation of policy achievements and shortcomings, along with some broad policy recommendations. Until very recently, however, there was no specific mechanism for following up on these recommendations. From time to time therefore, it has been discussed whether such a mechanism should be put in place. Specifically, in their report on the *Functioning of the International Monetary System*, the Deputies of the Group of Ten proposed among other measures to strengthen surveillance that:

the IMF should provide more candid assessments of national policies and their domestic and international impact as well as precise suggestions for policy changes ... For industrial and developing countries whose policies and performance are of greatest concern for the world economy, a confidential exchange of views between the Managing Director and the Finance Minister should be envisaged at the end of the consultation process. In addition, to ensure an adequate follow-up to the consultation conclusions, countries should be requested to present a report outlining the measures introduced or considered to deal with the problems identified by the IMF and to respond to specific policy suggestions (G-10 1985, para. 45).

In January 1992, the Fund's Executive Board approved a pragmatic and low-key follow-up procedure. This procedure would apply to all members, although the nature of the Fund contact could vary. In all cases, the summing-up of the consultation would be transmitted to the member's governor for the Fund. In some cases, where particular concerns had been expressed by the Executive Board, a separate letter from the Managing Director of the Fund could serve as a vehicle to stress certain points. And, in a few cases, where specific actions are expected or important issues, especially of systemic significance, have been raised, that letter could invite a response or suggest further discussions between the number and management or staff. This too is a modest step. But it has a number of attractions. It should help to increase the continuity of consultation discussions from year to year. It asks, in certain circumstances, for a specific follow-up response to the views of the international community on that country's policies. It involves the authorities at a high level. And it utilizes the traditional instruments of persuasion and peer pressure. On the negative side of the ledger, other than what one of my predecessors, Marcus Fleming, called 'the finger of public shame', there are no penalties or sanctions for non-compliance.

Notes

The views expressed are the author's alone and do not necessarily represent the views of the International Monetary Fund.

1 This definition of coordination comes from Wallich (1984, p. 85).

2 In this connection, it may be relevant to note that the Managing Director of the Fund began participating in the surveillance discussions of the Group of Five in 1982. Surveillance discussions shifted from the G-5 to the G-7 in 1987. The Fund's Economic Counsellor began participating in surveillance meetings of deputies in late 1986.

3 Recently, a more sophisticated attempt to apply this actual versus target approach to the policy undertakings at the economic summits of the 1975–89 period has been reported by Von Furstenberg and Daniels (1991 and 1992). In brief, they develop a method for scoring compliance with policy commitments. Their results suggest that for the fifteen economic summits taken together, G-7 policy authorities delivered on about one third of their commitments; they also find that the most and least successful summits were Venice II (1987) and Toronto (1988), respectively (average compliance scores for individual summit countries are likewise calculated). It turns out however that these results are extremely sensitive to whether one looks at changes in economic performance or at levels. In this connection, Christ (1991) cites the instructive case of the commitment to 'achieve low inflation' at the 1983 Williamsburg Summit. In the following twelve months, Japan achieved the lowest rate of inflation (1.4 per cent) among the G-7 countries but got the lowest score from Von Furstenberg and Daniels; in contrast, Italy recorded the highest inflation rate (11.2 per cent) but received the highest score. The reason for this seemingly non-sensical result is that their scoring method uses changes in performance as the relevant indicator (in an attempt to isolate the independent effect of the summit undertaking on the observed outcome). Obviously, if levels of performance were employed, the verdict about who succeeded and who did not would be completely different.

4 Even when considering just the comparison between optimal coordinated and uncoordinated policies, the gains to coordination emerge as larger when the game is a repetitive one and governments value their 'reputations' for carrying out policy commitments (Currie *et al.* 1987).

5 On the effects of coordinating when using the wrong model, see Frankel and Rockett (1988). Note, however, that if policymakers recognize that they do not know the true model and take this uncertainty into account, then policy may be set more cautiously, with positive effects on the gains from coordination (Ghosh and Masson 1991).

6 Average growth in the G-7 countries was 2.9 per cent for the 1986–91 period versus 2.2 per cent for 1980–5. For Consumer Price Index (CPI) inflation, the corresponding averages are 3.5 per cent for 1986–91 versus 7.0 for 1980–5. As regards average current account imbalances (expressed as a percentage of Gross National Product (GNP), and without regard to sign), the relevant figures are 2.3 per cent for 1986–91 versus 1.3 per cent. All these comparisons are robust to substituting unweighted for weighted averages (based on GNP).

7 One should also note that the policy coordination process is still maturing and that both the range of its activities and the relative priorities among them, may change over time. In this regard, Gyohten (1988) has argued that the G-7 exercise has already gone through three stages: an initial stage when the emphasis was on exchange rate realignment; a second stage when the emphasis shifted to macroeconomic policy coordination; and a third stage when structural policies took on added importance.

8 To get the flavour, recall that: (i) the Plaza Agreement (September 1985) concluded that 'some further orderly appreciation of main non-dollar currencies against the dollar is desirable'; (ii) the Louvre Accord (February 1987) noted 'Further substantial exchange rate shifts among their currencies could damage growth and adjustment prospects in their countries. In current circumstances, therefore, they agreed to cooperate closely to foster stability of exchange rates around current levels'; (iii) the G-7 Treasury Ministers' Meeting in Washington in September 1989 considered that 'the rise in recent months of the dollar (was) inconsistent with longer-run economic fundamentals'; and (iv) the April 1992 G-7 communiqué noted that 'the decline of the yen since their last meeting was not contributing to the adjustment process', as well as reaffirmed their 'commitment to close cooperation in exchange markets ...'.

9 Cooper (1984 and 1992) has in fact argued that looking towards the next century, the best regime would be the creation of a common currency for all the industrial democracies, with a common monetary policy and a joint Bank of Issue to determine that monetary policy. I must say that in the absence of larger (political) integration objectives, I would regard the establishment of such a regime as unlikely.

10 Obstfeld (1990), after examining the experience of the 1985–7 period, concludes that exchange rate changes for the major currencies were primarily related to monetary and fiscal policies rather than to sterilized intervention. Bordo and Schwartz (1990) argue that exchange market intervention since Plaza had no discernible short- or long-run effect on exchange rates. Dobson (1991) gives intervention policy during that period higher marks for effectiveness.

11 It is in this spirit both of providing a better link between underlying macroeconomic policies and exchange rate commitments and of reducing the overburdening of monetary policies, that Dobson (1991) and the Twentieth Century Task Force (1991) recommend that central bank deputies participate in meetings of G-7 finance deputies; the objection that is sometimes raised to this proposal is that adding seven more participants to these meetings would work against the preservation of informality and frankness.

12 This being said, I would not go to the other extreme and argue that quiet exchange rate commitments have the advantage that they permit the authorities to 'surprise' the market. To the extent that the actions of authorities come to be regarded as highly unpredictable, this can itself become a source of instability over the longer term.

13 See Mastropasqua et al. (1988) for estimates of intramarginal intervention in the EMS.

14 Consistent with this proposition, the empirical work of Frankel and Phillips

(1991) suggests that it took a long time (until early 1990) for most of the exchange rate commitments in the EMS to acquire strong credibility.

15 See Kenen 'Floating exchange rates reconsidered: the influence of new ideas, priorities, and problems', chapter in this volume.

16 In 1962, the United States accounted for 41 per cent of world output; by 1981, that share had fallen to 26 per cent. Over the same period, the industrial countries of Europe increased their share from 29 to 32 per cent, while Japan increased its share from 4 to 11 per cent. Changes in shares of world trade are somewhat less dramatic but tell the same story.

17 Reacting to this overburdening of monetary policy, both the Twentieth Century Task Force (1991) and Dobson (1991) recommend that measures be taken to increase the flexibility of fiscal policy in those countries where it is now inflexible. One such measure would be to extend 'fast track' authority – analogous to that on international trade legislation – to fiscal policy changes (within specified limits). My own preference would be to strengthen automatic stabilizers. Note that automatic stabilizers: can apply both to the revenue and expenditure sides; can add or withdraw stimulus from aggregate demand promptly at appropriate points in the business cycle; can be triggered automatically on the basis of cyclical indicators; can affect fiscal budget balance symmetrically over the cycle without affecting the medium-term orientation of fiscal policy; and can operate fairly directly and efficiently in restraining or stimulating aggregate demand (Goldstein and Isard 1992).

18 By not allowing automatic stabilizers to operate, I mean taking discretionary fiscal policy action in the opposite direction that offsets part or all of the effect of these automatic stabilizers.

19 For example, in 1990, about 35 per cent of US exports went to developing countries, and about 40 per cent of US imports came from developing countries.

20 For a more extensive discussion of 'good' and 'bad' current account imbalances (Frenkel et al. 1991).

21 See Cooper (1987) and Frenkel et al. (1990) for a discussion of the differences between the global economy and the standard competitive model that provide a rationale for policy coordination.

22 de Larosière (1991) has recently argued for introducing an objective element of discipline into the system via a compulsory mechanism of settlement in reserve holding that would be binding on all members.

23 In addition, every six weeks or so, the Executive Board holds an informal session on exchange market developments where the focus is on recent developments in financial markets, including the behaviour of the major currencies.

References

Baker, J. 1988. 'Economic Policy Coordination and International Monetary Reform', Remarks by the Honorable James A. Baker III, Secretary of the Treasury, Before the Council on Foreign Relations, Paris, 20 May, *Treasury News*, B-1419.

Bergsten, C.F. and Williamson, J. 1983. 'Exchange Rates and Trade Policy', in W. Cline (ed.), *Trade Policy in the 1980s*, Institute for International Economics, Washington DC.

Bordo, M. and Schwartz, A. 1990. 'What Has Foreign Exchange Market Intervention Since the Plaza Agreement Accomplished?', *NBER Working Paper*, 3562, Cambridge Mass., December.

Brady, N. 1990. 'Remarks by the Honorable Nicholas F. Brady, Secretary of the Treasury, Before the American Chamber of Commerce, London, 29 May, *Treasury News*, NB-825.

Bryant, R. 1990. 'Obstacles to Coordination and a Consideration of Two Proposals to Overcome Them: A Comment', in W. Branson, J. Frenkel, and M. Goldstein, *International Policy Coordination and Exchange Rate Fluctuations*, Chicago, University of Chicago Press.

Christ, C. 1991. 'Policies Undertakings by the Seven Summit Countries: A Comment', in *Carnegie-Rochester Conference Series on Public Policy*, 35.

Collins, S. 1988. 'Inflation and the European Monetary System', in F. Giavazzi, S. Micossi, and M. Miller (eds.), *The European Monetary System*, Cambridge, Cambridge University Press.

Cooper, R. 1984. 'A Monetary System for the Future', *Foreign Affairs*, 63.

1987. 'International Economic Cooperation: Is it Desirable? Is it Likely?' *Washington Quarterly*, Spring.

1992. 'What Future for the International Monetary System', in J. Frenkel and M. Goldstein (eds.), *International Financial Policy: Essays in Honor of Jacques J. Polak*, Washington DC, IMF.

Crockett, A. 1989. 'The Role of International Institutions in Surveillance and Policy Coordination', in R. Bryant *et al.* (eds.), *Macroeconomic Policies in an Interdependent World*, Washington DC, Brookings Institution.

Crockett, A. and M. Goldstein, 1987. 'Strengthening the International Monetary System: Exchange Rates, Surveillance, and Objective Indicators', *IMF Occasional Paper*, 50, Washington DC, IMF (this also includes the 1985 Report of the Group of Ten Deputies on The Functioning of the International Monetary System).

Currie, D., Levine, P., and Vidalis, N. 1987. 'Cooperative and Non-Cooperative Rules for Monetary and Fiscal Policy in an Empirical Two-Block Model', in R. Bryant and R. Portes (eds.), *Global Macroeconomics: Policy Conflict and Cooperation*, London, Macmillan.

Dobson, W. 1991. *Economic Policy Coordination: Requiem or Prologue? Policy Analyses in International Economics*, 30, Washington DC, Institute for International Economics.

EC Commission 1990. *One Market, One Money*, Brussels.

Feldstein, M. 1990. 'The Rationale for, and Effects of, International Economic Policy Coordination: A Comment', in W. Branson, J. Frenkel, and M. Goldstein, *International Policy Coordination and Exchange Rate Fluctuations*, Chicago, University of Chicago Press.

Fischer, S. 1990. 'The Coordination of Macroeconomic Policies', in W. Branson, J.

Frenkel, and M. Goldstein, *International Policy Coordination and Exchange Rate Fluctuations*, Chicago, University of Chicago Press.

Flood, R., Rose, A., and Mathieson, D. 1991. 'An Empirical Exploration of Exchange Rate Target Zones', in *Carnegie-Rochester Conference Series on Public Policy*, Autumn.

Frankel, J. 1991. *Is There a Yen Block Forming in Pacific Asia*, Washington DC, Institute for International Economics, unpublished.

Frankel, J. and Phillips, S. 1991. 'The European Monetary System: Credible at Last?', *NBER Working Paper*, 3819, Cambridge, Mass. NBER.

Frankel, J. and Rockett, K. 1988. 'International Macroeconomic Policy Coordination When Policy-Makers Disagree on the Model', *American Economic Review*, June.

Frenkel, J. and Goldstein, M. 1986. 'A Guide to Target Zones', *IMF Staff Papers*, December.

1988. 'Exchange Rate Volatility and Misalignment', in F. Reserve Bank of Kansas City, *Financial Market Volatility*, Kansas City.

1989. 'International Dimensions of Monetary Policy', in Federal Reserve Bank of Kansas City, *Monetary Policy Issues in the 1990s*, Kansas City.

1991. 'Macroeconomic Implications of Currency Zones', in Federal Reserve Bank of Kansas City, *Policy Implications of Trade and Currency Zones*.

Frenkel, J., Goldstein, M., and Masson, P. 1989. 'Simulating the Effects of Some Simple Coordinated Versus Uncoordinated Policy Rules', in R. Bryant *et al.* (eds.), *Macroeconomic Policies in an Interdependent World*, Washington DC, Brookings Institution.

1990. 'The Rationale for, and Effects of, International Economic Policy Coordination', in W. Branson, J. Frenkel, and M. Goldstein, *International Policy Coordination and Exchange Rate Fluctuations*, Chicago, University of Chicago Press.

1991. 'Characteristics of a Successful Exchange Rate System', *IMF Occasional Paper*, 82, Washington DC, IMF.

Funabashi, Y. 1988. *Managing the Dollar: From the Plaza to the Louvre*, Washington DC, Institute for International Economics.

Ghosh, A. and Masson, P. 1991. 'Model Uncertainty, Learning, and the Gains from Coordination', *American Economic Review*, June.

Giavazzi, F. and Giovannini, A. 1988. 'The Role of the Exchange Rate Regime in a Disinflation: Empirical Evidence on the European Monetary System', in F. Giavazzi, S. Micossi, and M. Miller (eds.), *The European Monetary System*, Cambridge, Cambridge University Press.

Goldstein, M. and Isard, P. 1992. 'Mechanisms for Promoting Global Monetary Stability', in M. Goldstein *et al.*, 'Policy Issues in the Evolving International Monetary System', *IMF Occasional Paper*, 96, June, Washington DC.

Group of Ten 1985. 'Functioning of the International Monetary System', *Report of the Deputies*.

Gyohten, T. 1988. 'Economic Policy Objectives and policy-making in the Major Industrial Countries: A Comment', in W. Guth (ed.), *Economic Policy Coordination*, Washington DC, IMF.

International Monetary Fund 1974a. *International Monetary Reform: Documents of the Committee of Twenty*, Washington DC, IMF.

1974b. *Report of Technical Group on Indicators*, Washington DC, IMF.

Krugman, P. 1987. 'The Bias in the Band: Exchange Rate Expectations under a Broad-Band Exchange Rate Regime', paper presented at conference on the European Monetary System, Cambridge Mass. NBER.

Lane, T. 1992. 'Market Discipline', *IMF Working Paper*, June, Washington DC, IMF.

de Larosière, J. 1991. 'Robert Triffin and the Reform of the International Monetary System', in A. Steinherr and D. Weiserbs (eds.), *Evolution of the International and Regional Monetary Systems: Essays in Honor of Robert Triffin*, London, Macmillan.

Mastropasqua, C., Micossi, S., and Rinaldi, R. 1988. 'Interventions, Sterilizations, and Monetary Policy in European Monetary System Countries', in F. Giavazzi *et al.* (eds.), *European Monetary System*, Cambridge, Cambridge University Press.

Mussa, M. 1990. 'Exchange Rates in Theory and Reality', *Essays in International Finance*, 179, Princeton, International Finance Section, Princeton University.

Obstfeld, M. 1990. 'The Effectiveness of Foreign Exchange Intervention: Recent Experience, 1985–88', in W. Branson, J. Frenkel, and M. Goldstein, *International Policy Coordination and Exchange Rate Fluctuations*, Chicago, University of Chicago Press.

Oudiz, G. and Sachs, J. 1984. 'Macroeconomic Policy Coordination among the Industrial Economies', *Brookings Papers on Economic Activity*, Washington DC, Brookings Institution.

Padoa-Schioppa, T. 1988. 'Toward a New Adjustable Peg?' in *The New International Monetary System: The Next Twenty Five Years*, Washington DC, June, Per Jacobsson Lecture, Per Jacobsson Foundation.

Poehl, K.O. 1987. 'Cooperation – A Keystone for the Stability of the International Monetary System', First Arthur Burns Memorial Lecture, at the American Council on Germany, New York, November.

Polak, J. 1988. 'Economic Policy Objectives and Policy-Making in the Major Industrial Countries', in W. Guth (ed.), *Economic Policy Coordination*, Washington DC, IMF.

Solomon, R. 1991. 'Background Paper on International Policy Coordination', in Twentieth Century Fund Task Force on the International Coordination of National Economic Policies, *Partners in Prosperity*, Priority Press Publications, New York.

Tobin, J. 1987. 'Agenda for International Coordination of Macroeconomic Policies', in Volcker *et al.*, 'International Monetary Cooperation: Essays in Honor of Henry C. Wallich', *Essays in International Finance*, 169, Princeton, International Finance Section, Princeton University.

Twentieth Century Fund Task Force on the International Coordination of National Economic Policies 1991. *Partners in Prosperity*, New York, Priority Press Publications.

Volcker, P. and others 1987. 'International Monetary Cooperation: Essays in

Honor of Henry C. Wallich, *Essays in International Finance*, 169, Princeton, International Finance Section, Princeton University.

Von Furstenberg, G. and Daniels, J. 1991. 'Policy Undertakings by the Seven Summit Countries: Ascertaining the Degree of Compliance', in *Carnegie-Rochester Conference Series on Public Policy*, 35.

1992. 'Economic Summit Declarations, 1975–89: Examining the Written Record of International Cooperation', *Princeton Studies in International Finance*, 72, Princeton, International Finance Section, Princeton University.

Wallich, H. 1984. 'International Cooperation in the World Economy', in J. Frenkel and M. Mussa (eds.), *The World Economic System: Performance and Prospects*, Auburn House, Dover, Massachusetts.

Williamson, J. 1985. *The Exchange Rate System, Policy Analyses in International Economics*, Washington DC, Institute for International Economics, revised edition.

Williamson, J. 1991. *Equilibrium Exchange Rates: An Update*, Washington DC, Institute for International Economics, unpublished.

Williamson, J. and Miller, M. 1987. 'Targets and Indicators: A Blueprint for the International Coordination of Economic Policy', *Policy Analyses in International Economics*, Washington DC, Institute for International Economics.

Discussion

RICHARD N. COOPER

A smoothly functioning international monetary system is not an end in itself. The international monetary system should serve the broader aims of society, and therefore should be instrumental in making life better for ordinary people. What do ordinary people want? Traditionally, their objectives and reasonable expectations from society and government can be grouped under three headings: physical and psychological security, high and preferably increasing material standards of living, and a sense of some control over their own destiny. For international economists, these aims can be abbreviated as PPP: peace, prosperity, and participation.

Most analyses of various international economic regimes focus, properly, on their macroeconomic performance. If that goes badly wrong, a regime clearly fails to serve the objectives of ordinary people. But there is also a microeconomic aspect to exchange rate arrangements that should not be neglected, although it usually is. I want to draw attention to two microeconomic disadvantages of the current arrangements of market-determined floating exchange rates, each from the perspective of the well being of ordinary people.

The first, less important but more visible, is the cost to travellers of having to convert currencies, usually at highly disadvantageous rates. Recently at London airport the difference between the posted buy and sell rates between the US dollar and the British pound, two of the world's leading currencies, was 14 per cent, a gross margin (before allowing for transactions fees) not much different from that for merchandise in an American supermarket. This amounts to a tremendous tax on travel. Fixing central rates within a wide band, as in the European Monetary System (EMS), does not help very much. *The Economist* several years ago ran the notional experiment of travelling from London to Athens through all twelve members of the European Community, converting currencies on entering each new country. The traveller started out with £100 and ended in Athens with less than £20 to spend, having done nothing but convert currencies. These cash transactions do not bulk large in international

transactions as a whole, which can typically be done by bank transfers at wholesale rates. But is worth keeping in mind that millions of ordinary people now travel outside their home country, and currency conversion is the only direct contact they have with international monetary arrangements. This highly visible aspect of the existing arrangements does not serve them well.

More significant from an economic point of view is the influence of floating exchange rates on the business decisions of the 10,000–30,000 business decisionmakers of the world whose collective decisions on investment will determine future standards of living throughout the world. The direct costs of currency conversion for corporations doing business *within* the European Community (EC) have been estimated at 0.5 per cent of EC Gross Domestic Product (GDP), a non-negligible amount (EC 1990, pp. 63–8). I am more concerned here with the indirect, long-term costs, and in particular the influence of exchange rate uncertainty on investment decisions. Many industries today are oligopolistic in structure. That means, in general, that firms and their customers like and expect fixed, posted prices, at least as a starting point for negotiation of discounts. It also means that few of the firms will deviate far from their competitors in their strategies of pricing, product innovation, capacity creation, and marketing. For a host of reasons, oligopolistic firms do not like to be far from the crowd of their fellow oligopolists. Making mistakes, even big mistakes, can be more easily justified to shareholders and other stake holders if their near competitors have made similar mistakes.

As international competition becomes more acute in oligopolistic industries, exchange rate fluctuations create a major problem for management. First, they cannot be ignored, since profits amount to only about 5 per cent of the selling price of many manufactured goods. Yet exchange rates can easily swing 5 per cent in a week, thus wiping out (or doubling, but that possibility does not fully compensate risk averting management) profits on an unhedged transaction, and for reasons that arise in the financial world and are largely beyond the ken of those whose specialty is manufacturing or marketing. It is increasingly easy to hedge any particular sale abroad through a variety of financial instruments. But it is not possible through financial instruments to hedge satisfactorily a capacity-increasing investment aimed at foreign sales. To allow prices in foreign markets to fluctuate with exchange rates irritates customers and runs the risk of losing sales. But fluctuating exchange rates make impossible steady local prices in each of several national markets without creating possibilities for arbitrage between markets.

How are firms likely to respond to these difficulties? First, and most benign, they will diversify their investments across currency areas where

they have major markets. Thus Japanese firms will want to 'hedge' by investing in productive facilities in the United States and in Europe, for instance, and similarly for firms headquartered elsewhere. This practice is not undesirable in itself, but insofar as it is motivated by currency uncertainty it implies that the hedging investments will have lower yields than they would if they could be made in the best location regardless of exchange rate uncertainties. That represents a loss to future generations.

Second, risk averse firms will reduce the total level of investment compared with a regime that, other things being equal, produces less uncertainty. There is little systematic empirical evidence linking investment to exchange rate uncertainty, although there is a certain amount of anecdotal evidence. It is noteworthy, however, that the ratio of investment to GDP in the industrialized countries of the Organization for Economic Cooperation and Development (OECD) fell by 2 to 3 percentage points following the introduction of generalized floating exchange rates in 1973, from roughly 24 per cent in the late 1960s to 22 per cent in the second half of the 1970s, and to 21 per cent in the 1980s. But the period following 1973 was subject to several major oil price shocks, a sharp rise followed by a fall in the rate of inflation in OECD countries, and the two deepest post-1945 industrial recessions, in 1974–5 and 1981–2. Too many things have happened to impute the markedly lower investment rates to exchange rate variability with any confidence, but neither can it be ruled out that they played a important role, particularly since the decline occurred more in tradable than in non-tradable goods, as one would expect from that particular causal influence.

Third, in the face of exchange rate variability that greatly complicates their pricing strategies, business firms will seek government assistance in separating markets, with a view to discouraging arbitrage from one currency area to another. We know from the experience of the mid 1980s that Japanese and European firms attempted to maintain their dollar prices in the US market, as well as local currency prices in their home markets, despite wide movements in the dollar exchange rate. A trade association was created in the United States to lobby for legislative and administrative action against 'grey market' goods, i.e., goods that (perfectly legally) were shipped by brokers or dealers outside of normal channels, taking advantage of the arbitrage possibilities. The low point of this response was reached when Duracell filed a trademark violation complaint in the United States against Duracell batteries produced in a 100 per cent owned Belgian subsidiary being imported into the United States by independent importers. Duracell properly lost the case, but only after tying the importer up in court for some time. Anti-dumping laws make no provision for movements in exchange rates, so they offer a field day for competitors to raise a case

against an imported product whose price does not follow the exporting country's currency appreciation. Successful protectionist action, or even harassing action, introduces microeconomic inefficiencies; and the possibilities of such action may also discourage investment.

These microeconomic considerations will not be, and should not be, decisive in the choice of an exchange rate regime. But they should not be wholly neglected either. The ultimate solution for them is to establish a single currency, at least among the major manufacturing nations, e.g., European Community, Japan, and United States. Such an idea raises a host of management issues, since a single currency must have a single monetary policy, one that in this case spans nations. That is challenging but not impossible to work out. An assessment of such an arrangement also raises a host of complex issues regarding the pattern of disturbances to which the participating economies are likely to be subject in the future, as well as their capacity to adjust to them. I will simply venture the opinion that, with monetary union, disturbances *between* these large and diverse economies, such as those that may call for exchange rate adjustment, are likely to be much smaller than the disturbances *within* them, where even today we do not rely on changes in exchange rates as part of the adjustment process. The main disturbances between these regions in the future are likely to be monetary in nature, creating complications for the real side of the economy such as those already discussed. With a common monetary regime and its accompanying integrated capital market, that type of disturbance would not be possible. Over time, the costs associated with flexible exchange rates among these three regions are likely to grow relative to the benefits of flexible rates, so it is not too early to begin thinking about alternative arrangements.

References

European Community Commission, 1990. *One Market, One Money*, Brussels, October.

Discussion

LAMBERTO DINI

The chapters by Bayoumi and Eichengreen and by Goldstein can be seen as complementing each other in a proposition that I could reformulate as follows: the functioning of the international monetary system needs to be improved, particularly in the field of the adjustment mechanism, but we should proceed with caution, avoiding ambitious reform projects and concentrating on concrete arrangements for international economic cooperation.

Indeed, the case for a major overhaul of the system has never emerged because, all things considered, the system has worked relatively well. Faced with such momentous issues as the oil shocks of the seventies, the debt crisis, and the process of financial integration, policymakers have been circumspect in questioning the foundations of the present system. Taking this into account, I should have to emphasize two points concerning the outlook for the international monetary system. First, I see a move towards tightening exchange rate commitments among the three major currencies as unrealistic in the foreseeable future. Second, I think that the present framework for international economic and monetary cooperation can be improved.

Macroeconomic and structural conditions as well as domestic policy objectives in the major industrial countries remain much too divergent to admit more stringent exchange rate commitments. The United States has just overcome one of the longest recessions in postwar history; Germany is contending with the unprecedented task of unification and its repercussions on the rest of Europe; Japan is coping with the effects of the restrictive policies required to cure a major asset price inflation. Under these conditions, I believe it is unrealistic to expect the leading industrial nations to relinquish part of their national sovereignty in economic and monetary matters and subordinate their internal policy objectives to the pursuit of exchange rate stability; in actual fact, policy coordination was pursued in the 1980s until fundamental inconsistencies emerged between the various countries' domestic objectives. Moreover, the flexibility of exchange rates

may prove beneficial in certain circumstances. The depreciation of the dollar until mid 1992 has provided a stimulus to economic activity in the United States. Once the recovery of the American economy has been consolidated, an appreciation of the dollar *vis-à-vis* European currencies would help the Community take advantage of the increase in US domestic demand. Conversely, an appreciation of the yen against the dollar and European currencies could help to reduce Japan's trade surplus.

To stress the advantages of exchange rate flexibility among the three main monetary areas is not to underestimate the risk of excessive reliance on the exchange rate for adjustments purposes. The risk is that exchange rate movements could be seen as a substitute for necessary changes of policy in other fields, particularly in fiscal policies. In turn, the lack of supportive policy actions could induce the exchange rate to overshoot equilibrium levels, creating a 'vicious circle' of depreciation and inflation, on the one hand, and of appreciation and deflation, on the other. The only way to prevent those developments is through international cooperation, but it should be clear that there are no 'quick fixes'. In considering the difficulties that confront international cooperation, one must first of all assess the gains it may be expected to produce. Analytical models often suggest that these are not very large, but it is widely recognized that empirical measures often underestimate them. The gains from policy coordination are unlikely to be achieved or even recognized if governments disagree about the 'true model' of the economy and the mechanism through which the effects of economic policies are transmitted to final targets. Lastly, coordination is costly in terms of the negotiating process and the time lags involved in reaching agreements.

Nevertheless, I believe some realistic and by no means insignificant improvements can be achieved in this field. In this respect, I broadly share the specific proposals analysed by Goldstein in his very balanced treatment. I agree, in particular, that exchange rate developments should be monitored closely by the International Monetary Fund (IMF), in line with the mandate of its Articles of Agreement. It is essential that exchange rate surveillance be conducted in an institutional setting and not by informal groups. In addition, IMF surveillance of members' macropolicies should be reinforced by making it more continuous and flexible. In this regard, I was glad to note that Goldstein quotes the 1985 Report of the Deputies of the Group of Ten (G-10) on 'The Functioning of the International Monetary System' which put forth several recommendations that remain valid today. Although those proposals are certainly less spectacular than meetings of the Group of Seven (G-7), I think they represent an important and promising avenue for the international coordination of policies.

Finally, I believe there is a need to consider how to broaden the scope of

policy cooperation among the G-7 countries. The first areas that come to mind are those of budgetary and trade policies. Both are very close to the concerns of national parliaments and therefore not likely to witness a relaxation of sovereign prerogatives. Still, it would be important for the cooperation process to help resist the protectionist pressures threatening the survival of the open trading system. Similarly, cooperation in the field of budgetary policies should aim at preventing the emergence of a generalized process of either fiscal consolidation or fiscal expansion, in order to contain their very serious implications for, respectively, economic activity and inflation.

Discussion

LEONHARD GLESKE

The Bayoumi–Eichengreen chapter is, in its substance, mainly an analysis of the past, indeed, a very sophisticated one. Of greatest importance in my mind, not least in assessing the possibility of reestablishing in whatever form a worldwide system of fixed exchange rates, is the final conclusion drawn from the comparison between the success of the pre-World War I gold standard and the breakup of the Bretton Woods system in 1971. What the authors are saying is this: 'The culprit appears to be the steady loss of macroeconomic flexibility over time. Maintaining a fixed exchange rate entailed few costs during the gold standard years because of the speed with which economies adjusted to shocks. In the post-World War II period, on the other hand, slower adjustment resulted in strains which eventually destroyed the Bretton Woods system.' This is a lesson we have to keep in mind when reflecting about the outlook for the international monetary system. We really should not ponder the future without first looking at the past. That is the merit of Bayoumi's and Eichengreen's chapter.

Goldstein's chapter is a comprehensive description and a lucid analysis of past efforts in economic policy coordination and at the same time a thoughtful and convincing evaluation of proposals for improving it. I find myself in broad agreement with most of what Goldstein says in his chapter and especially with what he says in section 3 against louder and more explicit exchange rate commitments by the largest industrial countries, or currency areas, towards which the international monetary system is developing. This will in all likelihood tend to change at least to a certain degree the nature of some of the problems we are discussing now. The most far-reaching change will be due to the establishment of monetary union in Europe and I will try to assess the impact of this development on the outlook for the international monetary system.

The process of European integration is an integral part of a broader development that will lead to a tripolar world economy, with the United States, the European Community, and Japan as the centres of gravity. Politically and economically the United States is now still the strongest

332

power in the world, but the days of its solitary dominance, which characterized the world economy until the second half of the 1960s, are over. There is nothing surprising in that. In the long postwar period of peace and security, during which the United States took the lead in fostering and sustaining a framework that promoted political and economic stability, the formation of other centres of dynamic power was to be expected once the reconstruction of the European and Asian economies had been completed. However, the end of the period of reconstruction of the European and Asian economies coincided with a marked rise in US inflation rates after the mid 1960s, thus bringing to a close the long period in which a domestically stable dollar had served usefully as an anchor for the whole international monetary system.

In all probability, the change in economic positions within the world economy and the resulting reduction in the weight of the US economy would anyway have had some impact on the role the dollar had assumed as a reserve and investment currency. But inflation in the United States caused the international role of the dollar to be impaired more than it would otherwise have been. The international position of the dollar was, of course, never really in danger (in contrast to the experience of the pound sterling which largely lost its status as a reserve currency in the 1960's). With a share in international reserves of close to 60 per cent, the dollar is still by far the most important reserve currency and continues to be the key investment currency in the international financial markets. In both functions, however, the dollar now has to compete with other currencies. Monetary authorities and investors in general now have attractive alternatives from which to choose.

Once Economic and Monetary Union (EMU) is complete, one of these alternatives will be a common European currency. In this respect it will take the place of the Deutsche mark, which since the 1970s has become the second most important reserve currency after the dollar. Some 20 per cent of global foreign exchange reserves are today held in Deutsche mark. A sizable part of this amount are in the official exchange reserves of European central banks. These Deutsche mark reserves will disappear as international reserves and become quasi-domestic claims. The introduction of a European currency will undoubtedly lead to a restructuring of international foreign exchange reserves and in international foreign exchange reserves and in international financial markets in general. The size and direction of this restructuring will depend in no small measure on whether the future European Central Bank (ECB) will be able to establish the kind of confidence in international markets that, for example, the Deutsche Bundesbank has earned at home and in international markets in the course of many years of a confidence-building monetary policy.

For me it is still an open question, with what speed and in what size the portfolio adjustment will take place. Central banks outside the EMU and investors in general will be, of course, confronted with the decision whether to change their assets denominated now in European currencies into ECUs or into other currencies, mainly the dollar and perhaps the yen. If they are strongly convinced about the quality of the ECB and its policies, their decision will be quite clear. But my guess is that many investors will for some time at least take an attitude of wait and see. So the dollar could even profit for some time from this shift to a European currency. To prevent such an undesirable movement out of European currencies it would be of great importance that European countries, before replacing their national currencies by a European single currency, made their continuing determination to pursue stability-oriented economic policies very clear to the markets, not with declarations but through their policy stances.

Although expectations regarding not only interest rate movements but also political developments play a role in the competition between currencies, stability of the domestic value of a currency is the most important factor for a reserve and international investment currency – at any rate in the long run. Provided that the United States succeeds in reestablishing and maintaining domestic price stability so that dollar assets continue to be a store of value, the dollar has every chance of remaining the principal reserve currency. Conversely, the future European currency will be all the more likely to take the place of the Deutsche mark, and gain importance as a reserve and investment currency, also *vis-à-vis* the dollar the sooner the markets are convinced that the monetary policy of the European System of Central Banks (ESCB) is successfully geared to domestic price stability. If that did occur, the role of the dollar in international transactions, and hence also as a reserve currency, may be reduced in relative terms by the emergence of a European currency as a major world currency. In all probability this will be a gradual development.

Turning now to the impact of EMU on exchange rate policy and international economic cooperation, one consequence of integrating the European economies into a large single market, and its culmination in a monetary union, will be a substantial contraction of the foreign trade sector. The share of foreign trade and capital transactions in the Community's combined Gross Domestic Product (GDP) and financial markets will be considerably smaller than the proportion, sometimes extremely high, currently recorded in individual member economies. At present, according to calculations by the European Community (EC) Commission, the average of total exports to and total imports from third countries accounts for only about 9 per cent of the GDP of the EC, only slightly higher than the corresponding US ratio. Therefore, fluctuations in the exchange rate will

have a smaller impact than hitherto on the Community's real economy. These effects have already been significantly reduced since the creation of the European Monetary System (EMS) and the gradual stabilization of exchange rate relationships in the Community. However, the various EC currencies are still affected to differing degrees by shifts out of or into the dollar and these shifts are a constraint on the individual member countries' monetary and interest rate policies. Such pressures on internal monetary cohesion will disappear once the EC has moved to irrevocably fixed intra-Community exchange rates and established a single currency and once, as a logical consequence, it pursues a common monetary policy. And although major dollar fluctuations will continue to influence the overall situation in the Community, any immediate adverse effects will become more tolerable than under present conditions. These comments should not be seen as a plea for an exchange rate policy of 'benign neglect' for the Community. But, as has been demonstrated by the United States with its repeated pursuit of a policy of benign neglect in the past, a large domestic market is able – at least to some degree and for a certain period of time – to absorb the impact of exchange rate movements better than economies with large foreign trade sectors.

International cooperation will nevertheless remain necessary, but it could be based less on the goal of keeping exchange rates stable and more on the primary goal of domestic stability and it should focus mainly on establishing macroeconomic and structural conditions that are necessary as a foundation of domestic stability. I fully share the view of Goldstein, when he thinks it is preferable to have monetary policy in the largest industrial countries give the highest priority to price stability. If the world's leading economies succeed in achieving and maintaining domestic price stability, they will at the same time make a strong contribution to exchange rate stability. The emergence of large exchange rate misalignments will under these conditions become very unlikely. The remarkable stability of exchange rates in the EMS for a number of years now is, after all, the result of price stability oriented fiscal and monetary policies in the member countries. I agree fully with Goldstein when he states: 'Stability of domestic policies is not a sufficient condition for exchange market stability but it comes close to being a necessary condition – regardless of the exchange rate regime.' And may I add – more in parenthesis – and in reaction to a point made by Bergsten: the EMS gained in credibility not because of the fixed exchange rate commitment of its member countries, but because of the growing convergence of domestic economic policies, which became more and more oriented towards domestic stability. This policy established a sound and strong basis for stable exchange rates within the EMS and made the fixed exchange rate commitment credible. The decision of EMS

partners to avoid a change in their exchange rate *vis-à-vis* the Deutsche mark has, as I understand it, never been a goal for itself, but was seen as a tool to support this stability-oriented domestic policy.

The statute of the future ECB includes a strong commitment to price stability as its primary objective. By pursuing such a policy at the Community level, monetary authorities in an economically unified Europe with a much smaller share in foreign trade than individual member countries now will be less likely to be confronted with the well-known dilemma of domestic versus exchange rate stability that has often been faced even by the larger member economies. This does not necessarily mean that the EC will become a hesitant participant in international monetary cooperation. As to intervention in the foreign exchange markets, the scope for influencing and stabilizing exchange rates may even become larger, since the impact on the liquidity of the banking system and the financial markets in general resulting from those interventions will be smaller in a large currency area than it is in smaller member economies. But even close cooperation will not always rule out the possibility that an attempt to stabilize exchange rates through intervention and even more through interest rate policy could impair the conduct of a monetary policy geared to domestic stability. There will therefore still be a need for some elasticity in exchange rates between large currency areas to allow for differences in policy options if, despite all efforts at cooperation, inflation performances diverge. But because of their size, these currency areas will be better able than smaller economies to absorb the impact of exchange rate movements on their real economies and to cope with such movements.

Discussion

TOYOO GYOHTEN

I would like to present a Japanese view on the outlook for the international monetary system. Present international monetary arrangements consist of two main elements. One is the reserve currency regime and the other is the exchange rate regime. The classical gold standard was a combination of a gold reserve regime and a fixed parity regime; the Bretton Woods system was a combination of a gold dollar standard and an adjustable parity regime; the post-Bretton Woods system we are now in is the combination of the dollar standard and floating exchange rates. I think the European Monetary System (EMS) is a combination of the multicurrency standard and the adjustable parity arrangement. My conclusion about the future of the international monetary system, if I may jump to that, is that for the coming decade or so, we will have to live with the system which is a combination of the tripolar reserve currency system and the floating rate.

In the post-cold war period, in spite of the increased homogenization of the world economic system, we have a strong tendency towards the regionalization of the world economy into three centres: European Community (EC), North America, and East Asia. In the process of regional integration, certainly Europe is by far the most advanced, and North America is following along a different path. Japan and East Asia are lagging behind in a somewhat different situation, because in East Asia we have no framework for a horizontal division of labour like in the EC and we do not have any simple structure of a single hegemony like in North America. In other words, East Asia is more divergent and less centripetal. However, East Asia has many dynamic subregional centres like Japan, the Korean peninsula, the southern coast of China, the northeastern part of China, the Indo-Chinese peninsula, and there are some countries which will emerge soon like Malaysia, Thailand, and Indonesia. Although these areas are quite diverse in the level of economic development and industrial structure, there is a common strong upward dynamics in motion, and particularly noteworthy at this moment is the rapidly increasing intraregional trade and investment. In this respect, Japanese and overseas Chinese

capital together with the manufacturing technology of Japan are playing a very crucial and central role. As is indicated in Goldstein's chapter, the role of the yen is slowly but steadily increasing. It is my view that if Japan continues to enhance its role as the supplier of capital and technology and the absorber of regional products, the yen will be able to perform the role of the third key international currency without any further specific institutional arrangement.

Under these circumstances, global trade and investment will be carried out under the broad framework of the trilateral currency system, while the exchange rate among these three currencies will continue to float. Certainly it is desirable to see that the present framework of the Group of Seven (G-7) will evolve into a kind of a triangular forum for broader policy coordination. It is also desirable that a reference zone arrangement, with a certain amount of automaticity and discipline, be agreed upon. However, I have to admit that, at least for a decade or so, the idea of a global EMS is not realistic. The main reason is that, in spite of the increased interdependence among the three economic centres, there is still a strong belief in these centres that it has not reached the point where exchange rate fluctuations between their currencies are no longer required. Among these three centres there is no agreement, as of now, towards eventual economic unity like the one which exists among EC countries.

What we can and should do is, in my view, to try to activate the coordination process so that we can reach at least a common assessment of the current world economic situation, reach a common acknowledgment of the list of problems to be addressed, and then agree on the priorities among them. I admit that the G-7 exercises of policy coordination during the last several years have not achieved all the aims and objectives we envisaged. Nevertheless I think they have been successful in making significant steps towards the goals I just described. In any event, the most important thing is to maintain a relationship among the three main poles which could be competitive, open, and non-confrontational at the same time. This is the kind of situation I would foresee for the medium-term future of the world.

Discussion

JACQUES DE LAROSIÈRE

In the chapter by Bayoumi and Eichengreen I was particularly interested by the following observations:

(1) The lasting exchange rate stability under the gold standard cannot be related to an exceptional stability of the economic environment (actually demand shocks were relatively stronger at that time).

(2) The crucial importance given by the chapter to the notion of flexibility of economic adjustment. The more flexible the adjustment process, the greater exchange rate stability. The authors underline, in this respect, the continuous erosion of the adjustment capacity after World War I and the major influence this phenomenon had on the demise of the Bretton Woods system.

At this point I would venture three considerations that could help explain the instability of modern exchange rate systems as opposed to the gold standard:

(i) The abandonment of the gold standard constraint after 1914 opened the way to more discretionary economic policies by governments. Inflation helped governments to develop public-sector and welfare systems. The indexation mechanisms engendered by inflation made the economies less flexible.

(ii) The lack of policy coordination between the United States, the United Kingdom, and France in the interwar period exacerbated the beggar-thy-neighbour aspects of economic policies and this explains, to a large degree, the exchange rate instability of the time.

(iii) It was the instability of American domestic monetary policies in the United States since the mid 1960s that provided the main explanation for the demise of the Bretton Woods exchange rate system. And this instability of exchange rates was a reflection, as I see it, of a more fundamental political inability – which is not unique to the United States but a worldwide phenomenon – to cope responsibly with the challenge of the Vietnam war and of the building of the welfare system. Historians will explain why our twentieth-century democracies have

been, on the whole, less disciplined, and more inclined to delay adjustment for political reasons than was the case in the nineteenth century.

I come now to Goldstein's chapter and I would like to say that I enjoyed reading it and that I share most of his views, with a few nuances, which I will explain below. On the whole, I believe his assessment of the results of economic policy coordination since 1986 is balanced, neither too optimistic – or perhaps just a little – nor excessively negative. I am also very much in agreement with his suggestions for improving the present surveillance procedures.

What he says on 'monitoring zones' seems to me particularly important. Not because I believe they are precisely and easily implementable, but because such 'zones' are a step towards introducing more objective criteria for assessment of – and action on – individual economic policies. In this respect they are a modest indication that what the system needs – as I see it – is a more 'objective', 'external' or 'automatic' set of rules applicable to all players. I also agree on the procedural suggestion put forward by Goldstein in relation to a better 'follow-up' of IMF Article IV assessments. Both suggestions – monitoring zones and follow-up procedures – are complementary. By the way, both are being used more and more in the European Community (EC). As you know, the multiple convergence criteria that are a condition for moving on to the third stage of Economic and Monetary Union (EMU), as well as the convergence programmes and their follow-up procedures are very much in the spirit of what is outlined in Goldstein's chapter.

Following are some specific observations:

(1) As a matter of method, I note that Goldstein's chapter assesses the results of policy coordination for the period 1986-on. But the starting date can be questioned. After all, following the Versailles Summit, the Managing Director of the International Monetary Fund (IMF) was invited to attend the Group of Five (G-5) exercises on surveillance from 1982 (I was first invited in Toronto in 1982). If that date had been the starting point of the assessment, the results would have been quite different: there would have been a subperiod of large exchange rate swings and misalignments from 1982 to 1985.

(2) This leads me to consider that the thrust of G-5/G-7 coordination policies has varied with the times and the players (Baker versus Regan). It changed in emphasis, learning by experience, and adapting to dominant preoccupations, fashion, economic and electoral cycles, and so on. In brief, it was an ongoing process which is less unified and more reflective than would seem at first sight. The appearance of a recession for the first time in Goldstein's chronology may also be influencing the process.

(3) My third observation is that the G-7 process has been most 'efficient' in its efforts to stabilize or orient exchange rates. I agree with Goldstein when he states that misalignments of key currencies were smaller on average in the post-Plaza era. I believe that the very existence of an 'activist' attitude and concern among monetary authorities *vis-à-vis* excessive exchange rate fluctuations provides, in fact, a 'psychological safety net' that has considerably contributed – although coordinated intervention has been relatively limited – to the stability of the exchange rate system since 1986. One of the reasons why we do not see more of a fall in the dollar nowadays – in spite of the unprecedented 650 basis point difference in short-term interest rates between the two shores of the Atlantic – is probably related in a significant way to the notion that there are 'out there', in the G-7 world, some borders that must not be espassed. On the whole, I think that the rejection of the old policies of 'benign neglect', the soft landing of the dollar, and the avoidance of exchange rate misalignments have been very positive factors for the system (in terms of containing protectionism and enhancing inter-national trade and investment). In the same vein, I feel Goldstein's chapter is somewhat too timid when it comes to the virtues – even for 'dominant' countries – of a firmer use of exchange rate stability as a tool for domestic stability and discipline.

(4) But exchange rate coordination was perhaps the easiest task. After all, international cooperation has usually been better at coordinating exchange rates than at influencing policies. That was the case of Bretton Woods: the parity grid was effectively preserved until 1971, but the deterioration of the fundamentals of the anchor currency had been overlooked to the detriment of the system.

I wonder if the present form of international economic cooperation is not, to a certain extent, liable to the same criticism. Let me make a few points in this respect:

(a) The G-5/G-7 exercises since 1982 have not led to a significant improve-ment of the fiscal imbalances in the United States. The accumulation of large fiscal deficits by the US since 1982 is in my view one of the major problems in the functioning of the system. The magnitude of the debt incurred through the sequence of yearly fiscal deficits has deprived the US policymakers of their normal fiscal margin of manoeuvre in times of recession.

(b) The surge in indebtedness throughout the system, and particularly in 'Anglo-Saxon' countries (as we call them in France) was not really detected by the G-7 policy coordination process nor were its recession-ary consequences – which we are now witnessing – adequately assessed.

(c) The activation of domestic demand in Japan – one of the achievements of the G-7 in the mid 1980s – led to asset inflation (not price inflation)

which had to be unwound one day, thus adding to subsequent strains.

(d) The overburdening of monetary policy – which is the result of the pervasive fiscal laxity and the downgrading of incomes policies by the G-7 combined with the price stability goal – is a source of many problems such as overshooting of interest rates, anomalies in exchange rates, distortions in capital flows, and so on. At a time when many budgets are so inflexible that they cannot even contribute to the automatic stabilization of the economy, this overburdening can lead to an excessive use of monetary instruments for short-term conjunctural purposes.

I will conclude. As I have tried to show, the coordination system is still too short-term oriented; its policy mix content is often unsatisfactory and its implementation is uneven. The chapter says somewhere that it is easier to ensure economic coordination when there is a dominant economy. I would agree, if the dominant economy were following a stable and domestically well-balanced set of policies in the long run. But there is a difference between hegemony and stability. There is a difference between a dominant currency and a monetary anchor. Peer pressure has, by nature, limited effects. Countries tend to pursue their own national objectives. The larger they are the more tempted they are to act in what they think is their own interest because they believe they are more immune to the consequences of their actions or their non-actions. The anchor function tends to be overcome, at times, by the domination factor. For these reasons I strongly believe that the system needs more objective constraints applicable to all and that this will only happen if the players become sufficiently equal. That is one of the advantages, in my opinion and from my standpoint, offered by the EMU. It can foster a truly tripolar system which is a prerequisite for the emergence of what could become perhaps one day a true 'world system'.

Index to 'The international monetary system'

348   **Index**